The
Graduate
Handbook

You Don't Know What You Don't Know

Russell J. Bunio

Order this book online at www.trafford.com
or email orders@trafford.com

Most Trafford titles are also available at major online book retailers.

Print information available on the last page.

ISBN: 978-1-4907-6221-0 (sc)
ISBN: 978-1-4907-6220-3 (hc)
ISBN: 978-1-4907-6219-7 (e)

Library of Congress Control Number: 2015911022

Trafford rev. 12/29/2015

North America & international
toll-free: 1 888 232 4444 (USA & Canada)
fax: 812 355 4082

ABOUT THE BOOK, OVERVIEW

The Graduate Handbook: You Don't Know What You Don't Know was written in response to a number of questions asked of me by my nephew, soon to be off to college. Those questions revolved around careers, college majors, and being successful.

This book attempts to provide graduates with proven best practices that will help them when they enter the day-to-day workforce. Most sources of the best practices are from the many successful bosses I was fortunate to work for. Also, some of the sources are people who worked for me, students, and some work associates I worked with along the way.

I was a sponge.

I watched these people, I listened to them, and I learned those practices that I felt would help me perform my job. I cherry-picked their best methods and, in many cases, modified and tweaked those practices and made them my own. I practiced them and improved them through the years.

This is a handbook that helps new workers by telling them what they should do in building their career-starting foundation. The fifty best practices are short and to the point. They are a quick read and will hold the attention of the reader. They are not philosophical; they are practical.

In the book I use *workers*, not *employees*. That is intentional. I want the graduate to recognize the importance of what they are there to do—work!

My subtitle of the book, *You Don't Know What You Don't Know*, characterizes many young people as they go off to that first real job—eight hours a day, five days a week, or even more. This book will greatly improve the speed by which the graduate learns the basics. As an example, practice 1: always be early and leave late sets the stage for basics that ultimately lead to more complex practices—i.e. practice 47: compartmentalization.

Even though this book's user-customer is the graduate, the target sales customers are those parents, aunts, uncles, grandparents, friends, and relatives who are looking for something to buy for the upcoming graduate.(*) Graduation gifts are often difficult to select. Many relatives give money.

A gift of *The Graduate Handbook* <u>and</u> some money provide the graduate with something special. That special gift is fifty best practices that, if consistently used, will provide a jump start for the new worker.

Those sales customers that have read some of the practices say, "Wow, these are common sense. I wish I had known many of them when I started."

Yes, *we don't know what we don't know*!

*100% of the net proceeds from the sale of *The Graduate Handbook* will go to not-for-profit organizations that help people enhance and advance their lives.

Contents

To Donald Snydel, my great friend who
personified success in so many ways.

(February 23, 1948-February 15, 2015)

"Russ Bunio's book is packed with wisdom and is an eminently practical and useful guide to success. Every graduate hopes to be mentored by the very best, and this book is a great start (It's a sometimes "gotcha"reminder for experienced adults, too. I made a few notes, myself). I enthusiastically recommend the book, and our children and grandchildren will be the first among many on my personal mailing list".

-James Henderson, former President and Chairman of Cummins Engine Company

"Students entering the workforce are interested in learning how to be successful in their first job. As educators, we often struggle with credibility issues. Russell J. Bunio provides that credibility in his new book, The Graduate Handbook. That is why I have decided to use this resource in some of the courses we offer at the University of Iowa."

-David Baumgartner Assistant Provost, University of Iowa

". . . . I most came to admire about Russ over the years of working with him was his ability to lead his bosses, peers, associates, and staff and especially the way he mentored young employees. This is a book to be read and reread by anyone wanting to become better at what he or she does, especially those graduates just beginning to enter the work place."

-Mark Chesnut former Vice President of Human Resources, Cummins Engine Co.

. . . . "this book is based on several of his (Mr. Bunio's) successful real life experiences in working his way up from "worker" to a very high level "worker". I personally witnessed Russ's transformation from an old school management environment to leading a renaissance of enlightened management change at every organization he 'worked'in.

-Carl Code former Director of Materials Management-GM

"Mr Bunio is one of the most experienced management professionals I know. He shares his experience and knowledge through 50 best practices, which provide a foundation for young workers. When I read the book I was thinking I could do better if I read this kind of handbook when I graduated. Thank you for giving graduates a wonderful and useful handbook.

-Ren Bing Bing Vice President of Weichai Power, Ltd., General Manager of Linde Hydraulics Co. (China)

"This book should be mandatory reading for all new graduates or built into the on-boarding processes by the companies that hire them.

-Dr. Daren Otten Dean, Applied Academics Yuba College

"If I had The Graduate Handbook when I started coaching, I would not have made so many unnecessary mistakes. Every young college graduate should use The Graduate Handbook as a Business/Career Bible."

-Boots Donnelly former Middle Tennessee Head Football Coach and inductee into the College Football Hall of Fame (2013), and Tennessee Sports Hall of Fame (1997)

"50 Suggestions, 50 Good Habits, 50 Friends . . . .
The first time I open it (The Graduate Handbook), I regard it as a handbook for new workers. Then I figure out this book absolutely suit for almost everyone. No matter you are a new worker of a multi-billion dollar company, or a graduate of world famous university, you will find something useful".

-Saiyu Ren recent graduate (23 years old) from the University of New South Wales, Australia.

INTRODUCTION

Why Did I Write This Book?

Through the years I have been very fortunate to work for, and work with, some very successful people. You might say they are very smart, well educated, hardworking, or just lucky or maybe some combination of all. Anyway, by most standards these professionals are very successful in their fields, and at one time, they, like you, were just graduates starting out.

One of my nephews asked me years ago, "Uncle Russ, I want to be like you. What do I need to do?"

Somewhat surprised, I smiled, laughed, and asked, "What do you mean like me?"

"I want to make a lot of money," he responded without hesitation. I smiled and then wondered, *Is he serious?*

His question made me reflect on this: how do we measure success, what is really important, and most importantly, how do I respond to his question? What advice can I give to a young person who is entering the day-by-day work environment? What have I learned, who have I learned the most from, and what advice can I give? After some serious thought, I began to document what I learned. This book is about advice; you can take it, apply it, adapt it, and/or ignore it. But it is advice based on *best practices* that work! These practices have worked for very successful people and have helped me along the way. Some of these practices you may already know about; others, not. The key is implementation, discipline, and making them part of your work ethic.

What Is Success (Money, Fame, Power, Happiness, Etc.)?

There is no one definition of *success*. The dictionary defines it as "something that ensures: the degree or measure of attaining a desired end."

There are several attempts to define success:

* Success is a dream come true after hard work.
* Success is to be rich and happy versus poor and happy—but the key word is *happy*.
* Success is reaching a place where your dreams were pointing to.
* Success is when you triumph over obstacles, barriers, and adverse situations.
* Success is a changing target or goal; it changes with time and conditions.
* Success is when you attain that which you sought.

Maybe success is a combination of these and other definitions; however, *you define success for you.* Many studies show that the successful person is generally characterized as happy, challenged, energized, focused, passionate, and persistent about his work.

> *Press on! Nothing in the world can take the place of persistence.*
> *Talent will not; nothing is more common*
> *than unsuccessful men with talent.*
> *Genius will not; unrewarded genius is almost a proverb.*
> *Education will not; the world is full of educated derelicts.*
> *Persistence and determination alone are omnipotent.*

—President Calvin Coolidge

Matching these attributes with *your* goals, aspirations, and dreams will make you successful. However, the end result, success, is defined by *you.*

What Are Best Practices? How Can They Help You?

Best practices
1) are a set of guidelines, ethics, and ideas that represent the most efficient or prudent course of action;
2) are methods or techniques that have consistently shown results superior to those achieved with other means; and
3) can be a baseline for continuous improvement, when you can better the best practice.

Key words here are *methods, ethics, techniques, guidelines, action, efficiency,* and *continuous improvement.* This book is about these and more.

Some may argue, what the best practice is for you may not be the best in the world. That is true. We don't have the ability to search the globe and compare the best to the better to the just good. The best is continuously moving and improving. Through benchmarking we are able to narrow that gap and continually drive closer and closer to the *best*.

What Is Benchmarking and How Does that Help?

Benchmarking is a quality tool that is a comparison of one organization's (or person's) best practices and performance against those of other organizations' (or persons').
Benchmarking seeks to identify standards, or best practices, to apply in measuring and improving performance.

When you benchmark, you document how you do something and then compare how others (usually someone that is noted for exceptional performance) do exactly the same process. You identify the differences and analyze the results (measurements).
If their process is superior to yours and the measured results are also better, then you may adopt or adapt to their approach.
Adopting or adapting those improvements to your process helps you improve and may lead to your creating a new best practice.

(*Note: Benchmarking allows you to learn or confirm. You may learn something new that you can apply to your process. You are continuously improving. Or you may confirm you are doing the same or better than the benchmarked person or organization. You know you are on the right track, and now you have confirmed it.*)

Where Do *The Graduate*'s Best Practices and Benchmarks Come From?

I have to admit, I did not create all the best practices in this book. Mostly I learned them; I sponged or borrowed them, modified them, and in some cases, improved the practices! Many successful people (I mentioned earlier) are the real creators of this book. I watched them in action, learned from them, and documented what they did to be successful and then tried to apply those practices to my work. Yes, I was a *sponge*.

At the end of this book, I listed many from whom I sponged, and I thank them for allowing me to do so, whether they knew what I was doing or not!

The Book's Customer

You, the graduates, are the customers of the book. The book is written to help you as you enter the workforce, as you initiate your career. I believe that by your reading, adopting, and practicing the fifty practices, you will shorten your learning curve and have the opportunity to use what successful professionals have created and used. This book will give you a jump start, an advantage, in that new, competitive workplace.

You will find that many of the best practices do not really focus on how to do something. They do clearly explain *what* you need to do. As an example, in the best practice "early in, out late" I explain what the desired result is, *what* you should do—always be at work early and usually leave a little late.

There are many books and training sessions on time management, and *The Graduate* does not take the deep dive into the how. I often give examples, recommendations, and explanations that focus on the *what*.

Best Use of *The Graduate Handbook*

My target was to write each practice to be clear, concise and easy to understand and to be a fast read. The goal was one page per practice. As you will see, I failed. I was not able to hold the one pager due to what was required to explain the practice.

However, to get the most out of the book, I recommend you read one practice, think about it, and try it out. Watch and see how others respond to your usage. Watch and see how your boss reacts. And see how the practice helps you with your job.

Some of the best practices may already be part of you or your approach. That's great, and you have a head start.

Your consistent use and adoption of these best practices will be recognized and appreciated. A hit-and-miss use will not. Your boss, fellow workers, and others will value consistency.

As you work your way through the list, you'll find some practices easy to implement, some more difficult. That's okay. Just remember, these practices came from very successful people, and I am sure their use did not always come easily or automatically.

What This Book Is Not, What It Is

This book is not a *how-to* book. It is not a *Dummies*, made-easy-type publication.

It is not a substitute for family, school, church, or other sources of learning. It is not an *end* that will allow you to be successful.

This book is a what-needs-to-be-done by a new person entering the workforce.

I hope this book will be one tool in your tool kit.

I expect it will be a *means* to your *end*.

That *end* is for you to be *successful*!

SECTION ONE: THE START

* Early In, Out Late
It does matter how much time you spend at work and when you come and go.

* Look Good and Smell Good
Your appearance makes an impression, no matter what job you do. Impressions do stick.

* Hardworking
Is there a difference between hardworking, working hard, or working smart?

* From Me to We
Your focus has to and will change.

* Customer Focus
Who is really your primary customer?

* Clear Job Expectations
You need them—understand them and excel at them.

* Mentored
It really helps to have a buddy, one who shows you the way!

* Do It Right the First Time
Being slow and correct beats being fast and wrong.

* Having Fun
Just because it is work, doesn't mean it cannot be fun.

* Write It Down
Remembering is good, forgetting is dangerous. Reduce stress and errors.

This is the only country in the world where today's employee is tomorrow's employer.

—Marco Rubio

The first day, week, and month of an employee's experience carries a lasting impression.

—Scott Weiss

The difference between who you are and who you want to be is the work you put in.

—Author Unknown

EARLY IN, OUT LATE

Some people are *always late*. Late for meetings, late for work, late for dinner, the movies, etc.

Even with activities that are very important to them, they seem to struggle to be on time. Being late is a serious problem when others rely on you, especially in a work environment.

Then at the end of the day, some workers practically *fly* out of work at the precise quitting time. Five o'clock comes and they storm out the gate.

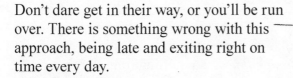

Don't dare get in their way, or you'll be run over. There is something wrong with this approach, being late and exiting right on time every day.

Background

There have been many studies done and books written on effective *time management*. Why are some people always late? What is the root cause of habitual lateness? Those having this problem find the problem often revolves around their identifying actions to be done, setting priorities for those actions, and placing the priorities into sequence. Getting to work on time or early should be simple; you do this first, second, third, etc., etc., and allocate the appropriate amount of time to accomplish each. Stack the time requirements, add some contingency for unseen situations (i.e., heavy traffic) and a little extra time to be early, and the lateness problem should be remedied.

Being early every day is a major *plus*!

Your boss knows you are here, your co-workers know, and the day gets off to a good planned start.

Most work doesn't get completed on a set schedule. There will be times when it is for the best of the business or your coworkers that you make sure all is done and complete before leaving for the day. That magic five o'clock quitting time should be more of the wrap-up time than the quitting time. Take some time at the end of each day to review anything possibly missing completion for that day, as well as to prepare a list of major items to do for the next day.

Galen (my boss) said, "Watch Billy G. sometime. Watch the way he comes in and leaves. Bill is here every day usually about half an hour early—practically running through the gate to his work area. At the end of the day, he is dragging, walking slowly, and is always beyond normal quitting time. What does that tell you?"

Best Practice

The Billy G. example told me that *being early* helps everyone in the workplace and *leaving later* than quitting time shows dedication to the work. How you handle both ends of the workday will be noticed.

Notes

_____

_____

_____

_____

_____

_____

LOOK GOOD, SMELL GOOD

Often, there is no real simple answer as to appearance and dress for the new employee. Some companies or organizations have uniforms or dress codes.

Many organizations say just about anything is okay, but not jeans. Others say business casual is expected, but on Fridays they allow casual dress.

Some organizations say nothing. Maybe they expect nothing. Or when the employee gets out of the (undefined) box, the boss will say something to the employee. ("Your uniform is dirty, please get it cleaned and pressed!")

Background

Working in a factory—requires one type of dress
Working at a restaurant—requires another
Working outdoors—another
In an office—another

Some insightful observations:

* I once heard a senior VP say, "Here comes another one of those 'look good, smell good' guys—looks sharp."
This was the first impression made, and a very good one. Even without any mention of position or job performance, the new person was recognized in a very positive way.

* In our Mexico operation, it was recognized that the ladies working in the plant always looked like a million bucks (maybe pesos) even though they were working on the assembly line.
The job at the plant provided them work, but also a daily social opportunity. They wanted to, and did, look great. The guys also improved their appearance—wonder why?

* You don't know when the boss is going to call you into his office, to maybe meet his boss or a customer. This opportunity could come any day. That opportunity needs to be met by looking sharp.

* At the end of the day, George was tired—clothes were dirty, George was dirty, and he didn't smell so good. This was the nature of his job.
However, at the beginning of the next day, George was ready—clean George, clean clothes, and George smelled good.

* When Ernie came for the job interview, he wore a new suit, white shirt, sharp red tie, and his shoes were shined. He walked in with a smile on his face even though, I knew, he was very nervous. That first impression was exceptional, a very positive impression even before he spoke his very first word.

* Harriet once commented, "She dresses more like a boss every day even though she isn't—yet! All things being equal, she deserves and will get that next promotion."
And she did!

Best Practice
It is generally best to overdress than underdress in your work environment. Looking good and smelling good for your fellow workers, the boss, customers, and yourself helps prepare you for that next opportunity.

HARDWORKING

While the other guy's sleeping, I'm working. While the other guy is eating, I'm working. While the other guy's making love, I mean, I'm making love too, but I am working hard at it!
—Will Smith, (actor, producer, etc. etc.)

As you enter your new job, you will be asked to do things you've never done before. You can't expect to be able to do all of them well or 100 percent correctly. Your boss will understand that and will expect you to learn as you go. This is hard work.
This is part of the normal learning curve for a new employee.

Background

Often there is confusion between *hardworking*, *working hard*, and *working smart*.
* Being *hardworking* means you are focused, diligent, industrious, and you always put a lot of effort and care into your work. Your effort is directed to the completion of a task that you want to accomplish in order to meet your objective.

* *Working hard* often means doing a task that requires a lot or too much effort. The task is often described as backbreaking, laborious, unpleasant, hard, or tedious. Working hard often provides an opportunity for job improvement.

* *Working smart* is the result of using the best tools, technology, processes, and procedures that simplify the task and reduce the number of hours or physical energy required to complete that task.

You, as a new worker, will experience and travel through working hard, being hardworking, and working smart. Ultimately, through *kaizen*, working hard can diminish, allowing more time for being hardworking and working smart.

(*Kaizen* is a Japanese term, foundational to the Toyota production system, that means gradual unending improvement, doing little things better, setting—and achieving—ever-higher standards.)

Some Quotes of Note
* "Hard work beats talent when talent doesn't work hard." (Author Unknown)

* "What separates the talented individual from the successful one is a lot of hard work." (Stephen King)

* "I'm a great believer in luck, and I find the harder I work, the more I have of it." (Thomas Jefferson)

* "Nothing worth having comes easy." (Teddy Roosevelt)

* "All roads that lead to success have to pass through hard work boulevard at some point." (Eric Thomas)

* "Good things come to those who work their asses off and never give up." (Author Unknown)

Best Practice

The boss will understand that you will have to work hard as you learn the job. However, he will watch to see how you progress at working smart while showing him you're a hard worker. Hardworking employees are recognized and rewarded.

Notes

_____

_____

_____

_____

_____

_____

_____

_____

_____

_____

_____

_____

_____

FROM ME TO WE

Questions

* I am going to have to do what? You have to be kidding.
* I am so new, will I know what to say?
* What if I screw up and embarrass myself?
* I know I am the new member of the team, but why do I have to present for the entire team?
* Can't someone else with more experience do it?
* How will I know what to say, or worse, if someone asks me a question, what if I can't answer it?

Background

Most of us have belonged to a team, club, band, or some form of working-together group. In most cases, we volunteered to be on these groups because we wanted to participate and contribute in some way. We wanted to, so we did.

Now that you are entering the workforce, you will quickly see that wherever you work, you'll be pulled into a group or team where you will be expected to participate and contribute as a team member. The reason teams are so prevalent is that results obtained by teams are generally superior to results obtained by the individual. What I've seen is that teams will outperform individuals when...

1. the task is complex,
2. creativity is needed,
3. the path forward isn't clear,
4. more efficient use of resources is required,
5. fast learning is necessary,
6. high commitment is desirable,

7. cooperation is essential to implementation,
8. members have a stake in the outcome,
9. the task or process involved is cross-functional, and
10. no individual has sufficient knowledge to solve the problem.

A team is a group of people working together to achieve a common purpose for which they hold themselves mutually accountable. Team members sacrifice their individual objectives and goals to the betterment of the team's or group's objectives and goals. The transformation is from *me* to *we*!

In the list of *'Questions'*, you can readily see, that to the new team member, it is *I, I,* and *I*. "What if I, how can I, how will I . . . ?"

That is normal and expected. Especially as you start a new career, you want to do well, and being part of a team is part of the job, not the entire one.

Example, if you work in production, you have a functional responsibility to the production department. Your day-to-day job is focused on production. However, if there are quality problems in production, you will start to interface with quality, engineering, and maybe purchasing departments, to help work together to solve those quality problems. Working with this team and establishing what the team (*we*) can do to solve the problem subordinates the functional area (production) to the benefit of the team, in this case, to the business team.

Best Practice

Being part of a team is inevitable. Participating and contributing to that team will be expected. You're shifting from thinking and acting from a *me* to thinking and acting from a *we* is what teams are all about. *We* generate the best results.

Answers to the First Paragraph
Don't worry, we will all help you. We'll all help create your presentation, and we'll be there when you present. If someone asks a question you can't answer, one of us, we on the team, will answer for you. Don't worry, you won't screw up; we won't let you! Notice all the we's!

Notes

_____

_____

_____

_____

_____

_____

_____

_____

CUSTOMER FOCUS

As you start that new job, new career, you will find you have many customers. Who are they? What will they want? Are their expectations reasonable? Will you get to meet your customers? How will you satisfy those customers or, as others say *delight the customer*?

You will find, generally, there are two types of customers, direct and indirect.

Direct customers are those that you provide a product or service to and you have daily interaction with. You know what they need and want, and part of your job is to meet their expectations—daily, weekly, and monthly. Most of these customers are your coworkers, your bosses, and others.

Indirect customers are those who you may seldom meet or have direct interaction with. As an example, if you work at an IT company, you may seldom speak to an end user specifically about the finished product you helped produce.[1]

Background

Your first, direct, and primary customer is your boss! This is the person with whom you need to establish clear job expectations, make sure you know how the boss will evaluate your performance against job expectations, and how you can strive to meet or beat those expectations.

---

[1] One of your best experiences will come when you meet an end user, or customer. This is a great opportunity to see and hear what is important to the end user, how you may affect what is important. Getting into the shoes of the customer is very valuable!

The boss is in the position of trying to get multiple tasks done. Usually he (or she) has a number of workers assigned to him. Because of this scope of responsibility and authority, the boss will rely on his people to do their jobs.

Don't ever hesitate to ask questions—about the assignments, timing, and how to do the work. The boss expects this! When you fully understand your job expectations, the boss will feel more comfortable about your ability, your ability to meet those expectations.

The boss will rely on *you* to be there, be on time, and get your work assignments done.

If you cannot meet some of the job expectations, let the boss know, and know in advance when the deadlines are. Surprises are not good and should be kept to a minimum, especially when your performance may affect someone else's in the flow of services or products you produce. Others will rely on you, and if your performance *can* affect theirs, you must let them know and work with them to resolve the issues. You are now part of the production flow, an important part. You don't want to be let down, and neither will your coworkers!

Best Practice

You will have many customers. *Your primary customer is your boss!* Work closely with him, make sure you understand his expectations of you, and strive to meet or exceed those expectations.

CLEAR JOB EXPECTATIONS

How do you know when your job, task, assignment is complete? Have you done all that is expected of you? If all isn't done and you walk away, someone could be disappointed (90 percent complete isn't okay or acceptable).

Background

Everyone likes to get the job done, out of the way, finished. It feels good to complete something and then move on to something else that is more fun, more challenging, or as many graduates say, move on to something more creative.

Understanding what the task expectation is, is critical. Don't take anything for granted, and do go to your boss and say, "Please explain that to me again so I have it. I want to know what the expected finished product is."

You may get answers like this from your boss:

* You'll know when you're done.
* If you don't know by now, maybe you just don't get it.
* See me later, I'm busy.
* Talk to Mary—she'll show you what to do.
* Just do a quality job and you'll be okay. I'll let you know if it's wrong.
* Read the instructions, and if you have questions, see me.
* Just do it like the others do it.

Do any of these responses really help you? Some probably help, but will they allow you to actually *make sure* you do an excellent job? No!

The best approach is to go back to your boss and ask him to make very clear what is expected, AND what IS the time frame to get it done.

Sure, the boss is busy and has a lot going on; however, if there is a performance expectation, that expectation must be clear in your mind.

I once heard a new employee have this conversation with her boss:

Employee: "I'm not really sure of what I am doing. I don't want to disappoint you, but I am falling behind and will have a tough time catching up."

Boss: "Who else is on your team, can't they help you? I'm off to a meeting right now."

Employee: "Jim does a similar job, but he's so busy I can't get him to sit down for five minutes."

Boss: "Okay, I will be back in an hour, and let's walk through your questions and I'll answer them for you. Okay? For now, watch Jim and see what he's doing."

Employee: "Great. Thanks. Where do we meet and at what time?"

Boss: "At 1:00 p.m., at my office."

Employee: "See you there. Thank you"

Now this employee has the opportunity to be clear with the boss as to what the expectations and time frame are and maybe even how he will measure the performance.

The employee should walk into the meeting at 1:00 p.m. with a complete list of questions. If all the questions are answered and now the employee is clear, then the objective is met. If there is still uncertainty, then ask more questions until you are clear. Do take notes.

Job performance is extremely important, especially for new employees. Make every attempt to obtain what you need. Asking questions is not seen as a weakness; it is seen as a strength!

Best Practice

Having clear job expectations is critical to excellent performance. You must understand those expectations! By meeting or exceeding *agreed-to* job expectations, you will be successful.

Notes

_____

_____

_____

_____

_____

_____

_____

_____

MENTORED

Welcome, you are now the new member of our team. We hope you enjoy your new job, and we all look forward to working with you. Let us know if there is anything you need, and we'll try to get it for you. Good luck to you!

Okay, now you are on the new job, and everyone seems nice, friendly, and helpful.
So when do we go for lunch? Where?
What time are breaks?
Can I have food in my cubicle?
Allowed to smoke anywhere?
What are the rules?
Who can answer all my questions?
These are normal questions running through the mind of any new person. How do you get these and many more questions answered? You shouldn't go to the boss for everything!

Background
The questions raised here are all normal questions for the new person. The best and simplest way to address this situation is to ask the boss, "Do we have a mentorship or buddy system in place to help new employees like me?"

Mentorship

A *mentor* is a person who provides guidance to a less-experienced employee. Often, the mentor is an experienced coworker who is well respected within the organization. Often called a buddy system, mentorship is a win-win. The employee benefits, as does the employer.

Benefits to person mentored. The mentor can:
1. Show how things work,
2. Help solve a problem,
3. Critique work,
4. Introduce others to the new person (reduce isolation),
5. Be an advisor, and lastly,
6. Show the ropes to the new person.

Benefits to the employer:

1. Greater employee productivity
2. Faster improvement on the job
3. Fewer mistakes made
4. Employee satisfaction generally better
5. Sure beats the sink-or-swim approach
6. Probably less employee turnover

Best Practice

As a new employee, you want to do a good job, grow on the job, and satisfy that primary customer—the boss. By asking if there is a mentorship program in place you are taking the initiative and showing your desire to do well.

If there is a program in place, great. If not, your boss may realize this is a good idea and implement one.

Ask to have a mentor.

Notes

_____

_____

_____

_____

_____

_____

_____

_____

_____

_____

_____

_____

_____

DIRFT: DOING IT RIGHT THE FIRST TIME

We all make errors and mistakes, have misfires, and even commit blunders—only those who do nothing, make no mistakes. Even the most experienced sometimes don't get it right every time or the first time. Later in the quality best practice, the emphasis is on knowing what the requirements of quality are and then working to meet or exceed that requirement.
DIRFT goes hand in hand with this practice. Our goal is zero defects!

Background

Fixes, repairs, reworks, rejections all result in time lost and increased costs. Philip Crosby, a quality guru, had it right. The four major principles that support DIRFT are these:

1. The definition of quality is conformance to requirements (*requirements* meaning both the product and the customer's requirements).
2. The system of quality is prevention.
3. The quality standard is zero defects (relative to requirements).
4. The measurement of quality is the price of non-conformance.

The key concepts are *conformance* to requirements, *preventing* defects, non-conformance has a *price*, and the goal is *zero defects*.

It doesn't matter if you are making a product, providing a service, or creating a report for others; your goal is to do an excellent job, on time, with zero defects.

Easy to say, not always so easy to do.

What may cause you to *not* create that zero-defect quality product?

* Not having a clear understanding of the work assigned

* Rushing the work and trying to complete it without sufficient time
* Being unprepared
* Not having a focus on the work
* Leaving the work unfinished or half-done
* Taking shortcuts

Here is a list of steps that will help do it right the first time:

1. Spend the time and make sure you are clear as to what the assignment is and there is agreement on what the finished product should look like.
2. Allocate the necessary amount of time to get the project done in addition to 10 percent for overruns or unforeseen issues.
3. Focus on the project; eliminate distractions.
4. Check your work as you go. Quality checks through the process will save time in the end.
5. Be methodical and not in a hurry.
6. Quality-check your finished product. Are you meeting the assignment expectation? Are there any obvious errors such as spelling errors, typos, or slight blemishes?
7. Have someone else's fresh eyes take a look at the work or project—anything missed?

Best Practice

Striving for zero defects in what you do will be supported by the seven steps listed above. Doing it right the first time, resulting in zero defects, not only reduces costs, but also improves the quality of your product or service. Your customers expect that quality!

Do it right the first time; you may not get a second chance.
—Author Unknown

HAVING FUN

Just because you have started work or a new career doesn't mean that your workplace cannot be fun. You should have some fun, and creating that environment with coworkers can be both socially rewarding and very supportive of job accomplishment.

Background

Some will argue that working is work and there is no time for anything but doing your job. They believe the boss doesn't want you wasting time, goofing off, or just plain socializing much. Work hard and that's it. That's what you are being paid to do.

Others will say enjoying your work, positively interacting with coworkers, having some laughs as you do the work will make you more productive in the long run. These folks argue that job fulfillment is the most important criteria for job success.

In reality, both approaches have some merit.

Most bosses want their workers productive and happy.
They do know that the *most productive* workers are
* punctual,
* focused,
* motivated,
* enthusiastic,
* happy and enjoy their work, and
* like their bosses.

The Complainer
Did you ever work around someone who hates his job, complains about everything, and really has nothing positive to say? I can't imagine being faced with this attitude eight hours per day.

The Loafer

Have you worked with someone who just goofs off any chance he gets? He looks for ways to avoid work. His days are very long, as are yours, since you must work with him. At quitting time, he runs from the work area and says, "I'm outta here!"

The Performer

It is easy to identify the motivated worker, who is on the job early, leaves a bit late, focuses on the job at hand, and finds ways to enjoy the work and the work environment. He is easy to work with and is recognized for his good attitude and performance.

Best Bet

Come to work to get the job done (first) while having some fun (second)! Most coworkers will enjoy being around you as someone who does a good job and enjoys doing it. Set the example and others will follow. And the group's performance will be what the boss will be looking for.

Best Practice

Find ways to have fun at work so you enjoy the workday. If you can't find some form of fun in your job, maybe you better look for another opportunity!

Do it well, make it fun—the key to success in life, death, and almost everything in between.

—Ronald P. Culberson, author

WRITE IT DOWN (RID)

It probably isn't very fashionable today to actually write something down on paper or keep notes. How often do we hear someone say:

* Oh, sorry, I forgot that. (Or as some say, "My memory didn't serve me.")
* No problem, I'll remember to take care of that.
* I keep turning over in my mind something I don't want to forget. Can't sleep.
* What do I need? I don't have a list—oh well, just wing it.
* Where is that telephone number? Who said they were going to take care of that assignment?

Background

Writing something down really does save time, energy, and frustration. Using random scraps of paper or just relying on memory can be unreliable and dangerous. The more you are expected to do and remember, the better your system needs to be.

Here Are Some Effective Practices
Ted always carried a very small notebook (about three by three) in his pocket, and as things would come up, he would write them in the book, as his reminder items. That book was always with him. At the end of the day, he would look at the book to make sure he would remember everything. Today, Ted is a vice president at Toyota.

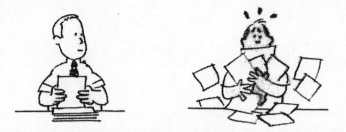

Charlie kept a list at his desk. As things that he couldn't take care of right at that time would come up, he would write them on his list of *to-dos*. During the day, Charlie would work from the list to make sure nothing of importance would be missed. At the end of the day, he would review the list before going home and prepare a priority list for the next day. His mind was clear, all was done, and a get-started list was ready for the morning.

Galen often would wake up during the night and be thinking, *I must remember to do this and that and that.* He would turn this over in his mind, over and over, for fear of forgetting it. Finally, Galen decided to place a pencil and paper near his nightstand so that if he would want to remember something, all he would have to do is write it down. He did this and his turning over and over stopped. His mind was at ease, and he didn't forget.

Best Practice

Don't always try to remember everything. It is very important to not forget, and the best way to avoid forgetting is to *write it down* and be *rid* of the worry of forgetting.

SECTION TWO: BUILDING YOUR ROLE

* Secrets, Gossip, Rumors
These are watch-outs! Sometimes it's just best to say nothing.

* Professional Communications
What you say, how you say it, and when to say it are all important.

* Eat, Sleep, Exercise
Make sure the right balance receives priority.

* Reliable, Trustworthy
You can become very valuable, leading to indispensable.

* Quality
Most think they know what quality is; few know how to clearly
define it. Here is a simple, easy definition for your use.

* Teams
Why teams deliver the best results and can help you move up.

* Hustle
Most believe it is better to do something versus nothing. Failure is
okay. Failure often provides a spring-board to success.

* That Interview
Here are four phases to follow to carry out a successful interview
(process).

Teamwork is the ability to work together toward a common vision. It is the . . . ability to direct individual accomplishment toward organizational objectives. It is the fuel that allows common people to attain uncommon results.

—Andrew Carnegie

Take care of your thoughts when you are alone. Take care of your words when you are with people.

—Unknown Author

Talent wins games, but teamwork and intelligence win championships.

—Michael Jordan

A boss promotes the reliable employee to higher positions, the professor offers research opportunities to the reliable student, (and) the team picks the reliable man as its captain.

—Brett and Kate McKay

SECRETS, GOSSIP, RUMORS

Is there such a thing as a secret in the workplace? When you hear someone say, "Can you keep a secret?" does that indicate that this person is passing a secret from another or just wants to confide in you?

Rumors, gossip, and so-called secrets are commonplace in most workplaces. We all want to know what is going on. We don't want to be left out in the cold. Or do we?

Background

Here are some safe guidelines to follow when being exposed to those rumors, gossip, and secrets:

Speaking

1. Treat secrets as not secrets—at best they are limited exposure of information to select people. If someone wants to tell you a secret, just say, "I'm really poor at keeping secrets, so if this is to be confidential, please don't tell me because I'm not so good keeping silent."

2. Gossip usually hurts people, not helps them. If you have something positive to say about someone, say it. If you are tempted to say a negative, just say nothing. Ask yourself, *Would I feel comfortable saying the gossip to the person's face, openly and honestly?* If you are, it is probably okay. If not, you should say nothing.
3. Rumors are like grass fires. They may start from a small spark, slowly spread, ignite more, and then rapidly burn out of control. Rumors can cause a lot of damage. Rumors can usually be dispelled by talking with your boss, checking your organization's policies, or sometimes just asking yourself, "Is this rumor too good, or too bad, to really be true?" And you know what, when it is *too good or too bad*, it is usually a bad rumor. Does that rumor pass the smell test?

Writing

1. By reducing something (a secret) to writing, you have become a partner in the secret-spreading flow. Now you will pass that non secret to others, and you are just as guilty as the secret's originator. Remember, you may be passing information that is bad, inaccurate, or just hurtful.

2. E-mails and social media are potential hotbeds for gossip and rumors. What you write can have your name attached to it forever. How you feel and think today will change. Relationships and friendships change, and you need to be cautious as to what you reduce to writing and share with

others. Over time, you may regret *publishing* so much for the world to see.

If in doubt, stop and think. *If what I am saying or writing would show up on the front page of my hometown newspaper, would my parents be proud of me or disappointed?* If there is *any doubt* in your mind, don't do it!

Best Practice

There are no real secrets in the workplace; gossip should be avoided, and rumors are usually a waste of time and energy.

Notes

_____

_____

_____

_____

_____

_____

_____

_____

_____

_____

PROFESSIONAL COMMUNICATIONS

Recently, while sitting next to a mother and daughter at a local restaurant (friends of our friends), I asked them where they were from (Tennessee) and what the daughter was up to other than being out to dinner at this restaurant. Smiling, the daughter replied, "I am a student at Colorado State University, and I am studying business and finance."
I asked, "What year are you?"
And she said, "I am a junior, *sir.*"
My wife then asked the young lady, "When you graduate, will you look for a job in Colorado, Tennessee, or here in Florida?"
She said, "*Ma'am*, I'm not sure, I do love my home state."

After other discussions around the table, I said to the young lady, "We do appreciate your *yes, ma'am* and *yes, sir.* It is refreshing!"
Again, smiling, she said, "Thank you, sir, but some of my friends at school make fun of me because I do say *sir* and *ma'am*. I can't help it. It's just the way I was brought up."

Our first impression of this young lady was very positive. *Yes, sir!*

Background

Every day we have many opportunities to communicate—face-to-face, text, e-mail, phone, letters, cards, and others. These opportunities are very important because they not only give us the vehicle to communicate content but also a vehicle to create an impression about ourselves.
Verbal and visual communication is generally accepted as the optimal opportunity for the most effective communication.

Here are some pointers:

One of my bosses would often say, "It's not so much about what you say, it's about how you say it. It's how you present yourself." How would you like it said to you? How do you get across the message so the other person listens and hears? Always try to be thoughtful, considerate, honest, and open. If you were on the receiving side, how would you want to hear the message?

Everyone likes to hear their name when being addressed. "Good morning, Jack! How are you, Kathy?" Looking at a person and saying "Have a great evening and see you tomorrow, Jan," will generally get a positive response back to you. A regular "hello" is always appreciated. Especially a "hello" with a name attached.

A common filler so often used is *like*. Some people will beat "like, like, like" to death and use the word to allow time to think or just fill in the blanks. This word and other repetitive words or phrases do become old very quickly. An easy way to stop their use is to slow down and think of other words to use in their place. Effective and professional communication is not a race. Slowing down and thinking about what you want to say will pay dividends.

Have you ever heard "It takes more muscles to frown than it does to smile"? I never confirmed that just because I never really checked it out. Whether it requires more or less muscles isn't the point. Smiles and laughter are contagious. Smiling at someone almost always gets you a smile in return. Laughing at yourself and with others creates a positive environment, an environment that others enjoy and want to be part of. A simple thing like smiling is an effective and positive form of communication.

Most everyone likes to talk and often talk about themselves. It is easy since they know about themselves and want to share with others what they are doing, what they think, or what others are doing that they know about. Being a good listener is sometimes difficult. It is hard to listen to someone ramble on and on. The challenge is to listen and then speak when it counts.
A good listener is rewarded with learning something (good or bad, fact or fiction) and can provide meaningful input (when he can get a word in edgewise).

Look 'em in the eyes! There is always time for tweeting, texting, and e-mailing. They have their time and place. When you have the opportunity to speak with someone face-to-face, take advantage of that opportunity. *Don't avoid it; embrace it!* Maintain eye contact through the discussion. This focused attention will be positively received.

When writing something, reread what you've written to make sure it says what you want (say what you mean and mean what you say). Lastly, are the grammar and spelling correct? Who knows where this document may end up. Make it clear and make it right!

Best Practice

These seven examples do add up to a best practice for professional, effective communication. Others do and will watch how well you communicate.

Notes

_____

_____

_____

_____

_____

_____

_____

_____

_____

_____

EAT, SLEEP, EXERCISE

Advice from a father to his son about work, school, and being off on his own:

You need to eat well, three good meals a day—breakfast is very important. Don't forget about enough sleep, maybe seven to eight hours per day. And last, you need exercise every day—some exercise.

Sure sounds like what we've all heard before—just common sense.

Background

On one of my visits to China, I had an opportunity to sit with a family over dinner and meet their son (home for the holiday), who is a student and who works in the USA. The son puts a lot of pressure on himself to do well. He is very dedicated to his studies and his job. He wants very much to create a good impression, make friends, and become part of the university life. He knows that his family is very invested in his education, and he doesn't want to disappoint them in any way.

The father said, "The only advice I gave my son was to take care of himself and make time for his health, sleep, eat, and exercise."

There was no mention of don't do this or don't do that. He didn't say don't go to wild parties, don't drink or smoke. All the words were very positive, and there was real focus on "taking care of yourself."

We talked about how difficult it was for the son to live by these guidelines. The pressure of the school and job often conflicted with the three easy things to do. There are days when there is just not enough time to do all of what is expected. There is a lot of give and take.

The father said, "All else is important but not as important as keeping the body healthy and working. Your first job is to take care of yourself then take care of school and the job. Invest in your health just like you do in school and your job."

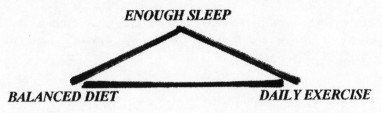

ENOUGH SLEEP

BALANCED DIET   **DAILY EXERCISE**

Best Practice

It really sounds so simple—eat, sleep, exercise. Who doesn't know that these three activities are very important? Who tries to intentionally ignore them? However, it is so easy to take the shortcut and move them to the back of the line. I have often talked about what you might add to your tool kit. Your personal health is a must!

Notes

_____

_____

_____

_____

_____

_____

_____

_____

RELIABLE, TRUSTWORTHY

*I do trust you. I want to trust you more and give you more
responsibility. I can't do it all myself, and I want you to take on
more each day.*

—The Boss

Background

From a boss's perspective, *reliability* is the passageway to trust.

Reliability is:

* "The ability to be depended upon, as for accuracy, honesty,
  achievement".
* "When you take on responsibility for your actions . . . and
  deliver".
* "When employees are reliable, when they are punctual, do their
  work with a minimum of errors, and put the job first".
* "When a person does what he says he is going to do."

Reliability>>generates>>trust.

Real-Life Example
Ron and his team were responsible for providing paint to the paint
line. Tonight the line was going to run short of paint, the line would
shut down, and thirty people would be sent home early—with
reduced pay.
No paint.
No work.
Not good!
Ron contacted the supplier and made expedited arrangements to
fly the paint from the supplier to a local airport and have the paint
picked up by a carrier. If all would go *as planned*, the paint would

arrive at the plant by 10:00 p.m. and the third shift of production would have the paint needed. Ron made all the necessary calls and connections with the paint supplier, their shipping department, the airfreight carrier, the trucking companies, the plant receiving inspection, and the production supervisor in the plant.

As Ron's boss left at 6:00 p.m., he asked Ron, "Are we okay on paint tonight, we going to get it?"

Ron said, "All is arranged, and I'll make sure it gets here."

The boss left.

Ron called the supplier again at six fifteen. "Is the paint ready?"

"Yes."

Ron talked with the carrier. "Are you on the way to get the paint?"

"Yes."

Half an hour later, to the carrier he asked, "Do you have the paint at the airport? The plane on time?"

"Yes."

He called the carrier at the arriving airport. "The plane arrived and you have the paint?"

"Yes."

"How long till you are at the plant?"

"One hour."

Ron, at nine, called the plant receiving inspection. "The paint arrived yet?"

"Yes, we're unloading it now."

At nine thirty, Ron called the production foreman. "You have the paint? All okay?"

"Yes, we have it, it's on the line and we're painting!"

Best Practice

Ron was reliable, and he had the trust of the boss to get it done. The reliable worker, one who does what he says he's going to do, develops trust with his boss, coworkers, suppliers, and customers. Reliability generates trust!

Notes

_____

_____

_____

_____

_____

_____

_____

_____

_____

_____

_____

QUALITY

That car is sweet and has super quality. We all know the Japanese make the highest-quality cars. J. D. Power confirms this. What do I know about quality?

My boss says he wants me to do a quality job, whatever that means!

Quality is in the eye of the beholder.

Quality is job 1!

Quality always comes first, cost second.

Quality is expensive.

If you don't have quality, you don't have customers.

And a favorite, if you have quality, the customer comes back; if you don't, the product comes back—*your choice.*

Background

Everyone talks about quality and how important it is.

The dictionary defines it as "an essential or distinctive characteristic, property, or attribute; high grade, superiority, excellence; producing or providing products or services of quality or merit." Hundreds of books have been written about quality, quality principles, and quality practices. These writings go into excruciating detail about building quality, the cost of quality, and how to design processes to reach high standards of quality in products and services.

There are many, many gurus who have contributed to the development of quality principles and practices.

1. W. Edward Deming
2. Kaoru Ishikawa
3. Joseph M. Juran
4. Philip B. Crosby
5. Malcolm Baldrige
6. Others

So when someone says you need to do a *quality job*, what does that really mean? A job done quickly and on time? A job done with no errors? A finished product that looks good and lasts? A product that works and doesn't break down?

One of the easiest definitions to remember, and maybe the most inclusive definition, is by Philip Crosby, from the Quality College, Winter Park, Florida: "Quality is conformance to requirements."

If you know what the requirements are (specifications of the finished product—the what—and timing to get the product complete—the when) and you meet or exceed (conformance) these two clearly defined requirements, you are providing a quality product or service.

Best Practice

Spend the necessary time with your boss to clearly define what a *quality job* is. Knowing the specifications of the finished product and the timing for completion will definitely help you do a quality job.

It is to your benefit and your boss's benefit to reach agreement.

TEAMS

Most all of us have been on a team of one sort or another. We celebrate our wins and try to forget our losses. *Get 'em next time.* And then we move on.

We learn important skills in the process, such as teamwork, relying on others, sharing a common goal, performing our role, competition, the importance of practice, and on and on. Those excellent experiences will carry over into the workplace. However, the main reason for using teams in the workplace is that the use of teams are usually the smartest way to achieve a goal.

Background

Most of the teams we associated with were sports, clubs, bands, or volunteer associations. These experiences were very important in our development and often allowed us to compete with others similar in age or interest. We often volunteered or tried out to be able to participate on these teams. We felt good about making the team and being accepted.

When you enter the workforce and there are teams, you will become part of a performance-driven group effort (like it or not). You will be expected to pull your load, contribute to the success of the team, and help others in the process.

No one sits on the bench if they can't or don't perform. Most teams are small (maximize efficiency and maintain low costs) and are very focused on their goal, usually a goal that cannot be reached by an individual.

Here are some similarities and differences between *sports teams* and *work teams*:

Sports	*Work*
1. Common goal	1. Common goal
2. Requires practice for best results	2. Requires practice for best results
3. *Major recognition for stars*	3. *Recognition for each team member*
4. *Promotes structure and tolerates creativity*	4. *Promotes and seeks activity*
5. Recognize and utilize leaders	5. Recognize and utilizes leaders
6. *Practice is before the contest*	6. *Practice is during the contest*
7. *Plays the game once or twice a week*	7. *Performs the work each day*
8. *Receive trophies or certificates for winning*	8. *Receive compensation for excellent performance*
9. *Best teams win and move on*	9. *Best teams win and move up*

Why do businesses and work groups use teams? Teams often are seen to cost more money, require more people, and are slower in getting results.
So what is the big deal? What are the benefits of using teams in the workplace?

* Teams provide a wider range
  of ideas and suggestions to solve problems.
* Teams that work together motivate one
  another as they focus on the task at hand.
* Teams often can accomplish much more
  than an individual can.

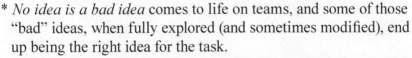

* *No idea is a bad idea* comes to life on teams, and some of those "bad" ideas, when fully explored (and sometimes modified), end up being the right idea for the task.
* Some workers are cautious and risk averse; gaining support and consensus of others on a team sometimes drives home the risky and best solution.
* Most teams contain some form of diversity in backgrounds, experiences, and cultures. This diversity brings new ideas and generates open-minded discussion and open-minded solutions.
* Teams help workers identify leadership skills and leaders on the team.
* Since team members are reliant and dependent on one another, team members more quickly help other team members. Team member growth and development help all on the team.
* Teams may appear to be slower (meetings, consensus building, negotiations, etc., etc.), and they may be; however, the results are usually superior, of higher quality, and easier to obtain support for implementation.
* Being on a team is more fun, and success is shared and celebrated together.

Best Practice

In the workplace, when called upon or asked to join a team, *do it*!
Volunteer!
The work experience will allow you to continue your job growth.
Whether a team member or a team leader, you will learn and grow,
and that growth will make you more valuable to other workers, the
boss, and the organization.
Volunteer!

HUSTLE

Every morning in Africa, a gazelle wakes up. It knows it must run faster than the fastest lion, or it will be killed. Every morning a lion wakes up. It knows it must outrun the slowest gazelle, or it will starve to death. It doesn't matter whether you are a lion or a gazelle. When the sun comes up, you'd better be running.

—Author Unknown

Background

There are those who will think about *it*, procrastinate about *it*, and will not get it done. There are those who will talk a good game, but when the time comes to play, they don't. And of course, there are those who say and believe "I just can't find time to get it done" instead of making the time necessary to get it done.

Action,
speed,
aggressiveness,
accomplishment
are not apparent
in their work spirit!
Are they overly tentative?

Versus

Others embrace action and focus on getting *it* done and getting *it* behind them. When it is game time, they are suited up, ready to play, and are early onto the field. These workers make time, complete the task, and look for more to do.
Action, speed, aggressiveness, *hustle,* and accomplishment are in their work spirit.

These sayings are dated but somehow continue to live on with meaning:

* He who hesitates is lost!
* The early bird gets the worm.
* It's not the size of the dog in the fight; it's the size of the fight in the dog.
* Don't put off til tomorrow what you can do today.
* A bird in the hand is worth two in the bush (back to the birds?).

These sayings reinforce the desire to get things done, make progress, and not hesitate or delay.
Failure by doing nothing is failure by omission.
Failure by doing something is failure by commission.
Most bosses I know, fully understand failure but have much less patience with failure by omission. Doing something and failing can result in the positive.

* "I have not failed. I've just found 10,000 ways that won't work." (Thomas Edison)
* "Failure is simply the opportunity to begin again, this time more intelligently." (Henry Ford)
* "It's fine to celebrate success, but it is more important to heed the lessons of failure." (Bill Gates)
* "When I was young, I observed that 9 out of 10 things I did were failures, so I did 10 times more work." (George Bernard Shaw)

Best Practice

In the day to day work environment, bosses would rather slow you down versus push you when it comes to completing assignments. By having an aggressive, hustled, get-stuff-done approach, you will get results (with some failures), and those results will be recognized and rewarded.
And when the sun comes up, you will be running!

THAT INTERVIEW

It's time for that job interview. "What do I say? What should I not say? What if I make a lot of mistakes and blow this chance? How do others get through this? Are there real secrets to having a good interview that gets me the job? I know I'll be nervous, and who wouldn't be? Anything I can do to stay cool?"
"I may get one shot at this, and I need and want this job!"

Background

Just about everyone can provide the interview candidate with ideas, and most are probably pretty sound recommendations based on some degree of experience. Most of us have been on both sides of the interview table and are aware of the stress an interview may place on a prospective employee. This stress and nervousness is taken into consideration by the interviewer, and generally, the interviewer will try to make the interviewee comfortable.

There are a number of phases that, if properly followed, will help you with a smooth, comfortable, successful interview.

* Phase 1: Preparation
* Phase 2: Practice
* Phase 3: Execution
* Phase 4: Follow Up

Preparation

It sounds simple (it generally is), but you need to do some homework.
Try to learn as much as you can about the organization, group, or company that you want to join. Search the Internet, talk with others who work for this organization, or visit the library (still a great

source of information). Document what you learn and prepare a list of questions you might want to ask the interviewer.

Think about some questions that might be asked of you and prepare your answers, such as these:

* Do you have any travel restrictions?
* Are you willing to transfer out of the town, state, or country?
* Can you work any shift and overtime?
* Where do you want to be in five or ten years? What position?

(Positive answers are generally a good sign of flexibility.)

Think about the job for which you are being interviewed. What are the expectations of this job, and how would you meet them? Is the job just a job or the start of a career? Besides money, why do you want this job (career growth, opportunity, field of interest, others)? Is there any prereading material provided by the interviewer that should be read before the interview? If none is provided, you might ask the interviewer if there is, such as...

1. a job description;
2. work plans and/or appraisal forms, etc.; or
3. organization's philosophy, principles, mission statement, any policies.

Anything provided to you by the interviewer should be read and studied, and any questions should be listed for the upcoming interview.

Practice

Now is the time to focus on practicing for the interview. The more you practice, the better you'll get. You will probably have one-half to one hour for the interview, and the interviewer will ask most of the questions. There is no list of standard questions or standard interview approaches. The person who interviews you will want to get to know you, get to know you over and above what has been supplied in advance.

I find the best way to practice is to spend time with someone who can play the interviewer role with you (know anyone in HR or with a lot of experience?).
Have them ask you interview-type questions.
Have them listen to your responses and give you feedback.
Have them tell you what went well and what could be improved upon.
Also, spend some time thinking about that first impression you will make. Practice with your interviewer friend and do the following:

1. Smile.
2. Try to relax as best you can.
3. Maintain good eye contact.
4. Listen intently to the questions.
5. Think before you answer; speedy responses are not the priority.
6. Answer the questions honestly, and be concise.
7. Be aware of the "like, like, like" trap in communications; slow down to answer the questions.
8. Select what you will wear and what you'll take into the interview (notes binder, notebook, iPad?).
9. Ask those questions you might have for the interviewer, and listen to the answers.

Execution

This is what you have prepared for and practiced for. Here are some observations of successful interviews:

* The candidate was prepared and knew about the organization.
* The candidate appeared relaxed, answered all the questions, and smiled through most of the interview.
* The candidate has a positive attitude, a good appearance, and appeared to be comfortable and flexible as to assignments.
* The candidate asked good questions and took notes.
* The candidate came across as open, honest, friendly, and sincere.
* At the end of the interview, the candidate thanked the interviewer for spending the time with him, said he hoped he made a positive

impression to meet the job expectations, and firmly shook the interviewer's hand, accompanied by a smile and a sincere *thank-you.*

Follow Up

After the interview, and allowing some time to take a deep breath, go off somewhere and make some notes on how the interview went, from your perspective.

1. What went well?
2. What would you do differently had it not gone well? How better could you have prepared?
3. How better could you have practiced?
4. What should you do differently at the next job interview?
5. What questions did you have a hard time answering?

That day or the next, take the time to send the interviewer a note to say something like this:

Thank you very much for spending time with me in the interview. Even though I was somewhat nervous, I hope I was able to effectively respond to your questions. Our interview just reinforced my desire to work for ABC Co., and I look forward to hearing from you in the near future.

Sincerely,
Cathy Wilson

If you don't hear anything back from the interviewer in a couple of weeks, a short note to the interviewer reinforcing your interest in the organization and desire for obtaining the position would be quite appropriate. Sometimes the process drags on or is delayed. Your follow-up is a positive sign.

Best Practice

The first interview is difficult just because it is the first. You will get better.

Using the four steps—*preparation, practice, execution, and follow up*—will help you land that first job and others in the future.

Notes

_____

_____

_____

_____

_____

_____

_____

_____

_____

_____

_____

_____

_____

SECTION THREE: FOCUS YOUR EFFORT

* Multitasking versus Focused Effort
Both approaches are effective, if used appropriately.

* Focus, Focus, Focus
Getting rid of all those distractions is the key to best results in a shorter time.

* Attention to Detail
What's on the surface may not tell you the whole story. Peel back that onion and dig!

* A Place for Everything and Everything in Its Place
How organization saves you time, speeds up your work, and reduces frustration.

* Look, Listen, Learn
You too can learn to be a sponge. Utilizing the three Ls in an active versus passive way will speed up your ability to become more and more productive.

* Close the Loop
It's not over til it's over. Getting the job completely done is what you are after. Being satisfied with 70–80 percent may result in failure.

* PPP: Prepare, Practice, Present
Here's a simple approach to make an effective presentation. All steps are important, especially the *practice* one.

* Ethics and Ethical Behavior
These are ten principles of ethical behavior. They will work in any work situation or environment. Doing the right thing is your guide.

* Building Relationships
Listed are some pointers to help you belong and participate.
Developing good relationships on and off the job will make work
more rewarding and playtime more fun.

* Be the Best
The fastest and most direct road to success is being the best you
can be at whatever you do. This will be recognized and rewarded.
No matter what the job, no matter what the career, by being the
best, you will achieve job satisfaction and advance.

Notes

_____

_____

_____

_____

_____

_____

_____

_____

_____

_____

_____

Treat your colleagues, family and friends with respect dignity, fairness and courtesy.

—Lorii Myers

The best teamwork comes from men who are working independently toward one goal in unison.

—James Cash Penney

Doing the best at this moment puts you in the best place for the next moment.

—Oprah Winfrey

The difference between who you are and who you want to be is the work you put in.

—Author Unknown

The only way to do great work is to love what you do. If you haven't found it yet, keep looking. Don't settle.

—Steve Jobs

MULTITASKING VERSUS FOCUSED EFFORT

Everybody multitasks. Why not? We can get things done faster and waste less time. Doesn't everyone say "time is money"? Why not fill every minute as best we can? I can easily do two or three things at a time. I can read, listen to music, check e-mail, text, and talk on the phone all at the same time.

Background

Most studies dispel the notion that multitasking automatically saves time or is really an effective way to get things done.
"It has been successfully demonstrated that the brain cannot effectively or efficiently switch between tasks, so you lose time. It takes four times longer to recognize new things, so you're not saving time. Multitasking actually costs time."[1]

Multitasking is not always the answer to getting things done faster, more efficiently, with the highest level of quality.
In today's world of ADD (attention deficit disorder), you might think that multitasking accommodates those who have a hard time focusing. Studies also show that too is incorrect.[2]

When to Multitask
For those who like to do many activities at once, multitask when...

1. the quality or outcome of the activity isn't critical;
2. the result of the activity doesn't affect others, especially customers;
3. the activity doesn't require a lot of thinking; and

---

[1]   R. Rogers and Moresell, *Journal of Experimental Psychology: General* 124 (1995): pages 207–231.

[2]   Joshua S. Rubenstein, "Executive Control of Cognitive Processes in Task Switching," (2001): pages 763-797.

4. the finished product, if needing a fix, isn't hard to fix.

When to Focus Your Effort
There is a time to really focus when...

1. the quality of the work performed is critical,
2. your outcome will affect a customer or others,
3. the activity does require thought and analysis, and
4. the outcome needs to be right the first time.

Best Practice

Multitasking can help get several things done concurrently, such as those not requiring serious thought, a lot of coordination, or a high level of quality.
Focused effort requires concentration and thought, which delivers a higher-quality product. Both approaches have effective applications. Their balanced use will benefit you in the long run.

Notes

_____

_____

_____

_____

FOCUS, FOCUS, FOCUS

As stated in a previous best practice, there is a time to multitask and a time to focus. Understanding when to use one approach or the other is important.

1. When quality is critical, focus.
2. When the outcome affects a customer or others, focus.
3. When the activity requires thought or analysis, focus.
4. If the outcome needs to be right the first time, focus.

Why is it often difficult to *really* focus your time or efforts? Your work environment may not lend itself to allow it. Sometimes your workload is so heavy you can't find the time to focus. Continual distractions make it difficult (e-mails, phones, texts, social media, meetings).
Setting priorities and meeting expectations is a balancing act that's tough to accomplish.
Can focusing on one project cause you to miss completing another?

All these and other reasons may be affecting your ability to focus. Those reasons can be mitigated, avoided, or even eliminated. When you feel that you have too many balls in the air, or, you can't do it all, or you are making too many mistakes with what you have, try these approaches to help focus your efforts and get stuff done.

Environment
Find a place where you can go to hide from distractions. This can be a place where you aren't known, a place that

has a door, or just a place you won't be bothered or interrupted. Select a place that is comfortable. If others are around, let them know you need this time to focus and ask them to "please do not interrupt." Try to eliminate other potential interruptions. Turn off the world around you! Headphones can help.

Time
Allocate a block of time each day or week that is for focused work. That time is sacred, with no interruptions, and your time is dedicated to focus on the subject at hand. I have found sixty to ninety minutes is often the maximum for good, uninterrupted, focused work. Then stop. If more time is needed, take a break and return after coming up for air.

Organize
Gather all you need to use your focused time effectively. Take your lists, computer, documents, etc., etc.—all the tools and resources— that will be needed.
Select from your to do list what you want to complete first. Prioritize accordingly:

* Must do
* Want to do
* Like to do
* Someday will do
* Scratch it—won't do!

Zoom in and then drill down and work on that highest-priority item. Work on it until it is complete or you have accomplished what you want to complete in the allocated time. If this task is a large and complicated one, try to break it down into smaller pieces and bites and work on them. After one item is complete, move on to the next.

Best Practice

You can't focus on everything. That's not focus.

Selecting the most important task at hand and driving it to completion is not only an efficient use of time but also rewarding. You got it done, and it is a quality product.

These successful people have it right:

* "To create something exceptional, your mind set must be relentlessly focused on the smallest detail." (Giorgio Armani)

* "Stay focused, go after your dreams and keep moving toward your goal." (LL Cool J)

* "Concentrate all your thoughts upon the work at hand. The sun rays do not burn until brought to a focus." (Alexander Graham Bell)

* "Productivity is never an accident. It is always the result of a commitment to excellence, intelligent planning, and focused effort." (Paul J. Meyer)

Notes

_____

_____

_____

_____

_____

_____

_____

ATTENTION TO DETAIL

Deadlines are tough to meet!
Often, there is a natural tendency to have to settle for "run with
what I have, that's as good as I can make it."
Do you find there is never enough time? Enough time to do it right?
Enough time to get into the details?

Background

Understanding the big picture is usually easier, more expedient,
more fun, and less difficult to comprehend. Looking at the headline
stories on the Internet or *USA Today* gives you an overview, a high-
level interpretation of what the writer wants to communicate. It
usually is a thirty-thousand-foot view that is designed to tell you
something within a limited time frame or limited number of words.

However, in performing your work, getting *into the details*
provides you with the necessary information that will help you
make right decisions and do the best overall job. Doing it right
is what you are paid to do! The more detail, the more focus, the
higher probability you will effectively complete the task.

*Don't let your big-picture thinking stop you from caring about
the small stuff. Paying attention to the details could give you a
competitive advantage. Details matter. It's worth getting it right.*
—Steve Jobs, Apple Inc.

The larger the project, the more important the decision or task, the
more *attention to detail* will help you ensure success.

When drilling down into the details, here are some things to think about:

1. Focus and *eliminate distractions* or other projects. Think only of this task or project. Focus, focus, focus!
2. Do big things in small chunks. Try to *break the task down* into small digestible pieces.
3. *Allow enough time* to drill down into the details. Your objective is to get it right. Speed is important; being thorough is more important.
4. *Peel back the onion* as you proceed. What you see on the surface may not be the reality or the truth.
5. *Document* and make lists of what you learn.
6. If you get tired of digging, *take a break* and walk away for a while. Come back and reread what you've learned and continue.
7. And last, *have another person take a look* at your work; a new set of eyes may see something and may find some errors.

There are many axioms, phrases, or quotations that emphasize the importance of paying attention to detail:

* "Watch the pennies and the dollars will take care of themselves." (Unknown Author)

* "The devil is in the details." (Unknown Author)

* "The devil is in the details, but so is salvation." (Hyman Rickover)

* "The *pursuit of excellence* [Lexus] comes with attention to details." (Toyota policy)

* "If you are going to achieve excellence in big things, you develop the habit in little matters." (Colin Powell)

* "When you work on the little things, big things happen." (Rodger Halston)

Best Practice

Attention to detail—by digging for and obtaining the detailed information to support your decisions, recommendations, or actions, you will greatly enhance the probability of doing it right. Remember, what is often on the surface may not be the whole story.

Notes

_____

_____

_____

_____

_____

_____

_____

_____

_____

_____

A PLACE FOR EVERYTHING, AND
EVERYTHING IN ITS PLACE

Organizing and making visible important things will save you a lot of time, anxiety, and frustration. It is easy to do, it requires some effort and discipline, but it's worth it!

Background

We all have a lot of stuff. Some of it is needed every day, some not. Wasting a lot of time looking for the same things (over and over) is not very effective or efficient. Some examples:

1. Where are my keys, in my jacket, on my desk, in my chest of drawers?
2. I think I have enough cash in my wallet. Where is it?
3. My desk is a complete mess. I know the bill is there somewhere. Is it due? Past due?

4. I just can't find anything in my work area.
5. I am always running and can't find what I need.
6. And there are surely many more examples!

What is needed is a designated location so there is a place for everything and everything is in its place. After each use, the item is then returned to its place.
As I said before, this does require discipline.

Find a place to charge and keep that cell phone.
Ensure house and car keys are always returned to that same place.
Organize your desk so there is a place for each group of papers.
Post-its, notes, stickies—consolidate into one follow-up page; date
it. Keep old pages as a record.

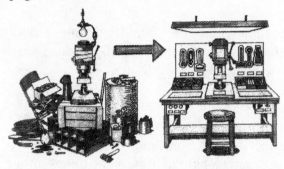

Look at that work area, can it be better organized? Take a look at
your files and see how you can separate and organize them.
Where does that purse or wallet go when not in use?
A place for everything and everything in its place seems to be
common sense, and it is. Doing it is another story. Failure to do it
can have consequences.

"[Twenty-eight percent] of employers say they are less likely to
promote someone with a disorganized workspace."[1]
"A coworker is judged based on the cleanliness of his or her
workspace."[2]

Best Practice

Create a place for everything and put everything it its place. Save
time, improve housekeeping, and reduce frustration.

---

[1]   2011 CareerBuilder Survey of 2662 hiring managers.

[2]   2012 Adecco survey, 1015 adults surveyed.

LOOK, LISTEN, LEARN

School is finished, so let's get on with it. No more studying, testing, practicing. Wrong!
You are just starting, maybe using some different methods, but you are just starting. Now you can have some fun without just reading, studying, and testing.

Background

Starting a new job can be interesting and difficult at the same time.
"What is really expected of me?"
"When I am stuck, who do I talk to?"
"If I ask too many questions, they'll think I am stupid or unprepared."
"Who really knows what's going on around here?"
"How am I going to be accepted by my coworkers?"
Sure, you'll have lots of questions and aren't expected to know everything as a new employee. No big deal.
But how you react to this *inexperience* will help determine how fast you get up to speed and what kind of performance you'll have.

Look
Watch those around you; pay close attention to the boss.
Look at your coworkers. They sure have more experience than you do.

Look at how others do their job and how they interact among themselves, with the boss, and with customers.
Look for reactions of others to others, to yourself.
You have just joined a new group or team—look at what they do.

Listen

Hey, there is a lot of stuff going on around you. Listening to what is important is the key. Listen to what the boss says. Listen to your coworkers. And listen to your customers. Sorting through what is important and related to your job *is* the trick. This will come from experience, sometimes the experience of the first day.

Don't get trapped into listening to rumors, criticisms, negatives directed at the boss, coworkers, others.

With time and experience you will have time to form your own opinion about others. It is best to keep those opinions to yourself.

Learn

By looking and listening, you will learn. You will see what works and what may not. You'll learn that some people you work with are excellent (great performers, they enjoy their work, are hard workers, and are a *positive* influence in the workplace). Coworkers like to be around them, and you will too.

Others, you'll learn, are just the opposite. They can be very *negative*, criticize the workplace, the boss, the world, and usually aren't as productive as others. That is their choice. It surely should not be yours.

Best Practice

Walking into that new job looking, listening, and learning from others is an easy and effective way to quickly get up to speed, become part of the team, and determine what the best practices are, those best practices you might want to adopt.

Notes

_____

_____

_____

_____

CLOSE THE LOOP

"Boy, I was disappointed. I thought all was taken care of, and it wasn't. When I came in, it wasn't there. I thought you told me all was done and there was no problem. You said it'd be there."
"I am sorry. They told me it was all taken care of. When I left, they said all was set and it would be here for sure. I don't know what happened, but I'll find out."
What happened here? Or better yet, what didn't happen?

Background

When we join a work team, we become more and more reliant on others, and they on us! Getting a job done often requires a lot of coordination, timing, effective communication, and trust. When we make a promise or commitment, others will rely on it. Others will make plans or commitments on their own based on what we have said or promised.

Promises or commitments need to be locked in.
Promises or commitments should be *fail-safe*.[1]
Promises or commitments establish our credibility with coworkers and the boss or anyone receiving them.

Example
The young student had some timing difficulty obtaining the needed student loan that was due in two weeks.

Student: "My loan is approved, and it needs to be to the school by January 15. The money isn't available to them till February 1. The loan is approved but not available."

---

[1]   "A system or plan that comes into operation in the event of something going wrong or that is there to prevent such an occurrence" (*The Oxford English Dictionary*).

Uncle: "Will the school accept a letter from the loan agent saying the loan is approved and that the school will wait till February 1 for the money? And if they agree, make sure you get the name and telephone number of the person you talked to who said it is okay."
Student: "I don't know, but I will call and get the information and the name."

Later in the day . . .

Student: "Yes, the school will accept the letter from the loan agent, and I'll be okay till February 1."
Uncle: "That's great. When will the letter be sent to the school?"
Student: "They promised to send it Wednesday, January 13 and will be at the school by January 20, and I'll be okay."
Uncle: "That's good. Who did you talk to, and what's his number?"

All seems set, there are no problems, the letter is to go out in three days and be at the school in plenty of time. The actual loan will be at the school before February 1—no problem. On January 12, the uncle calls the student.

Uncle: "Do you know if the letter will be sent out tomorrow, January 13?"
Student: "That's the plan. I assume they will do as they promised."
Uncle: "What is the name and telephone number of the person [Tim] you spoke to?"

Uncle calls Tim, the loan officer. After three attempts and no replies, he calls the general number of the bank.

Uncle: "Hello, I am calling about loan number xyz for my niece to see if Tim has sent the letter to the university, as promised. *Today* is the date for it to be sent."
Bank Officer (Jane): "I am sorry, I don't know anything about it. Tim has been off, ill for a week, and his work has been piling up. I am sorry, I know nothing about a letter."

Oooops!

70

After the uncle's lengthy explanation, Jane searched through Tim's desk, found the approved student loan application.

Jane: "Today is January 13, and I'll need to have someone draft the letter and send it to the university. That will take till January 18, and probably won't be to them by January 20

Uncle: "Please fax it to them, and I'll get you the fax number, okay?"

Jane: "Will do, but you do know that now because of the delay, we will not be able to get the money to the school by February 2! It just can't be done."

Uncle: "This defeats the whole purpose of all we have tried to do. The school must have the money by February 1, or my niece won't be able to enroll."

Jane: "I will have to see what I can do and will be back to you."

Uncle: "When?"

Jane: "Tomorrow."

That same afternoon . . .

Uncle (to the school admissions officer): "Our loan has been approved, and because of their loan officer's illness, they may not be able to have funds to you by February 1. What can we do?"

School Admin. Officer: "Once you talk with the bank officer tomorrow, let me know what she *can* do and give me her name and number, then I can see what I *can* do."

Next day . . .

Uncle: "Any news, any progress?"

Jane: "We can speed up the process, but the money will be delivered February 4 at best."

Uncle: "I will have the school admissions officer call you, okay? Maybe we can work something out."

That day, the bank officer and the school admissions officer spoke
and agreed that 2/4 would work
and the niece could enroll on
February 1. The uncle
asked for and obtained a
faxed letter confirming
this agreement, the
niece enrolled on
February 1, and the

admissions office received the funds on February 4 as promised!

Best Practice

Sometimes the best intentions run into unintended problems or
poor performance by others. We can't let these variables affect our
ability to get things done.
By anticipating what can or will go wrong, we learn to not assume
all will work to plan. By identifying failure points and checking
on them or eliminating them, we can reduce our risk. In the case
of the student loan, after much expediting and follow-up, we were
able to close the loop and guarantee the niece's admission. The
final agreement document sealed the effort.
"It's not over til it's over," some wise person said.

Notes

_____

_____

_____

_____

_____

_____

PPP: PREPARE, PRACTICE, PRESENT

At some point you will be asked to make a pitch, presentation, or report to a group. Maybe it is a pitch to the boss, your coworkers, or a customer. Everyone gets a bit nervous when they have to stand up in front of a group (all alone!) and sound like they know what they are talking about.

These thoughts may run through your mind:

"What makes me the expert?"
"Do I really know what I am talking about?"
"What am I going to say?"
"What if I forget something?"
"What if someone asks me a question I can't answer?"
"How am I going to talk for five to ten minutes?"

Background

There are three phases to being effective in making a presentation:
One, prepare for the presentation.
Two, practice what you have prepared.
Three, present with support and confidence.

Prepare
Draft out a list of all the points you want to make in the presentation, the messages you want to deliver, in a few sentences or phrases.
Next, take this draft of points and decide what the best sequence for these points is so they are in the order in which you want to present them.
Look at the list again. Any points missed? Does this sequence seem to be the most effective for delivering your message?
(Don't hesitate to put some notes or reminders on your sheet related to your points.)

Practice

This is probably the most important step in preparing for a presentation. It is time to practice, practice, practice.

First, stand up alone and practice by yourself. Say a few introductory words about your topic and then start going through your presentation points.

Second, find a friend or associate (someone that is objective and somewhat knowledgeable about the topic) and ask them to listen to the pitch. Have them ask you questions about the presentation. Ask them to give you honest feedback as to what went well and, maybe, what did not go well. Ask them, "What three things am I doing well in the pitch, so I can keep doing them, and what three things can I do better or improve upon, so I can sharpen the presentation?" If there are no improvements recommended, push back until you get some suggestions (or find another friend or associate to help).

(Remember: Practice is the most important part of a presentation. You will feel more comfortable, more confident, and more relaxed as you do the final presentation. High school basketball teams practice four to five hours for every one hour of playtime. Band members practice six to eight hours for every hour performing.)

Present

So now it is show time. You have a solid presentation. You have practiced and know what you will present. The content of your presentation is clear to you, and your comfort level is high. You are the expert on your presentation.

* Follow your key points and sequence.
* Have your notes with you for reference.
* Anticipate questions with answers.
* If asked a question and you know the answer, fine—reply. If you don't, say, "I don't know, but I will find out and get back to you."
* Avoid words like *always*, *never*, and *all* since most things aren't absolute.
* Keep your presentation on track; you are in the lead and in control.

* Close the presentation with a thank-you (probably a thank-you because it's over).

Best Practice

The experience of delivering a report or presentation does not have to be a bad one. Since it is *you that has been asked* to present, it is an *opportunity for you*, a positive opportunity. By diligently *preparing*, repeatedly *practicing*, and with confidence *presenting*, you will give an effective presentation, and don't be surprised if you will be asked to do one again!

Notes

_____

_____

_____

_____

_____

_____

ETHICS AND ETHICAL BEHAVIOR

In your workplace you will learn there are some behaviors that are acceptable and some unacceptable. Then again, there are behaviors promoted to help the organization meet its goals and objectives. You may even receive a list that spells them out for you—the dos and don'ts.

Background

There are some ethical principles that will guide you as you initiate your work experience. I call them the top ten for workplace success that, if followed, will provide you guidance no matter where you work and no matter what job you perform.

1. Honesty
2. Trust
3. Respect
4. Truth
5. Honor
6. Integrity
7. Understanding
8. Tolerance
9. Fairness
10. Kindness

As you read through the *definitions* and a boss's view, you'll quickly see that many of these are connected or interconnected. That's good, because they are.

Honesty
"Sincere, genuine, upright, and fair; honorable in principles, intentions, and actions."

I want my people to be honest. We rely on one another. If they aren't honest, how will we be able to work, solve problems, and get stuff done? Honesty is the best policy—should be the only one!

Trust
"Firm reliance, confidence, and belief; faith; custody and care of."
I trust you to take care of that. I trust you will make the right decision. What I am saying is, you take care of it—it's taken off my agenda. I'm not going to worry about it; you will.

Respect
"Deferential or high regard; to have esteem for—to pay one's respects."
Whoever you deal with—customers, suppliers, coworkers—listen, be fair, use good manners; treat others as you want to be treated. As Roger Federer (Swiss tennis champion) stated, "I fear no one, but I respect everyone."

Truth
"Conformity to knowledge, fact, or actuality; veracity; the real state of affairs."
When we know the truth, we can solve problems. We all make mistakes; don't cover them up. Make them visible, and we'll fix them. Tell the truth, or someone will tell it for you.

Honor
"Personal integrity maintained without legal or other obligation."
When it's decision time, do the right thing, honor the truth. It hurts everyone less in the long run.

Integrity
"Strict personal honesty and independence."
If you know the truth, stand by it. Stick to it; don't waver. Again, do what is right, no matter the pressure. How others see you is on the line! There is respect involved here.

Understanding
"A reconciliation of differences; an agreement reached between two or more persons or groups; tolerant or sympathetic."
Understanding your coworkers' point of view is important. It's good to listen to and understand their perspective. You won't always agree, but you should appreciate how they look at things. We can agree to disagree, and that's okay too.

Tolerance
"The capacity for or practice of recognizing and respecting the opinions, practices, or behavior of others."
You will meet a lot of interesting people along the way—a lot of different, interesting people. Showing respect and understanding of others will go a long way. Put yourself in the other guy's shoes and see how they feel!

Fairness
"The quality or state of being fair; impartial treatment; just or equitable; consistent with rules."
Sure, life's not always fair, so we have policies, processes, and procedures (PPP) to help us run the operation. Follow them and you'll be okay. The three Ps help provide everyone a level playing field and the same chance. Play by the rules!

Kindness
"An act or instance of being kind; governed by consideration and compassion: friendly, obliging."
A simple smile, friendly hello, followed by a helping hand, sure goes a long way. Being tough, aggressive, and driven doesn't mean you can't be kind to others.
"It is nice to be important, but it is more important to be nice" (Alan Mulally, president of Ford Motor Co.).

Best Practice

The top ten for workplace success, as it relates to ethics and ethical behavior, are best practices in their own right. They provide a solid foundation as you build your work career. They will *not* always be

easy or convenient to follow, and others may not be so inclined to adhere to these principles. It's not a perfect world.
However, by their use, *you are doing the right thing*!

Notes

_____

_____

_____

_____

_____

_____

_____

_____

_____

BUILDING RELATIONSHIPS

You probably won't believe this, but when you start working every day, you'll find you spend more time with fellow workers than with your friends or even your family. You can expect to spend eight to ten hours per day, sometimes six days a week, on the job.
It is important that you focus on developing good working relationships. If effectively done, those relationships will:

1. allow you to be happier and more productive;
2. make work more enjoyable—yes, even fun;
3. help you develop your career;
4. allow you to create good relationships with customers, suppliers, and other stakeholders;
5. position you for pay raises and promotions; and
6. help you attain your goals and provide real job satisfaction.

Remember, work is eight to ten hours per day, every day. Job satisfaction is very important.

Background

"You can submarine your career and work relationships by actions you take and the behaviors you exhibit at work. No matter your education, your experience, or your title, if you can't play well with others, you will never accomplish your work mission."[1]
Think of this, as a new member of the workforce, and maybe even a team, you will have a role to play. That role will be dependent on others as others will be depending on you. The maximum

---

[1]   Susan M. Heathfield, *Human Resources Management*. Acknowledged human resource expert.

or ultimate level of accomplishment will come about through effectively working together.

These are some cornerstones of building good working relationships:

* Trust
* Mutual respect
* Open, honest communications
* Listening
* Truthfulness

With these in mind, and with the appropriate application, here are fifteen practices that will help you develop those good working relationships:

1. Talk with your coworkers, not always just about work.
2. Smile and others will smile back.
3. Call people by their name; we all like it when we are recognized.
4. Be friendly and helpful.
5. Be cordial and positive. No one likes a whiner or a habitual complainer!
6. Be interested in your coworker. What is going on in their life, family, and friends?

7. Be generous with praise and stingy with criticism. Celebrate successes.
8. Listen to others. Listen twice as much as you speak.

9. Be thoughtful of others' opinions. Opinions are opinions.

10. Develop a sense of humor—laugh at yourself. Laughter shows you are human and maybe a bit humble.

11. Accept that you will make errors and mistakes. That's okay. Don't hide or cover up mistakes. Learn from them and move on.

12. Acknowledge others with a "Good morning," "How's it going," "What's up," "See you tomorrow," and "Thank you!"

13. Consider others' feelings when you speak and act; put yourself in your coworkers' shoes.

14. Avoid gossip, and only speak positively of others; if you can't, it is best to be quiet.

15. Don't try to find time, *but make time*, to get to know your coworkers. You *make the effort*. Visit their work area and see what they are doing.

Best Practice

Your work results and career are really dependent on being able to effectively work with others. Making the effort to grow and develop good working relationships will make you, your coworkers and team more successful.

BE THE BEST

"I want to be the best. I want to make a lot of money, like you. What is the secret? What should I study, major in? I want to be on my own. I want to be creative. I'd like to own my own business so I don't have a boss. I want to be my own boss and come and go as I please. I want time to do the things *I want to do*. How do I get there?"

Background

There are a lot of desires and questions here and a lot of wants. As a graduate, you probably have these questions and more running through your mind. Graduation day comes with a *big door* opening to you. How smoothly and effectively you pass through that door and where you go will change over time. Your path (education, jobs, careers, family) will evolve and change as you go.
Success story examples:

* I have a friend (a good student) who went to night school and community college and, after many years, finally graduated. He landed a job with a waste management company as a dispatcher. Through the years he was promoted to foreman, then manager, district manager, to vice president. *Being the best!*

* Another friend of mine survived college, served in the military (flew navy jets), went to work for the government, and moved up pay grades through his roles in the government. Years later, he joined a consulting company as vice president. Then he joined a think tank (as senior vice president) that services the government.
Many jobs, many great successes! *Being the best!*

* A relative of mine didn't graduate. After ninth grade, he had to go to work to support his family. He did this job, did that job. He went to work in a brewery—he drove a lift truck. He became a foreman. He moved to another business, learned the business, and years later he bought out the retiring owner. It took many years but he became his own boss, with his own company, with his own responsibilities. His career went from a ninth-grade graduate to president of his own small company. *Being the best!*

* I worked with a lady who, after high school, went to work wherever she could find a job. After some time, she was able to join the largest employer in the community as a clerk. She soon was promoted to a position requiring more responsibility as an administrative assistant. This person became the administrative assistant and coordinator for an executive vice president. She was at the top of her field and was recognized for it! *Being the best!*

* Edward was just an average student in high school. However, he was an excellent football player, always a starter, always the best. He became a teacher and coach. Eventually he became a college coach and won numerous championships. After retiring from working and coaching, he was recognized for outstanding coaching performance in the university's hall of fame. Three years later, he was recognized for outstanding performance (inducted into the hall of fame) as a player from the university from which he graduated. As a player and coach, he was *being the best!*

There are thousands, if not millions, of success stories like these. This is America!
What made these and others so successful? Is there a common thread? Common attributes? Education? Luck? Motivation? Job Satisfaction? Patronage? Money? Persistence? Perseverance?
How did they find their way, their right path, their path to success?

Best Practice

These people were hard workers at being the best in their job or their field. They differentiated themselves from others. Their work ethic, plus some of the attributes listed, helped them become very successful.

Being the best at whatever you do, no matter what you do, will lead to recognition, reward and success.

Notes

_____

_____

_____

_____

_____

_____

_____

SECTION FOUR: MOVING FORWARD, STEPPING UP

* Meetings! Meetings! Meetings!
Whether you are running the meeting or just attending, make sure
there is value in the time spent off the job. Getting something out
of the meeting is up to you. It is *your time* off the job.

* Up Close and Personal
Being in the best position to listen, learn, participate, and be
recognized. No back row for you!

* Volunteer: Be a Leader
Don't hesitate to volunteer if you feel you can contribute and make
a difference. If asked to lead, why not?

* The Black Hole
You don't want to go there. Once you do, your reputation will be
hard to repair, and those depending on you will hesitate to trust
you.

* Step-by-Step
How do you handle a big project that is complicated and complex?
How do you get it done in the designated time frame? Let me
introduce the elephant.

* Practicing CPI
Never give up. You may be slowed down. There may be
obstructions before you. Others may fail you. The target may
change or be delayed. But you never give up till it is done.

* Measure It
Five steps to help you reach that goal, that target. Keeping score
and keeping results visual works in sports, education, health, etc.,
etc. In your work environment, measures are critical.

* The Five Whys
Here is a basic process created and used by Toyota in all their
operations. The process works and is easy to use in searching for
the root cause.

* Give Me More
Shock the boss and ask for more work when you are ready for it.
Why not use that free time and get something done?

None of us is as smart as all of us.
—Ken Blanchard

When you get into a tight place and everything goes against you, never give up then, for that is just the place and time that the tide will turn.
—Harriet Beecher Stowe

Tell me and I forget. Show me and I remember. Involve me and I understand.
—Chinese Proverb

If you are only doing what you are getting paid for, and doing it no better than the average employee, then your pay is most likely right where it should be.
—Bo Bennett

MEETINGS! MEETINGS! MEETINGS!

"Why should I, we, spend so much time in meetings? They take so long and are a waste of time. I have my job to do and meetings put me behind, and it will be hard to catch up. So what's the big deal with so many meetings (team meetings, staff meetings, planning meetings, communication meetings, etc., etc.)? Should I go, or skip them?"

Go!

Background

Meetings do take time and energy, and they take you away from your immediate job, your responsibility. However, meetings prove very valuable if handled correctly and efficiently. Here's why. Most bosses, leaders, or coworkers call for meetings to...

1. gather or impart information to a group (this is done more efficiently and with less chance of error if done one by one);
2. exchange ideas, views, opinions and suggestions (open discussion also generates ideas that may not be created by one person alone—diversity of inputs is powerful);

Creating a Plan

3. discuss options, narrow those options, and obtain support and buy-in;
4. collectively solve problems;
5. make decisions and move forward;
6. create a plan to do what is necessary (in an organized way) to make decisions; or
7. communicate, communicate, communicate (this is talking, listening, and discussing; meetings are chances to give *your*

input and help provide direction that affects the organization and *you*).

In these meetings you can learn a lot more than by just using e-mails, texts, or other non-face-to-face methods.

In face-to-face meetings, you will:

1. see the body language of others (this form of communication provides insight sometimes as valuable as verbal communication).
2. be engaged (just by being in the meeting, you will be expected to participate and contribute).
3. be able to ask questions, hear the questions of others, and hear the answers.
4. get all to participate, if the meeting is handled properly (also, buy-in is often easier to obtain in meetings and usually more timely; a sense of belonging grows, and usually, a form of bonding is developed).
5. often have opportunities at visualization (charts, graphs, handouts, use of whiteboards, etc., etc.) that will help with understanding and explanations.
6. sometimes find the time spent is less—collectively spent—than alone for both you and the person running the meeting.

From many perspectives, meetings are value added if properly organized and managed. If senior management felt they were a waste of time and they were making you less productive or efficient, they would not support or drive them. Go and participate in meetings.

Here are some suggestions for meeting effectiveness—whether you are calling the meeting or you are helping with a meeting implementation. These are simple but effective:

1. Create an agenda with timelines. Keep the meeting as short as possible. Short is better (fifteen minutes, thirty minutes, one hour, two hours—beyond this, it gets risky).
2. Invite participants, not spectators. Keep the size of the group small.

3. Start on time. If this is to be a regular (weekly, monthly, etc.) meeting and participants are often late, install a fine system. At 1:00 p.m., the meeting starts, the door is closed. Late arrivals pay a dollar for late arrival. This dollar could be put into some celebration fund for future use. Lateness will cease to be a problem.
4. Have someone be the note taker, someone who isn't running the meeting.
5. Focus on the topics on the agenda. Stop any straying discussions. Turn off phones!
6. Try to engage all in the discussions. Call on those who say nothing or aren't engaged.
7. Capture and summarize what is decided on each topic so everyone understands and there is no later disagreement.
8. Where action is required after the meeting, seek out volunteers to carry forward the work needing to be done before the next meeting.
9. Create a draft agenda for the next meeting and send to all after the meeting.
10. After the meeting has ended, spend some time to evaluate the meeting as to effectiveness (after-action review):
   a. What were the objectives of the meeting? Were those objectives met?
   b. What went well in the meeting? Make sure you continue those practices or approaches.
   c. What could be improved on in the meeting? What should we do differently?
   d. What will we do in the next meeting to make it more effective?

Best Practice

There is a place for e-mails, texting, and teleconferencing. These tools are usually fairly effective at passing along information. However, they are rather restrictive at capitalizing on interactive inputs, collective use of intellects, and the problem-solving capabilities of the group. *Attend and participate in meetings.* And when you lead a meeting, follow the guidelines listed. Successful meetings generate successful solutions and generate better results!

Notes

_____

_____

_____

_____

_____

_____

_____

UP CLOSE AND PERSONAL

Here we go, back to those meetings. Do you ever wonder who is doing all the work around here? All we seem to do is go to meetings.

Most meetings are really focused on communication of one sort or another. The boss (or someone) feels it is important to pull the workers together and pass on some information or instructions. So someone thinks it *is important* to take you off the job and communicate.

Background

Since you are now off the job and *have to* sit through another one of these meetings, should you take advantage of the free time and slip to the back of the office or room and sit with *your* buddies as a way to get through this? Catch up on e-mail?

No!

Sit up front, preferably in the front row. Get to a position close to the speaker so you can clearly hear and see everything.

Here are some of the advantages of being up close and personal:

1. You will plainly hear what the speaker is saying.
2. You will have less or no distractions between you and the speaker.

3. You will focus on the speaker and be able to see his expressions and emphasis points.
4. You will better see charts, graphs, or other visual tools used.
5. You will be able to take better notes.
6. Questions are more easily handled coming from the front row.
7. And the speaker will see you and see *you are engaged*!

Here are some disadvantages of being up close and personal:

1. It will be hard to not follow the speaker.
2. Your mind won't so easily wander.
3. If you doze off, you'll be seen or noticed.
4. Your friends will miss you back in the last row.
5. The speaker will see you way back there and wonder *if you are engaged* or not.

Obviously, the advantages of being a front-row participant greatly outweigh all disadvantages. And besides, you may learn something, something important.

Best Practice

In meetings, lectures, and presentations, be a front-row participant. You will hear more, see more, learn more, and be better informed. *Up close and personal* works!

VOLUNTEER: BE A LEADER

I always liked the situation created when the commander said, as ten soldiers lined up before him, "I need a volunteer to lead a small team. It is an important mission, and I need someone to lead. So those of you who'll volunteer, please take one step forward."

All took one step *back*, except one person, who was caught off guard. The commander said, "Well, I guess I have my volunteer!"

Background

There will be opportunities to lead, and some will step forward, others hold back. Of course there is anxiety related to leading. *Where do I start? Will I know what to do? Will I be able to get the job done? Will the team listen to me? What happens if we fail? Do I have the skills to lead? Why should I volunteer? Let someone else do it!*

You are asking the right questions, questions that will get answered as you lead an effort or team.

Leading can be viewed as an inborn skill set or one that comes about through a process of teaching, learning, observing, and practicing. Many experts believe that leadership is one-third born and two-thirds made. And those in the one-third born supposedly inherited attributes such as being extroverted, highly organized, effective at communications, and/or other special traits. Note, these traits also can be learned, practiced, and fine-tuned.

Volunteering to lead an effort will give you an opportunity to take initiative, work with others, develop your organizational and people skills, and take on an assignment that the boss sees as important. This is an opportunity, not a burden!

Getting Started: Getting Organized
Before calling the team together, make sure some of the basics are in place with the boss as to what exactly the assignment is:

1. What is the project description and scope?
2. What is the timeline? When is the job to be done?
3. What is the expected finished product?
4. Who is the customer of the product?
5. Who is on the team?
6. Other.

Once these are clarified with the boss, follow these steps as you work through the leadership project.

Premeeting
The assignment will take time and effort. Make time for it. Allocate the necessary time for planning, meetings, communications, etc. The key word is *make*.
Establish a place for meetings—away from other distractions.
Get to know your team, their background, skills, interests, time availability.

First Meeting
* Schedule that first meeting to get organized and communicate the assignment information from the boss. Clarify, listen, discuss, again listen, and seek input from all on the team about going forward. That first meeting should be casual, open, and a time to share information. Have a crisp short agenda—not too long.
* At that first meeting, some assignments should be made to gather information or to plan the next steps. At minimum, you need to establish when and where the next meeting will be (I like to make a shift from calling them meetings to *huddles*!)
* Between huddles, continue to communicate progress, learnings, issues, and other factors associated with the assignment. Keeping the assignment center stage is important.

Subsequent Meetings, or Huddles

* Repeatedly emphasize and reinforce that you want all to participate. Ask all for ideas and input.
* Being open and honest is necessary for all. Everyone will participate, and the work will be shared. Delegate and don't try to do all the work yourself.
* Working as a team is what's required since the team solution will be better than just an individual's; if the boss didn't think this, he'd just give the assignment to one person.
* The team members who get their assignments done, recognize them with "Great, thank you." Those who don't get them done, ask questions as to why, when they will get the assignment done, and if they need help. Some assignments will be more difficult than others, but all are important to the success of the team.
* Keep the focus on the assignment. When someone gets off track, pull them back in or ask them to *park that topic* till the end of the huddle—when time will be available.
* Discuss and make decisions and move forward.
* Keep records of huddles and assignments. Assign someone the job.
* Periodic reviews and updates with the boss prove helpful and can ensure alignment.
* It is absolutely a good idea to have some fun as you work in the huddle. *High fives* can go a long way to signify progress or success.
* With every huddle, make assignments and set the next huddle time and date.
* It is always a good practice to end the huddle with a quick reminder as to what the assignment is and the target date for completion.

Completing the Assignment
As the leader, you should be the first to recognize the completion of the assignment. Go back to what the boss gave as basics and confirm with the team if *all objectives were met*. If so, then schedule a huddle with the team and the boss for review and celebration of the completed project. Each team member should

participate in reviewing the work done and credit should be shared by all. The team leader often takes a backstage role and allows each team member to be recognized by the boss.

Say something to say to each team member, *congratulations and thank you. This* will be appreciated by all.

Best Practice

Volunteering and volunteering to lead is an opportunity to learn about the organization, about or from the boss, from others, and about yourself. Leadership skills come from getting over the anxiety of the unknown and from practicing what you've observed and learned.
Taking that step forward becomes easier, and your volunteering effort *is recognized* by the boss.

Notes

_____

_____

_____

_____

_____

THE BLACK HOLE

We all know what it is. Sometimes stuff seems to go to that *imaginary place in which things are lost*, that ever-lurking, dangerous black hole!

Background

The boss asks you to do something, take care of something, or make sure something happens. That something is important to the boss. He has entrusted you to get it done.

The boss thinks you are working on it, expects it will be done, and is waiting for its completion. Finally he remembers he asked you to take care of this weeks ago and now confronts you with, "Whatever happened to that project I asked you for? I need it for tomorrow so I can finish my report!" Ooops, the project fell into that black hole.

Your coworker gives you her report that you need to prepare for your joint project. You know she gave you her section, but where is it? It will be embarrassing to ask her for another copy. You seem to ask her often to redo her work, to help you.

You are right, your coworker is already saying, "Here we go again, it's lost in that black hole. His black hole is going to affect my performance too if our project is late!"

The black hole is not really a place. In fact, it is the opposite of a place; it is an unknown. It is a mysterious void. You really don't want to visit the black hole—whatever it is.

Some simple rules that help you not to visit there:

1. When someone asks you to do something, *write it down* and follow up on it. If you have a target date, or not, and if that request is not fulfilled, let the requestor know the status.
2. Get *organized* and have a place for everything and everything in its place. Keep the assignment visible and in front of you.
3. Assignments should have target *completion dates*; mark your calendar with the assignment and the date to be done.
4. Plan and work to get all assignments done *early*. I have never been criticized for getting something done a day or so early.
5. And lastly, *never* say "It must have gone into that black hole." It's just an excuse. Not knowing where something is looks bad and is bad. Your credibility will be affected and others' confidence in you will diminish.

Best Practice

When you get an assignment, write it down, keep record of its progress, work to a target date, get it done early, and keep the customer of the assignment up-to-date as to the status. *Don't use or visit that black hole!*

STEP-BY-STEP

How many times have you been asked to do something that seems overwhelming, complicated, and unrealistic? The job is so big and you don't have a clue where to start. You may ask yourself, "How am I ever going to get that done in the time I've got? There is just no way."

Background

"I want you to inventory everything in the entire warehouse. I want nothing missed. I need to know what's in there, no mistakes, and I don't care how long it takes. Just get it right."
This is what the boss wants and expects. Where do you start, and what needs to be done? This is a *big* project and, to the boss, a *big* deal!

Do remember, "You can't eat the elephant all at once." You need to establish a good plan, one that is realistic and doable, and carry that plan forward, step-by-step. See the section on *what's your plan.*

The boss has set your goal: complete, accurate inventory.

You can establish your strategy.

You can establish your plan.

You can determine the tactics.

You can set a target date for completion.

You can measure your results and progress.

Possible step-by-step plan:

1. Step 1 (overall strategy): *I don't want to take the inventory on the weekend but could take some each evening. Maybe two to three hours per day after work. I can get two others to help with the counting, the scales and inventory tags.*
2. Step 2 (basic plan): *Our small team will go and determine (estimate) how long this project will take. We'll estimate all the equipment, tools, tags, etc., etc., based on what we see as the project's scope.*
3. Step 3 (tactics): *We will order all the stuff needed for the inventory. Once we have it all, we'll schedule the inventory. We estimate it will take five days to do, and we'll divide the warehouse into five equal sections. Everyone will be notified to save that two to three hours per day.*
4. Step 4 (measures and target date): *Starting on Monday next week, we should have it done by late Friday. One-fifth of the inventory should be done each day. If by some chance our estimates are off or we run into problems, we can spill into Saturday or the next Monday.*

This is a good step-by-step plan. You have taken what seemed to be a huge project and have broken it down into small, manageable steps. The overall plan is shown to the boss; he approves it and is impressed with your thoughtfulness and coordination.

Best Practice

Creating a good plan with a *step-by-step process* grabs that elephant and brings him down to size!

PRACTICING CPI

Most of us know what CPR stands for and how it helps in an emergency. Practicing CPI is quite different. It just means "never giving up"!

Background

There will be times when you'll face so many obstacles to meeting your assignment, goal, or target that you'll feel it is unattainable and you might as well give up. "I've wasted so much time already trying to get it done, no use in wasting more time." You may say, "I've hit that brick wall and that's it!" "Maybe I'll turn it over to the boss!?"
CPI can help.
The *C* stands for being *consistent* ("marked by an unchanging position"). As you try and try to get something done, if you are consistent with your effort and drive, the goal will become clearer and one that is within sight. Your position will become visible to others.
The *P* stands for being *persistent* ("continuing in a course of action without regard to opposition or previous failure"). Aggressive follow-up often refers to persistence. Some may call this stubbornness. Others may call it focused on purpose and results.
The *I* stands for being *insistent* ("standing or resting on something; not budging"). Here we are taking a firm position, one based on facts and one from which we will not waver.

Example of CPI Use
Our supplier has periodically failed to ship our supplies to us on time. Some weeks he is two or three days early. Others he is a week late, sometimes jeopardizing our production line and maybe affecting customer delivery. We can't continue like this. My job is to have what is needed every Monday. My performance depends on Monday deliveries.

C—Each week I give the supplier my scheduled needs. On Tuesday I will provide the schedule of materials needed. I will have the schedule to my supplier by 10:00 a.m. every Tuesday. *Every Tuesday at 10:00 a.m.*

P—On Tuesday, I will call my supplier at ten thirty and confirm that he has received the schedule, that all is understood on the schedule, and that he confirms there is no problem meeting the schedule for next Monday's noon delivery. Issues are discussed and resolved, ending with the supplier's commitment for Monday's delivery. If there are any unresolved issues or concerns revealed by the supplier, I'll ask, "Who do I talk to that can guarantee me my deliveries?" If required, I will then talk to the more responsible person who confirms delivery. If that confirmation isn't established at this level, I will continue *climbing the ladder* until I will get the commitment.

I—On Friday, I will call my supplier and confirm the shipment is on schedule and okay for Monday. If all is okay, I will plan another call for Monday to confirm the shipment is in transit and will be delivered. If for some reason the shipment will be late or maybe missed till Tuesday, I will call the person who made the commitment and find out where the problem is and when it will be fixed. If not satisfied with the answer, I may continue to *climb the ladder* to the president's office, if needed.

Remember, my performance is pegged to the supplier's performance. I must get the material needed; others are depending on me. By being consistent, persistent, and insistent, I am letting the supplier know I am after the material and I will not give up till I have it.

Best Practice

Having a balanced approach that shows you are consistent (reliable and regular), you are persistent (won't take the eye off the ball), and insistent (just won't give up) instills a high degree of confidence in your performance and ability to ensure the job will get done. CPI gets results!

If you have an important point to make, don't try to be subtle or clever. Use a pile driver. Hit the point once. Then come back and hit it again. Then hit it a third time—a tremendous whack.
—Winston Churchill

Notes

_____

_____

_____

_____

_____

_____

MEASURE IT

It seems like anything very important is supported by measurement. We measure sports (scores, individual performance averages, win-loss records), education (grades, SAT scores, GPAs), diets (calories, fats, carbohydrates, weight), medical labs (cholesterol, blood pressure, etc., etc.), and work (attendance, project deadlines, performance).

We are surrounded by measurements that provide us a track record.

Background

It is hard to imagine putting a lot of effort toward anything and not measuring *how you are doing*. This applies to not only our work environment, but also with our personal goals and objectives. There is a lot of truth to "If you measure it, you'll get it; if you don't, you won't." That sounds pretty absolute, and of course, it is not. However, when we measure, we do the following:

1. *Focus*—attention is paid to the most important.
2. *Improve vision*—trends, problems, and variation jump out and opportunities are identified.
3. *Make good or better decisions*—seeing in black-and-white provides us with the facts and data needed to make good decisions, decisions that are not just opinion based.

One of the best approaches to create measures to help you is
* first, defining your goal or target (what is it that you want to accomplish or attain?);
* second, creating a metric (for each goal or target, define how you can measure your progress and be able to see if you are moving in the right direction);
* third, establishing a system (keep a scorecard, a tracking system, where you can measure where you are against your goal);

* fourth, posting the results (do this daily, weekly, whatever makes sense, so you can see the trend; keep this visible—right in front of you—so it isn't missed); and
* fifth, reviewing the results and adjusting (if your progress is satisfactory, keep on; if not, make a change that might get you back on track or speed up the progress).

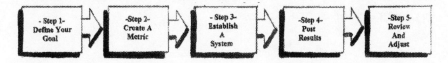

Simple Real-Life Example
John, a coworker, wanted to lose weight and get to 200 pounds. For him this was an admirable and aggressive target (he was at 247 pounds.).
He used these five steps:

1. Goal: 200 pounds
2. Metric: pounds
3. System: weighing himself first thing in the morning every morning
4. Posting of results: a little chart near the scale where numbers are written
5. Review of results and adjustments: from 247 to 245, 240, 239, 241, 238, etc., etc. He got down to 220, then John went on vacation (ooops). John shot up to 225.

There was an adjustment needed (no pizza and beer). Back on track, John went to 224, 220, 210, etc., etc.
Eventually his plan worked as he reached the 200-pound goal. He continued the system, and now his weight stays around 200, with periodic *adjustments*!
You will sooner or later hear the term *KPI* (key performance indicators). This is a phrase to emphasize the use of measures and not have too many. The goal is to measure the few and only the important.

Best Practice

Measuring and keeping score are important tools that will help you know where you are, where you are going, and determine if you are making the progress you want. Many organizations have realized that using continuous improvement systems like JIT, Lean, and Six Sigma rely heavily on measures and measurement, and their use is key to an organization's success.

Notes

_____

_____

_____

_____

_____

_____

_____

THE FIVE WHYS

Toyota Motor Company is regularly recognized as the "best, highest quality" automobile manufacturer in the world.[2] In the last five years, Toyota produced more automobiles than any other manufacturer.[3] The Lexus (*pursuit of perfection*) each year wins awards as the best-built, highest-quality car.

When you analyze the reasons for this tremendous and consistent success, you will quickly realize that a key ingredient is the Toyota Production System (TPS).

There are many documented elements to TPS—build quality in, just-in-time, kanban, elimination of waste, and many, many more that created a fully integrated system. I want to tell you about one of those elements.

Background

Training of Toyota team members and teams goes on consistently within the Toyota plants. The individual and the team play important roles in building the automobiles, and this is recognized and enforced in each plant operation. Problems are a continual fact of day-to-day life in an assembly plant. Therefore, each team member is trained and provided tools to help solve problems. One basic tool is *asking the five whys*.

The five whys is a process of arriving at the real problem cause through investigation of all possible causes. Here we filter through the superficial causes and arrive at the root cause. Once that root cause is identified, the appropriate fix can be established and installed.

---

2   *Forbes Magazine*'s Top 10 Quality Cars 2011 (five out of the ten).

3   *The Telegraph*, March 19, 2014 (Number 1 in the world 2008–2013).

Remember, with TPS, team members are after the ultimate source of the problem. The way to do this is to keep asking why (get a response), another why (get a response)—starting with the problem—and keep asking the *why*, going from the possible cause to the real cause.

A couple of examples
Late Deliveries
Problem statement: *We continue to miss customer deliver dates, and the customer is upset!*
Why 1: *Why do we keep missing the schedule delivery dates? (Because parts aren't produced and ready to ship on time.)*
Why 2: *Why aren't the parts produced and ready to ship on time? (Because production says they don't have the material to produce the parts early enough.)*
Why 3: *Why doesn't production have the parts on time to produce the parts? (Because the supplier ships the parts too late.)*
Why 4: *Why does the supplier ship parts too late? (Because the supplier doesn't know what we need until it's too late.)*
Why 5: *Why doesn't the supplier know our needs and their timing? (Because we stopped giving the supplier forecasts with lead times.)*
Why 6: *Why did we stop forecasting needs to suppliers? (Because Mary retired and we stopped forecasting needs when she did.)*

These *six* whys uncovered the root cause of the problem. We were not giving the supplier forecasts of our needs and adequate lead times to meet those needs.

Stranded
Problem statement: *You are on the way home from work and your car stops in the middle of the highway.*
Why 1: *Why did your car stop? (Because I ran out of gas.)*
Why 2: *Why did you run out of gas? (Because I didn't buy any gas on the way to work.)*
Why 3: *Why didn't you buy gas on the way to work? (Because I didn't have any money.)*

Why 4: *Why didn't you have money? (Because I lost all my money last night in a poker game.)*

Why 5: *Why did you lose all your money in last night's poker game? (Because I am not very good at bluffing when I don't have a good hand.)*

Root cause for this particular problem: a poor bluffer! The fix: learn to be a good bluffer or give up poker! (Maybe what was initially seen as a technical problem, in reality, is a human problem.)

There are some obvious benefits to using the five whys:

1. It is a simple, easy-to-use process.
2. It is an effective way to separate symptoms from causes, which will lead to the root cause.
3. The process provides you a comprehensive way to determine and expose the relationships between various problem causes.
4. You can use this process with a group or by yourself.
5. The process isn't expensive—you need your team, a flip chart, and time!

Best Practice

We all encounter problems in the workplace. Some of these problems appear to be simple and easy to correct. Those that are, we fix and get on with it.

However, those reoccurring problems may be the result of not finding the real or root cause. The five whys (or six, or seven, etc.) will allow you to uncover the cause and apply a fix that sticks!

GIVE ME MORE

"Do I really need eight hours to get the job done? The last lady that did this job took eight. If I start getting it done too early, they'll think the job is too easy and give me more work. If I get it done too quickly, others will say, 'Slow down, you are ruining it for the rest of us. We won't get our overtime.'"

Background

I can remember a coworker coming up to me and saying, "You are the new kid. You are working too hard, you better slow down. Leave some work for the second shift." At the same location on another day: "That work is not your job, that is another job classification. You need to stop what you are doing." Since I was the *new kid*, I did listen to the fellow workers, followed their advice, because I wanted to fit in.
Another job, while scheduling a department, I was able to *continuously improve* my work routine, and after some months, I completed my job in just six hours. Now I have two hours available to do what? Should I stretch the work out for eight hours or what? Should I tell someone? I told my boss; he smiled and gave me additional work and responsibility.

John was to go on vacation, and Phil was designated to fill in for two weeks. After some training, John left, and the job requirement was to make 150 pallets each night. Night one, Phil produced 145, the next 160, then 190, 220, 240. With a little sweat, Phil made 250 a night. Phil continued to make 250 a night while it got easier to do so. The foreman, Ziggy (nice name), regularly saw the results of Phil's work and said to John on his return, "Why can't you get me 250 pallets per night?"

After some discussions, Phil and John got together, and John was able to easily increase his output to 200 pallets. The company and the boss benefitted.

Lastly, I remember a GM vice president (talking to a small group of young employees at the factory) tell us some stories about how he developed his career at GM. He said, "I wasn't the smartest, nicest, most polished guy, but I was always there to volunteer, to say 'I can do that. I'll do that too.' No matter who I worked for, I was able to say, 'Give me more,' and I'll take it on. I did a good job on each assignment, and I practically became indispensable to my boss and the organization. And here I am talking to you young folks. See, I told *my* boss I'll do that."

Best Practice

It is a best practice to ask for more. Getting your assignments or job done early, meeting all expectations is not a reflection of others' efforts or abilities but is reflective of you and your efforts. Those efforts afford you the opportunity to say, "I have completed my job and am ready for more—*give me more*."

Notes

_____

_____

_____

_____

SECTION FIVE: THE BIGGER PICTURE

* Saving to Invest
Those first paychecks may seem small (after all those deductions), but taking advantage of some savings pays dividends, especially in the long run.

* What's Your Plan?
Why are plans so important, and what are the ingredients of a good plan? How do I create that plan?

* Sequencing
Setting priorities will become more and more important to you. Allowing the right amount of time to get stuff done and putting that stuff in a logical order will ensure you will get all done on time. Being late is sometimes okay; early or on time is best!

* Make Visual
Using visualization techniques reduces confusion, enhances understanding, and provides guidance and alignment. Management by seeing is used everywhere.

* Make Accomplishments Known
The boss wants to know what his employees are doing. When you do more than what is expected or do something outside your job description, it is okay to let the boss know.

* Suppliers as Partners
Effectively matching customer wants to supplier wants creates a relationship of win-win. Developing supplier *partnership style relationships* deliver the best results.

* Those Bosses
Here we have a list of fifteen different boss types. Where does your boss reside, and how best do you respond to that boss?

Don't save what is left after spending, but spend what is left after saving.

—Warren Buffett

When enthusiasm is inspired by reason, controlled by caution, sound in theory, practical in application, reflects confidence, spreads good cheer, raises morale, inspires associates, arouses loyalty, and laughs at adversity, it is beyond a price.

—Coleman Cox

Financial peace isn't the acquisition of stuff. It's learning to live on less than you make so you can give money back and have money to invest.

—David Ramsey

SAVING TO INVEST

Most millionaires have obtained that wealth from their parents. Others have created something special, invented a new technology or a unique gadget. Or maybe they are mostly star athletes or movie stars. Anyway, they are the ones who have the most money. These assumptions are all wrong!
Yes, they do account for a very small amount of millionaires. However, the majority of millionaires are normal, hardworking career people who...

1. live well below their means, consistently spending less than their income;
2. allocate their time, energy, and money efficiently in ways conducive to building wealth;
3. believe that financial independence is more important than displaying high social status;
4. didn't have parents who provided funding for their success;
5. have children that are economically self-sufficient;
6. are proficient in targeting marketing and business opportunities; and
7. chose the right occupation, one they like and are dedicated to (80 percent of America's millionaires are first-generation rich).[1]

Background

When you graduate and enter the workforce and earn some (your) money, you can do the things you want to do and you will now make choices as to how to spend that money. Don't be surprised or shocked by that first check or deposit! Once all the deductions are taken out, you'll see the net coming to you around 50–60 percent of the total wage.

---

[1]   Thomas J. Staley and William D. Danko, *The Millionaire Next Door*, 3–4.

One of my first bosses said, "You better save some of that money before it gets into your hands and out. Once there, it will be gone before you know it. The company does have a savings plan that automatically deducts a percentage of your wage before you ever see it. And they contribute to that savings and help you invest it. You tell them how much to withdraw—say, 10 percent—and they'll do it for you. It's a great deal. And you'll find you really don't miss it. Do it now!"

This was some of the best advice a new wage earner could receive. Whether it is an automatic savings plan, retirement plan, or 401(k), take a good look at it, study it versus other savings options, and sign up for the one that is best for you.

If you start saving $3,000 a year (at age twenty-two), at an average rate of return of 8 percent, you will accumulate $1,070,000 by the age of sixty-five! This is based on your money contributed. If your organization or business also contributes to the investment, the wealth generated will be substantially larger.

(Albert Einstein said, "The most powerful force in the universe is compound interest.")

Best Practice

Your goal may not be to become the millionaire next door, but you will want to develop some degree of long-term financial security. Early and consistent savings with prudent investments will help you create that wealth. The earlier you start, the larger the return.

WHAT'S YOUR PLAN?

There are many plans. We have all heard of health-care plans, business plans, lesson plans, financial, marketing, production—so many plans. So what is a *real plan*? What are the key elements, and how do I create one for me or my needs?

Background

It is easy to become confused with these foundational planning terms. How do they fit? What is the correct sequence of their use?

1. Plan
2. Goals or objectives
3. Measures
4. Strategy
5. Target dates
6. Tactics

Let's switch them around and put them into sequence:

1. First is your goal or objective: What is it you want to accomplish? What is your end game or desired result?
2. Next is your strategy: What is the macro or overall method you will use to reach your goal?
3. The plan: Spell out in detail what you will do to meet your strategy and how you will measure your performance.
4. Tactics: These are the actual steps, processes, actions, or procedures you'll follow to meet your plan.
5. Measurements: Throughout the planning process, you must measure, measure your performance and progress.
6. Target dates: Target dates are desired end or completion dates. They are usually somewhat flexible but should be aggressive and realistic.

By understanding and using these six *components*, you can develop a plan and know where you are going and see if you are on or off that plan.

Example
You may decide your long-term goal is to become principal of your high school (remember, this is just an example; who would want this?).

1. My goal is to become principal. This is what I want to be. To reach this goal, I will need a long-term strategy of obtaining the education necessary to qualify.
2. My strategy is to attend a college or university, major in education or education administration, and get good grades.
3. My plan is to apply to schools that I can attend, obtain the financing to complete the required major, and obtain the grades necessary to continue the process—master's degree or PhD in education. So what are the steps (tactics) necessary to achieve this?
4. The major part of my plan revolves around the tactics I will use in my plan. These are necessary steps I must take:
    a. I need to obtain good grades that will help me get into the right schools.
    b. I need to score well on ACTs and SATs.
    c. I will need to apply to multiple schools.
    d. I will need to obtain funding.
    e. I need to develop the right curriculum that will qualify me for the job of principal.
    f. I need to obtain excellent grades to qualify me for the next steps (master's degree and then PhD.
    g. I will go to the library or other place every day to focus on my studies.
    h. Others.
5. So how am I doing? I've got my goal, my strategy, plan, and tactics. (Measuring your results at each step of the plan is critical to *making your plan*. Measuring, keeping a scorecard, and keeping your progress visible makes the plan happen. Of course, you may need to change your plan or tactics. However,

the strategy should remain constant if the actual strategy will allow you to reach your goal.)

6. Through the entire planning process, you must set target dates. By measuring and setting target dates at all times, you'll know if you are on track to meet your goal. Your first target date may be to graduate in four years. Another is to graduate with a 3.5 grade point average, preparing you for the next step.

Effectively using these six components can help you reach your goal. The next time your boss asks you, "What is your plan?" you can say, "My goal is this, strategy this, the plan and tactics are this, and I will be measuring myself against these target dates." He will be impressed, very impressed, as you reach that goal!

Best Practice

We all have dreams, visions, aspirations, and goals. Being very thoughtful about establishing a goal should be matched with establishing a thoughtful plan with all the components. Without a good plan, your goal may become elusive or even unattainable.

Notes

_____

_____

_____

_____

_____

_____

SEQUENCING

Sequencing means placing a priority on what needs to be done first, second, third, etc., etc., and then doing it. Sequencing is a very important part of time management—maybe the most important.
It helps you decide what should be done first and last.
It helps you decide what is the most important and the least.

Background

How often have you heard these:

1. "I just ran out of time, I couldn't get it all done."
2. "I had so much to do I just couldn't complete everything on time."
3. "He is always late, no matter how much he tries to be on time."

How often have you witnessed these:

1. That last-minute scramble or crash to get something done, where one would have to wing it.
2. The boss or customer standing there, waiting, waiting, waiting for something to be delivered.
3. The promise date being missed, thus disappointing someone— worst case, a customer.

Part of your job as a new worker is to manage your time and manage it so the work that is expected of you is done right and done on time. The process of *sequencing* can help you accomplish both.

Example
You are given a list of to-dos by your boss and you're expected to get them done in one shift. You have ten tasks expected to be done today and each day.

First, define and understand the ten tasks. List them in priority as to the most critical, first to be done to the last. Then assign (estimates) time needed to perform the task.

* Task 1 is the most critical and takes 30 minutes.
* Task 2 is next, 40 minutes.
* Task 3 is next, 40 minutes.
* Task 4 is next, 120 minutes.
* Tasks 5, 6, 7, 8, 9, 10 _____ minutes assigned.

By doing this, you have a game plan to do the work in a logical sequence that assures the completion of the task on time. Working your way through the tasks, you will confirm your work estimates (make adjustments) and get the work done.

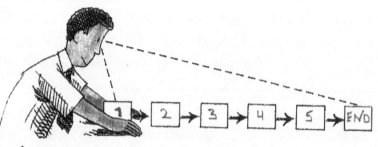

Example
Creating lists of stuff to do can also lend itself to effective sequencing. Keeping the list in front of you and marking what needs to be done first—top priority, *red*; lower priority, *yellow*; least priority (nice to dos), *green*—help you make sure the most important gets done. This color visualization of priorities works! These examples favor use of written actions to help sort and prioritize. The less-complicated, easier tasks may only require sequencing in your head. As an example, getting to work on time sure doesn't require a documented list. But if you are regularly late, maybe you should think about what needs to be done, how much time it takes, and if it is a must or want task that keeps you from being at work on time. Get the musts done, and be on time.

Best Practice

Organizing your work or tasks and putting that work in priority will help you make sure you allow enough time to complete that work in a timely fashion, allowing enough time to do a thorough, quality job. We all have time constraints that must be managed effectively. Sequencing will help do this.

Notes

_____

_____

_____

_____

_____

_____

_____

_____

MAKE VISUAL

Computers, iPhones, smartphones are all great tools, tools we rely on and use every day. How can we get along without our computers or cell phones? Can't!
Another tool to help us remember, keep track, communicate, and be informed is *visualization*.

Background

I like this definition for *visualization*: "visualization is when you transform the invisible to the visible. Its purpose is to communicate data."

Every day we experience visualization; it is all around us.

1. Speed signs tell us how fast we can legally go.
2. In a store, sales signs tell us how much we can save.
3. Crosswalks (zebras, as the Chinese call them) show us where it is safe to walk.
4. Scoreboards at sporting events tell us who is winning at the time.
5. Visual flight schedules at airports tell us where to be and when to be there.
6. Go, Stop, No Parking, Closed, Open, Men's, Ladies', and on and on are all examples of visualization.

They help us make decisions, save time, and keep us aware of what is going on.
Just as visualization is an effective tool in our everyday environment, visualization is an effective tool to use in our working experience. Here are some examples of how to use visualization in your day-to-day work:

1. Besides just talking about issues and problems, support that talking with the use of flip charts, eraser and whiteboards, anything that can communicate with pictures or data. Go beyond just talking. When we *see* information, we can better understand and remember it!

2. Identify where important items are to be (mark the area) and keep the items in those areas so you can see them and find them quickly when needed (a place for everything and everything in its place). If that area is empty it is also a visual signal.

3. Keep scores for yourself as to what *you* might want to accomplish. A personal scorecard, or scoreboard, not only keeps you aware of progress but also alerts you to changes in priorities or approaches to attain the desired score.

4. Making, using, and following up with visual lists positioned in a place you can't miss help with *forgetting*. Some leaders use legal pads.

5. Get a calendar (one that you can keep in front of you) and post the important events on that calendar.

6. What is important on your job? What is the boss expecting as results? Find a visual way to keep score on his expectations and measure your results.

7. There are always applications for visualization in your work environment that can be used for scheduling, sequencing, inventory, safety, and on and on. When all can see, all can better understand.

Pareto chart
showing relative importance of
different components of the problem

Best Practice

Making the invisible and complicated visible promotes better understanding and highlights priorities. Making important information visible helps develop the best decisions. By adding visualization to your tool kit, your approach becomes more balanced.

Notes

_____

_____

_____

_____

_____

_____

_____

_____

MAKE ACCOMPLISHMENTS KNOWN

Fay: "I do my job every day and a lot more. They don't even ask about the extra stuff I do, and I don't think they really see or know what I do. I figure I am here for eight-plus hours and I'll do what I think is right. Besides, I'd rather do something versus nothing. It makes the time fly, and I do have fun."

or

Alan: "I'm only going to do what they expect me to do. They only pay me for what they ask me to do, and that's all I will do. They want extra, they need to tell me what they want and pay me for it. At five, I'm outta here!"

These are two very different views of work. One is "I do and will do more than is expected, no matter if it is known or not." The other, "I am only going to do so much, unless I am paid extra to do more."

Background

Experience shows that those who draw the line (Alan) and only do so much also may be drawing the line on their advancement and potential promotion.

Fay is showing initiative and an independent, self-motivated work ethic. Fay sees work that needs to be done, has the time to do it, and does it. That initiative will be recognized and rewarded. But do others know what she is doing? Does her boss know?

Carl (the big boss) said, after a visit to look and see, "Fay, you are doing a lot of great work here, more than we are expecting. I see you have had many unforeseen and unique problems and you fixed them and kept on going. Great job! *But* nobody knows about all of what you've done and how you did it. They surely don't know about all the challenges you've faced. If others don't know about this, they'll think all is fine, the job is pretty easy, and there is nothing special going on here."

Fay: "I don't want to brag about what I have done. I feel uncomfortable about tooting my own horn. I am only doing what is needed to get the job done, whatever it takes."

Carl: *"Nonsense,* you need to tell us, report to us, and let us know all that you are doing—especially getting work done over and beyond the normal daily work. Don't try to be so humble. Do you want others here at the home office thinking you are doing nothing down there? Tell us the facts."

Best Practice

It is always a good practice to do more than what is expected— whether paid for it or not. However, when doing work over and beyond the normal, *make that work effort visible and known.* Doing more than what is expected is a good thing and should be recognized and it will be rewarded.

You are not tooting: you are enlightening!

SUPPLIERS AS PARTNERS

There are many strategies as to what is the most effective way to work with suppliers. They range from "suppliers are a dime a dozen" to "suppliers are critical to our success." Over the years, the role of the supplier has changed as organizations rely more and more on the supplier as an integral part of their total supply chain.[1]

Background

In today's world where supply chains may cross countries or even continents, the importance of suppliers has grown. That importance has grown as the global marketplace has grown. We compete where we never have before, and customers become more demanding for selection variety, for high-quality products, while expecting delivered costs to become lower and lower.
In the customer-supplier relationship, there are expectations.

Customers Want	*Suppliers Want*
Cost—the lowest price or costs. They want suppliers' prices and costs low and trending down.	*Cost*—prices that will provide the desired profit margin needed to grow the business; to be paid on time.
Quality—100 percent quality all the time, every time, with no exceptions.	*Quality*—to produce 100 percent acceptable parts.
Delivery—always on time, no misses, no backlogs, with shorter lead times.	*Delivery*—to meet schedules agreed to; longer lead times.

---

[1]   *Supply chain*—the interconnected movement of materials and information as they flow from the source to the end customer.

Continuous improvement—never-ending improvements in cost, quality, delivery, etc.	*Continuous improvement*—improvements that are to the benefit of both the customer and supplier.
Technology—new ideas, improvements, and breakthroughs to help the customer.	*Technology*—revenues or profits that allow for investments and improvements to help the customer.
Attitude—an open, honest, trustworthy relationship.	*Attitude*—an open, honest, trustworthy, long-term relationship.

(Note: Many of the expectations are similar, if not the same. Differences are normally open to negotiation and modified or agreed to. These negotiations, if successful, will generate a win-win agreement or contract that will provide the framework for both parties to meet their goals and objectives.)

Some customers only focus on cost, quality, and/or delivery. Depending on the product or service (office supplies, readily available consumables or services, commodities, etc.), this narrow approach may be adequate. The product or service is easy to obtain, and any failure or poor performance by the supplier is easily remedied—switch to another.

However, as suppliers become more and more critical to the success or failure of your business or organization (often accounting for 50 percent or more of *your* total cost), the customer must rely heavily on supplier performance. Any break in the supply chain can be catastrophic, and suppliers are critical to that chain's performance.

A customer who develops trust, respect, openness, honesty, and a partnering approach with key suppliers will have a propensity to be more successful. A supplier who can also develop this relationship with key customers will greatly enhance their probability of success.

Best Practice

Treating suppliers as you would want to be treated sounds logical and simple. It isn't. Problems, emergencies, and issues arise on both sides of the relationship. Being able to address those issues openly and honestly solves most problems.

Being a good supplier should be matched with being a good customer. Being able to say "You are one of my best suppliers" would only be surpassed if the supplier can say "You are my customer of choice!"

> *As I hurtled through space,*
> *one thought kept crossing my mind—*
> *every part of this rocket was supplied*
> *by the lowest bidder.*
> —Astronaut John Glenn

Suppliers are very important!

THOSE BOSSES

What should you know about your boss? What style of boss is he? How much time should you spend with the boss? Does it make a difference how you interact with the boss as long as you get the job done? Is the boss always right?

Background

As your career progresses, you will have many opportunities to learn about bosses, their techniques, their characteristics, and their style of management. The emphasized word here is *learn*. Even though it may seem easy to categorize the boss into one style or another, you will find that most bosses have mixed styles and are not dominated by one in particular.
Here are some examples of bosses you may have the opportunity to work for, and learn from.

1. **The Pal/Buddy.** This boss wants to be friends with everyone. He believes that having a friendly relationship with workers is the most important attribute to getting the job done. He avoids conflict and wants to develop a personal relationship during and after regular work hours.
2. **The Missing**. It is often difficult to know where this boss is. He seems to avoid his office or work area and is always in 'meetings/conferences/off site". He seems to leave his work group on automatic pilot and can seldom be found when decisions are needed.
3. **The Procrastinator.** In the next section of this book you will learn that 'facts and data will set you free'. However, this boss just can't move forward without more thought, preparation, analysis, and decision making. He seems to frequently drive up to, or past, deadlines. He doesn't make quick or snap decisions. He is very cautious.

4. **The Traditionalist**. This boss is trapped in his old practices and ideas. He would say,"If it has worked in the past, why not stick with it?" He very much values looking back at history versus looking for new approaches or ideas. He values consistency and avoids taking risks. Procedures and policies are of the utmost importance.

5. **The Workaholic.** This person is a machine. He lives for work and if he could get away with it he would be working 7 days a week. He is usually in the office first and leaves last. There is no one more dedicated than this boss. His performance is excellent, his workers respect and admire him, and he knows what is going on in the work area.

6. **The Micromanager.** This guy really gets into the details and watches very closely the output of his workers. He believes in perfection and whether it is his work or yours, he will check, and double check to insure 100% accuracy. He feels he must get into your work details just to make sure all is done correctly.

7. **The Underqualified-not Ready.** You may hear this in the work place, "how did this guy ever get the job, he doesn't know what he's doing". The new boss may fit this characterization. The new boss has a learning curve too.
More seasoned bosses may also find themselves in over their heads and need help and support.

8. **The Do it all**. Some bosses have learned through the years how to do all the jobs they are now responsible for. He feels it is easier to step in and just do what needs to be done. Getting the job done is faster, the task will be done correctly, and in some ways provides a level of security for the boss. The boss can do it all, and at times he does.

9. **The Coach**. We all love the effective coach. He shows the worker what to do, how to do it, and reinforces positive performance. The coach is a developer. He enjoys taking raw talent and molding that talent into independent, functioning workers. He enjoys teaching and values learning. The coach empowers and monitors results.

10. **The Great Boss.** This is the ideal boss. He is open, accessible, honest, trustworthy, and fair. He too sees the value of coaching and does it.

His door is always open and he creates a workplace environment that is both positive and rewarding. He empowers his workers and is available to help, when needed. This boss knows what is going on in the workplace, and engages his workers in running the business. He is open to new ideas and is willing to take some risks.

He is a good listener and his decisions are well thought out.

11. **The Innovator.** There are no boundaries to what is possible with this boss. He embraces change and newness. To him, what happened in the past is old news. Workers ideas are listened to and acted upon. He wants to get ahead and stay ahead of the competition.

    He gets bored with policies and procedures and sees them as necessary evils (at best).

12. **The Politico.** When this boss makes a move or reaches a decision first and foremost in his mind is the political impact. Doing what is right or correct takes a second position behind political considerations. His decisions will often revolve around.....

    what will my boss think

    how will this decision impact my career,

    and will my decision be seen as a positive or negative decision?

    The Politico makes decisions based upon the me, not the we.

13. **The Bean Counter.** Everything is about the numbers. This boss believes in measurement and tracking performance at every step. The human side of the work environment comes in second to the financials. Costs, cost savings and expenditure control are the major areas of focus. Creating a budget and sticking to it is paramount.

14. **The Unprepared**. Some bosses just can't help themselves. They do not do their homework or prepare for that next meeting or that next day. They tend to be quick on their feet and often are seen as 'winging it'. Practice and preparation are not important to them.

15. **The Antagonist.** Most bosses attempt to have their groups work together. Teamwork and supportive participation are their approach. The antagonist is different. He promotes

discord between workers in an attempt and belief that conflict will create energy, develop enthusiasm, and generate open discussion that will more effectively solve problems. Conflict and stress are his tools to precipitate confrontation, participation, and progress. Creating an antagonistic, competitive environment is his goal.

Luckily or unluckily, I have not had the opportunity to work for all fifteen types of bosses. However, there are five that are somewhat common, and I may have learned something of value that will help you with adapting to their style:

1. *Workaholic*
   Of course, there is a lot to admire when the boss is a workaholic. However, most of us want to focus on our job, meet or exceed the boss's expectations, and do what is needed to be successful—and have a life. The best recommendation here is to be very clear on what the boss's expectations are, and for you and the boss to have a shared understanding of those expectations. It is important for the boss to know (reviews, reports, meetings, e-mails) you are focused on the work and you are getting it done. Absolutely do not become a clock-watcher. Quitting time is making sure all is covered for the day and you are well lined up for the next day. As I noted in practice 1, *in early out late* shows your dedication to the work without being a workaholic.

2. *Traditionalist*
   The traditionalist will expect you to do your work, as it has been done, to procedures, to process, or to policy. That is what he expects, and you should work hard to comply to them. As you obtain additional experience and find a more efficient way to do the work, take this new idea to the boss as an improvement or enhancement to the current procedure. Explain the benefits and show how you've considered any negatives to the change. With a thoughtful, well-analyzed improvement proposition, the boss may take a chance on it. He will be cautious and have to think about it. That's okay.

If that suggestion is accepted and works, your boss will be more receptive to change ideas when coming from you. If that suggestion is accepted and it fails, you will have a more difficult time getting the boss to listen to change ideas.

3. *Micromanager*

Usually, a micromanager is concerned with perfection and having no errors. Of course, he has more experience than you and may be better trained in this work. The best approach is to make sure your work is of the highest quality and has no errors. Each time the micromanager finds something (and they will search for that something) with errors, it will reinforce his need to check on you and your work. Therefore, check and double-check your work. Also, let the boss know that he should feel comfortable with the minor stuff you do (you always check it 100 percent) and you look forward to learning more about the more complicated work he does.

Remember, do not take micromanaging of your work as personal. The micromanager does this with his other people.

4. *Underqualified*

Whether you're a boss or a worker, there will be times (as you move up) you too might be considered underqualified. The underqualified can be a good boss, and the best approach is to help the boss be successful. What you bring to the job can help the boss better understand the work and make him more and more qualified. This assistance or partnering will not be forgotten by the boss. Many feel that their job is to make the boss a success, to never let him fail. Not a bad idea!

5. *Great*

This is the boss we all want—the listener, the team builder, the coach, the boss that motivates the entire group to excel. He creates a work environment that is task oriented, recognizes success, and promotes having some fun on the job. With this boss you should take notes and document all the approaches and practices he uses that makes him a great boss. Those that you can apply to your work area, do so. Practice what you are learning from this boss and make those practices yours.

Sounds like this is what this book is all about.

Best Practice

You will have many bosses, and learning about and understanding these bosses will help you in meeting your work objectives. The five I selected were the ones that, more likely than not, you will experience. To be the most effective in understanding and managing your boss,

1. try to understand your boss's style of management and work within that style—spend a fair amount of time to watch and learn his style;
2. focus on your work and its objectives—no matter the style of the boss, there is always a way to succeed under his management, and doing what is expected 100 percent of the time will make you successful; Knowing what the boss expects and wants is very important
3. find better or smarter ways to do your work as this will be accepted by all bosses—some acceptance comes faster, some slower; and
4. remember, you can learn from anyone—take note of the habits of the boss you've liked and not liked.

SECTION SIX: THE NEXT LEVEL

* Continuous Improvement Beats Postponed Perfection
This is a long title to say making incremental improvements (step/
step) usually delivers the best results as you learn and grow. It
usually beats waiting, waiting, waiting for undelivered perfection.

* Facts and Data Will Set You Free
What is a sound process for making those decisions before you?
When do you draw the line and make the decision and go for it?

* Compartmentalization
This is a technique to help you manage many tasks and allow you
to complete them one by one as needed. Get those drawers ready.

* Customers Rule
Customers are people; most are nice and reasonable, while others
will challenge your patience and endurance. Is the customer always
right? The customer does pay you.

* People Make the Difference
In most cases, we can all buy the same materials, buy the same
machinery or tools, install the same methods or procedures. What
makes the difference of how everything works are the people.

* Attitude Feeds All
There is nothing more important to attaining success than
displaying a good and positive attitude. This is the *best* of the best
practices.

Excellent firms don't believe in excellence—only in constant improvement and constant change.

—Tom Peters

There is little difference in people, but that little difference makes a big difference. The little difference is attitude. The big difference is whether it is positive or negative.

—W. Clement Stone

When you choose to be pleasant and positive in the way you treat others, you have also chosen, in most cases, how you are going to be treated by others.

—Zig Ziglar

Do more than belong: participate!
Do more than care: help!
Do more than believe: practice!
Do more than be fair: be kind!
Do more than forgive: forget!
Do more than dream: work!

—William Arthur Ward

CONTINUOUS IMPROVEMENT BEATS
POSTPONED PERFECTION

Change is rather uncomfortable for some people (maybe even most people). We all get into routines, into comfort zones, and when someone or something rocks the boat, we have a tendency to recoil or even push back on that change. Real change is seldom easy. Most people do not resist change; they resist being changed.

One of America's most successful business leaders, Lee Iococca, said this about change: "We are in serious trouble, and we are going to make change, and that means we are going to take risks. I need all of you on board. I expect you to *lead, follow, or get out of the way.*"

He is rather blunt about his view of change. It is needed and coming, and the choices of roles are spelled out.

Background

The successful organizations that I have been affiliated with promote and actually embrace change as a way to grow and flourish. If you don't change, don't make improvements these organizations recognize, you just won't survive.

As you start that new job, at first you'll just want to survive at getting the job done. What to do, when to do it, and to make sure what you do is right are the first priorities. However, shortly you'll have that job down pat and will realize, *I can do this better if I make such in such a change.*

Making *incremental improvements* to your job, to your process, allows you to...

1. get the job done faster,
2. get the job done with less labor,
3. improve the quality of your work,
4. improve your accuracy,
5. get more efficient,
6. probably reduce costs,
7. have more fun and get a little creative, and
8. maybe go back to your boss and say, "I've got that job done with some improvements. What more can I do?" (The boss likes improvements and values someone wanting to do more.)

Once you get into the habit of looking for improvements and making those improvements work for you, you'll find that change is not so uncomfortable or threatening. Change becomes a way of life, the norm, and comfortable. It becomes an opportunity for you to be a leader in support of your organization's success.

Many organizations employ various improvement or change processes. They do this to survive and stay alive in their competitive marketplace. Six Sigma, Kaizen, Lean Manufacturing, TQM, Baldrige Performance Excellence are but a few of them. Their goal is to incrementally improve the organization, not just talk, think, or procrastinate about improvement (postponed perfection).

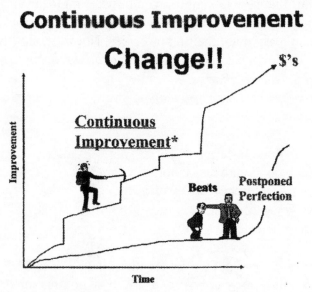

One extremely successful manufacturing plant came up with a JDIT program—just do it. All employees were trained in the program, and each person was expected to participate at making improvements and helping the organization's survival. The organization did survive and it has flourished!

Best Practice

By incorporating in your thought processes and then your actual implementation a mind-set of incremental continuous improvement, you can instill this best practice. Some can do this, some not.
If you can, you will have a major advantage over *your* competition.

Notes

_____

_____

_____

FACTS AND DATA WILL SET YOU FREE

In walks our new boss, all smiles and ready to soothe everyone about the current job situation. It was bleak; that's why so many lost their jobs. The boss started by saying how unfortunate it was for those who did lose their jobs. He said, "We must do better, or we too will lose our jobs. It's nothing personal, just business." Hmmmmm, not personal?
That sure soothed everyone!
Then after about an hour of reviewing the situation, the boss said, "We will succeed as long as we work together, focus on our customers, and when we make decisions they will be thoughtful and fact driven. *Facts and data will set you free.*"
I turned to the guy next to me and said, "I wonder what that means?" Soon I learned!

Background

Every day we are afforded the opportunity to make decisions. Many of these decisions are almost automatic. We aren't required to spend a lot of time or energy to make them. And since many aren't all that important or critical, we make them and get on with it.

1. What do I need to do first today?
2. What am I going to wear to work today?
3. What meetings are scheduled for today? Do I attend all of them?
4. Where are we going for lunch?
5. What time do we meet after work?

These decisions are somewhat important, but if made incorrectly, there is probably little or no consequence as a result of them. And they can be remedied relatively easily.

This now leads us to *facts and data will set you free*. What does it mean?

As we attempt to make more important decisions, we are often faced with "Is this the right decision or not? I keep thinking about it, but I'm not sure. How can I be sure? Others are counting on me? Should I ask others what they think? How long do I wait?"

The more critical the decision, the more data you need to gather. Asking questions of others and doing some homework is a good start. Write down what you hear and learn.

Any and all sources are good. Try to sort through the information you've gathered and evaluate the following:

1. Is what I gathered true?
2. Is the source reliable?
3. How can I confirm what is correct?
4. What have others done in the past, and how did that turn out?
5. What does my boss think of what I've learned?
6. What are my ideas? What are the ideas of the others?
7. Do I have enough resources, data, inputs, and even opinions?

There is a lot to factor into making good decisions. Here are seven basic steps to help you through this process:

1. Before doing anything, *stop* other tasks, slow down, and focus on this decision.
2. Establish the goal of the decision. What do you want to accomplish? What is your desired deliverable?
3. Bring forth all those facts, data, inputs, and opinions you've gathered; study them.
4. Develop options that *could* meet your goal; there should be numerous potential options.

5. For each option, consider the consequences of implementing that option. What are the potential results, good and bad?
6. Choose what you believe is the best option. This option attains your goal. This option has the best probability of success. Implement this best option.
   a. Set yourself free!
7. Watch and monitor your results. If modifications are needed, make changes.

You should now feel comfortable; you've done your homework, looked at all the data, analyzed the facts. You've made that decision; therefore, you are free. The decision is made based on best information and evidence at that point in time.

Best Practice

By doing your homework, gathering data, then analyzing that data (verifying the facts) and making a decision, you can now feel comfortable. Remember at that decision time, you've made the best decision, a decision based on what you know. Therefore, facts and data did set you free!

Notes

_____

_____

_____

_____

_____

_____

COMPARTMENTALIZATION

One of your work challenges will be keeping all those balls in the air that seem to come your way. Or another way to say it, "getting a lot of pots on the fire and trying to keep them from boiling over." So how do you deal with the pressure—people, workload, family, projects, social life, home—all at once? *You don't!*

Background

There is a technique called compartmentalization. Some people are born with this capability and really don't know it. Others learn it, apply it, drastically reduce their job pressure and obtain excellent results. It does require discipline, self-training, and focus. Here is how compartmentalization works: *in your mind and/or in your workplace environment you learn to segregate, isolate, focus, and complete the task.*

You often hear, "You can't let your personal life spill over into your work. You have to keep them separate, and you don't want either of them affecting the other." At least that is the goal.

Compartmentalization takes this illustration to the next step and has you organize your projects (for lack of a better term) into freestanding, distinct items that do not spill over and that allows you to focus on that one project when you want to or need to. Think of it this way: each project gets a drawer in a chest of drawers that holds that and only that project.

When you need to work on that project, you pull out that drawer, focus on that project, and when time is up, close that drawer and go to the next project.

This allows you to isolate multiple areas, focus on that area when needed, and put it away when not needed.

Here are some steps to get started:

1. Select a focus—isolated it away (drawer) from all other issues you might deal with.
2. Select other focus topics.
   (There might be 4-8 areas (drawers) deserving focus -your call on the number)
3. When you open that drawer, apply extreme focus and work on that topic. That focus should be for a relatively short time to make progress, not necessarily complete the project. When finished, close the drawer.
4. Move forward through the drawers in slow, regular steps— maybe make sure you open each one daily and always keep an eye on the project target completion date or promise date.
5. When working in that drawer, don't beat that project to death— remember to think step by step as you move toward that completion date. Open the drawer, do the work, close it, and move on.
6. If you designate eight drawers, hold the line and say no to adding more till one of the eight is empty. Then fill it, if you need.

This systematic separation approach has many advantages:

1. You set your priorities—you organize and segregate them.
2. You become more focused, pay better attention to detail.
3. You won't jump from one topic to another; you won't shift gears unnecessarily.
4. You will get more done.
5. Boredom of staying on one project too long is eliminated.
6. Quality of your product will be improved.
7. You will regularly *see* and meet target dates more effectively.
8. Your actual output and productivity increases.

9. Compartmentalization runs counter to multitasking. There is a place for each. But what compartmentalization does is require focus, focus, focus!

Best Practice

Compartmentalize when you need to segregate and focus on multiple topics or projects. Compartmentalization will reduce spillover, task interference, workplace disruption and reduce stress!

Notes

_____

_____

_____

_____

_____

_____

CUSTOMERS RULE

"That guy is a real jerk. He comes in here every day, never says hello, thank you, or anything. He's a real grump."
"Do you think she would have her money out when the bill is totaled—with a long line waiting on her. Oh no, she finally opens her purse, searches for her wallet, gets out her money, and counts out to the penny the exact amount. Did she think the stuff was free?"
"I have to say, *may I help you and thank you,* so I do. Who cares!"
"That meeting with the customer was terrible. He told us what he wanted and didn't care how we got it done. If we don't get the problem fixed, he said we're out!"
"Who does she think she is? Her requests are unreasonable and can't be met. She'll find that out when she doesn't get it filled!"
So how is your day going?

Background

These few examples do reflect some of the frustration when dealing directly with customers. Whether you are dealing with customers in the open marketplace, in meetings, or engaging them across the negotiating table, you will learn one fact.
Customers are very unique. They are people, and no two are alike. Some are easy to deal with, some not. Some are engaging, some not. One customer will say, "How are you, and thank you," and mean it. On the other end, the customer will say nothing and mean it. Some will treat you with utmost respect, and others will almost ignore you.
As a new worker, having the opportunity to participate with customers, you need to be professional, confident, and non-combative. The best approach is to use the customer contact opportunity while harboring no preconceived ideas or opinions.

Customers are diverse, and so are servers and suppliers (like you). How a customer responds can be directly attributable to how the server or supplier responds.

1. Is the customer always right? If he isn't, should I avoid telling him?
2. Can a customer be insulting and get away with it?
3. Do I need to always be at the customer's beck and call?
4. Do I tell the customer what he wants to hear? Do I lie?
5. Do I shield the customer from the truth?
6. Are customers always unreasonable?

The answers are no, no, no, no, no, and no.
First we need to establish the basic concept of who pays. As Henry Ford said, "It is not the employer who pays the wages. Employers only handle the money. It is the *customer* who pays the wages." With no customers, there is no revenue; no revenue means no wages, and no wages means no job! Very simple, very direct, and very real. Therefore, with all the challenges you may face dealing with customers, the reality is the customer pays *you*!
What should a new worker keep in mind when dealing with customers? What are sound basic principles of being customer led?

1. First, recognize all customers are not the same. Treat each as an individual and treat each professionally and with respect.
2. Get to know your customers. In some cases, actually study them, their business, their goals and objectives. The more you know about your customer, the better. Getting into the shoes of your customer may help you get into step with his needs and challenges. You can learn a lot about customers outside the day-to-day work area. Invest the time to do this.
3. Listen to your customers. Customers want to be heard, be understood, and know that you are listening. Keep notes and document the customer's key points. Any customer insult should be ignored or at best categorized as "unintended poor choice of words."
4. Ask questions. Make sure you are clear as to customer expectations. The clearer they are with you, the better chance you have of meeting those expectations.

5. Be honest with the customer. Good news is easy to convey. Bad news is just plain uncomfortable. Just the same, the customer will appreciate the truth, especially when he knows you are telling him about the real situation.

6. Keep yourself calm. Unreasonably demanding customers will not be neutralized with anger or aggressive responses. Sometimes those unreasonable demands, once fully understood and analyzed, are not only not unreasonable but quite doable.

7. Prepare for the meeting with the customer. You do represent your company or organization. The customer will value seeing his supplier team as knowledgeable, focused, and responsive. Be prepared to be very responsive to the customer's needs. "Does he expect me to turn on a dime?" (*Yes.*)

8. Being humble won't hurt. There will be times you will be more knowledgeable or more up-to-date than the customer. How you effectively convey that information to the customer will be important to the relationship.

9. Make recommendations to help the customer. Your ideas, if well thought out and based on learning, experience, and data, will be well received.

10. Last, always follow up. Any assignments made or expectations established with the customer should be captured, documented, and acted upon so the customer knows you are working for him. Never, never allow customer follow-up assignments fall into that *black hole*!

Now, back to those no, no, no, no, no, and nos. The ten principles listed address these no's and more. Customer satisfaction is a key underpinning of supplier success. It takes understanding, work, dedication, and commitment.

Best Practice

Understanding that you are paid by the customer and making that customer successful makes you successful. This is universally recognized and accepted—no customer, no job, no pay. When you have the opportunity to interact with a customer, make it a positive one for the customer and yourself. Your pay may depend upon it.

Positive Customer Satisfaction Comes in Many Forms
A few years ago, our family went to a small mom-and-pop restaurant for breakfast. There were but ten tables and one busy waitress. After we surveyed the menu, the waitress approached and just stood there, not saying a word, awaiting someone to start the orders. My brother-in-law said, "I'll take number 2—the traditional breakfast." My wife said, "Number 4, the waffles." All of us followed. Last to place the order was my sister, and she said, "I don't see what I'm looking for, so I'll take 3, pancakes."
The waitress stopped writing, looked at my sister, and finally said her first words, "No, you don't!"
In shock, my sister looked up at the waitress and stumbled with "I-I-I just wanted three pancakes."
"*No, you don't!* You won't be able to eat them. Each pancake is larger than the plate, and no one eats three. You want one."
"Yes," my sister said, "I want one!"
My sister barely finished the *one* pancake. She was delighted by the food and the unique method used by the waitress to help the customer not make a mistake.

* * *

A young man was selling frozen ice cream, soft drinks, and popsicles as he walked by the hundreds of people on the hot New Jersey beach. As he strolled from blanket to blanket, umbrella to umbrella, his attention-getting phrase was "Ice cream, ice cream. The best in town, cold, and refreshing," and with a *big smile* on his face, he yelled out, "Give your chick a lick a on a stick, give your tongue a sleigh ride. I'm your man with a plan, stay cool getting that tan."
Even those who really didn't initially want an ice cream bought one because of the unique pitch.

* * *

Customers are important; they pay you!

PEOPLE MAKE THE DIFFERENCE

In most businesses or organizations, four basic groups are expected to be in alignment and perform effectively:

Man, material, methods, and machinery

Toyota's basic principle is to develop these groups to work in harmony and balance. This best practice focuses on *man*.

Background

Whether you are in business, education, government, or another field, all four of these groups (M-M-M-M) are available.
With the right selection and adequate funding,

1. we can all buy the same materials,
2. we can all buy the same machinery, and
3. in most cases, we can all buy or develop (benchmark) the same methods.

Man is different—*unique*. Man is the integrator of the other three. Man can adjust to changing circumstances. Man can adjust the machines, the material, and of course, the method. Man can adapt.

Therefore, man is the special group. *People make the difference.*

Most organizations attempt to recruit people that

1. have a positive attitude;
2. can adapt to and even promote positive change;
3. work hard, aggressively, with speed;
4. are engagers and doers, are action oriented;
5. are willing to listen, learn, and grow on the job; and
6. are team players who value and respect others.

Most organizations continually *invest* in their people by

1. providing regular on-the-job training;
2. sending their people for further formal education;
3. sending their people to training session, seminars, and conferences; and
4. providing job rotation and expanded experience and opportunity.

Man, the human resource, plays the most important role in the long-term success and viability of any organization. Investment in the human resource consistently delivers the best results.

Best Practice

Learning to effectively work with others, whether you are a follower or a leader, is a key because *people make the difference.*

In organizations, small or large, the key ingredient to success is the people.

Alaska Airlines[2]
Advertisement in the *Wall Street Journal*, May 17, 2014
"Alaska Airlines Awarded Highest in Customer Satisfaction Among Traditional Carriers in North America by J. D. Power Seven Years in a row."

"It's our employees who make the difference."

Man is recognized here as the success factor; people made *the difference!*

---

[2]   At Alaska Airlines they have the following:

Machine—uses Boeing 737s available to all airlines.

Materials—uses standard jet fuel, oils, lubricants available to all airlines.

Methods—uses the same basic FAA guidelines and other operation methods followed by all airlines.

ATTITUDE FEEDS ALL

I have saved the most important practice for last. All the best
practices explained in this book are important, and their collective
use will greatly enhance your ability to be successful. Some of
these practices you may already use, while others need to be
thought through, understood, practiced, and made part of your day-
to-day routine.

Attitude stands on its own and permeates each of the other forty-
nine practices. How often have you heard "Boy, she sure has a
great attitude" or "Don't have such a bad attitude, look at the bright
side"? It is your choice to be made; promote a good or positive
attitude that can help you be successful, or accept a neutral or
negative attitude that (at best) doesn't help you.

Background

How do you define a positive attitude? What differentiates a
positive attitude from a neutral attitude or even from a bad
attitude? Some common definitions of a positive attitude are as
follows:

* Those displaying a disposition of optimism and
  encouragement.
* Those individuals that possess a glass full versus half-empty
  mentality.
* Those who don't ignore problems when they crop up. Instead,
  they face the problems head on and do something productive to
  change the outcome.
* Those who speak of the positives and avoid speaking of
  negatives.
* Those who readily say "Good morning," "How are you," and
  "Good evening" and mean it!

So on this last best practice, you have an opportunity for a short quiz as to what attitude you possess. Be honest because this quiz is to help you.

Yes = 2, Sometimes = 1, Seldom or Never = 0

1. When something doesn't go your way, do you accept that disappointment and move forward? Do you look at why this happened and try to figure out how to avoid this disappointment in the future?
2. As you come across coworkers, customers, even those you don't know, do you look them in the eye and smile? Are you friendly?
3. When your group or team loses, do you have a tendency to try to lift them up and help them move forward?
4. Are you happy with others' successes even when you don't benefit from that success?
5. When others succeed, do you enjoy saying "Great job," "Congratulations," and "Let's celebrate"?
6. Do you focus on the future and looking forward versus the past and looking backward? Are your best days still ahead of you?
7. Do you avoid gossip and joining in or agreeing with negative talking about coworkers or the boss?
8. Do you avoid negative people?
9. Do you address problems when they come up and avoid delaying action?
10. Do you listen to others' point of view and value their inputs?

Most graduates will see their score somewhere in the middle 10–15 from a maximum of 20. Those areas where you give yourself a 0 are opportunities to improve your attitude portfolio.

Since attitude is so important and a major underpinning of the forty-nine practices, here are some suggestions that will help you and help you create an environment of positive attitudes:

1. Remember, you create your attitude, no one else does. What is handed to you and how you respond is the basis of your attitude. No excuses. Your attitude is yours. Take charge of it.
2. Face failure and disappointment as the normal part of life. There are always winners and losers.

Failure is simply the opportunity to begin again, this time more intelligently.

—*Henry Ford*

Success is a lousy teacher. It seduces smart people into thinking they can't lose.

—*Bill Gates*

It is fine to celebrate success, but it is more important to heed the lessons of failure.

—*Bill Gates*

3. With all the negatives around us, find or search out the positive. Frowns are often met with frowns, smiles with smiles. You will be surprised how smiling and laughing uplifts others and yourself.

4. Avoid angry, negative people. Don't let their attitudes spill upon and affect you. Don't waste your time trying to change their attitudes; focus on yourself. Associate with others that are positive.
5. Language plays an important part in attitude:

   a. Avoid: "I can't, impossible, no way, won't work, never,
      always."
   b. Promote: "I think I can do that, that's possible, that could
      work, sometimes, usually."

   How do you respond when someone asks, "How are you?"
   a. Avoid: "Okay, hangin' there, not bad, tolerable."
   b. Promote: "Terrific, fantastic, couldn't be better."

6. Allocate time for yourself to step out of the daily race and have
   a few laughs with coworkers or even the boss. Laughing is
   contagious. As I said in practice number 9, you are allowed to
   have fun at work.
7. Look for good, positive qualities in others; appreciate them,
   understand them, and see if they can apply to you.
8. Slow down and think twice and act once. You are not expected
   to make snap judgments. Mistakes will be minimized, your
   performance enhanced.
9. Do some pre work exercise; listen to some uplifting music
   and try to get fired up for work and seeing your friends there.
   Think of something positive or fun for the day. Don't show up
   half-asleep.

Best Practice

Having a positive, can-do attitude not only will serve you in the
workplace but will also become contagious and help create a
positive attitude within your group.

The longer I live, the more I realize the impact of attitude on life.
Attitude, to me, is more important than the past, than education,
than money, than circumstances, than failures, than successes,
than what other people think, say, or do. It is more important than
appearances, giftedness, or skill. It will make or break a company,
a church, a home. The remarkable thing is we have a choice every
day regarding the attitude we embrace for that day. We cannot
change our past, we cannot change the fact that people will act in a
certain way. We cannot change the inevitable.

The one thing we can do is play on the one string we have, and that is our attitude. **I am convinced that life is 10% what happens to me and 90% how I react to it.** *And so is it with you.*
   We are in charge of our attitudes.
—Charles R. Swindoll

Today will be the ***best day ever!***
If you can start each day with this short phrase, you are off to a great start with a positive attitude! Others will see it, appreciate it, and will want to join in.

Notes

_____

_____

_____

_____

_____

_____

_____

_____

_____

_____

THE END
IS REALLY THE BEGINNING

Now that you have read the fifty practices, the next steps are up to you. As I said at the beginning of this book, these practices have been gleaned from and improved upon from some very successful people. Today you have an opportunity to take advantage of their skills and learning.

As a high school graduate, advanced education graduate, or military service person who is transitioning into the day-to-day civilian workforce, you now have before you some of the best approaches that will help you develop your career. You will find some of these are easy to implement, some more difficult. The speed by which you can adopt these practices is up to you. However, the sooner you start implementation, the better. And as said before, consistency is very important.

One of the best practice contributors recently said, "I wish I had known all of this when I was in my twenties. I could have saved a lot of time. Some of it was just wasted time."

A recent Purdue graduate spoke of what she learned in a very short time as she entered the competitive workforce. Not surprising, her findings are very consistent with the *Graduate Handbook:*

1. Be nice and ask others for help.
2. Work harder than you need to work.
3. Success runs parallel to happiness.
4. You are not entitled.
5. Enjoy what you are doing and do it well.
6. You are not as busy as you think.
7. My new priority:
   a. Customer first
   b. Company second

c. Business third
d. Organization fourth
e. Me last

At the start of this book, we discussed what *success* is. You need to decide what success is for *you*. What you decide today may differ in the future. However, remember, what you decide is your decision.

Today, if someone asks me what I need to do to be successful, I can say read *The Graduate Handbook*. It will surely help you!

With use of *The Graduate Handbook*, your probability of success will increase, reaching your goals will be accelerated, and truly you will have more fun as you travel that road.

I wish you the best as you start that new work experience.

Now you do know some of what you didn't know.

And, remember,

"When the sun comes up, you better be running!"

—Russell J. Bunio

ACKNOWLEDGMENT

I wish to thank all of you who have helped and guided me through this book. I am very grateful for the time, effort, and inputs you provided:

Brain Appleyard
Mary Bunio
Connie Bunio
Suzanne Cannon
Jackson Cannon
Cindy Code
Pepper Deschantel
Ralph Holroyd
Thomas Hoag
Laura Lightstone
Larisa Lightstone
Emily Myers
Jamie Snydel
Nancy Drinkhall Snyder

I also want to acknowledge and thank Oriel Stat a Matrix for permitting me to use drawings from the book *The Team Handbook, Third Edition* (www.teamhandbook.com). Reprinted with permission.

SOURCES OF BEST PRACTICES

Bosses
Charles Terry ....Foreman, GM
Galen Myers......................General Foreman, GM
Hap Grieshop....................Superintendent, GM
Ron Vonderheide ....Administrator, GM
Carl Code ....Director, Materials Management, GM
Gary Woodall....................Plant Manager, GM Mexico
Robert Schuler ....Plant Manager, GM Mexico
S. Uchikawa......................General Manager, NUMMI (GM and Toyota JV)
H. Kinoshita......................General Manager, NUMMI (GM and Toyota JV)
Mark Chesnut....................VP, Human Resources, Cummins Engine Co.
James Henderson ....Chairman, Cummins Engine Co.
Joseph Loughrey................Executive Vice President, Cummins Engine Co.
Tim Solso ....President, Cummins Engine Co.[1]
Alan Mulally.....................President, BCAG, The Boeing Co.[2]

Coworkers
Ron DeCarlo ....Purchasing Manager, GM
Joseph Schrantz ....Manager, GM Mexico
Dave Cairoli......................Manager, GM Mexico
Preston Crabill ....Manager, GM Mexico

Employees
Rodney O'Neal ....General Motors Institute, Student in Training[3]
Ted Agata..........................Manager NUMMI Office, Detroit[4]
Larry Husmann..................Director of Purchasing, Cummins Engine Co.
Hope Cantrell.....................Director of Materials, Cummins Engine Co.

---

[1]   Present Chairman of the Board of General Motors Corporation.

[2]   President of the Ford Motor Co. (retired 2014).

[3]   CEO Delphi Automotive, PLC. (Retired 2015)

[4]   Present Vice President Toyota Motor Co.

Kathy Banks ....Director of Quality, Cummins Engine Co.

Rebecca Swift....................Administrative Assistant, Cummins Engine Co.

Eldon McBride..................Director, Human Resources, The Boeing Co.

Associates

Lee Cutrone ....President and CEO, Trustmark Bank, Houston, Texas

Don Snydel........................VP, Creative Printing Services

Les Andersen.....................VP, Human Resources, Longs Drug Stores

Anthony Torcasio...............Vice Chairman, The May Department Stores Company

Robert Rohrbaugh ....Chief Prosecutor, State of Maryland

Ren Bing Bing ....Vice President, Supply Management, Weichai Power Co.

Cheng Huiming..................Manager of Technical Department, Weichai Power Co.

Carmen Castillo.................President, Superior Design International

Steve Broback ....Thunder Lizard Productions and Parnassus Group

William Biel.......................VP, Merrill Lynch

Harriet Michel...................President, National Minority Supplier Development Council

NOTES

NOTES

NOTES

NOTES

NOTES

NOTES

NOTES

NOTES

Printed in the United States
By Bookmasters

Reading, Writing, and the Rhetorics of Whiteness

Wendy Ryden and Ian Marshall

Routledge
Taylor & Francis Group
NEW YORK   LONDON

First published 2012
by Routledge
711 Third Avenue, New York, NY 10017

Simultaneously published in the UK
by Routledge
2 Park Square, Milton Park, Abingdon, Oxon OX14 4RN

*Routledge is an imprint of the Taylor & Francis Group,
an informa business*

© 2012 Taylor & Francis

The right of Wendy Ryden and Ian Marshall to be identified as authors of
this work has been asserted by them in accordance with sections 77 and 78
of the Copyright, Designs and Patents Act 1988.

Typeset in Sabon by IBT Global.
Printed and bound in the United States of America on acid-free paper by
IBT Global.

Library of Congress Cataloging-in-Publication Data
Marshall, Ian.
    Reading, writing, and the rhetorics of whiteness / Ian Marshall and
Wendy Ryan.
        p. cm. — (Routledge studies in rhetoric and communication)
    Includes bibliographical references and index.
    1. Language arts—Social aspects—United States.   2. Discrimination
in education.   3. African Americans—Education.   I. Ryan, Wendy.
II. Title.
    LB1576.M37895 2011
    371.829'96073—dc22
    2011013234

ISBN13: 978-0-415-88865-3 (hbk)
ISBN13: 978-0-203-80298-4 (ebk)

Contents

Figures

Introduction

Where Has All the Whiteness Gone? Reading and Writing Race in a "Postrace" Era

A COLOR-BLIND AMERICA: ALL WHITE ALL THE TIME

In his examination of impoverished urban schools in *Shame of the Nation: The Restoration of Apartheid Schooling in America*, Jonathan Kozol sadly concludes, with respect to integration, that he "cannot discern the slightest hint that any vestige of the legal victory embodied in Brown vs. Board of Education or the moral mandate that a generation of unselfish activists and young idealists lived and sometimes died for has survived within these schools and neighborhoods. I simply never see white children" (10). Kozol cites statistics for urban schools showing upwards of eighty percent of the student population as black or Hispanic with the poorest areas showing well into the upper ninetieth percentiles. Indeed, he tells of a Bronx high school population where "a mere five tenths of 1 percent were white" and anecdotally includes a South Bronx teacher's testimony as she muses over the presence of a white student in her class: "I've been at this school for 18 years. . . . This is the first white student I have ever taught"(9).

Kozol's description of urban public schools squares with Matthew Bettinger's claim that in New Jersey half of all minority students attend schools where they are the majority. This bleak portrait of *de facto* segregation conflicts starkly with America's ostensible disavowal of the last century's Jim Crow racism (Bonilla-Silva 25). With the exception of white supremacists, most white-identified Americans when pressed in a public way will say they are not racist, so successful has Civil Rights rhetoric and multiculturalism been in influencing the shape of the American discourse on race. In the classrooms of those of us still old-fashioned and impolitic enough to bring up the issue, we frequently encounter this profession of antiracism from students resistant to such discussions as they impatiently parrot mainstream color-blind rhetoric about racism's demise or irrelevance. But what do we make of this seeming contradiction between people's expressed ideology and the material reality? How can the early twenty-first century boast more segregated demographics than a pre-Civil Rights era of legalized segregation? And how can so many (white) people assert, with a straight face, that racism and discrimination are things of the past?

Racism, on the surface, is out of style these days—we all agree it's bad—and consequently even the notion of race as a topic of discussion is passé as evidenced by our students' yawning, doodling, and eye-averting when the questions are broached in the classroom—reactions that are not without justification, as we will discuss later. But (neo)liberalism[1] decrees that it is not *de mode* to make openly racist avowals as public positions. And in exchange for this "progress," it seems, polite folks of all racialized groups agree not to focus on race at all, that anachronistic concept that marred our past, like slavery, but does so no more. TV sitcoms and other venues of popular culture show integrated friendships and workplaces without mention of racialized subject positions as though we all agree that drawing attention to such things is now gauchely beneath us and completely "old school." But contrary to this harmonious vision, the fact is there are many white people who have never even had a black person into their homes let alone sustained social relationships with any person of a different color. Popular depictions of an integrated, "postrace" U.S. allow white America to maintain a self-serving construction: "While I may not have black friends, clearly there are white people who do."

But who are these racialized others who populate our TV screens and white America's imagination? One falls easily into the multicultural notion that they are simply "there," but careful attention suggests they serve a purpose, too; something beyond having to do with assuaging white guilt about a society which is still deeply, "inconveniently" racially divided. For along with discussions of race and racism, guilt and shame too have left the fashionable domain, except for those progressive white folks who still, as Julie Ellison points out, define their whiteness by their liberal guilt. But one of the promises of the Obama era has surely been to release postracial America from that burden. After all, why would one feel guilty about something that no longer exists? What Toni Morrison has referred to as the metonymic displacement of black subjectivity (*Playing* 68) that we see in popular entertainment creates the impression that we have achieved the oft-quoted MLK yardstick of "content of character" versus "color of skin."

This contemporary understanding of racism, then, appears to be analogous to the American attitude about feminism humorously evoked in a *Sylvia* comic years back: feminism has not resulted in men actually doing more housework, but it has made them *think* that they do. Likewise liberal multiculturalism and civil rights rhetoric have not so much eliminated racism as made people *think* we have and in the process prompted the morphing of American racism into something with a "smarter" veneer that is ever more difficult to penetrate than the overt proclamations of white supremacy. Thus, despite the fact that many white people maintain they are not racist or that discrimination and racial inequity no longer are significant factors in our lives, racism continues. For, undeniably, racialized inequality in America is rampant despite a significant increase recorded in the 90s in an African-American middle class (Aronowitz 189).[2] According to sociologist Eduardo Bonilla-Silva, for example:

> racial considerations shade almost everything in America. Blacks and dark-skinned racial minorities lag well behind whites in virtually every area of social life; they are about three times more likely to be poor than whites, earn about 40 percent less than whites, and have about a tenth of the net worth that whites have. They also receive an inferior education compared to whites, even when they attend integrated institutions. In terms of housing, black-owned units comparable to white-owned ones are valued at 35 percent less. (1–2)

He questions "How is it possible to have this tremendous degree of racial inequality in a country where most whites claim that race is no longer relevant?" (2).

This is the issue that faces contemporary whiteness studies where the most incisive questions about whiteness await examination. Indeed it is this contradiction between perception and reality that in part spawned, in the last decades of the twentieth century, the burgeoning, interdisciplinary field as distinct from the earlier critical inquiries into race mounted by Du Bois, Wright, and Baldwin.[3] Scholars have remarked on the ubiquity of whiteness studies and its wide-ranging infiltration of the academy (see Kolchin) since its emergence from earlier approaches and the focus on construction of race, such as cultural studies and Critical Race Theory (CRT), a movement that began within legal studies as an effort to problematize the supposed neutrality of the law with considerations of whiteness's normative supremacy in society and legal theory (Valdes et al. 1). The contribution of whiteness studies to the legacy of CRT's racially conscious perspective has been the critical acknowledgment of whiteness's paradox as an "absent presence" (Prendergast) in the creation and maintenance of racial dominance. Rather than the margins, whiteness studies highlight (i.e., "make visible") the normative center of racial oppression.

This notion of focusing on whiteness as an unremarked racialized category has been invaluable, for as the twentieth century progressed and doctrines of white supremacy diminished, whiteness's hegemony became increasingly reliant on its normative invisibility. While critical attention has been paid in the academy to marginalized groups, whiteness has loomed large—and silently—at the center. Thus whiteness studies implicitly promised to address racism at its source by studying the culture—the habits and tactics—of a white-identified population and its privilege, how it comes to be so constituted, and at whose expense. In this way, "racing" whiteness opened the door for further exploration of the constructed nature of race and its social deployment. All of these developments held great promise for rhetoric and critical pedagogy: as educators and citizens working toward social change, we seek not only to understand the way discourses of whiteness shape our societies and permeate our classrooms but also how to equip ourselves and our students with the critical tools necessary to identify and confront these interpellations.

"SO WHAT'S GONE WRONG?"

The title of Mike Hill's *After Whiteness* provocatively and ironically raises the specter of obsolescence in discussions of race while at the same time alluding to some of the core contradictions within the wide-ranging "field":

> Perhaps whiteness studies might better be dubbed *after*-whiteness studies, thus keeping the temporal irony of its absent presence at the forefront and in play. Scholarship on whiteness typically begins with the awkward premise that the very object it presumes to study is something less to be preserved than to be uprooted, if not abolished, one happy day. (9)

Certainly one of the premises of studying whiteness has been that race is a social rather than biological concept whose construction is not inviolable but rather subject to change and thus possible to reconfigure, even eliminate. The work of the historians and sociologists has been quite insistent in this regard: whiteness is not a *de facto* condition but rather an organizing category that emerges in response to specific material circumstances, its principle effect being the social control of the working classes through racialized division. Thus the psychocultural as well as socioeconomic dimensions of whiteness[4] are best understood as contingent phenomena with political utility and not (as we often see in the introductory paragraphs of student essays on prejudice) an inevitably omnipresent manifestation of human nature. Lerone Bennett (76), Theodore Allen (16) and Noel Ignatiev (47–48) offer examples of how the emergence of class division along racial lines is observable in the seventeenth and eighteenth and early nineteenth centuries.[5] Contemporary analyses such as Karen Brodkin's *How the Jews Became White Folks and What that Says about Race in America* and Ruth Frankenberg's *White Women, Race Matters: the Social Construction of Race* argue for a similar understanding of whiteness as social process linked to the complexities of assimilation and upward mobility.

While by now a commonplace, this counterintuitive notion of race as chimera has been no small disruption to America's unconscious process of racialization. And what follows from this notion—that what can be made (i.e., whiteness) can be unmade—is, as Hill points out, at the core of whiteness studies' antiracist agenda. But apart from the epistemological difficulty of studying that which one hopes will vanish or is actively working to eliminate (see Hartigan, "Establishing" 498), the triumph of the concept of race as construction ironically abets a reactionary notion of race as irrelevant, a belief which, it has been argued, is a cornerstone of liberal whiteness's "color-blind" reconfigured hegemony.

Hill's title suggests a paradox of two trajectories: America is moving toward a homogeneity where race is irrelevant, and yet despite *and* partially because of this situation, white people have become an "endangered species," a minority in need of protection due to the injured status of their whiteness. Both ideas, as we shall see, are able to do duty on either end of the political spectrum, while still managing to shore up white hegemony in either case, an aspect of the phenomenon Robyn Wiegman calls the elasticity of white particularity. For liberal and progressive constructions of whiteness too will invoke the notion that whiteness and white people need a kind of saving and restoration in these multicultural times, a notion that may be understood as a key component in the constitution of contemporary American whiteness. The extent to which whiteness studies is able to examine and affect this state of affairs is a crucial question facing the field today.

For among the critiques of "what's wrong with the study of whiteness" is the charge that the effort is so imbricated in the phenomenon it hopes to study that the field can't help but reproduce the very structures it wishes to expose, critique, and dismantle and that its own discourse participates in the same racism that is the object of interrogation. In short, whiteness scholars have, perhaps inadvertently, found a way to reinvigorate whiteness and recenter the white subject by paying attention to the particularity of whiteness in its various incarnations. In a right-headed attempt to reconceptualize that notion of white identity as a monolithic constant existing independently of historical and material conditions, scholars have focused on ethnic groups and how they became white, admittedly to show the construction of whiteness and complicate our understanding of its nature.

But such efforts dovetail with the rhetoric of multiculturalism and identity politics to grant a new ascendancy and aura to the ethnic, hyphenated white.[6] No longer do we have simply white people and culture but rather a smorgasbord of, largely working-class, whiteness: Jewish-Americans, Irish-Americans, Italian-Americans, Hungarian-Americans, all with their own unique historical locations and trajectories and all able to claim their place at the banquet table of multiculturalism. In so doing, they are able to disown white privilege via an embracing of working-class status. Even as their whiteness is exposed, their legitimacy as ethnic groups is in effect authenticated and their whiteness rehabilitated. Working-class studies have made no small contribution here in recuperating the significance of the working-class masculine subject. "By the mid-1990s it seemed to some that the phrase 'working class' operated as code for talking about white men" (Linkon and Russo 82) who, it is feared, are being left behind as whiteness fades into insignificance.[7] We see this fear evoked particularly, albeit perhaps inadvertently, in well-intentioned, progressive pedagogical and composition scholarship that frets over alienating working-class whites, especially the male, and seeks to find a place for them in our brave new postracial era by offering the hope of an alternative nonracist, pride-instilling white identity, for otherwise "the inability to locate a positive articulation of whiteness mean[s] a negation of identity, of self, of humanness" (Seibel-Trainor, "Critical" 645).

But as Robyn Wiegman convincingly argues, the working-class white male, in the form of the minoritized designation of "white trash," establishes ethical authority through claiming a "harmed and discriminated whiteness" (146) that, according to progressive liberal discourse, can best be alleviated by claiming an antiracist subjectivity through class alliance. Although clearly the intent is to find a way to combat divide and conquer politics, one of the effects of such scholarship is to restore the significance of this whiteness that we purport to be dismantling and to aid in the creation of "white identity formation that has no compensatory racial debt to pay" (Wiegman 147) because of its own injured status.[8] Despite the critical dimension of college seminars such as "Rednecks, Crackers, and Hillbillies: White Trash Deconstructed and Reconstructed" (Beech 176), one of the effects of such inquiry is to reclaim white identity even as we seek to situate it in racist discourse.

"EVERYTHING OLD IS . . . : THE 'NEW' WHITENESS"

In her critique, Robyn Wiegman asserts that it is the focus on particularity in whiteness studies that undermines antiracist agendas in part because of the cultural discourse in which "the language of civil rights is mobilized to protect whiteness, which is cast not only as a minority identity but as one injured by the denial of public representation" (116). It is precisely this notion of the possibility of benign, nonracist whiteness eclipsed by our multicultural landscape that allows for whiteness's new hegemonic formation and the ideological claims that we live in a postracial era devoid of past inequalities. Indeed, as Wiegman puts it, "the hegemonic formation of white identity today must be understood as taking place in the rhetorical, if not always the political, disaffiliation from white supremacist practices and discourses" (119) so that "many Americans can now join efforts to undo civil rights reform without recognizing their activities or opinions as participation in the contemporary reconfiguration of white power and privilege" (120). In the case of whiteness studies in the academy, the attempt to unmask the invisible universality of whiteness for the sake of retrieving "a prewhite ethnicity," a condition deemed necessary in much of whiteness studies in order that "the antiracist subject be invented" (139), ultimately "reinscribes the centrality of [the] white masculine" (140). The monolith of invisible whiteness is broken down only to be multiply refracted in particularities that reestablish its presence and the presence of white people in a downsizing academic labor market. Thus whiteness can be studied, and contained, without producing any significant social change while at the same time featuring and thus celebrating a white agency upon which the antiracist agenda of whiteness studies relies.

So it is precisely and ironically at the point of its activist dimension—the commitment to produce social change—that whiteness studies finds itself in the most trouble. Other critiques also focus on the activist nature of the field but from different perspectives. Both the historian Peter Kolchin and the anthropologist John Hartigan worry that the principal insight of whiteness studies—the constructed nature of race—is in practice effectively erased and replaced with a reified notion of whiteness devoid of critical usefulness (to explain social relations) that comes "close to portraying race as a ubiquitous and unchanging transhistorical force rather than a shifting and contingent 'construction'" (Kolchin 13). Hartigan expresses the concern that too often the effect of whiteness scholarship is "to promulgate an assumption that whiteness simply exists and is real thus undermining a potentially productive opportunity to reframe the long contentious debate over what race is and how it matters" ("Establishing" 497). In other words, despite the insistent recognition of construction that appears foundational to all whiteness inquiries, whiteness too often functions in analyses as an objective, "external" signifier of racism rather than as an embedded construct whose meaning is dependent on, and significant to, particular actors and social relations, or what Ruth Frankenberg calls "ensembles of local phenomena complexly embedded in socioeconomic, sociocultural and psychic interrelations ... as a process, not a 'thing,' as plural, rather than singular in nature" (*Displacing* 1). This tendency to reify whiteness occurs most notably in effecting the antiracist agenda where the nuances of whiteness are collapsed into a single category that needs to be disavowed and eliminated.

Bonilla-Silva defends this practice by arguing for a "changing same quality" (9) of whiteness, a term he borrows from Michael G. Hanchard, to justify the need to view racism as an omnipresent and continuing social force. Even so, this tendency to essentialize whiteness in order to repudiate it does come at a critical cost and (as argued later in Chapter 3, "The Kitsch of Liberal Whiteness and Bankrupt Discourses of Race") might be a key contributor to our inability to transcend our impoverished public discourse about racism, where:

> a certain mind-numbing redundancy characterizes most widely circulated representations of race: scenes of intergroup conflict predominate, to the exclusion of the array of social interactions between whites and people of color that are not conflictual; an "extreme gulf" generically summarizes the contours of interracial coexistence; and analytical views offered by commentators, newscasters, reporters, and politicians are woefully simplistic in comparison with the nuance and complexity manifest in many "racial" situations. (Hartigan, "Establishing" 495)

While there is still plenty of "un-nuanced" racism to go around, Hartigan's call for an examination of "complexity" merits attention, and it is often just such attention to complexity that is sacrificed in calls for abolition.

In our classrooms, students—and not just white students—used to exactly the rhetoric that Hartigan describes often quickly become impatient with their teachers' attempts to engage critically with the subjects of racism and whiteness. Student resistance to critical discourse is much discussed in the scholarship of critical/radical pedagogy with reasons abounding to explain student disengagement, most of which can be paraphrased as: folks don't like being told things they don't want to hear. No doubt this is true enough, but perhaps these explanations also serve a narcissistic justification for scholars and teachers invested in their own agendas at the expense of what we might learn from student feedback—that much of what passes for analysis in the popular conversation and perhaps even our critical discourse is in fact marred by models that have not adequately taken into account the way whiteness has remade itself to ensure exactly the continuity that Bonilla-Silva references. Perhaps our students are at least partially right: our discussions of race are indeed in some ways irrelevant and badly in need of an "upgrade." But for all the flaws and liabilities, whiteness studies perhaps still hold the potential for just such a fresh insight into "postrace" America.

"And Now? Reading and Writing Race in a 'Postrace Era'"

> [T]he sciences, into which our knowledge may be said to be cast, have multiplied bearings one on another and an internal sympathy, and admit, or rather demand, comparison and adjustment. They complete, correct, balance each other. . ... There is no science but tells a different tale, when viewed as a portion of a whole, from what it is likely to suggest when taken by itself, without the safeguard, as I may call it, of others.
>
> Let me make use of an illustration. In the combination of colors, very different effects are produced by a difference in their selection and juxtaposition; red, green, and white change their shades, according to the contrast to which they are submitted. And, in like manner, the drift and meaning of a branch of knowledge varies with the company in which it is introduced to the student. (76)
>
> John Henry Newman, *The Idea of a University*

We introduce the passage from John Henry Newman for two reasons. First, consistent with Newman's conception of knowledge, we understand whiteness to function variously depending upon context. Second, we believe the best way to make sense of the scholarship on whiteness used in this introduction, and throughout the book, is as a circle of knowledge—not unlike Newman's—with whiteness as the focal point. In this arrangement, we see each scholarly approach as contingent upon the others to establish epistemological ground, meaning, and definition. In this arrangement the borderlines between disciplines are always contested spaces, subject to geographic, historical, spatial, and temporal variables. This book, then, hopes to begin a mapping of whiteness as an interdisciplinary epistemology through a palimpsest; a putting together of various perspectives on whiteness to determine what kinds of questions and, indeed, what kinds of answers are possible when specifically centered on matters of writing, pedagogy, and classroom practices in a university setting. Discovering how whiteness functions in such settings; how students, administrators and faculty participate in the production of whiteness is our aim here.

In "Rhetoric and Ideology in the Writing Class," James Berlin famously championed social epistemic rhetoric as the "better" choice for the field of composition studies because of its inherent self-consciousness regarding political and ideological placement: "social epistemic rhetoric contains within it the means for self-criticism and self-revision" (490). But Berlin, in his studies of class, ideology, and rhetoric did not—perhaps could not—account for (his own) whiteness. As Keith Gilyard points out, despite the strength of Berlin's work, Berlin failed to address adequately what Gilyard calls "the race code." Gilyard says:

> It is strong testimony to how potentially invisible, or invisibly potent, that particular code signifies. Furthermore, because rhetoric is inherently ideological, as Berlin himself declared, he compromised his own teaching project by not attending to the issue of race more critically. From the subject position of a white teacher, a label he did not reject, how could he teach students to "resist" and "negotiate" the controlling discourse that whiteness is? (Higher Learning 48)

And yet we imagine that Berlin would not have been averse to a correction—indeed he would have seen it as an indication of where the social epistemic would lead.

So we conceive of the state of whiteness studies: despite/because of important critiques, the field remains vital and continues to transform. It is in this spirit that we continue our own work here in the face of the cultural premises of "postrace" and "after white," the most recent challenges facing a field, which has yet to fulfill its promises and potential. We envision the essays that follow in *Reading, Writing, and the Rhetorics of Whiteness* as a conversation, not one that purports to "solve" the epistemological and ethical difficulties facing whiteness studies, but rather one that takes place against the backdrop of crisis and critique we describe above, with a view of whiteness as contingent, contested, interdisciplinary, dependent upon time, space, and geography and, as Newman would have it, is mindful of the "safeguard" that different approaches can provide. In these six chapters, each with a distinctive commentary on American culture at large, we address the process by which one is both educated formally and educated culturally into whiteness by focusing on rhetoric, pedagogy, and institutional practices of higher education. As we confront the nuanced constructions of white supremacy, we resist a move from inquiry to prescription and instead acknowledge not only the fallibility of our positions but also their tentativeness.

For instance, we recognize that much of our inquiry focuses on a black/white binary that, although not simplistic, is specific to our limited scope of an American context of whiteness, in which "mirrored white identity is virtually dichotomous, constructed according to a black/white paradigm" (McKinney 100–101).[9] Even within this American context, this binary has been increasingly complicated as we witness, for example, whiteness's chameleon form emerging in the protectionist immigration rhetoric of Arizona and elsewhere and the desire to establish two-tiered criterion for citizenship that distinguishes between American born children of "citizens" (read, "white") and immigrants. Our racialized discussions can now occur without any mention of race at all as we oppose the building of a "ground zero mosque" that desecrates "sacred" (read, white) space, not on the basis of anti-Arab and Asian sentiment but ostensibly on its socially acceptable metonymic displacement: racially coded "Islamophobia" and patriotism. In other words, the phenomenon of whiteness is implicated in and relational to a myriad of "otherings" that have extended the American baseline of racism. But even as globalization and space-time convergence threaten the provincial black/white demarcation, yet it remains stubbornly intact. The question of reparations for Africa and descendents of slaves, for example, produces a rhetorical paralysis of reactionary response that reveals just how entrenched Jim Crow remains in the American ethos. The division of black and white is, we believe, a significant and historically charged one for America's "peculiar" racial legacy, the effects of which, we implicitly argue, set the terms for the American discourse on race and continue to be relevant. Indeed, we often privilege this binary in our discussion because we think the "color line" identified by DuBois as the twentieth century's "problem" is as much a "problem" in the twenty-first, despite a kind of wishful multicultural thinking that imagines us having moved beyond that binary's corrosive effects to a world happily peopled with folks of undetermined racialized origins. This belief in the genetic melting pot that holds itself out as both a threat and a promise to the American future is, we find, another manifestation of "color-blind" rhetoric and, as such, another form of masquerading whiteness that has repositioned itself in response to a rhetoric of multiculturalism where whiteness becomes exoticized and alleviated of its blame in creating a deeply inequitable society. It is this desire to unravel the "new" whiteness that threads its way through our conversation and informs the essays of this volume.

1 Confessing Whiteness
Performing the Antiracist, Liberal Subject

We have . . . become a singularly confessing society. . . . The obligation to confess is now so deeply ingrained in us, that we no longer perceive it as the effect of a power that constrains us.

Michel Foucault (59–60)

Liberal guilt is about race, and it always was.

Julie Ellison (345)

(A)m I not reproducing the relegation of non-white people to the function of enabling me to understand myself?

Richard Dyer (13)

No matter how progressive our own intentions might be, when we affirm whiteness we automatically draw on and reinforce its insidious history.

AnaLouise Keating (83)

The details of the scene are vague—I must be very young, five years old? I have gone fishing with my brother at the Brickyard Ponds—they are called that because this was once the site of a brick factory that blew up resulting in the creation of the town's landmark bodies of water—there are three, good-sized ponds surrounded by woods and the remnants of the kilns of the brick factory—suburban American versions of ancient ruins. This is a powerful place for me—the landscape of many memories—so much will happen to me in connection with these ponds in years to come.

This particular memory is an early one and has to do with fishing with my brother. He is four years older than I, and I am the little sister who wants to do all that he does. My father has bought us fishing poles, inexpensive rods and reels that for him are a great expense. After all, everything is, and that need for money and the imperative never to waste anything is burned into me forever during those years. I am absolutely thrilled with this rod and reel, this indulgence, this marker of my father's love and regard. He has driven us to the ponds, I'm sure, but I don't remember that. I'm not even sure of the time of year, but it must be at a time when the foliage is thick because that's important to what happens later. I'm pretty sure it's a rainy day—not pouring but damp. Possibly, I'm dressed in light slacks—my specially bought chubby girl pants I so loathe? Both my brother and I are overweight—products of our starch-filled diets. But I am happy now, being here with my brother although he doesn't much want me along, but it's not personal, just a fighting for a space, a carving of niche. We are fishing on the banks of the second pond—each pond back is a further retreat from unwooded civilization. The second pond is not quite the heart of darkness the third pond is, but it is by far a more serious encounter with the wilderness than the first pond, which borders the road. Real fishermen never are content with the first pond—that's for little kids.

But still I'm not much of a fisherman, not really worthy of second pond status—the details are hazy here but somehow I lay down my rod and reel and become distracted—probably I started playing on the bank in the mud, wandering off, getting lost, maybe briefly. But the result is, I no longer have my rod and reel. What happens next? I must really resort to conjecture now because I don't remember—my brother probably is frantic, trying to figure out where the pole is because he will get blamed if it is lost. I have all the emotions of a child who is scared about incurring the wrath of her parent and crest-fallen at the possible loss of the prized object. If I have lost it, I will not get another, I know.

Eventually, we must leave the woods and seek out my father to confess and ask for help. So I am not sure who voices the idea first—my brother or my father, but I do know it was not me.

The proclamation: "The niggers took it."

For what I have not yet mentioned is that during the time my brother and I were fishing, our paths crossed with two other children, two black boys, my brother's age or older. There were only a few black families in the town I grew up in: these children were not from town, but it was not unusual for out-of-towners to come here to fish. I remember another time when my brother had caught a fish, a bass. (My family did not eat fresh water fish, and somehow this consumption was complicatedly racialized: white people did not eat sunfish, according to my father, although he acknowledged some did eat trout and bass and pickerel, but not us—I think it was somehow a mark of poverty in his mind to eat freshwater fish, but I'm not sure.) Normally my brother would have thrown the bass back, regardless of size, but it was hooked in the gills and bleeding to death. I remember my brother taking it over to a black man fishing nearby, explaining what happened, the man taking the fish to keep and eat. Thus these ponds were a kind of neutral zone, normally, where segregated societal boundaries toyed with each other in carnivalesque ways only to reaffirm just how unporous those boundaries actually were.

Perhaps I remember some vague tension in the encounter between the two boys and my brother as we passed each other in the woods that day, something remotely masculine; something recognizably boy-like; clash of antler nubs shedding velvet fuzz. Perhaps that is why my brother reported it to my father that way—the niggers took my sister's fishing pole. Did that make him less culpable; make us both more victims? Maybe it made him more of a failure, unable to protect his white sister. And maybe the boys did take the pole. I don't know, and most certainly I did not care. My father's anger is searing at the loss of the rod and reel and that's all that I know. I would never contradict him, this terror of a man, not until much later in life, but vaguely, only vaguely at the edges of my fear do I remember thinking there was something inadequate and off-base in the assertion: "the niggers took it." For me the phrase lacked the explanatory power it seemed to hold for my father and brother. But my father is not angry at these phantom boys he never even saw—he is angry at me, I sense that clearly—what I don't yet understand is how he is angry at the whole world, I'm just one part of it. And what I come away with from the incident is this profound feeling of shame that I could be so foolish as to have been parted from my luxury possession, whether stolen or lost. That I am so stupid and negligent as to have let niggers take my fishing pole. I suppose that, above all, is what I learn.

Forward to many years later, another story. Simply put, I am a frustrated white teenager suffocating in the repressive household dominated by my father. Again, I'm not sure of my age, but I am old enough to feel the stultifying effects of living under the regime but too young to have the resources or wherewithal to do anything about it. It is Saturday night, I am stuck at home, sitting in the living room with my father, forced to watch his selection of TV program, although there isn't really anything on that I would watch anyhow. I am merely here, waiting, waiting for the day that my life will begin. It's Saturday, and I long for some kind of autonomy that would put me anywhere but here, out with friends recklessly experimenting with drugs and sexuality. That sounds frivolous but it is anything but. To add insult to injury, we are watching the Lawrence Welk Show, a variety show featuring the eponymous band leader, which my father has perversely adopted as one of his favorite programs in response to the rising licentiousness that he feels has infected the world. This insipid display is his idea of wholesomeness. But one of tonight's acts features a dance routine with a black man dressed up Bojangles-style and a white Shirley Temple-type but older girl or rather, young lady, I suppose. This infuriates my father, and he begins to rail against the pairing, managing the impossible feat of eroticizing the hopelessly asexual Lawrence Welk Show. I had learned the strategy of keeping silent in the face of his tirades but am never able to maintain it for long. I finally respond, "Oh for God's sake, they are just dance partners!" This sets him off and allows him to focus his rage on me, or rather on my burgeoning sexuality, which I suspect was his target all along: "Well, you better not bring any partners like that around here," he manages to sputter inanely.

When my father makes statements such as these, I feel embarrassed for him, for me—and I feel sorry for myself that this accident of birth has placed me here with him. This racialized invasion of my own sexual privacy—I despise him for this even though I don't understand it all yet. I feel disgust. In my mind, this is just one more confirming example that he is an idiot holding me back from a rightful destiny, and I can't wait for the day that I can get away from him.

The above stories about my life can be understood as belonging to a type of nonfiction narrative that has become a staple of whiteness studies. As Peter Kolchin observes, many of the authors who work in the interdisciplinary area of critical whiteness studies often foreground their scholarship in personal narratives that first identify the writers with, examine, and then disaffiliate them from a personal racist past (2–3). To describe this genre, Jill Swiencicki has coined the term "awareness narrative," which she defines as "a narrative of awakening, one in which the writer sees for the first time the unearned privilege their skin color affords them and *one that reveals the historical, familial, and cultural trajectories of race difference they are linked to and perpetuate*" (337, emphasis added). While not all predicated necessarily on "first time" glimpses into white oppression, the autobiographical narratives we find in whiteness scholarship generally tend to locate the author's personal life in the discourse of whiteness in an attempt, as all personal narrative does, to combat the evasion of theoretical abstraction and to start from the premise that "particular subjectivities of authors are crucial and should be textually embodied rather than effaced" (Hesse, "Creative Nonfiction" 239). Whiteness, then, (hopefully) emerges from these narratives not as monolithic generalizations but rather as what Ruth Frankenberg calls "ensembles of local phenomena complexly embedded in socioeconomic, sociocultural and psychic interrelations . . . as a process, not a 'thing,' as plural, rather than singular in nature" ("Displacing" 1).

Given that a founding premise of critical whiteness studies involves this kind of moral accounting from white people, such narratives potentially can be powerful tools in whiteness's unmasking and unmaking. As Lynn Worsham explains about her decision to recount a story from her childhood: "Working through this story . . . represents a provisional response to feminists of color who have challenged me . . . to tell the truth and be accountable, to name the enemy within, and to examine the specificities of the role race has played in this white life" ("After Words" 335). The formation of such stories appears to proceed inevitably from the foundational epistemology of whiteness studies that differentiates this project from other (earlier) forays into the study of racism. Rather than turn the gaze outward to the constellation of "othered" racialized subjectivities, the study of whiteness intends to focus on the pernicious, unnamed source of that othering (and, in most cases, the black/white binary that has characterized American discourse on race): "much current work in the burgeoning field of whiteness studies notes the political significance of the white ability to avoid perceiving whiteness as a racial position" (Carter 28).[1] As Dyer explains it, given that "being white is not an issue for most white people, not a conscious or reflected on part of who they are," whiteness scholarship begins a cultivation of "the awareness of being white" (5). From this perspective, not only is the awareness narrative genre inevitable but also a valuable rhetorical strategy that assists in the moral assessment of white identity. Mab Segrest summarizes the impetus in this way: "Because racism normalizes whiteness and problematizes 'color,' we whites as 'generic humans' escape scrutiny for our accountability as a group for creating racism and as individuals for challenging it" (43). This imperative for accountability in "second wave" whiteness scholarship has dovetailed with the academic turn toward the personal as a valuable (albeit not unproblematic) phenomenological methodology.

But in the context of whiteness scholarship, these stories serve an additional purpose, one that can be described as ritualistic in nature. As Maurice Berger writes, "The fear of revealing these dirty secrets [about whiteness] has hindered race talk for decades. The irony is that it is only by revealing these dirty secrets that race talk can be effective. It might make better sense . . . to encourage self-inquiry on the most personal, rather than the most public, level" (180). Again we see the attempt to go beyond the monolith of whiteness, but the salacious quality imputed to revelation in this statement, as well as the emphasis on personal fear, is telling, as the description conjures an image of a secret society to which daring petitioners seek admission, the price of which is the disclosure of secrets made available for scrutiny. While intended to help the white-identified subject own up to the experience in/of whiteness, these narratives effectively function as authenticating *rites de passage,* "an entry to the discourse community of antiracist pedagogues, scholars, and cultural workers" (Swiencicki 337), whose recitation then permits the "initiates" to enter the liminal space required to embark on enacting the antiracist agenda at the core of whiteness studies. Without the narrative renouncement—this "coming clean"—the white-identified subject would otherwise ostensibly be precluded from participation due to his or her very immersion in whiteness's repudiated discourse. Together these narratives comprise a rhetorical tradition of "confessing" whiteness,[2] a prerequisite act of self-actualization[3] that seemingly lays the groundwork for dismantling white racist identity, a kind of "truth and reconciliation" strategy of responsible owning of experience from which one can then move forward to become a member of the new group of antiracist workers.[4]

But the proliferation and generic qualities of these tales warrant a consideration beyond merely allowing the stories to "speak for themselves" and their announced intent of problematizing whiteness and combating racism through personal interrogation. What do such stories really tell us, and what purpose do they effectively serve? What is the cultural work that they do? For, in some ways, these narratives, whether we classify them as being about awareness, interrogation, conversion, confession, or something else, become, as is often said about whiteness itself, "everything and nothing" (Dyer 39) in relation to white identity, concealing as much as they reveal, and in the process they emerge as a way of rehabilitating the white subject and reclaiming that which we ostensibly hope to dismantle: whiteness itself. Even though such narratives purport to aid the white subject's interrogation of whiteness, to function with the intention of what Victor Villanueva has called "critical autobiography," not as "confession and errant self-indulgence" but rather as "a way of knowing our predispositions to see things certain ways, of understanding what it is that guides our intuitions in certain ways" ("Politics" 51), this narrative performance of guilt and shame is not unproblematic, despite the contention that "liberal guilt can be folded into a productive antiracist cultural or political position" (J. Ellison 347). For these stories also permit, in effect generically demand, the recentering of the white subject as a cultural and scholarly concern via the "spectacularization of white humiliation as a mode of political insurgency" (Wiegman 143) in which the psychic "penalty" of whiteness (Thandeka 8) is exposed in order to provide "insight into the profound damage racism has done to us [i.e., white people]" (Segrest 44) for the purpose, to be sure, of providing white people incentive to give up what paltry advantages racism has afforded them at the expense of their own mental and spiritual health. For if Villanueva's understanding of "the autobiographical as critique" is correct, the narrating subject necessarily becomes the focus of inquiry, and so we must consider what (whose) subjectivity is being thus situated and, regardless of intent, to what effect. We must consider not only the cultural and individual reflection aided by such narratives but also the way they serve to enhance the ethical authority of the white subject—precisely through the metacognitive performance of self-reflection and interrogation. Ultimately, such narratives function to constitute white identity and as such bear ironic rhetorical resemblance to the confession in the coming-out story of lesbian/gay narratives: the narrators in effect "come out" as white. Before elaborating further on this comparison and its implications for whiteness scholarship, I want first to look back at and frame the issues at hand in terms of narrative subjectivity as it has been explored in past scholarship. I want to raise questions about the generic limitations of personal narrative in performing antiracist analysis.

PERSONAL NARRATIVE: AGENCY AND AUTHENTICITY REVISITED

Indeed the "problem" with confessing whiteness, as part of performing an antiracist liberal subject position, is locatable generally in the parent genres of the personal narrative and essay and the relationship of such genres to the function of cultural criticism and the construction of identity. What is the nature of the "truths" that such writing produces, and what is the effect of naming them? These issues, of course, have been hotly debated within the field of composition and rhetoric and have been a focus of post-structural narrative theory, and it behooves us to revisit some of these questions in the present context. Central to these discussions are concerns about the relationship of the personal to an "authentic" self. A quote from Barbara Kamler's *Relocating the Personal* should suffice to remind us what is at stake: "The idea that there is a real authentic self that can be expressed in writing is, at best, a partial notion grounded in an Enlightenment conception in which the self is imagined to be stable, coherent, unitary and autonomous" (38) and, I would add, *a priori* to the narrative construction, a notion Candace Spigelman dubs "the myth of authenticity, the illusion that an individual can feel, understand, and capture in writing socially and culturally unmediated or decontextualized experience" (61). In this context, Jane Hindman identifies "the conflict between opposing conceptions of an expressivist, autobiographical self whose autonomy creates coherence out of inchoate experience and a socially constructed self who is always already constrained by the conventions of discourse" ("Making Writing" 89). The post-structural corrective to authenticity reminds us that personal narratives are to be understood not transparently but as "a representation of experience rather than the experience itself ('not authentic')" (Kamler 46); they are textual constructions, not "direct" expressions of identity or reality. Such perspectives had their effect on writing pedagogy and led to criticism of the bourgeois subject position reproduced and valorized in the "honest," "authentic" writing of expressivist paradigms. But these insights into the nature of narrative also paved the way for the recuperation of personal writing via the post-structural rationale of interrogating and refashioning identity, vis à vis cultural location, through narrative subjectivity. The latter has figured importantly in social constructivist and critical/radical pedagogies, such as in the deployment of literacy and educational narratives. Indeed, this rationale in part underpins the epistemology of the awareness narrative: the instability of the narrative white subject permits, through writing, a dismantling and reconstruction—a decomposing and recomposing—of that identity.[5]

This premise of constructed subjectivity should be considered alongside the development of pedagogical interest in the scholarship of the personal essay. An example of the kind of attention paid to the personal essay in the previous decades can be found in Paul Heilker's *The Essay: Theory and Pedagogy for an Active Form*, where he summarizes the critical work done in relation to the genre and the implications for the writing classroom and college curriculum. Proponents of the personal essay cite it as an alternative to the effaced subjectivity and conclusive authority that undergird models of academic discourse. The essay, as opposed to the academic article, is steeped in particularity and ethos: "Truth of the world is inseparable from the truth of the personality in the essay"

(Heilker 60). It is also lauded for its open-ended form and exploratory method, which "transgresses disciplinary and discursive boundaries" (Heilker 53) in the tradition of Montaigne's antischolasticism. This latter notion of transgression is particularly relevant in the present context in relation to the question of a constructed versus an authentic self. For the claim of transgression against formal and ideological boundaries relies in no small part on the dramatized subjectivity of the essay's persona and is very much linked to the LeJeunean "pact" of autobiographical nonfiction that the narration be "true"; the narrator, "real." Thus it would seem the faith placed in the essay's transgressive nature is largely steeped in romantic conceptions of the authentic, truth-seeking self, a paradigm at odds with the notions of constructed subjectivity and "planned authenticity," to use Trinh T. Minh-Ha's term (89), as the governing ethos of representation. Even as such writing grants increased representational control, it paradoxically limits the agentive possibilities of exploration and truth-seeking, despite the writer's rhetorical moves to include metacognitive interrogation of the narratized experience (i.e., demonstrated awareness of the narrator's constructed position in the text). Personal narrative is (only ever) a controlled exploration of self and experience even when it purports to be an "honest" one.

While personal narrative and personal essay are not simple equivalents, both genres, despite efforts to pin them down, remain (productively, I believe) amorphous and mutually informing, and thus a consideration of the personal essay form is apt and useful in analyzing the autobiographical elements of whiteness scholarship to help us understand the construction of identity that occurs in such narratives and the cultural work that they perform. In turn, such an analysis can inform our understanding of the pedagogical uses and limits of such writing in the classroom and beyond. In order to do this, I consider the ideas of transgression and authenticity, so important to the imputed potential of the awareness narrative, by looking at a particular essay in relation to ethical authority and narrative structure: Orwell's well-known "Shooting an Elephant," an awareness narrative about colonial British whiteness as well as a quintessential example of the personal essay. I use two composition critics, Thomas Newkirk and Douglass Hesse ("Stories"), who both, in the course of different analyses, consider the generic nature of Orwell's piece, in which he describes his days as a police officer in colonized Burma. His meditation evolves around an incident where he is expected to shoot a rampaging elephant and the ineffectual debacle that the event becomes as Orwell destroys the becalmed creature merely to save face in front of the local people. In Newkirk's estimation the essay establishes Orwell as "a formidable opponent of colonialism" (14), a conclusion that bodes well for "the political work that creative nonfiction could do," and suggests that "the authorial subjectivity constructed through those genres" (Hesse, "Creative Nonfiction" 239) is ideally suited for discursive antiracist work. But my contention is that a closer look at

Orwell's piece will qualify this assessment of this rhetorical effect to reveal a much more sobering view than Newkirk's exuberant description suggests. The implications for awareness narratives in whiteness scholarship are, perhaps, equally sobering.

THE PERSONAL ESSAY: WHAT MAKES IT TICK?

Newkirk identifies an epiphanic formal feature in what he describes as "the expected conventions of the confessional personal narrative" (12), and he sees "Shooting an Elephant" as providing "The paradigmatic example of this form of self-presentation" (13). Newkirk identifies the construction of "two time positions: a self that commits the act, and an older 'wiser' self that looks back to judge that action. We are asked to believe that this act of looking back has created a chastened and morally sensitive individual" (12). Newkirk goes on to identify in the structure of such personal narrations what he calls a "turn." As he discusses Orwell's example, Newkirk bullets out the following points about the so-called "turn" that acts as a fulcrum to a "before and after" subject positioning:

It (the turn) creates a "before and after" moment that is dramatically satisfying. This was not an understanding arrived at slowly; it is represented as a flash of realization, an epiphany arrived at in a moment of extreme psychological pressure.

It provides thematic weight to the essay. It allows us to consider a major issue, the motives for oppressive action in colonial governments, through his examination of this "tiny" event.

It illustrates a mind at work, moving from particular to general, making sense of experience. It is therefore a model of learning, an illustration of what John Dewey called "intelligence."

The essay has a confessional urgency. Orwell is "guilty" of a sin that is expiated in the writing. The reader senses a personal need to confess not only to the killing itself, but to racism bred by colonialism. This willingness to reveal something disagreeable enhances Orwell's ethical appeal—here is a man willing to show himself at his worst.

It shows the writer moving to higher moral ground. The early Orwell, young and "poorly educated," plays the role of oppressor without knowing why. The Orwell that emerges from this experience is more conscious of motivation and more capable of opposing the colonialist system. The act of writing the essay itself shows Orwell now to be a formidable opponent of colonialism. (13–14, emphasis added)

Excepting Newkirk's insistence on sudden epiphany (as opposed to a conclusion reached through slow deliberation), the generic features he extrapolates from "Shooting an Elephant" serve as an accurate description of whiteness awareness narratives and are indeed similar to what Swiencicki sees as a three-part structure in awareness narratives: admission; circling around the lack; an awareness (351). Take, for example, the autobiographical introduction of David Roediger's *Wages of Whiteness,* in which he describes the racist landscape of his youth with such details as boyhood bonding over a knife referred to as a "nigger jigger" (3) and his parroting of beliefs that "Blacks paid no taxes and therefore ought not vote" (4). He ascribes a kind of preconscious state to this younger version of himself that eventually gives way to an aware self to whom "Racism just increasingly made no sense" (5) as he reflects on the effects of the civil rights movement on the communities in Missouri where he was growing up. Just as Newkirk sees Orwell emerging as a formidable opponent of colonialism, so too can we see the narrating subject of Roediger's tale emerging from the child's preconscious pall of inherited whiteness to become a champion of racial equality and social justice. We can see at work here the confessional quality that Newkirk identifies, correctly I believe, in Orwell's essay as being an important part of the representational dynamic of awareness narratives—a confession that accomplishes both repudiation and reclamation of the white subject under an antiracist mantle.

But unlike Roediger's piece, Orwell's essay is both more and less than an awareness narrative—more in the sense that it exceeds the generic purpose of the antiracist/imperialist agenda to focus on the existential condition of the psychologized Orwell (in much the same way, perhaps, that Frederick Douglass's narratives exceed the generic features of abolitionist propaganda)[6] and less in that it fails as an initiating confession that clears the way for Orwell to embark on antiracist work. Newkirk's formula establishes the new and improved Orwell that emerges from this narrative to be fit to assume duty as a "formidable opponent of colonialism." But in what sense? What is the source of these grandiose claims that Newkirk makes on Orwell's behalf? Indeed I find myself wondering if the essay Newkirk describes is the same one I know. For rather than the formidable opposition of which Newkirk speaks, I come away from Orwell's essay immersed in the modernist sense of powerlessness that the narrator feels. Hesse's assessment here is instructive and one I share: "Orwell's realization of the oppressor's plight is an event in the story [rather than the "point" of the story—see below]. . . . the horror of 'Shooting an Elephant' is that this realization does not alter the course of events after it. He still pulls the trigger" ("Stories" 187).

Instead of being "more capable of opposing the colonialist system" as Newkirk would have it, the Orwell of the story experiences himself vacant of agency, and he leaves us with the contemplation of that incapacity. Yes, he is perhaps "more aware of motivation" and the existential futility of domination, but such awareness does not make him "more capable." I agree that there has been a "turn," which is to say merely *something* has happened in the course of this essay, but I find the "something" far less blatant and quantifiable than Newkirk makes it out to be in his formula, and it is this subtlety that puts the narrative at odds with an unambiguous antiracist agenda even as it makes it a compelling story.[7] "Shooting an Elephant" is certainly not an example of what Connors has called "the I-learned-a-lesson story" (150) replicated so frequently in student narrative essays where the chastened, converted subject goes forth to sin no more. Newkirk's blatant assertions miss Orwell's, and perhaps in general the essay genre's, nuance—as well as its ineffectuality. The contemplative subject does not here translate into an agentive one, at least not in the sense of an antiracist subject. What the essay does accomplish eminently is to create a focus on the white narrating consciousness.

Before continuing further with the implications of Newkirk's analysis, I want to elaborate more on the basis for Douglass Hesse's observations, primarily because, as I discuss below, I find Newkirk's perspective somewhat deficient and profitably supplemented by Hesse's. Hesse's intent is to develop a theory of narrative that transcends the composition paradigm as "story as example," where narrative is used for the purposes of illustration of a main point or thesis. His assertion is that narrative functions less reductively and in a far more complex way than is often taught or portrayed in writing textbooks. He suggests that narrative does not *contain* points as much as it *leads* to points, the difference being crucial in understanding the rhetoric of narrative. He characterizes the textbook treatment of the rhetorical deployment of stories as follows: "stories are seen as furnishing evidence for the truth of a proposition. Whether point is extracted from incident or incident is supplied to verify an already-existing point, the two are presented as having an equation-like relationship, with story on one side of the equals sign and point on the other" ("Stories" 178). But in Hesse's more elastic view, the story is not the point itself but rather the occasion to make points. In his words,

> I am not arguing that we abandon the idea that stories prove points but that we understand proof as rooted in making, the bringing of points into plausible existence. Making a point is not "balancing the equation." I mean it more literally in the sense of establishing a juncture on the line of words that comprises the essay, a place at which the stating of propositions becomes possible. . . . (185)

For Hesse, "point" is less a synonym for example or thesis or theme or kernel of meaning and more literally a place in the narrative space of the essay where assertions can be put forth. The story itself might not "prove" or illustrate anything, but it may provide the structure of an opportunity, even excuse, for the narrator to ruminate.

If we take Hesse's idea that narratives provide occasion for making points and consider "Shooting an Elephant," we can view the essay differently than Newkirk does through the formula of his "turn," a concept that seems to rely on the "balanced equation" metaphor that Hesse attempts to supplant. For starters, the perspective shift to anticolonialism that Newkirk sees as central to his theory does not develop in Orwell's piece over the course of the essay but rather is infused in it from the beginning. Orwell indicates as early as the second paragraph that "at that time I had already made up my mind that imperialism was an evil thing." What's more, Hesse's model implicitly calls into question the neat structure of Newkirk's "turn," which, in the case of "Shooting an Elephant," Newkirk assumes to be self-evident in as much as he does not specify its location. Is it in the middle? The end? I see not one but perhaps several "turns" or "points" in the story. Perhaps Newkirk privileges the one that occurs with the quintessentially modernist ethos expressed in the statement that evokes Eliot's "The Hollow Men": "It was at this moment, as I stood there with the rifle in my hands, that I first grasped the hollowness, the futility of the white man's dominion in the East."

But if this is the statement that "matters" (and notice the recentering of whiteness that occurs at that moment), what happens to the rest of the story that details Orwell's indecision and impotence? For we could very well say, as Hesse does, that the important thing about this essay is not so much Orwell's realization but his inability to change the course of events. Well after his epiphanic declaration, he relates the following: "The sole thought in my mind was that if anything went wrong those two thousand Burmans would see me pursued, caught, trampled on, and reduced to a grinning corpse like that Indian up the hill. And if that happened it was quite probable that some of them would laugh. That would never do." An ambiguity here arises with regard to the location of the narrator's ironic stance: which Orwell displays this detached insight? The young Orwell or the older who looks back? Arguably, this is a later epiphany achieved through reflection, but Orwell presents the sentiment as belonging to the moment. And in that case, his earlier realization does not allow him to alter his thinking or change his actions; he is not emancipated from his racism. Certainly this is a "point," *of* and *in*, the narrative as important as Newkirk's turn and one again, notably, that reproduces the centering of whiteness. What too in Newkirk's scheme do we make of the detailed account of Orwell's inability to dispatch the elephant in any efficient and merciful way, an event that seems to elicit more horror for the dying elephant than a dead human being and is a sentiment underscored in Orwell's parting conclusion that he was "very glad the coolie had been killed" because the death provided legal pretext for his actions?

Newkirk's formula reduces the above narrative details to filler, but it is precisely such detail that undermines his argument about the essay's epiphanic structure as agentive in relation to the narratized Orwell achieving higher moral ground. For, arguably, the essay details no moment of sudden insight but rather the recounting of an experience whose meaning is only gathered in hindsight after years of reflection. The insight is not galvanizing but instead incapacitating. Furthermore, it would seem that the Orwell of "Shooting an Elephant" is doing his level best to discredit his moral authority because this strategy of debasement serves ironically to enhance ethos, as Newkirk in effect points out. But the convolution further attests to the complexity of the essay's form that Newkirk's analysis fails to credit, despite the acknowledgment that Orwell is "willing to show himself at his worst." It is that "willingness" that requires our careful consideration—the way it presents itself "as a way to renounce mastery" (Hindman, "Thoughts on Reading" 11)—because of the role that an ethos of humility plays in the "planned authenticity" of Orwell's narration and the focusing on Orwell and his whiteness that the rhetorical strategy effects. The idea here is that, as an awareness narrative, "Shooting an Elephant" does not succeed in producing a sudden insight that makes the narrator more capable of resisting the evils of empire. Rather it is a highly successful personal narrative that problematizes its subject in nearly ineffable ways even as it most certainly reconstitutes the centrality of whiteness to the moral universe of the piece.

If Orwell's piece is not accomplishing the epiphany-based resistance that Newkirk ascribes to it, what is happening in the narrative's structure? In Newkirk's formula, this supposed movement to higher ground is paralleled by a structural movement from specific to general. I would suggest that Newkirk has this inverted: the structure is precisely the reverse and moves from general to specific.[8] Rather than the story being an example of what's wrong with imperialism, as Newkirk suggests, I think the essay moves (perhaps, one could argue, in a conservative fashion) from the abstract political analysis of imperialism toward the narrator's lived experience of that "ism." Indeed the narrator's early announcement that he was already decided about the evils of imperialism suggests a certain dissatisfaction with exactly the kinds of pronouncements made by Newkirk. We get a signal here (a turn; a point?) in Orwell's essay that he will be moving in a different direction. Orwell distances himself from the blanket commitments of dogma contained in such phrases as Newkirk's "fierce opponent of colonialism" when he devalorizes the "rampant anti-European feeling" in Burma as "aimless, petty." The Orwell of "Shooting an Elephant" is less a crusader and more an observer of complexities and nuances surrounding the banality of evil. In Montaignean fashion, the narrator will be, as Hesse would say, "storying readers to propositions" ("Stories" 189) in a shift away from the tradition of rational argument based on abstraction and analysis.[9] This is important because, although Newkirk acknowledges ethos in the personal essay, I see an implicit example/theme structure in his analysis that, in its reliance on rational appeal, is essentially logocentric, denying the pathetic and ethical dimensions of the essay's rhetoric. I am suggesting that the story and essay are functioning in a less reductive way than the theme/example mode, or what Newkirk is calling the "turn," would allow for, and it is precisely this complexity that undermines the pedantic efficacy of the confession of whiteness.

Because the essay resists this reduction, it also resists the claims of higher moral ground that Newkirk attributes to it. The undermining of narrative authority that takes place in "Shooting an Elephant"—an admittedly complex undermining that ultimately affirms through skepticism what it attempts to tear down—is an ironic strategy, one that Newkirk, as noted above, does rightfully identify as Orwell's willingness "to show himself at his worst," a rhetorical move of confession typical of the genre, and one, that I believe, becomes problematic for whiteness studies. For ultimately "Shooting an Elephant" becomes a tale less about the evils of empire and more about the narrator who tells the story, in much the same way that *Heart of Darkness* treats Africa as a backdrop for the narration of the individual European and how he is affected by colonialism: Orwell's accomplishment in the essay is not his opposition to colonialism per se but rather his ability to "grasp the hollowness . . . of the white man's dominion." Thus it is a modernist tale of alienation that focuses on European futility. The recentering of whiteness that occurs here is significant and is accomplished through a narration emphasizing the effect of colonial positioning on the subject Orwell, a nearly inevitable outcome for a genre in which, as Heilker says, "Truth of the world is inseparable from the truth of the personality."

My point here is not to argue that Orwell's politics were faulty or that "Shooting an Elephant" is a bad personal narrative full of shortcomings. Far from it. Orwell's political views are well known, and I agree with Newkirk that this particular essay is "paradigmatic." But as such, the "job" of "Shooting and Elephant" is not to show Orwell as a formidable opponent of colonialism or even to function as propaganda for anticolonialism, regardless of Orwell's political stances. Its "job" is to render irreducible lived experience through a depiction of the "ordinary" self and a narrating consciousness that is based on establishment of a (calculated) ethos of honesty—a "planned authenticity." As Adina Hoffman has said of memoir, "The stories of individual people who live and breathe the sweeping choices made by prime ministers and presidents . . . offer readers the chance . . . to grasp the flesh and blood implications of all those generalizing gestures made on high" (23). But I do think that the reader of personal essays should know how to read such work—not as logocentric arguments or honest interrogations but contrived explorations both enhanced and limited by subjectivity and particularity. The essay is less about calling us to action and more to thought. And that is the price we pay with the personal essay. Its strength is its weakness. In its resistance of conclusive prescription, it often leaves us rudderless. If these characteristics are tendencies of the genre, it raises questions about the extent such narrative, when performed competently, can fulfill its hoped for role in whiteness scholarship as a reckoning. In order to succeed in that capacity, these stories would "fail" as personal essays that problematize and resist the closure of authenticating structure. They would not be "true" personal narratives at all but rather exercises in social realism simplified to rely on a point/example structure. For one way to understand personal writing is that it is less about interrogating the subject and more about creating a narrative of the self—even in their most guileless and private forms, the acts of externalization and meaning making that take place through writing may inevitably put us on the trajectory of identity formation and the creation of a public narrative for the self to live by.

COMING OUT WHITE: CONTROLLING SUBJECTIVITY

The question of narrative identity is closely linked with the issue of revelation and disclosure. What is made public and what is closeted becomes central and inevitable to any personal narrative, despite the fact that the personal narrative would seem ostensibly to be based on an epistemology of disclosure. In her essay about the role of the personal in academic writing, Melissa Goldthwaite quotes her puzzled friend asking her why she writes personal essays:

> "You're the most private person I know," she said. "Why would you choose to write about your life?"
> "Because I choose what's revealed and what's not," I answered. (55)

Although Foucault's observations on sexuality spawned an entire school of thought regarding the constraining and compelling nature of the confessional structure, the genre also, perhaps ironically, produces a confessing subject that retains at least a degree of agency in the choice of what can be revealed. Thus in this way the confession of the personal narrative with its planned authenticity *is* agentive in the sense of a preemptive strategy that gives the narrator authority over the interrogation within generic constraints. The resulting subjectivity is both compelled and authorized, as we see in the case of "coming out," a concept with utility beyond gender/sexuality narratives as "queer theorists have argued that analyzing closeting narratives may be useful for understanding not only gay and lesbian culture and politics but also for understanding legal, cultural, and political discourses more generally" (Burgess 128). As Eve Sedgwick points out, "'The closet'" and 'coming out,'" are "now verging on all-purpose phrases for the potent crossing and recrossing of almost any politically charged lines of representation" (71). Deborah A. Chirrey, quoting the definition of Swain and Cameron, offers the following:

> "self declaration of identity is a coming-out process when it is a declaration of belonging to a devalued group" (1999: 68). In these terms, the individual in western society who discloses, for example, their mental

illness, their survival of sexual abuse, their underage pregnancy, or their drink or drug dependency, has 'come out.' These broader groups share many of the fears and anxieties, responses and reactions that gay men and lesbians experience around the process of coming out. . . . There are other discourses of disclosure that have a good deal in common with coming out, but are not labeled as such. (34)

Chirrey further states "Coming out is typically viewed as the action of individuals on the margins of society whose lives, lifestyles, or personal characteristics are subject to social disapprobation. However, . . . it has been possible to see parallels between these discourses and the pragmatics of any discourse in which an individual constructs a new facet of his/her identity or discloses any personal information" (35). Thus awareness narratives about whiteness can be understood as coming out about a racist identity and negotiating the same porous public/private divide as minoritized/ stigmatized sexual identity. Such narratives open the door of what may very well be a glass closet on "secret" white identity in a way that allows for the recentered white subject to maintain control of the revelation and thus the white identity in question. So we see in "Shooting and Elephant" how Orwell discredits himself in order to emerge as the existential hero of his story who wrestles with the wound of colonialism. In this case, coming out need not be an affirmation or defense of identity but merely an acknowledgment of complicity.

Awareness narratives reveal how the white subject's past is implicated in racism, but in reality such a revelation is what we might call "the open secret" (Burgess 129; Sedgwick 80). Similar to the way the homosexual identity may be known but not acknowledged, so the racism of the awareness narrator is understood but not talked about publicly until the confession is made in its particulars. Under such circumstances, "coming out" is not a true revelation in the sense of a surprise but rather an insistence on an inconvenient identity whose assertion has the power to disrupt the status quo or authorized discourse and, importantly in the case of whiteness narratives, to allow a purging and reclaiming of the white identity. On the other hand, since the white racist identity is unmarked, "invisible," the white subject always has the option of concealment through silence, again similar in some cases to the nonheterosexual subject whose revelation is in effect voluntary and in contradistinction to other stigmatized groups who do not have the choice of "passing"—such as most black people, for example. So to be white, through its invisibility, affords a certain privacy and privilege surrounding identity, and yet relinquishing that privacy does not necessarily result in disruption of the privilege but rather a claiming of existential status. For whiteness's hegemonic invisibility also effects the feeling of loss in the white subject similar to that perhaps experienced by the closeted gay who lacks supportive affiliation with either the gay or straight community: "The nature of the silence required for the formation of . . .

white identity [has] yet to be noted in the chronicles of our nation's psychic life" (Thandeka 10). Coming out, then, embodies the hope of "salvational epistemological certainty against the very equivocal privacy afforded by the closet" (Sedgwick 71). Coming out is very much about the subject agentively establishing a place in the world in order to avoid the alienation of silence and invisibility.

The epistemology of the awareness narrative is consistent with the epistemology of the closet and the obverse coming-out narrative when we consider the invisibility of whiteness, one of the founding premises of whiteness studies, for "The closet serves as a metaphor for invisibility" (Burgess 129). If whiteness is present but invisible, then it is indeed in the closet in the way LGBT identity is present but unauthorized and therefore unseen. The identification here is ethically ironic in that "hidden" in closeting discourse implies subjugated; in this case the white racist identity is being revealed in order to be shed, not embraced, and to reveal the scope and scale of whiteness's reach. In the LGBT coming out, the subjugated identity/discourse exists in defiance of the default of gendered heteronormativity. Whiteness, on the other hand, is the normative and oppressive "master narrative" in its various incarnations. In her discussion of whiteness as modern heterosexuality, Julian B. Carter observes,

> a primary goal of gay, lesbian, and queer scholarship has been to carve out a space in which queer representations and interpretations have epistemological and political value, with a focus on making oppositional discourses register as disruptions in the relentless display of normative heterosexuality that goes by the name "American culture." The kind of "invisibility" that most concerns queer scholarship, in short, is of a different order than that which is of central interest in critical whiteness studies: it is the abject invisibility of having been eradicated from the representational field, not the powerful invisibility of the wizard pulling levers behind the curtain. . . . Whiteness studies and gay/lesbian/queer theory thus engage issues of visibility and invisibility from different directions and from different needs. (27–28)

Yet in the rhetoric of awareness, whiteness must be confessed in order to become visible. The implications of this are significant because, with a decided lack of irony, the white subject is positioning itself as injured (even as it has injured others) and in need of reclamation through ritual initiation. (Indeed there is a question here as to whether the racist or antiracist stance is being positioned as the default. For whom is coming out being performed? The self? The white racist community? The liberal community for whom racism itself is invisible? The antiracist community of which the "new" antiracist self is a part?) The wound of whiteness must be revealed, "confessed," and this is perhaps a reason why such narratives often focus on the disempowered child on whom whiteness is inflicted. The white subject is traumatized into existence, as I will discuss further below, and the traumatized subject here recovers through the construction of an antiracist identity and reintegration into the community.

Coming out is an important affirmation for the LGBT community but also figures significantly in the identity formation and the liberation of the subject. Coming out, then, is about creating a self-narrative. According to Deborah A. Chirrey, the LGBT coming-out narrative, while a political action, is also a construction of identity (24). Likewise Esther Saxey emphasizes dialectical identity formation as the focal point: "these stories work to construct identities. . . . individuals tell coming out stories, but the coming out story 'tells' us" (2–3). As Yong Wang puts it, "the act of coming out marks a significant phase in the formation of the homosexual subjectivity both for the individual and for the formation of gay/lesbian communities" (235). The casting of identity formation as political action is of course at the core of the impulse to confess whiteness. The belief here is that acknowledgment of the closeted whiteness is disruptive to both overt racism (in its repudiation) as well as the hegemonic color-blind discourse of liberalism and postracism (in its invisibility). Even though the ostensible aim of coming out white is to discredit rather than affirm whiteness, the confessing white subject leaves one identity behind in order to enter a new community, a necessary move to protect the self that is being cut off from its former identity. This too, however, is consistent with the LGBT coming-out story in that "Another perspective on coming out is to interpret or recast it as an admission of former wrong-doing, not necessarily in a sexual sense, but in the sense that the gay or lesbian person has not been truthful about who they are. . . . the coming out is interpreted as a shameful one: as an admission of guilt, a confession of wrong-doing, or the revelation of deceit" (Chirrey 32). In an inverse parallel to the stabilization of LGBT identity that may occur in the coming-out narrative, coming out white relinquishes one shamed white identity for a new and improved one, thus producing the reclaimed white subject. Just as "newly outed gays and lesbians trade one rigid identity for another and unwittingly prop up heterosexuality, which needs homosexuality as a foil so as to maintain its dominant position in the political status quo" (Burgess 140–41), so too perhaps the antiracist's need for the racist to establish identity maintains rigid hierarchies. The question then arises, to what extent do whiteness narratives destabilize whiteness? In other words, to what extent are they "queer"?

Even though, as Sedgwick maintains, the process is never quite so neat or reified ("To come out does not end anyone's relation to the closet" [81]), generically, the coming-out narrative provides for "a shift from the private sphere to the public, and also a shift from silence into speech" that ostensibly liberates the subject from the closet (Bacon 251). In the case of whiteness narratives, the fiction of liberation of the subject is accomplished through a confession that confronts and "outs" the experience of white identity formation as a private wound and then controls the representation of the revelation and the investment in whiteness itself. We see this pattern in "Shooting an

Elephant" when Orwell positions himself as being injured by colonialism and the role he is "written" into. Orwell confesses the "truth" of this predicament, allowing us to glimpse just how base and self-serving his motivations were. But telling the secret, coming out, appeals to the reader as an act of integrity, even if his actions at the time were less than noble. In telling the truth, Orwell redeems himself precisely because he assures us that redemption is not his goal—indeed that he is beyond it. As mentioned above, the self-effacement strategy ironically moves Orwell into the role of Modernist hero.

A similar strategy is enacted in my opening narration for this chapter when I tell the two childhood stories involving my father, where I lyrically focus on the setting of doomed romantic ruins (in anticipation of the white melancholia evinced by the later adolescent self) and confess the private painful truth of my white upbringing while assuring the reader with my feelings of shame and dislocation about my desire to break free from white patriarchal rules. I have positioned myself as an innocent child caught up in the racist/sexist world of adults who must, in order to survive, make the tragic choice of joining the white order and then feel the shame and anger that would motivate me to break free. I further establish ethos with metatextual commentary, which shows a struggling consciousness trying to reconstruct a memory, and by presenting this child as a victim of patriarchy and a sympathetic member of the working class—indeed I even position the father and brother as victims of something beyond their control in that regard. That all of these things are true is beside the point—I am not accusing myself or anyone else of lying, posturing, hoaxing, or having bad intentions in the quest to interrogate whiteness. Instead I am pointing out that the need to confess is understandable as a generic construction and as the need to find an ordering narrative for what is often perceived and represented as trauma—a survivor's narrative to live by, one that involves the reconstitution of a palatable—and empowered—white subject, palatable to both the self and the society to which the self seeks entry. And I am then asking how useful can such narratives be in combating racism when one of their primary functions necessarily produces a refocusing on the injured white self? And do they, however inadvertently, in their promotion of the rehabilitated white identity, dangerously contribute to the erroneous idea that we currently inhabit a postracial era merely haunted by the gothic whiteness of the past? Antiracist work is reduced to the romance of excavating white psychic ruins, what David Aaron Gresson refers to as "white pain" and what Anne Anlin Cheng has identified as "white racial melancholia" (12).[10]

WHITENESS AS TRAUMA

The extent to which white identity formation is connected to trauma is taken up by Thandeka in her discussion of awareness narratives. Thandeka's work involves interviewing white people, which she identifies as Euro-Americans, about their first memories of being "raced" in order to help her understand the formation of white subjectivity—in a sense, how white people are "made." She points to one particular story of Dan, who as an adult recalls a school trip to the segregated South and tells of his dismay at seeing the "colored" and "white" signs. He reports knowing that this was very wrong and feeling confusion over the silence maintained by his teachers at this manifestation of racism. He waited in vain for someone in authority to disrupt this capitulation to the status quo. As a result, he came to experience this silence surrounding "America's racial policies" as "his personal secret" (7–8), a stance that Thandeka found startling, given that she remembers experiencing segregation as a decidedly public phenomenon. Dan goes on to tell a story about how in college at the behest of his fraternity brothers he told a black student to leave the local chapter:

> With [Dan's] . . . prompting, his local chapter pledged a black student. When the chapter's national headquarters learned of this first step towards integration of its ranks, headquarters threatened to rescind the local chapter's charter unless the black student was expelled. The local chapter caved in to the pressure, and Dan was elected to tell the black student member he would have to leave the fraternity. Dan did it. "I felt so ashamed of what I did," he told me, and he began to cry. "I have carried this burden for forty years," he said. "I will carry it to my grave." (1)

Thandeka says,

> I felt empathy for his suffering but was troubled by his lack of courage. Dan's tears revealed the depth of the compromise he had made with himself rather than risk venturing beyond the socially mandated strictures of whiteness.
> I realized that being white for Dan was not a matter of racist conviction but a matter of survival, not a privilege but a penalty. . . . As Dan's tears revealed, the internal price exacted from him for his ongoing membership in the "white" race was psychic tension and discomfort. (8)

Thandeka generously makes a distinction between being racist and complicity in racism (perhaps parallel to a distinction we might make between homophobic and heteronormative) when she argues that "Dan did not cry . . . because he was a racist. He cried because his impulses to moral action had been slain by his own fear of racial exile" (9). Her belief is that the white subject is formed when the child (in this case the young adult) is threatened with the loss of family and community when he/she (inadvertently) transgresses the boundaries of whiteness. She has collected numerous stories attesting to the cognitive dissonance the white person feels when antiracist impulses in their formative years put them at odds with the values of those who succor and nurture them. The white subject is forced into a position of sacrifice and must give up any "desires for a more inclusive [nonracist] community" (9) if he/she is to maintain ties with the "primary group" (10). In the case of Dan, she argues that he is not crying for guilt over his racism—indeed she takes pains to argue that the conventional move to characterize Dan's actions as racist seriously misrepresent his status—but rather a more primary wound, what she calls a "deeper loss and regret": the loss of the white community that his feelings have put him at odds with:

> The nature of the agony brought on by his refusal to risk exile thus could not be grasped using the standard racial categories of judgment and damnation that assume discriminatory racial acts against others by Euro-Americans always arise from racism, prejudice, and bigotry. Such an approach would simply racialize the deepest level of Dan's distress: his need to retain membership in his own community of caretakers and peers. The charge of racism would thus act like a prisoner's stun belt used to exact a confession. . . . Although he is not a racist, Dan might confess his guilt as a racist because this was the only way to stop the charge of racism for his act and also because racism was the only category he had to express . . . his stifled feelings and blunted desires. (9)

In effect Thandeka posits two sites of trauma: the fear that Dan feels at the potential loss of his group identity and the shame he feels at his inability to transcend that need in order to act in a more ethical way. Thandeka's identification of this first wound as nonracist is interesting because it points to a way in which awareness narratives function generically outside the agency of the confessing subject. The narrator confesses to racism because that is the rhetoric available to represent the nature of the trauma. But from Thandeka's standpoint, the source of the trauma is not racist feelings but rather the wound of separation that the "pre-white" child feels when it manifests preconforming feelings. The white community quickly teaches the child that such feelings are wrong, and the fear of exile from having disappointed family and community is what in reality accounts for the strong feelings of white shame in recollection. Thus failure to be white as a kind of original sin is at the emotional core of awareness narratives.

Thandeka's explanation of the formation of the white subject as occurring through the individual's inability to sever connections to family/community is compelling, but there is no reason to suppose, based on the description of Dan's admission about the fraternity, that he is not crying in response to the shame he feels at not being able to stand up to the fraternity—in other words, his past racism and his capitulation to whiteness. He is confessing his failure here to Thandeka, a black woman who rhetorically stands in metonymically for the group he has wronged, and thus feels his shame particularly acutely. He is in effect offering his disgrace to her as an apology. But even so, he is experiencing his whiteness, to use Thandeka's words, as a "penalty" or wounded identity. We see a similar move offered in the awareness narrative of Julie Landsman in her book, *A White Teacher Talks about Race,* when she recounts her experience of using the word "nigger" in front of the black woman who works for Landsman's family in Texas, 1948. She repeats the rhyme, taught to her by her father, about "Eeny meeny miney mo." The caretaker, Lillian, tells her that the word hurts her feelings. Landsman describes how recalling the moment in the present makes her feel:

> And even now, as I stand here, quiet for a moment before the view of the long, winding river, I can feel my body stopped there in that kitchen. I can feel the new sensation of coldness that ran through my arms and legs. I can still smell the dusty wind that blew on me out on that porch, still hear the sound of Lillian back at the sink, emptying a pan, running water over the baby bottles that waited to be cleaned.
>
> This was a time when my body registered pain all through the pathways to my heart. It felt worse than anything I had felt before, to be told that I hurt someone.
>
> I believe now that it is in these moments . . . that we are formed. In the heat of our kitchens, in the back of a car, in the check-out lines in stores. . . . (5)

Landsman's piece exhibits features typical of personal essay/narrative, including the lyricism of detail and the aestheticizing of experience endemic to the genre, as well as the landmark/epiphanic significance of the experience, what Newkirk, as discussed above, dubs a "turn": "It felt worse than anything I felt before." As a good practitioner of creative nonfiction, Landsman includes the details that allow us to understand what it is like to see through the lens of the narrator's subjectivity: "In creative nonfiction . . . we are not making universal claims of Truth, but rather presenting one person's truths about the nonfiction world" (Perl and Schwartz 76). Landsman exposes a construction of the vulnerable self here and thus establishes her ethos of honesty—and in so doing focuses us on the white subject. She confesses the secret of the racist white father, how white people are suckled on racism, and thus shows us a wounded child who is a victim of whiteness and who has unwittingly reproduced the effects of whiteness and inflicted its wound on another. (What is not said is equally important, for we are not told what the child understood or thought about the word "nigger." Did she use the word without understanding? Did she know that the domestic worker was one of the possible referents? That the word was pejorative? The lacuna allows us to read the child as innocent—to suppose that she was unwittingly wielding the weapon of whiteness.) Whiteness is experienced as penalty, and the telling of the tale reveals the formation of the wounded white subject that allows for the narrator's ritual reclaiming, even as it attempts to "out" the localness and particularity of whiteness.

But here we see too the "open secret" of whiteness's glass closet. Landsman is careful to point out the time and location—Texas, 1948—of the incident, again, without explanation, as though the fact tells us all we need to know. And it does. The time and place work enthymemically—we can all read in the rest. For as Thandeka says of roughly the same time and location, "Segregation had never been a 'personal secret' in my life. . . . I lived in . . . Dallas in 1952 and at six already knew which stores my parents and I could enter and be treated decently" (8). That Landsman's father would have taught her the racist rhyme, that she would have repeated it in front of the black caretaker, in other words, that the structure of her family was steeped in whiteness, is not startling. In fact, we might suppose it to be so typical as to wonder what could produce the feelings of intense shame. The incident becomes in effect, a "safe" secret to confess, in as much as everyone already knows about it. Offering its particulars up to the ritual of confession perhaps conveys a degree of sacrifice of the white subject greater than what actually is.

We might say, however, that Landsman is not so much confessing to the use of the word "nigger" here as she is recording a moment when she first became aware of her power to hurt someone else, in particular, the black domestic worker who appears to have functioned as a nanny for the family. Fair enough, but the existence of the black caretaker, the narrator's relationship to her, is another secret implicitly being confessed here. Again, the existence of the domestic worker is succinctly explained, perhaps excused is a better word, with "Texas, 1948." The figure of the black nanny who raises white children is a potent representation of whiteness and a great liability for one who will come to identify as antiracist. The relationship with the nanny in the closet must be accounted for in order to rehabilitate the liberal white subject, and her presence poses particular difficulty.

The stubborn fact of the black caretaker is a feature of Lynn Worsham's awareness narrative, "After Words," which she wrote as the afterword for the MLA collection *Feminism and Composition Studies: In Other Words* as part of her feminist and antiracist efforts: "to unbecome white—to work to end white supremacy through an interrogation of whiteness and an articulation of antiracist forms of whiteness" (345). Like Landsman, Worsham expresses a faith in the quotidian: "it is in the interstices of the everyday that identity and experience are produced" (345). Worsham's account has been praised as a model piece of writing that blends the academic and the personal (Spigelman 77), and in it she revisits an instance of family iconography known as the story of Blue Betty set, yet again, in "the mid-1950s . . . in a small town in the piney woods of east Texas . . . as deep into the deeply segregated South as one could go" (336). It is the story of how an African-American woman named Betty came to work in Worsham's household and ended up acquiring the moniker "Blue Betty." Worsham explains that there are both pedagogical and political reasons for her to recount the tale:

> When I was two or three years old, my mother returned to what passes in this society as real work—full-time paid employment outside the home. (She had been doing both paid and unpaid work at home.) My parents were desperate to propel themselves squarely into the middle class. . . . A few weeks before she started her entry-level clerical job, she began to talk to me. . . . Because I was, in her words, an overly sensitive child, she anticipated that I might not handle these changes well. She explained that someone would be coming to our house each day to take care of me. She said the woman's name was Betty, and, she added, Betty was "colored.". . .
>
> In the days before her return to work, my mother asked me . . . who was going to take care of me. . . . I replied, without hesitation, "Blue Betty. " Nonplussed by this response, my mother always suggested . . . that perhaps blue was the only color I knew . . . so I must have figured that "colored" meant blue. . . . In her account, I was happy and content as I awaited Blue Betty's arrival, and my mother made no effort to educate me, although this was not because she thought it best to leave well enough alone. (It would be years before I held enough pieces of my mother's history to begin to understand her chosen silence.) In my mother's account, Betty was amused when she first heard her name transformed—so much so that from that day on she also called herself Blue Betty. (334–37)

Worsham's account about her caretaker differs significantly from Landsman's story in several respects. Unlike Landsman, Worsham herself has no recollection of the event in question. Indeed the focus of her astute analysis is the way the story functioned in family folklore—the service the narrative performed as her mother would retell it. The story was not a mark of shame, as in the case of Landsman's unwitting falling into whiteness. The child's mistake in Worsham's case is instead a kind of transcultural catachresis (see Spivak 60) that disrupted the racism implicit in "colored." Worsham speculated that her mother's telling of the story was an attempt to call into question with limited means the whiteness of the time: "my mother found evidence . . . that racial terms and gender constructions are entirely artificial and arbitrary" (338); and to bolster her child's agency: the story "nourished the starving girl-child of a father who aggressively denied his daughters the power of naming and the right to choose a vision" (337).

But Worsham asks about the cost. She speculates about "The violence enacted through this blue-eyed story" when "it is the white woman who occupies the center of an alible narrative" (339) and describes the story as "vulgar in its fanciful and sentimental coloring of a cliché, indecent and base in its self-congratulation" (338). She recognizes that the story reflects "a world in which white people learn to expect that they . . . take center stage" and that her mother's story casts her "in the role of an innocent in a corrupt world, the color-blind child whose ignorance is recast as superior knowledge" (341). She says we must recognize Blue Betty "as a racist story, one that perpetuates as surely as it resists white supremacy" (342) in its silent erasure of Betty as a narrating subject. But what Worsham seems less able to recognize is that insight into this racism is an insufficient strategy to avoid its replication in this academic iteration of the story. Despite (or perhaps in some ways because of) the metatextual apparatus that is replete throughout the essay, in which Worsham authenticates her ethical author-ity by relentlessly questioning and theorizing motives and effects, the story of Blue Betty is not rescued from the pitfalls of the awareness narrative genre that reinvigorates the white subject as a focus of inquiry, in this case the narrating consciousness of Worsham. For while the essay is an inter-rogation of the intersections of whiteness and patriarchy and the power relations of naming and claiming, at the heart of the story is once again confession of the open secret: confession of the way the family is impli-cated in 1950s Texas racism and the intimate reliance on African-American domestic labor: the nanny in the closet. And thus the liberal white subject struggles to find representation within this treacherous domain, in this case by engaging in postmodern narrative strategies of legitimation that allow for a controlled representation and reclaiming of the subject.

In the effort to contextualize this particular manifestation of whiteness, Worsham, as we see above, makes a typical rhetorical move and locates the white nuclear family's reliance on the black caretaker within patriar-chal capitalism–the mother's own domestic labor is not valued, which in effect requires her to rely on cheap labor provided by African-Americans in order to effect upward mobility. Worsham's language in these passages, masterfully nuanced, creates a sympathetic portrait of the white mother figure whose own domestic efforts are disqualified from "real work" while (through?) acknowledging the debt of racialized labor:

> *blue* may have accurately named the color of an African American woman's pain . . . forced by economic necessity to cross into hostile ter-ritory to take care of some white woman's pampered child for a meager wage. *Blue* may have accurately named Betty's lived relation to the bru-talizing realities of a racist, patriarchal society where postwar affluence made possible the rise of the black bourgeoisie while also successfully maintaining the unequal distribution of economic opportunities along lines of race and gender. (338–39)

Speculation about the meaning of blue here, while intended to restore Betty's subjectivity, actually further obfuscates, for we are treated to the insights of the narrating consciousness here which has a vested interest in establishing an ethos of responsibility while also protecting the nurturing mother figure. Betty was exploited but in a qualified way, and the reader experiences the willingness to talk about this as a noble effort on the part of the white subject. Worsham must, reluctantly it seems, "out" a mother who has been filled with good intentions toward her daughter. She offers us a coming-out narrative that is not much of a surprise at all as she presents a protofeminist-inclined mother who too is a victim of whiteness's all-encompassing blinding glare. The child of Worsham's narrative is doubly victimized by whiteness since her story has been appropriated by the mother in order to shore up the white family. Whiteness, to use Thandeka's term, "costs" Worsham, and she has born the burden of it: "At times I could not bear to hear the story spoken, would not hear the recitation of what it carried in its words. At times, the story has been a dead thing in my hands, and I wanted no part of it to touch me. . . . Yet the story has always had a hold on me, worrying a piece of my mind, and my peace of mind, the way a hunting dog worries the throat of its prey" (339).

Spigelman, in her discussion of Worsham's essay as a model of hybridization between personal and academic writing, points out that "Worsham establishes ethos by citing other respected writers and researchers. Demonstrating her own generous appreciation of the literature and its application to the current situation, her text and her reputation in the field mark her as an established scholar" (76). But in terms of a narrative on whiteness, there is an even more important strategy at work here for establishing ethos. For the story of Blue Betty has a surprise ending. Worsham "finally" (343) reveals that as an adolescent, she discovered her maternal grandmother was Native American, a fact that the "white" mother attempted to keep closeted as she herself accrued the benefits of passing, which extended then to her daughter. The disillusioned Worsham understands this even as she wants to "know this grandmother's story and place it alongside mine" (344), a statement that claims for her the feminist tradition of connecting her life with silenced female ancestry, such as we see in Maxine Hong Kingston's "No Name Woman."

Why, however, does Worsham wait to tell us about this part of her story? Why use this rhetorical structure of establishing herself as white only to come out Native American? Why not, for example, divulge this information at the beginning instead of "passing" throughout the narrative? One answer is that by holding the identity in abeyance she is complicating the white landscape and our conceptions of racialization just as her mother used the story of Blue Betty to do. By allowing us to become comfortable with a notion of her as white, she disrupts reified racial discourse with this new piece of information. But another rhetorical effect also accrues from delayed revelation of the Native American grandmother in the closet, and that is claiming the benefit of the exotic to rehabilitate the white subject as a postracial projection (the ideal for which we see in the case of "Eve" discussed by Mike Hill in his introduction). Intended or not, for better or for worse, the Native American grandmother becomes a kind of ace in the hole who in effect sweeps in at the end of the story to rescue the mother and daughter from their whiteness and the narrative judgment of unrelenting Texas racism. Thus the thornier questions of Blue Betty, methodically engaged throughout the story, are scuttled and obscured (even as they are complicated and elucidated) by the multicultural presence of the grandmother—precisely the opposite of what seems very clearly to be Worsham's intended effect.

Garner reminds us that the whole point of exposing white invisibility is to show how the white "capacity to be universal and disembodied cannot be separated from the capacity to be an individual. . ., to be the liberal and liberated Enlightenment subject" (39), a fiction of subjectivity white people reserve for themselves. To what extent do the autobiographical elements of whiteness scholarship fail to disrupt this elision and instead reestablish this subjectivity? I have ended this section with a discussion of Worsham's "After Words" precisely because of its erudition and sophisticated awareness about the issues in question. Because even as this writing successfully interrogates dimensions of whiteness, it nonetheless participates in its reproduction, as do the other narratives mentioned. I am not talking here about what one reviewer has labeled the potential "self indulgence" of such stories (Storrs 571), for that term implies an excess that can be corrected with informed, conscious intent. I have argued that the genre itself fosters this reproduction of whiteness in its promotion of a *bildungs* oriented self-narrative. Even (especially?) narrative that strives to resist the simple epiphany of Newkirk's "turn" will replicate the ethical authority of whiteness through a variety of strategies endemic to the genre, as discussed throughout this chapter, thus limiting (and, indeed, focusing on) the agency of the white subject to a self-reflective gaze that is always necessarily performing self-rescue, or what Frankenberg calls "the narrative deployment of Others in such a way as to secure one's own 'redemption'" ("When We Are" 6).[11] We see in these narratives an example of how whiteness resourcefully reconstitutes itself, not just in the writing but in the *reading*, for the narcissistic reproduction of whiteness may account for the appeal these narratives have for a white audience, which of course is a significant part of the rhetorical exchange that gives birth to this particular genre.

Rather than a question of bad faith on the part of the authors, we find here an example of "the degree to which a white gaze is reinstated even as efforts are made to displace it" (Frankenberg, "Mirage" 79). In some respects, we are facing the very problem of language itself as it constructs the experience of whiteness for us. I don't mean to suggest that subjects are helpless in the face of linguistic hierarchies, but Ruth Frankenberg's analysis of an introductory passage by David Roediger demonstrates the extent to which language is steeped in whiteness. She describes Roediger's attempt to use the plight of an imaginary slave to draw attention to the way racialized analysis perpetuates othering. In his scenario, Roediger asks us to look at the slave but then reminds "us" that she is looking back. "Yet, as Roediger continues, it is as though the blinders fall back over his own eyes. Who is or are the group designated 'us' in his next sentence when he notes that 'little prepares us to see her as looking out, as studying the bidders'?" ("Mirage" 78). Frankenberg goes on to observe the various tropes and turns of phrases that show Roediger is writing from a position of whiteness even as he self-consciously tries to draw attention to the very phenomenon of racism. She assures the readers that her criticism is not personal but instead a reminder of how difficult it is for the white subject to transcend its subjectivity.

I would add that this is a question of language that seems to be a matter beyond mere consciousness and will. Thus I have not been arguing that white people shouldn't engage in self-reflection about their racism: in Chapter 5, I discuss the need for emotional epiphanies in white lives that expand the parameters of white identity through cathartic recognition and thus the importance of charting emotional rhetoric in the construction of whiteness. But I have come to believe that to enshrine these reflections in narrative performances under the ethical auspices of confronting whiteness becomes another matter entirely, as I have discussed throughout this chapter, and raises questions about the limits of autobiography to confront the narrative kitsch of whiteness (see Chapter 3) both in the classroom and beyond. Ultimately, what Ian and I call for and try to enact in this book is a study of whiteness based in dialogue rather than what might be termed the "tyranny of narrative" that continues to prevail as the preferred mode of academic discourse. It is our hope that dialogue can perhaps act as a corrective to the "failings" of narrative. This is an idea that we will return to, but first, in the next chapter, Ian continues with a metacritique of reconstituted whiteness from an institutional perspective, specifically that of higher education and basic writing.

2 Whiteness (as) in Basic Writing

"He soun white!"
"I like how he talk!"
"Say dat againe!"
"Say somthin sexy!"
"Yo, man, listen to dis guy. He soun like a faggot!"

It's September 1983 and I'm at Clifford J. Scott High School in East Orange, New Jersey standing in line outside the nurse's office. The group, black like me but mostly girls, observe me from head to toe. My drainpipe jeans and brogue loafers, the "in" style of the England I had left days earlier, must have surprised as much as amused them. I'm called in. The nurse's dark skin contrasts imagistically against her white lab coat.

"Name, please?"
"Ian Marshall."
"Scuse me."
"Ian Marshall" I say again.
"Spell that first name."
I enunciate, "I. A. N."
"Is that one "L" or two . . . on Marshall." She says squaring her gaze.
"Two." I reply wondering if I've ever seen it spelled any other way.

I'm questioned about my shots, found compliant, and then I'm routinely examined with a blood pressure machine and tongue suppressor. Compliant again, apparently. Minutes later, as I turn to walk out, "Young man" the nurse says, "You speak so beautifully. Don't ever lose that." Out the door the gaggle who found my speech so engaging moments earlier barely notice me as their interests flit elsewhere.

Clifford Scott High, and East Orange itself, was no warm and welcoming place for cultural diversity in the early 1980s. Its reputation was only slightly better than East Orange High, the city's other high school. It's a city which, ironically, serves as partial setting for Philip Roth's novel *The Human Stain*. That novel's central character, Coleman Silk, and I have almost exactly opposite trajectories with respect to whiteness and racism in the U.S. although we end up in remarkably similar places. While Silk must leave the East Orange of the 1940s in order to re-create himself as a white Jew enroute to becoming a professor, he does so by "simply" passing into white society. There is no hybrid identity or racialized public uncertainty to contend with. I, however, enter the East Orange of the 1980s and am regarded as white, in contradistinction to other people of color in the largely African-American community, enroute to becoming a professor. My passing was a kind of precursor to the present "postracial" era having to do with my language and culture that set me apart from both the African-American community and the burgeoning Caribbean community that together comprised the racialized "other" of that time. Although I'm darker in skin tone than most people I know, the closest cultural approximation given me by my classmates was a very peculiar *white*. Unlike Silk, passing for me has always been a linguistic phenomenon. My dark skin color, then, was strangely overruled by a "white" accent, thus complicating color alone as a basis of "white skin privilege" as Peggy McIntosh (291), Marilyn Frye (126), Noel Ignatiev (*Irish* 82) and others have proposed where their notions of whiteness are probably best thought of as an initial precursor to understanding how whiteness functions today as a kind of injured identity as Wendy argues in chapter one and Robyn Wiegman and Mike Hill propose.[1]

My dark skin at least fit the color of both Clifford Scott and East Orange High—and of course the city of East Orange itself—all "black" then as now. Back then they were black in a way that was wholly new to me since my arrival from Bristol, where I grew up in the working-class district of Easton and spoke what is considered there a working-class dialect. In Bristol, while I would readily be marked as working-class because of where I lived and how I spoke, I would not as easily be marked as specifically black in the way I am marked here because unlike in the U.S., England's social class system is less segregated by race. For instance, my family lived among white working-class families, something rare in the intensely segregated U.S. In fact, Bristol's working-class districts have historically been racially mixed, and largely unsegregated. I don't mean to suggest that England (or Bristol for that matter) is a model of racial harmony—far from it as I remember the race Rebellions of St. Pauls, Bristol, and Brixton, London—but since there is no legacy of racial segregation it is easier to see how what we in the U.S. often take for patent racism is often the way the U.S. hides its deeply rooted class structure where a division of the working class (white towns and black towns within the same county often separated by streets marking borders) encourages the illusion of upward mobility not having black neighbors appears to encourage. In Bristol my working-class dialect reflected my working-class identity which was indistinguishable from the working-class identity and speech of my white neighbors. This raises specific questions for me about *African-American Language* (AAL) about which I will have more to say.

In East Orange, my speech was something different. It marked me as an "other" other. I was exotic. From a distance (my clothes aside of course) I was as vulnerable as any other black youth in an urban setting at that time.

I was subject to a kind of metonymic displacement as described by Victor Villanueva ("New Racism") and Toni Morrison (*Playing* 68) where my color, that is to say, the key point of similarity with my African-American and Caribbean classmates, stood in for and elided my differences. At a distance, I was just a plain black kid. However, up close in conversation I couldn't easily be mistaken for African-American, and therefore I couldn't easily be metonymically displaced.

Villanueva, following on Burke's four master tropes, takes the idea of metonymic displacement a step further by connecting it to the idea of individualism. He says:

> The ultimate reduction, as far as I can see, is individualism. If everything is reduced to individual will, work, and responsibility, there's no need to consider group exclusion. "Identity" plays into this one quite well, because then it becomes an individual assertion of a group affiliation, the individual taking precedent. ("New Racism")

By this I understand Villanueva to be asking us to consider how groups get excluded from mainstream culture. That is, he seems to be saying that there is a tricky relationship between an individual's actions and how those actions (and utterances) get connected to the group from which she or he comes. Consider this: an African-American student, not unlike those from Clifford Scott High, takes the college placement test for English and language skills. They place into Basic Writing after twelve years of schooling. Their placement may be described as metonymic displacement because of how African-American Language itself tends to stand in for, and signal, "Basic Writer."[2] Basic Writing, the institutional academic location, is seen as a chance to improve her writing and join the rank and file college student in regular college courses. The student's ability to get *out* of Basic Writing is reduced to her "individual will, work and responsibility." The fact that she is being asked to write in a language that does not reflect her experiences or reality and that the vast majority of her fellow black classmates will follow her into Basic Writing (group exclusion) though not necessarily out of it, becomes secondary to their displaced metonymic identity as "black," which in this case is organized around their writing and language.

Another example of metonymy: My immigration to the U.S. wasn't my first experience with AAL, but it was my first experience with how to *read* it. My first experience was when I was no more than five or six years old. *Hong Kong Phooey*, the American children's cartoon from the 1970s was syndicated on British television. Hong Kong Phooey was a super hero puppy dog whose day job was janitor at a police station in a fictitious U.S. city. His alter ego, however, couldn't solve any crimes without his cat partner. The laughs from this cartoon came from his complete ineptitude and his equally complete dependence upon his cat friend to solve the crimes that he, as a superhero crime fighter, would invariably be credited for. What is remarkable about this isn't just that Hong Kong Phooey's cat partner was completely mute; his exasperated expressions were enough to convey his thoughts, and simultaneously allow them and him to be read as white. Or that Hong Kong Phooey's speech had a distinctly black cadence. What is most striking for me today is that I did not connect his speech patterns to a group or class of people at that time beyond recognizing that it was *American*. Nor do I believe most people in England would, and the reason for this is obvious but important to note. Hong Kong Phooey's speech is that of a 1970s urban black guy. He was not a metonymically displaced character for any culture I was a part of. Hong Kong Phooey for me, then, wasn't stupid because he spoke a particular way or used a particular language; he was stupid because he was a particular character. His speech was perfectly acceptable to us listening to it an ocean away. His speech patterns, then, were just as phenomenal as his ineptitude and were a marker for nothing, and no one else, but him. Coming to the U.S. taught me how to read him as specifically *African-American*.

A related take on this issue involves my three-year-old son who has an absorbing attraction to the present-day cartoon, *The Backyardigans*. The characters—not coincidentally created by a black woman—also have linguistic racial markers. Unlike Hong Kong Phooey none of them are buffoons, and the most obviously black character by speech pattern, Uniqua, is smart, insightful, and often leads the other characters out of their imaginary scrapes. However, this cartoon does not have a character who speaks in the language or dialect of urban black America. African-American Language, as defined by Dyson and Smitherman (973), the speech at the heart of the African-American community, is completely absent from *The Backyardigans* and in its place is a sanitized black intonation most closely resembling the speech of the black middle class. While the show does not participate in the racist displacement of black identity typical of cartoons of the 1970s, it does participate in the racial discourse of language by appropriating specific dialects for each of the five characters in the show and assigning them specific character traits which tend to challenge the old prevailing stereotypes. I draw your attention to this not as a special criticism of *The Backyardigans*, but to point out that such choices about children's cartoons still, apparently, need to be made. *The Backyardigans* as an artifact of present-day cartoon production seems to be speaking to, and about, cartoons like *Hong Kong Phooey* by attempting to reverse the effects of that older cartoon, which consciously or not, seems to occupy the mind of its creator. In a sense, then, the cartoon industry has a subtle kind of racialized discourse imbricated into it, which my son now participates in when he watches *The Backyardigans*. It seems to me that the project of Basic Writing has a racism similarly imbricated into it because it routinely codes nonelite writing as error, and in particular tends to code African-American language as error. That is to say, the project of Basic Writing still carries the essential nature of its racist beginnings as a project to sanitize the language of the "other" even (and especially) in our so-called postracial era.

As I indicate above, England is no model of racial harmony, but there are themes in popular discourse there that are worth mentioning because of the central role working-class dialects have held in popular culture for decades. Besides *Till Death Do Us Part*, the British sitcom that *All in the Family* and later *Archie Bunker's Place* are based upon, there were also shows like *The Duchess of Duke Street* and *Upstairs Downstairs* which dealt pointedly with issues of social class in ways I've yet to see on U.S. television. One show in particular, *The Duchess of Duke Street*, is important in this regard because its central character, Louisa Trotter, has a decidedly working-class dialect: one which would place her in roughly the same socioeconomic and political class as, say, the African-American community of East Orange where I lived.

Whereas her dialect identifies her as working class—even working poor—she is never identified as stupid or buffoon-like as Hong Kong Phooey might be. My point is that while British TV can broadcast powerful working-class characters—with their attendant working-class dialects and at least a serious attempt at portraying and dramatizing working-class life, I have yet to see this done on U.S. TV where African-American Language and working-class black life is concerned. African-American Language simply isn't visible in popular U.S. culture unless channeled in very particular ways, which causes it to be reified and metonymically cast as in, for example, music videos or comedy shows.

As I recount these experiences and observations, I recognize my own prejudices against AAL; its various oral intonations and its users. These prejudices were learned in the early days after my arrival here. Is my having not a single close friend of African-American descent all through high school an indication of my own internal racism? Is my shock at scouring the hallways of Clifford Scott for a single white face and finding none evidence of New Jersey's educational whiteness? Could this still be how immigrants become part of U.S. culture—by ostracizing African-American life and African-American Language? My family members come to the U.S. and still marvel at how they can spend an entire weekend on my parent's porch in East Orange and not see a single white person walk or drive by. I also wonder if many Rhetoric and Composition instructors have had feelings about AAL similar to mine but have normalized and internalized them such that they are invisible but not inconsequential in their writing classrooms, writing programs, and their pedagogy. Certainly one of my objectives here is to point out that the apparent *absence* of AAL in both the academy and mainstream media suggests that the consequences are real and more than likely related to the invisibility of whiteness in these places too.

Today I see my high school nurse's urging me to never lose my working-class Bristolian dialect as a form of internalized racism on her part and an encouragement to me to embrace a certain kind of individualism similar to what Villanueva articulates. Her comment, "don't ever lose that" suggests that she knew then what I had yet to fully understand: that my accent could be a real material asset because of the way it distinguished me from my African-American classmates. Or, perhaps more importantly, that acquiring AAL could severely limit my life chances in the U.S. This was just one of many ways that I was taught to despise the AAL of the Northeast by whites, blacks, friends, and family alike. Indeed, one of the first things this culture ever taught me was how to eschew those very speech patterns.

These early experiences with AAL and my recognition that it is a deeply despised language cause me to question the role of Basic Writing on college campuses today despite its ostensible purpose to help students succeed in academic institutions, because it is here that AAL has confronted—and continues to confront—greater U.S. culture in stark and revealing ways. In the northeast, where I live, these Basic Writing classes are overwhelmingly populated by African-American and Latino students. These students effectively pay a premium at the beginning of their college careers because of the day-to-day realities of their lived-experiences as revealed through the language they use. It was my early experiences at Clifford Scott High that taught me my first lessons about the politics of language in the U.S., and particularly in institutions of higher education. These experiences helped me understand that while individual Basic Writing programs differ, the project of Basic Writing itself and how it has been instituted throughout higher education in the U.S. rests on highly questionable premises having to do with notions of language and intellectual deficiencies in mostly nonwhite student populations, and most significantly, is evidence of a studied meditation on whiteness in higher education. That is to say, the aims and purposes of Basic Writing, tied as they are to the economics of higher education and the servicing and serviceability of racialized others in these institutions, do not seem at all reclaimable from their white supremacist underpinnings.

I use the term "servicing" and "serviceability" in the same sense that it is used in critical whiteness studies to demonstrate how racialized others are rhetorically positioned socially, politically, and ultimately economically in the creation of a white identity. For example, Karen Brodkin, in her book, *How the Jews Became White Folks and What that Says about Race in America*, discusses the desire for upward mobility on the part of working- and middle-class Jews at the turn of the 20th century. This desire, she argues, was satisfied by juxtaposing Jews as "model minorities" with a servicing construction of the African-American that posited them as degenerate and dysfunctional. It is at this point that a constructed "whiteness" emerges to posit Jews as *normal*. The servicing construction of the African-American, then, was an indispensable part of the whitening of Jewish life in America. Jewish writers could—and did—construct narratives of the African-American family against which they juxtaposed the Jewish family. This maneuver contributed to the integration of Jewishness into mainstream American life thereby creating a "new normal" which simultaneously included Jewishness as it underscored the exclusion of African-Americanness.

In making this argument I do not minimize the important observations and concerns of scholars who argue in favor of preserving a space on college campuses for Basic Writing if only for political and strategic reasons. Deborah Mutnick, Keith Gilyard, and Lynn Quitman Troyka come to mind most immediately; people who have taught basic writing and advocated for students in Basic Writing for years. They each argue in various ways for the opportunity offered by Basic Writing courses as gateways into higher education despite its malignment by many in and outside of the field.

Mutnick, for example, argues for a nuanced understanding of the political climate within which the project of Basic Writing exists, recognizing attacks from both the left and the right in her article, "The Strategic Value of Basic Writing: An Analysis of the Current Moment." I sympathize with her assessment of Basic Writing of a decade ago, and would argue that despite innovative developments in the field, such as the implementation of the studio model across many campuses, and the application of universal design into pedagogical practices, the analysis she proffers remains, essentially, as true today as it was then—abolitionists on the right arguing that Basic Writing courses and students who populate them do not belong on college campuses, and abolitionists on the left who argue that Basic Writing does not belong on college campuses, but the students who populate it do.

Yet I find it difficult to support her position wholeheartedly since her assessment of those she positions on the "left" seems problematic to me. For instance, she cites Bartholomae's assertion that Basic Writing had become 'a grand narrative of liberal sympathy and liberal reform.' Further, Bartholomae began to question Basic Writing's place in the curriculum (76). My reading of Bartholomae in the essay, "The Tidy House: Basic Writing in the American Curriculum," published based on the keynote speech Mutnick cites, does not mark these comments as particularly revealing or central. Rather, it is where these comments lead that is essential in his argument. He seems to want us to consider how the project of Basic Writing participates in a narrative of education that does nothing to challenge the prevailing definition of education as we understand it, but rather participates in it. That is to say, while Mutnick points out that some of Bartholomae's theories became pedagogical standards at all levels of Composition (76), she fails to take his argument a step further to see that what he was actually advocating was the use of nonstandard dialects to point the way to new ways of knowing and new uses of language in writing classrooms rather than their deployment in these classes where teachers and students understand that the objective is, ultimately, to bring the nontraditional student to the "normal" of standardized white middle-class dialects of English that Freshman Composition in its form then, as now, teaches (Bartholomae 18).

Gilyard, in his essay, "Basic Writing, Cost Effectiveness, and Ideology", similarly, though more cautiously, offers a defense of Basic Writing on the grounds that good writing can be—and is—produced in such courses even as he seems to settle for an uncomfortable middle ground where he sympathizes with many of the assertions put forward by abolitionists of the left such as Crowley and Shor, but nevertheless sees Basic Writing as "a place of potentially radical spaces. . ." (37). The decade since the publication of his essay, however, tells a tale that is unlikely to lead to radicalism of any note. For instance, the development of online courses, three week semesters, the corporate takeover of higher education, most vividly illustrated by the shifting of Basic Writing courses to community colleges, and the merger contemplated by Blackboard and K12 to offer Basic Writing classes online[3] suggests an outsourcing of these courses which will no doubt alienate students in Basic Writing rather than acclimate them to a college community and environment.

Quitman Troyka's open letter to the editors of *JBW*, published in the same issue as Mutnick's and Gilyard's essays, laments the lack of political will on the part of Basic Writing scholars. Of the four areas she outlines as failures on the part of Basic Writing faculty and researchers—poor public relations, an inability to resist traditional academic culture, the "hasty retreat" from the "Black English" debate, and the overreliance upon unexamined research from earlier decades—the one that draws my attention is the third, having to do with the treatment of African-American Language by researchers in the discipline. As Quitman Troyka herself argues, the attacks on Geneva Smitherman's work by the mainstream media were stunning in their racism, and the silence from Basic Writing scholars in response was deafening in its absence.

Quitman Troyka's assessment speaks to Mutnick's reading of Bartholomae in that it highlights the ways in which Mutnick may be unwittingly supporting a pedagogy that is, at its roots, white supremacist since she does not adequately account for the critical inquiry of language Bartholomae seems to advocate, and which Gilyard seems to suggest is possible in Basic Writing; she is silent on that score. We could argue, then, that whiteness in language has been so successful that it has succeeded in presenting itself as normal, even to those who might be sensitive to the racism that often accompanies the arguments over literacy in higher education.

Does African-American Language, then, represent some aspect of what the U.S. seeks to repress? I often wonder, for instance, if President Barak Obama's successful candidacy for president in 2008 wasn't in part due to his ability to code switch so effectively and not be solely dependent upon his natural speech patterns, which seem more in line with his white mother's culture than with his black Kenyan father, or with the African-American community he made his own. He is no Jesse Jackson as the current senate Majority leader, Harry Reid suggests, pointing out that President Obama was well suited for a presidential run because he is a "light-skinned" African-American "with no Negro dialect, unless he wanted to have one" (Reid). Clearly Reid understands something about the way AAL triggers fear and anxiety that is yet to be fully explored in greater U.S. culture or in the profession of Rhetoric and Composition.

In the "postracial" age of Obama, most New Jersey towns remain stubbornly segregated, and therefore so do most of its 591 school districts.

There is nothing postracial about this blue state's Essex County and the disparity in school systems evident there where over eighty percent of all black children go to schools in which they are the significant majority.[4] This pattern is repeated almost uninterrupted statewide from one county to the next. These statistics serve to underscore the very different realities African-American children live, at least in the state of New Jersey, vis-à-vis their white counterparts.

The language differences we see between these groups, then, may properly be understood as a reflection of how these different communities must articulate the different realities that they live. This is one reason why I question the logic of an argument that would favor acquiring the ever elusive "Standard English" as the solution to the issues language presents to us in our writing classrooms. Not only does it fail to address the economic and social disparities (and realities) that AAL represents, but it also refuses to address the intrinsic racism of a school system and social order incapable of accounting for the language patterns of so many in the U.S. today.

WHITENESS AS CRISIS AND ABSENCE IN BASIC WRITING

> . . .*given the fact that the overwhelming majority of research within composition studies is written by white researchers and that the teaching force in the United States is increasingly white while the student population is increasingly not, I feel it is imperative to acknowledge that constructions of whiteness are inherent in how we teach and do research. . .*
>
> —*Amy Goodburn* (83).

Amy Goodburn's appeal, written some ten years ago, is as true today as it was then. She asks us to acknowledge the constructions of whiteness within composition studies, and this is at once inviting and daunting. It is inviting because anyone who wishes to understand how and why so high a percentage of minority students are segregated into Basic Writing classes in higher education would want to understand how 'whiteness' plays a role in the apparent apartheid. It is daunting because whiteness in Basic Writing is characterized not only by the presence of these students in these classes, but by the absence of a critical discourse that examines how whiteness functions, and indeed, by how *absence* itself functions to create whiteness in composition studies generally. Absence, along with the notion of *crisis,* has characterized the history of Basic Writing in higher education since its inception some forty years ago and gives compelling evidence for its complete reconceptualization. Neither Basic Writing nor basic writers have ever been adequately defined (Otte and Williams Mlynarczyk 64). Both exist as abstraction when we generalize too much beyond the borders of our own institutions which, perhaps, is a central reason why the field is so given to crisis. Just what (and who) is the discipline serving?

Another related reason the field is given to abstraction is that Basic Writing and whiteness may be seen as similarly situated within colleges and universities. The lack of a standard definition of the "basic writer" enables Basic Writing to be enforced locally, broadly, and promiscuously in the subjective eyes of the authorized beholder much like definitions of race where categories are subjectively identified by the authorized gaze of already-invested white people who do the identifying—like state police teachers. Whiteness and blackness in skin color, as in speech, are actually socially inherited categories based on already-dominant whiteness in any given social or discourse community.

Mike Hill, in his book, *After Whiteness: Unmaking an American Majority*, argues that one form of whiteness in universities may, on the one hand, be seen as a lamented absence because of how the defenders of the hallowed halls of higher education characterize the masses of working-class people who came to school during Open Admission and "ruined the university," but on the other hand, whiteness in universities may be seen in scholarship in whiteness theory itself as a vocation for white scholars of literature (predominantly male) who had jumped on the diversity bandwagon and had resolved to position their identities as exactly that—diverse. Hence there was the flourishing recognition (and publication) of ethnicity among the erstwhile white faculty in the 1990s—Italian-American, Irish-American, Jewish-American, and the like. "White," then, was not only the invisible abstraction, but it was also imbricated into the hyphenated. It allowed people to claim a marginal identity in greater U.S. culture and to have suffered there on the margins—or so the argument seems to have gone.

What has never been well articulated or mapped is how Basic Writing as a discipline may also have served similar purposes years earlier. In this sense, like the scholarship in whiteness of the 1990s, it may well be defined as a colonial "career" as articulated by Edward Said in his defining book *Orientalism*, where he argues that the region known as the orient was a career for young Westerners, men usually, made possible by a set of ideas and notions, a compartmentalized bound archive of knowledge shared by Western colonial powers to dominate and control their empires (40–41). As a field, Basic Writing far more dubiously may be said to appropriate its students, and be appropriated by its advocates and detractors who increasingly find their own professional identities in its unstable history. This provides an interesting take on Mina Shaughnessy's characterization of the field as "a new frontier like the American West" (Shaughnessy 4).

Whiteness as Crisis

As the history of our field has well documented (most recently and lucidly by George Otte and Rebecca Williams Mlynarczyk in their book, *Basic Writing*) both Composition and Basic Writing began life in crisis. The shocking revelation that the elite, who otherwise were appropriately suited to higher education, could not string two sentences together in writing without grammatical error necessitated the creation of the first Composition courses at Harvard University in the late nineteenth and early twentieth centuries. This, coupled with the increasing enrollment in universities of the not quite white Jews in particular[5] to satisfy the demands of a rapidly expanding industrial capitalism, allowed the newly created Composition course to serve double duty as both a writing course and a gatekeeper regulating who and how many people passed the course, got their degree, and entered the workforce. Thus, we are told, begins the history of Composition in the American university (Brereton qtd. in Otte and Williams Mlynarczyk 44; Shor, "Apartheid" 91; Crowley 89). Ira Shor's provocatively titled essay, "Our Apartheid: Writing Instruction and Inequality," more than most that had come before it, connects the Basic Writing crisis of the 1970s with the concurrent economic crisis by explicitly linking what he termed "the fake literacy crisis" to the industrial state, labor exploitation, and racism, implicitly arguing that together they form a powerful mix that functioned in remarkably similar ways to that of the Harvard course by regulating the workforce and functioning as a gate-keeping mechanism so as to promote current social inequalities of race, class, and gender (92).

"Crisis" is the prerequisite of a lamented absence as Mike Hill articulates in *After Whiteness*. He effectively underscores and extends Shor's critique showing how the notion of crisis was intimately related to the culture of universities in the U.S. beginning with the post-World War II G.I. Bill of the 1950s through Open Admissions of the 1970s up to the present. This crisis, Hill tells us, had several effects on the university having to do with a decline in public funding, the corporatization of the university, and the firm entrenchment of adjunct labor which precipitated declining numbers of full-time tenured faculty (138–40, 153). The "adjunctification" of the profession clearly contributed to the paranoia surrounding faculty sovereignty and the threat they saw to their privileged status, but what is important for us to note in Hill's critique is how his assessment of both Clark Kerr's *Uses of the University* and Bill Readings' *University in Ruins* racializes this crisis, which they both frame as an invasion of the "mob" (Kerr's word) that "ruined" (Readings' word) the university by its presence (Hill 159). The mob, of course, is not just a more militantly active student population, but a dramatically diverse one as a result of Open Admissions.

The university in crisis meshes precisely with Min-Zhan Lu's observation in "Conflict and Struggle: The Enemies or Precautions of Basic Writing?" that the students were often seen as unqualified college material. For instance, she discusses Geoffrey Wagner and Louis G. Heller's questioning of the "educability" of Open Admissions students—the very students whom Kerr and Readings refer to as the mob. Their description of these students as militants and hostile (Lu 892) make their fears palpable, and puts them in the camp of those who see the university as somehow in ruins as a result of their presence. My point here is that like Morrison's Africanist

Presence, the presence of racialized others along with an inassimilable student body (Hill 156) triggers responses that lament the ruin, the mob, and militancy on college campuses. Both Kerr and Readings as discussed by Hill, and Wagner and Heller as discussed by Lu, lament the loss of a golden (white) age before the masses arrived. Indeed, in the case of Readings and Kerr, Hill tells us, the lamenting of this golden age *preserves* the idea of the golden age as a kind of absent presence (Hill 157). Hill's emphasis on the productiveness of *absence* underscores rather than suggests Catherine Prendergast's notion of the absent presence of race in composition studies, as I will show.

A similar kind of preservation occurs specifically around the question of Basic Writing as detailed by Lu. One of the main arguments in her essay is that Basic Writing came about, in part, because of an unwitting alliance over the question of acculturation between pioneers of Basic Writing and those who saw it as a threat, namely Wagner and Heller. That is to say, the call for acculturation was simultaneously recognition that Open Admissions had somehow ruined the scholarly community that had existed before the mob had arrived: the kind of institution Oxford was (Lu 891). She writes:

> [Kenneth] Bruffee's and [Thomas] Farrell's eventual success in establishing the legitimacy of their knowledge and expertise as Basic Writing teachers, I believe, comes in part from a conjuncture in the arguments of the two Basic Writing pioneers and those of Wagner, Heller, and [Lionel] Trilling. (893)

She goes on to point out that Farrell, for instance, sees the principal goal of Basic Writing as the acculturation of students. The implication here is the general acceptance that the students have already—or are in danger of—ruining the school, and must be prevented from doing so. The primary mission of Basic Writing, then, was never to address the issues and complexities of language as a sociopolitical phenomenon let alone as a reflection of the lived experiences and realities students come from, but rather as a kind of colonial enterprise to mimic the language and habits of the white established power structure—to render the Basic Writing students tolerable as a university presence. Thus, the very political act of declaring the end (and absence) of this political power structure, as Wagner and Heller do, participates in the reproduction of it and so helps to enshrine whiteness in Basic Writing.

In his essay, "The Birth of Basic Writing" Bruce Horner discusses another aspect of the crisis in Basic Writing in his discussion of Open Admissions which, while tangential to my line of argument with respect to whiteness, is nevertheless indicative of it. Here whiteness is an absent presence in the political materiality of the Basic Writing project. Speaking in the context of student demands and violence during CUNY's Open Admissions process, he points out that the discourse surrounding it:

posited two types of students set in opposition to one another: the Open Admissions students, associated with politics and minority activism, and the ideal college students, assumed to be interested in and capable of pursuing academic excellence because they were not distracted by political interests. . . .

A second, related myth marked Open Admissions students not only as being activists but as belonging to ethnic minorities. For example, all evidence showed that the majority of CUNY Open Admissions students were whites of working-class background . . .Yet the myth persisted in popular media discourse that all or most Open Admissions students at CUNY were black or Puerto Rican. . . . Unimaginable within the framework of the binary were the so-called "white ethnics": working-class whites, many of them at CUNY of Italian or Irish Catholic background, and many of them conservative in their political views. While the invisibility of white working-class ethnics speaks most obviously to the pervasive blindness of Americans to social class and the persistence of racism, it speaks also and more specifically to the constitutive power within and outside the academy of the public discourse linking minority students, political activism, and academic underpreparedness, a power which made invisible students who might lack both academic preparation and interest in political activism. (8–9)

What is important to note here is Horner's observation that the white working-class student "who might lack both academic preparation and interest in political activism" because, as he says, "many of them [are] conservative in their political views" are "invisible." Their invisibility, I would suggest, is not incidental to the CUNY crisis, but constitutive of it and of the Basic Writing project since it not only appropriated the CUNY administration and minority students in a particular power dynamic that transformed the white ethnic student into the white "normal," it did so by appropriating blackness and the minority student as aberrant, not unlike the way Jewish families became "white" against a representation of a dysfunctional black family as Brodkin argues. "Basic," then, became synonymous with "racialized" in higher education almost from the inception of Basic Writing programs, at least in the Northeast.

Also noteworthy is the link between political activism and whiteness that Horner makes suggesting that to act white is to act within political boundaries of the status quo. Not only does whiteness claim "normal," it also demands political conformity thereby underscoring its ubiquitous power since to challenge it is, by definition, to be abnormal.

Whiteness as Absence

In the last section we saw how lamenting the passing of a golden age of the university, coupled with hostility toward the masses in terms of their educability and the perceived threat they posed to the viability of the institution, becomes a palpable demonstration of whiteness in education culminating in a compromised Basic Writing project from its very inception.

In their essay, "Critical Literacy and Basic Writing Textbooks: Teaching Toward a More Just Literacy," Patrick Bruch and Thomas Reynolds discuss another example of whiteness as an absent presence. However, their discussion is centered on writing pedagogy in Basic Writing. They argue that cultural studies (and by implication its pedagogical counterpart, critical pedagogy), pioneered by James Berlin, Ira Shor, and others, may have unwittingly reinscribed the very dynamics of power that they set out to challenge (Bruch and Reynolds). Specifically,

> [James] Berlin and [Michael J.] Vivion conclude their introduction to *Cultural Studies in the English Classroom* by pointing out a major weakness in the collection—that 'people of color did not choose to submit materials for consideration' (xiv). While Berlin and Vivion do register the significance of this absence, stating that 'The silences created here speak loudly of a need to examine how we constitute ourselves as a community' (xiv), their characterization of the constitutive gap in their collection as a product of what 'people of color did not choose' to do potentially minimizes their own insight that the deafening silence is a product of the well-intentioned choices and actions of cultural studies theorists ourselves and the social relations of race inscribed in the discursive practices we value. (Bruch and Reynolds)

What Bruch and Reynolds refer to is the apparent inability of critical pedagogy to account for how it produces its own blind spots with respect to race both as a political strategy on college campuses and as a pedagogical practice. Critical Pedagogy, they argue, has not produced student texts and literacy that are sensitive to "racially segregated and hierarchized communities that by default promote white language." They further point out that:

> the racial disembodiment of literacy that links it to whiteness happens on material and ideological levels. On the material level, critical literacy underserves members of marginalized racial groups by downplaying the significance of the fact that, as Eugene Wolfenstein has pointed out, "languages have skin colors.". . . On the ideological level, literacy continues to underserve marginalized groups by implementing the belief that valued institutional practices like literacy are neutral with respect to social group relations of power. This ideological effect is accompanied by using literacy in ways that ignore its historical context and participation in racial dynamics.

Literacy, then, for Bruch and Reynolds, seems not just to be a question of acquiring another dialect since language, as they suggest, is nothing if not ideological and therefore political, but is also an apparently race-neutral way of teaching white linguistic codes that ignores the highly charged social and political history of the production of those codes. They go on to point out that

> Since their [Berlin and Vivion's] discussion of what is in the book—the chapter summaries—is disconnected from the critical comment regarding who is not—people of color—race is framed as something absent from cultural studies rather than as a dynamic that structures cultural studies and critical literacies it values.

Bruch and Reynolds suggest, then, that the most progressive pedagogy formulated by composition theorists is itself subject to whiteness where racialized others (and raced language) is the absent presence that frames and circumscribes this pedagogy. That is to say, the absence of people of color in the discourse of critical pedagogy is a constitutive part of the pedagogy itself.

Keith Gilyard, in his essay, "Higher Learning: Composition's Racialized Reflection," while acknowledging the importance of critical pedagogy to Composition and Rhetoric, nevertheless gives a similar critique of Berlin and critical pedagogy arguing that

> if a rhetorician as critically sensitive and astute as Berlin, who was obsessed with how cultural codes implicitly operate, failed to crack the "race" code for us, it is strong testimony to how potentially invisible, or invisibly potent, that particular code signifies. Furthermore, because rhetoric is inherently ideological, as Berlin himself declared, he compromised his own teaching project by not attending to the issue of race more critically. From the subject position of a white teacher, a label he did not reject, how could he teach students to 'resist' and 'negotiate' the controlling discourse that Whiteness is? (48)

One gets the sense that this last question for Gilyard is purely rhetorical. He seems to suggest that Berlin is unable to resist the controlling discourse of whiteness precisely because of its imbrications in U.S. culture, and subsequently in Berlin himself.

The forgoing analyses present significant problems for those who argue in favor of bidialectialism, the argument that students who come from nontraditional families and communities can (and should) simply learn the codes of Standard English: a principal goal of most Basic Writing programs. If languages are not simply codes but are also ways of being, what is at stake here is the role of African-American Language on college campuses. Put another way, how should we address the 'servicing' role that African-American Language has played—and continues to play—in higher education?

BIDIALECTALISM AT THE TURN OF THE TWENTY-FIRST CENTURY: REDRAWING THE BOUNDARY

> *The argument [over the legitimacy of Black English] has nothing to do with language itself but with the role of language. Language, incontestably, reveals the speaker. Language, also, far more dubiously, is meant to define the other—and, in this case, the other is refusing to be defined by a language that has never been able to recognize him . . . It is not the black child's language that is in question, it is not his language that is despised: It is his experience.*
>
> —*James Baldwin*

I'm often struck by the fact that no one in the U.S. has ever addressed me with anything less than approval where my speech is concerned, or has ever asked me to acquire the linguistic code of the academy, yet I'm not convinced that my speech was ever any closer to academic discourse, or that academic discourse itself was any less foreign to me than it was to those whom I went to Clifford Scott High School with, none of whom, as far as I know, are university professors teaching English today—a profession I doubt I would have had if I had stayed in Bristol, with its own peculiar social class and racial hierarchy. It's worth asking, then, why we're not more surprised that African-American Language still exists in the way that it does in the U.S. today, because its existence, it seems to me, is strong evidence of a social, political, and, of course, academic system less equitable and democratic than we might at first suspect. I cite Baldwin above to underscore my suspicion that in the U.S. "it isn't the black child's language that is in question, it isn't his language that is despised: it is his experience." I wonder, then, if the project of bidialectalism isn't equally as problematic where whiteness is concerned as the project of Basic Writing seems to be.

One notable defense of the bidialectical position is David G. Holmes's "Fighting Back by Writing Black." I want to spend some time discussing his article because I want to show how someone who clearly understands the power of rhetoric both politically and in the discipline of Composition and Rhetoric can be moved by what appears to be institutional and social demands to a position that seems paradoxical. Indeed, his argument appears to undermine his own project by endorsing the view that students need to learn the language of power because as well as making them more linguistically versatile—a goal I agree is worthy—it also gives them an opportunity for greater academic success and better prepares them for the market outside of school. While Holmes doesn't say this, he nevertheless seems to be arguing for a kind of cosmopolitanism that had not yet materialized when he was writing and has yet to materialize some eleven years after the publication of his article.

The essay, written in 1999 as a chapter in *Race, Rhetoric, and Composition* edited by Keith Gilyard, is a carefully constructed and nuanced assessment of the way black intellectuals in art and politics—and subsequently academia—have come to view themselves and their respective movements in terms of racial identity. Holmes begins by positing that the Black Arts Movement of the 1960s and 1970s that espoused a deep connection to the black community was a more deliberately political movement than the Harlem Renaissance. However, according to Holmes, the Black Arts Movement simultaneously espoused propaganda that delimited the identity of the African-American artist as a single kind of thing. His rhetorical question: who should be the arbiter of authentic black identity with respect to the Black Arts Movement is a prelude to the question at the heart of his argument which is: why should African-Americans who learn and use Standard English be considered any *less* black than those who speak in nonstandard dialect? (54). While I agree with Holmes that the acquisition of Standard English by all students is a good thing in almost all circumstances, we should nevertheless consider how such students acquire this language—the context and pretext for learning it, the role of other dialects, and the consequences of it. We should also consider what, exactly, Standard English is. The term "Standard English" seems to elude definition just as the terms "Basic Writing" and "Basic Writer" do. Indeed, perhaps its most consistent definition may be what it is *not*, which appears to be the dialect of the masses in any given locale. I am less convinced by Holmes's argument, then, when I consider Baldwin's assessment of language where Baldwin argues that what is really at question is the experience language conveys. I therefore not only question Holmes's conclusions, but also the premises of his argument which, it seems to me, are more enmeshed in the politics and history of language in higher education than his readers might first suspect, and that my experiences, growing up outside of the U.S., have allowed me to see from another point of view.

Juxtaposing Nikki Giovanni and Amiri Baraka as exemplars of the Black Arts Movement on the one hand and Ralph Ellison and James Baldwin as alternatives on the other, Holmes argues that both Ellison and Baldwin held to a dialectical take on black culture specifically and American culture generally. This is unlike, for example, Baraka who Holmes argues saw only one way to be black as well as the impossibility of integration into greater U.S. culture. Holmes says of Ellison:

> For him, the melting pot did not represent the loss of ethnic identity . . . but the tense yet essential interplay between minority cultures (and Ellison would include white culture within this definition) in the melding together of a new, American culture. Further, this mutual influencing (between whites and blacks, for instance) would exist regardless whether it was recognized by either group. (55–56)

Historical evidence can be used to show that the split Holmes identifies between Ellison's more assimilationist position on the one hand and

Baraka's more isolationist position on the other with respect to who should be the arbiter of black identity and art isn't an either/or proposition. Indeed this issue might be traced back to the tension between house slaves and field slaves, between Washington and Du Bois, between the early Malcolm X and the early Martin Luther King Jr. My point is that we might reasonably argue that the split itself is a central and historical feature of black life in the U.S.; not incidental to, but constitutive of, it.

The "splits" I mention are much more revealing when viewed through the lens of social class. If Baraka, for instance, sees little hope for assimilationist ideas, it is perhaps because his experiences in working-class urban Newark, New Jersey, teach him these things. Similarly, if Ellison sees the potential for such hopes it is because his experiences in rural Oklahoma, where he learned to love reading and rarely, in those early days, thought of himself as black, taught him the possibility of such (R. Ellison ix). I think the split between Malcolm X and Martin Luther King, and Washington and Du Bois, can be seen in much the same way respectively. What is crucial to note about these examples is that they all fit within the logic of social class formation in the U.S., which remains largely invisible behind the logic of race. While there is truth to the idea that the U.S. may be considered a "melding together of cultures to produce a new American culture," it is equally true that it is the distribution of power that determines and delineates that melding. That is to say, while each of those mentioned in my examples may represent different castes, they nevertheless are all constitutive of the permanent laboring class as defined by Du Bois[6] in the U.S., a class reserved for African-Americans since the firm entrenchment of slavery in the 1660s. As I will show, learning the linguistic codes of the dominant majority will not change this material fact for the masses of African-Americans whose experiences, Baldwin tells us, are despised.

Holmes next critiques the 1974 CCCC document, The Students' Right to Their Own Language, to make the case that the document inadvertently creates the same shaky ideological foundation for Composition pedagogy as the Black Arts Movement did for literary studies because, he argues:

> the existential investment students have in their respective dialects restricts pedagogical discussion. Accordingly, teachers are primarily responsible for cultivating the students' 'self esteem and self image' by giving ample respect to their dialects. (58)

Holmes's last sentence here is important. Is he right that teachers, mostly white, mostly adjunct in Basic Writing or Composition classes, have "cultivat[ed] the students' 'self esteem and self image' by giving ample respect to their dialects"? Or do these teachers' actions represent the twin problem of being unwilling (or unable as adjuncts) to confront the politics of language in their classrooms on the one hand and the implicit hypocrisy of trying to unproblematically produce white middle-class writers out of racialized others on the other?

Holmes's discussion of the students' rights to their own language precipitates another related discussion having to do with the language of the marketplace which is what these teachers are more than likely thinking about as they listen to their African-American students communicate in writing and in speech. Here is the closest Holmes gets to connecting the deeply ideological and class-based notions of rhetoric with language when he indirectly suggests that learning the dialect of the marketplace—his term for Standard Edited American English—is not only academically and intellectually beneficial to the student by adding another linguistic code to the students' quiver, but also essential if one is to defend oneself from the dominant culture, hence "writing black and fighting back" (59).

There is no question that Standard English, whatever we decide it is, has value because all dialects do. There is no argument that students are enriched by acquiring this dialect if for no other reason than the fact that it is another dialect. The questions to ask are: to what extent do we account for the controlling discourse that this English is? And can we teach Basic Writing and bidialectalism without participating in the racialized (and racist) discourse of language acquisition and dissemination in higher education?

These are the central issues addressed by James Sledd in his article, "Bi-Dialectalism: The Linguistics of White Supremacy." In this pithy assessment of bidialectalism and, by implication Basic Writing, Sledd, writing in 1969, accurately predicts the problems inherent in both projects. He says:

> Because people who rarely talk together will talk differently, differences in speech tell what groups a man belongs to. He uses them to claim and proclaim his identity, and society uses them to keep him under control. The person who talks right, as we do, is one of us. The person who talks wrong is an outsider, strange and suspicious, and we must make him feel inferior if we can. That is the purpose of education. In a school system run like ours by white businessmen, instruction in the mother tongue includes formal initiation into the linguistic prejudices of the middle class. (1307)

An extrapolation of Sledd's argument here suggests that the existence of African-American Language as a relatively insulated form of communication among African-Americans in the U.S. constitutes a kind of segregation which speaks for itself. Sledd also points out a key by-product of bidialectalism in his recognition that there are contradictions built into assuming the language of another, particularly of a hegemonic power structure. These contradictions may well—and in the case of African-American Language probably does—direct prejudices toward the home language of the minority. What is also noteworthy is Sledd's observation that there are linguistic prejudices (and we can include the term *white* here) built into the process of education perpetrated by white businessmen. Indeed, Sledd tells us, the purpose of education is to make these outsiders feel inferior even as the class-based exploitation of their instruction was being formulated. Sledd continues:

> Black English provided the most lucrative new industry for white linguists, who found the mother lode when they discovered the interesting locutions which the less protected employ to the detriment of their chances for upward mobility. In the annals of free enterprise, the early sixties will be memorable for the invention of functional bi-dialectalism, a scheme best described by an elderly and unregenerate Southern dame as 'turning black trash into white trash.' Despite some signs of wear, this cloak for white supremacy has kept its shape for almost a decade now, and it is best described in the inimitable words of those who made it. Otherwise the description might be dismissed as a malicious caricature.
>
> The basic assumption of bi-dialectalism is that the prejudices of middle-class whites cannot be changed but must be accepted and indeed enforced on lesser breeds. Upward mobility, it is assumed, is the end of education, but white power will deny upward mobility to speakers of Black English, who must therefore be made to talk white English in their contacts with the white world. (1309)

Sledd points directly to the profit motive inherent in the project of bidialectalism and by implication, Basic Writing. He simultaneously identifies an industry of remedial education that may be considered the superstructure upon which, in Villanueva's terms, may be constructed a colony of Composition. We are reminded again of Shaughnessy's characterization of the field as "a new frontier like the American West" when Villanueva says:

> when we demand a certain kind of language, a certain dialect, and a certain rhetorical manner in using that dialect and language, we seem to be working counter to the cultural multiplicity we seek. And I think that means that we will have to rethink the whole thing. The demand for linguistic and rhetorical compliance still smacks of colonialism. ("New Racism" 183)

Both the white supremacy that Sledd speaks of with respect to the industry of remedial education and the colonialism Villanueva speaks of inherent in Composition imply a profit motive that should be considered alongside any potential benefits bidialectalism and Basic Writing are said to have since, as Sledd and Villanueva suggest, this profit motive seems imbricated in the very projects themselves.

African-American Language in Higher Education

While Holmes correctly questions the intellectual ground of those who essentialize black speech, he does not adequately envision a role for it in higher education though his provocative title suggests one. This, however, is not something he is unmindful of. In his critique of Valerie Balester's book, *Cultural Divide: A Study of African American College-level Writers,* he points out that "One of the most important dimensions of Balester's study is her observation regarding how [the students she studies] to greater or lesser degrees, looked upon the use of Black English Vernacular as improper. . ."(61). He goes on to say:

> While it is true that negative attitudes held by educators toward black dialect can certainly be harmful, to pity African American students (such as her student Thomas) for being 'unaware that his academically oriented writing bears some hallmarks of African American rhetoric' is extreme. (61)

Given Sledd and Villanueva's arguments, we have to wonder why Balester's student shouldn't have the right to use Black English Vernacular (or African-American Language) without "negative attitudes held by educators toward his rhetoric"? The answer, I suspect, is similar to the one having to do with the racism that accompanied my experiences with African-American Language at Clifford Scott High School, which Sledd underscores. It would severely limit Thomas's chances of success in the U.S. marketplace. Isn't it possible, then, to question the viability of bidialectalism and Basic Writing out of recognition that language presents and represents valuable experiences rather than, as Holmes argues, just a desire to essentialize black language? I take, then, Villanueva's charge seriously that we "rethink the whole thing" and redraw the boundary of Basic Writing—and composition studies—to include African-American Language, as well as other diverse dialects, as a viable discourse in institutions of higher education on their own terms; something J. L. Dillard argued in his influential book, *Black English*, a text which informed the 1974 Student's Rights to Their Own Language resolution of the CCCC,[7] and something David Bartholomae may have been advocating in his essay, "The Tidy House: Basic Writing in the American Curriculum."

LIZA JANE AS AFRICANIST PRESENCE IN BASIC WRITING

> [Basic Writing] is that kind of student writing which disturbs, threatens, or causes despair in traditional English faculty members
> —Robert Connors (quoted in Otte and Williams Mlynarczyk 55).

While the debate over the uses, and indeed the role, of African-American Language—and African-Americans—on college campuses at the turn of the twenty-first century are hinged almost exclusively on the ability of students to master a particular kind of code switching, at the turn of the twentieth century the debate over the presence of African-Americans in the upper echelons of American society was much clearer and remarkably similar. One of the central issues then was how the masses coming out of slavery would relate to the burgeoning upwardly mobile minority of the black community. An almost equally important consideration was the general uplifting of the erstwhile slave in what can only be described as a brutally hostile culture. It isn't difficult, then, to see the loss of a golden (white) age in the university as critiqued by Hill and Lu some ninety years later as a kind of rerun of the struggle to integrate the black masses into greater U.S. society after Lyndon Johnson's Great Society. In this sense, Basic Writing is aptly termed by Ira Shor "an Apartheid educational system" where it becomes part of a new kind of Jim Crow. This metaphor is, in fact, consistent with much of Michelle Alexander's thesis in her book, *The New Jim Crow: Mass Incarceration in the Age of Colorblindness,* where she questions why and how so many men of color are being incarcerated at such alarmingly high rates today. What her study and this essay underscore is how racism reconstitutes itself in apparently race-neutral ways without naming what it's doing in a kind of twenty-first-century grand narrative enshrining a whiteness that is both normative and exclusionary.

The name "Liza Jane" in the subheading of this section of this chapter is inspired by Charles Chesnutt's short story, "The Wife of His Youth," written at the turn of the nineteenth century not long after Harvard's first Composition course had been established, and the failure of reconstruction was apparent. Chesnutt's story fascinates me because of how he deploys language use by his characters to help underscore his narrative objectives as well as demonstrate, through his central character, Liza Jane, the veracity of the African-American masses she represents. This representation captures the "Africanist Presence" Toni Morrison describes in her book, *Playing in the Dark: Whiteness and the Literary Imagination,* since Liza Jane's oral utterances appear consistent with "that kind of student writing which disturbs, threatens, or causes despair in traditional English faculty members."

Indeed, the quote from Robert Connors in his description of Basic Writers is strikingly similar to Toni Morrison's description of the fear that is struck into twentieth-century white writers as they contend with the Africanist presence in their work. In her book, Morrison argues that it requires hard work not to see that the best scholars of literature go out of their way *not* to confront the consequences of race in their critical analyses of texts (*Playing* 17). I am arguing here that the project of Basic Writing and bidialectalism are themselves meditations on the white space in composition studies; an inability to fully and completely face the consequences of racism not just in language, or on college campuses, but in U.S. culture generally. I am suggesting that it requires hard work not to see this.

Chesnutt's Liza Jane

Chesnutt's symbolic use of Liza Jane is sophisticated. Married to the significantly younger Sam Taylor, a mulatto, while they were both in slavery, she fares much worse than he does after the Civil War. While he escapes to the north just before the commencement of the war on the suspicion that he will be sold south, she spends the war years in slavery until Emancipation. After the war, Sam looks for Liza Jane for some time, but does not find her. Giving up his search, he leverages his light skin complexion and intellect to settle in the North, working his way up to stationery clerk for a railway company in a well-to-do segment of a black community symbolically called "The Blue Veins Society." The Blue Veins Society was so called by dark-skinned blacks of the community because it was said that if your veins could not be seen through your skin, you could not gain entrance to it although no rule of that sort officially existed. Indeed, dark-skinned blacks critical of the Blue Veins often became its most ardent supporters after they themselves were admitted. Chesnutt continues,

> When such critics had succeeded in getting on the inside, they had been heard to maintain with zeal and earnestness that the society was a lifeboat, an anchor, a bulwark and a shield,—a pillar of cloud by day and of fire by night to guide their people through the social wilderness. (2)

This description on Chesnutt's part is highly ironic. Just who and what were the Blue Veins being shielded from if not the very dark-skinned masses they themselves were once a part of. It is important to note that no white characters are present in this story yet the actions of the darker-skinned blacks to first criticize and then be ardent defenders of the Blue Veins Society speaks to a racism that both envelops and permeates the black community that Taylor has made his own. This is not unlike the advice offered me by the nurse at Clifford Scott High, since in both cases the objective was the separation; the creation of "a bulwark and a shield" from the African-American community at large.

Changing his name to Mr. Ryder, Sam Taylor embraces the American tradition of reinventing oneself. However, as Lorne Fienberg points out in her essay, "Charles Chesnutt's 'The Wife of His Youth': Unveiling of the Black Storyteller," this reinvention involves ". . . a denial of origins and the obligations of the past . . . The exhilaration the Blue Veins have of achieving autonomy to create one's social roles," she continues, ". . . may be accompanied by a profound state of anxiety" (4). This idea is consistent with Thomas Farrell's observation of Basic Writing students entering the university and being prepared for their acculturation. As Min-Zhan Lu says:

> Farrell recognizes that such a move will inevitably be accompanied by "anxiety": 'The psychic strain entailed in moving from a highly oral

frame of mind to a more literate frame of mind is too great to allow rapid movement' (252).

Interestingly, Fienberg identifies the anxiety as a "denial of origins" coupled with the "obligations of the past." Both, it seems to me, are hinged to the role and uses of language when I consider the excerpt from Farrell which suggests a particular linguistic hierarchy. Mr. Ryder has none of the linguistic markers of an African-American let alone an ex-slave. He appears to be, for all intents and purposes, *white.*

Similarly, the Basic Writing student must also deny her linguistic origins in order to successfully navigate Basic Writing. This is made clear by the description of the writing produced by such a writer as "error." While a term Shaughnessy herself would question, it nevertheless remains a principal purpose of Basic Writing: the *erasure* of this writing in university settings in order for the student to move through the university.

After the war, Liza Jane searches earnestly for Sam for twenty-five years and finds him at the very moment he is to be engaged to the beautiful, light-skinned, wealthy, and widowed Mrs. Dixon, thereby securing his social and economic future at once.

Liza Jane and Ryder meet on his front porch as he scans the pages of a Tennyson poem in order to find a suitable line to recite to his fiancée. The irony is impossible to miss as the scene dramatizing the reunion with Liza Jane suggests. Reading from the text in his hand, Ryder says:

> She seem'd a part of joyous Spring:
> A gown of grass-green silk she wore,
> Buckled with golden clasps before;
> A light green tuft of plumes she bore
> Closed in a golden ring.
>
> . . . .
> She look'd so lovely, as she sway'd
> The rein with dainty finger-tips,
> A man had given all other bliss,
> And all his worldly worth for this,
> To waste his whole heart in one kiss
> Upon her perfect lips. (12)

It is precisely at this moment that Chesnutt's narrative and rhetorical objectives coincide in the text as he introduces Liza Jane to us and to Ryder at his gate describing her as follows:

> As Mr. Ryder murmured these words audibly, with an appreciative thrill, he heard the latch of his gate click, and a light footfall sounding on the steps. He turned his head, and saw a woman standing before the door.

She was a little woman, not five feet tall, and proportioned to her height. Although she stood erect, and looked around her with very bright and restless eyes, she seemed quite old; for her face was crossed and recrossed with a hundred wrinkles, and around the edges of her bonnet could be seen protruding here and there a tuft of short gray wool. She wore a blue calico gown of ancient cut, a little red shawl fastened around her shoulders with an old-fashioned brass brooch, and a large bonnet profusely ornamented with faded red and yellow artificial flowers. And she was very black—so black that her toothless gums, revealed when she opened her mouth to speak, were not red, but blue. She looked like a bit of the old plantation life, summoned up from the past by the wave of a magician's wand, as the poet's fancy had called into being the gracious shapes of which Mr. Ryder had just been reading. (12–13)

While Liza Jane's physical description is meant to be seen in stark contrast to that of the idyllic woman in the poem, we see in her character that which we might associate with Queen Guinevere in terms of her humanity and nobility. While Ryder has successfully re-created himself in classical American terms, Liza Jane carries with her a narrative that is dependent upon her past and is a visual and oral history as illustrated by the narrative she relates to Ryder, whom she does not recognize as her husband. "'My name's Liza'" she begins, "'Liza Jane. W'en I wuz a gal I wuz married ter a man named Jim. But Jim died, an' after dat I married a merlatter man named Sam Taylor'" (13).

The form of Liza Jane's speech is significant for my purposes as Chesnutt seems to anticipate the ways in which language itself might become a new front on the color line by textualizing her testimony. In many ways, the textualizing of Liza Jane's oral utterances anticipates much of what Gloria Anzaldúa, one of James Sledd's former students, was after as she refuses to deny any of her eight languages in her intellectual work, and indeed, presents all of them as equally valid and as a reflection of her identity.[8] Her book, *Borderlands/La Frontera: The New Mestiza,* has always fascinated me because in many ways she embodies the kind of intellectual rigor with language that Bartholomae seems to point to in his essay, "The Tidy House: Basic Writing in the American Curriculum," and simultaneously points the way to how we might reenvision the Basic Writing project.

The form of Liza Jane's speech is also important in the story as it is consistent with her dress. Indeed, they may even be said to be consistent with her slave past and her twenty-five year sojourn. Coarse and gritty, the speech pattern does not relate a life of ease or one prepared for upward mobility as defined by the society Ryder now represents. However, a careful look at the content of her speech reveals something different. Consider, for instance, the rhetorical position she puts herself in and what this might suggest about her relationship to Jim vis-à-vis their marriage. As she narrates the story, her subjective position is subordinate to that of the marriage and to Jim himself. She even identifies herself as a "gal." Consider how this rhetorical position changes as she relates the details of her marriage to Sam Taylor as her subjectivity takes prominence and provides her with a certain agency and investment in the arrangement. *She* marries Sam.[9] The shift is subtle but important to note because it is consistent with her character as counterpart to Tennyson's Queen Guinevere whom Ryder is reading at precisely the point Liza Jane arrives at his gate. While she does not exhibit the form of Guinevere we expect, she does exhibit the content. Liza Jane's language and history, as the Connors' epigraph and Baldwin quote remind us, are both threatening to the Blue Veins represented by Mr. Ryder, and institutions of higher education today, for precisely the same reasons. Her presence and presentation threaten Mr. Ryder's marketability and consequently his upward mobility. Similarly, these markers would place her in Basic Writing without regard to the experiences they convey or the ways in which her identity is manifest in them.

If Liza Jane is the image of the Basic Writing student, then Mr. Ryder is the image of one who has successfully navigated its gates. Consider this description of Ryder, for instance, which with respect to language, is remarkably similar to what most Basic Writing teachers might want to expect from a graduate of their writing course,

> While [Mr. Ryder] was not as white as some of the Blue Veins, his appearance was such as to confer distinction upon them. His features were of a refined type, his hair was almost straight; he was always neatly dressed; his manners were irreproachable, and his morals above suspicion ... Although the lack of early training had hindered the orderly development of a naturally fine mind, it had not prevented him from doing a great deal of reading or from forming decidedly literary tastes. Poetry was his passion. He could repeat whole passages of the great English poets; and if his pronunciation was sometimes faulty, his eye, his voice, his gestures, would respond to the changing sentiment with a precision that revealed a poetic soul, and disarm criticism. (7)

In this quote I recognize an uneasy similarity between myself and Mr. Ryder. Neither of us had a particularly remarkable early education; we both migrated and took advantage of opportunities presented to us through our similar love of language and our ability to approximate our respective languages of power. Clearly, this puts me in an uneasy relationship with my students in the Basic Writing program I direct who often speak nonstandard dialects since I'm asking them to undergo a transformation I didn't have to, nor would necessarily want to. As an immigrant to the U.S., I have no home language in direct conflict with the prevailing power structure to negotiate as they do or as Ryder no doubt did. After Liza Jane leaves his garden, Mr. Ryder retires to his bedroom and "stood for a long time before the mirror of his dressing-case, gazing thoughtfully at the reflection of his own face" (17). A face in which he no doubt sees the image of Mr. Ryder, the man he has become, as well as the image of Sam Taylor, the man he once was.

Mr. Ryder's dilemma, then, reflects the dilemma of the bidialectical student in that the question of identity and individualism is central to both. Returning for a moment to Victor Villanueva's discussion of individualism as a form of metonymic displacement, recall that he argued a result of this individualism is the eliding of group exclusion. We could argue that individualism is a response to a society a person rejects, just as community or humanism is a response to a society a person accepts.[10] If Ryder accepts the wife of his youth, he simultaneously rejects individualism over community and would claim common cause with Liza Jane and all whom she represents. If he rejects her he simultaneously endorses individualism and his market-driven ambitions. Sam Taylor, his former self, will simply disappear, or worse, remain an aberration to him.

Mr. Ryder's dilemma comes to a head when he has to confront the Blue Veins Society. At the dinner party that was ostensibly organized to announce his engagement to Mrs. Dixon, he surprises everyone, and introduces Liza Jane as the wife of his youth, forgoing the particular form of upward mobility that would be his if he had married Mrs. Dixon.

Chesnutt's rhetorical skill is noteworthy. He uses Ryder's proximate dilemma to clearly highlight the general obligations of the Blue Veins toward the black community at large. Ryder's introduction of Liza Jane at the dinner party effectively trapped them between what they espouse, and what their daily actions suggest they believe. To Ryder's question about what an honorable man should do when confronted with a lost wife who has searched faithfully for twenty-five years for her husband even though their slave marriage would be legally binding only if they both chose to make it so, they all echoed, following Mrs. Dixon's lead, "He should have acknowledged her" (23). Therefore, they too must acknowledge Liza Jane. They could not now, after hearing Ryder's rendition of his life story told in third person, reject his slave wife. The table ostensibly set for Mrs. Dixon must now accommodate Liza Jane and all she represents.

"All she represents" is the critical idea here. I've been arguing that whatever else Basic Writing has been over the past forty years, it has not been a neutral player in the colonizing effects universities can be said to have. So the questions surrounding what actually happens to Liza when she sits down at the table and what the Blue Veins are doing when they ask her to sit are crucial. What kind of invitation is it? Is it made so that they can all feel they've honored their obligation and having her there at the table is a way for them to feel good about themselves for shouldering the burden of having this person that they don't really want there? Will they deploy her presence there as a kind of construct against which they can construct a whiteness for themselves, similar to how Brodkin tells us Jews became white against a constructed and servicing blackness, thereby making it clear to her, and to themselves, that she really isn't one of them? Are they tolerating her because they want to be understood as good, liberal people as Wendy suggests in Chapter 1? We could accuse Basic Writing of doing all of these things with regard to the basic writer's presence at the ruined university. Liza Jane can never be Ms. Dixon—no amount of code switching or bidialecticalism will make it so. In fact, it seems likely that Chesnutt is suggesting just how obscene that would be—to try to "dress her up" like a Mrs. Dixon.

There are those who might suggest hybridity as a possible and positive alternative to the acculturation Liza Jane faces. In this arrangement, if there is a genuine invitation for Liza Jane to take a seat at the table—a seat at a university with all of her attendant experiences and linguistic richness, the "table" will be altered by her presence, and Liza Jane, too, will change as a result of being there. She won't become Mrs. Dixon but neither will she statically and simply remain the "ex-slave." There is a chance for real growth here for Liza Jane and, significantly, the institution as well if the invitation is genuine rather than assimilationist; if there is a dialectical relationship among the participants. Liza Jane won't keep her speech as is, and she won't "code switch" to Blue Veinese. A hybrid language, a hybrid Liza Jane, and a hybrid institution would emerge, and in turn this possibility would affect the Blue Veins, those whose erstwhile job it was to protect the institution from such people as Liza Jane.

Unfortunately, the notion of hybridity does not work well in unequal power relations and has all too often produced the evil twin to this idyllic arrangement in academia, which is best summed up by Victor Villanueva who says,

> 'Hybridity' has come to replace 'internal colonialism.' Hybridity can mean a creative transcendence, an affirmation of cultures and histories that are both of the mainstream and the other, but it tends to include the cultural mimicry that the other is forced to undergo before creative transcendence is allowed expression ("Colony" 187).

He continues his critique borrowing from Ella Shohat who is equally sharp in her assessment of hybridity calling it "forced assimilation, internalized self-rejection, political cooptation, [and] social conformism" (qtd. in Villanueva, "Colony" 187).

Liza Jane never gets an opportunity to show what she knows and how she knows it because the process of acculturation is so embedded in the process of presenting her to the Blue Veins that she—her agency—inevitably gets lost. Indeed, the inequality embedded in this form of hybridity begins to show in the story as Ryder has her in a changed suit of clothes "neatly dressed in gray and wear[ing] the white cap of an elderly woman" (23).

Part of the point of this essay, then, is that the bedrock[11] upon which Basic Writing sits is fundamentally flawed so as to privilege white mainstream U.S.

culture. The objective should never have been to educate Liza Jane in the sense that we think—basic, remedial, deficient, disadvantaged—it should be to influence the fundamental nature of what it means to be educated. Liza Jane is extraordinary because her lived-experiences *are* her education in ways academia can only hope to approximate. That is to say, borrowing from Freshman Composition, her form and content are completely consistent with one another, and they inform her public and, as far as we can tell, personal identity in remarkably astute ways. If given an opportunity to sit at the table *as* Liza Jane, I have little doubt that she could contribute to the integrity and uplift of the race, which is the Blue Veins' ostensible *raison d'être*, just as basic writers, if allowed to exercise their own language in a reimagined course which takes seriously the notion of multilingualism, would contribute to an institution's integrity and uplift.

Basic Writing professionals recognize that students come to our classrooms proficient in their own language and could shape not only their experiences at institutions of higher education, but the institution itself. These students often come with a rudimentary understanding of the grammar and mechanics of the language of power, a language intrinsically connected to the white middle-class and the market.

As the product of a working-class family, and as a black educator, it is clear to me that language acquisition is more complex politically and pedagogically than Composition and Rhetoric has yet fully articulated. We seem to be at cross-purposes when we teach and demand Standard English from our students and at the same time ask them to speak from a position of agency as Liza Jane does. Basic Writing teachers and program directors would do well to continually ask, as I try to, if they are in the business of creating and participating in the production of Mr. Ryders when we might have an opportunity to participate in the rehabilitation of Sam Taylors. Can the academy be constructed in such a way as to have us not dismiss the Liza Janes, but accept them, their languages, and the experiences these languages embody?

3 The Kitsch of Liberal Whiteness and Bankrupt Discourses of Race

> If (racial) harmony at home is truly a goal in the United States, as knee-jerk responses to nearly every media-controlled controversy here have concluded, perhaps, in lieu of that extended, extensive, and healing conversation on race we've been promised since the riots of the 1960s or since the Rodney King beating and subsequent L.A. uprising, O.J.'s murder trial, or Imus's use of a phrase that every report on the controversy recognized was so tame that it printed and reprinted it, played and replayed it, over and over and over again, *perhaps we should try another tactic.* (emphasis added)
>
> Michael Awkward, *Burying Don Imus* (166–68)

> ... brotherhood of men on earth will only be possible on a base of kitsch.
>
> Milan Kundera, *Unbearable Lightness of Being* (251)

> In order to transcend current race relations, which is a concrete possibility, we must first go *through* race in order to have any hopes of going *beyond* it.
>
> Zeus Leonardo (125)

Ed, a student in a class I teach on creative nonfiction, reads aloud from his essay, in which he deploys terms and phrases like "ginzo" and "Gotti wannabes" to describe Italian Americans. He qualifies this description, in what he calls a "side note," by assuring everyone it is OK for him to talk about "wops" this way as he is "100% Italian." The class warms to the intended humor of the piece and accepts at face value the "100% Italian" rationale. When I push them to probe the idea rhetorically—what does he mean? What's the potential offense the narrator seems aware of? Why does the ethnic identification change things for him and for his audience?—I am met with resistance from these white students, who act as though I am nagging them to eat more vegetables or stop smoking (both of which I've been known to do from time to time). Despite my attempts to look at some specific dynamics, they can only feel a boilerplate discussion about racism coming on in which they are going to be chastised in some way and silenced into monolithic agreement that racism is bad.[1] I feel them rushing and mobilizing to head the whole thing off at the pass, and I don't blame them. Too often, such discussions get us nowhere, in part, it's true, I think, because of the moral failures of liberal guilt but also because, as the students seem to intuit, there is something very stilted and disingenuous about our evaluations of race that often turn into scripted recitations rather than dialogue. When informed by our public discourse on race, these discussions are governed by a rhetoric of kitsch.

RACISM, CRITICAL PEDAGOGY, AND THE WRITING CLASS: EXAMINING IDEOLOGY

This is not to say that my class is not badly in need of some kind of discussion. In all fairness here, the students' reluctance to discuss their racialized identity stems from a broader question concerning conflicting views of the epistemological domain of the writing classroom, a conflict which embroils not just writing teachers but also their students. My class's hesitancy to take on the issue of racism can be seen as part of that greater debate (that perhaps has been most recently popularized by Stanley Fish's *Save the World on Your Own Time*).[2] We have, in other words, an ongoing feud about the roles of content and style in the writing curriculum, at least according to Richard Fulkerson's summary of composition and rhetoric's ideological discord. Fulkerson's survey of the state of the field at the dawn of the twenty-first century confirms (but does little to add to) the taxonomy that Berlin described for instruction in writing and rhetoric decades earlier. According to Fulkerson, the contention between social epistemic rhetorics and pedagogies (what Fulkerson identifies as "critical/cultural studies" or "CCS" [655]) and other approaches, such as expressivism and current traditionalism, is alive and well (see for example Ian's discussion in Chapter 4 on the institutional convergence of New Criticism and Platonic rhetoric). That is to say, the debate rages on, unproductively according to Fulkerson, over whether it's appropriate for writing courses to take on "politics," and leftist politics at that, or whether we should be teaching "writing." (He dismisses out of hand the assertion that all writing instruction is implicitly ideological.) If Fulkerson's assertions mirror general public opinion, then we can understand student resistance to talking about the rhetoric of race as steeped in the conservatism of current traditionalism and linked to broader perceptions of the writing classroom as an ideologically free, New Critical zone where meaning-making and the moves of rhetoric can or should be taught as though they are as devoid of social values as mathematical proofs. Any attempt to use rhetoric as a cultural tool to help us unpack the constructed nature of belief systems is met with rebuff.[3]

But before I continue considering the specific resistance to confronting whiteness within traditional writing pedagogy, I first find I must say more about this same old question begged in current traditionalism (or what Fulkerson refers to as his "genre" approach): in a writing class, we should be teaching *writing*, but writing about what? What does "writing" devoid of content look like? In fact, Writing Across the Curriculum (WAC) theory, for one, provided an answer to this question some time ago: "writing," a highly contextualized activity embedded in different rhetorical circumstances, doesn't look like much of anything without content. How to know the dancer from the dance? John C. Bean, for example, in his influential *Engaging Ideas*, a book written to foster composition pedagogy across the curriculum, characterizes the dilemma as one in which students believe that writing teachers are out of bounds when they comment on students' *ideas*. By the same token, students are taken aback when their professors from other disciplines seek to comment on writing issues in their work. This bifurcated view of writing that treats writing as "packaging" and separates it from thinking underlies the pervasive view of writing as discrete skill that can be learned through arhetorical drills and apolitical teaching, a view that students often hold when they arrive at college. "It is," as Bean tells us, "the challenge of faculty across the disciplines to show them other ways of imagining writing" (19).

Indeed. Nonetheless, Fulkerson, in his argument against critical/cultural studies (CCS) courses, whether he realizes it or not, adopts exactly this discredited rationale of the content-less course. He argues against CCS courses, claiming that in such classes that might take on questions such as societal racism

> writing is essentially a display of valued intellectual inter-actions with the relevant texts and is judged accordingly. Ungenerously, one could argue that this does not produce a writing course at all—any more than a sociology course in race relations that uses extensive writing is a writing course. Certainly it provides students with extensive practice in writing and with getting feedback—although it isn't clear whether the feedback is mainly about writing or mainly about culture and how to "read" it. (663)

He adds "most CCS course seem [sic] inappropriate to me. . . . First, reading, analyzing, and discussing the texts upon which the course rests are unlikely to leave room for any actual teaching of writing. So we get a 'writing' course in which writing is required and evaluated, but not taught" (665).

What Fulkerson willfully leaves out here in his explanation of the "state" of writing instruction is the field's shift to emphasize rhetoric so that "writing" becomes part of the study of discourse generally. Under such a scenario, the dichotomy between "feedback" about writing or culture that Fulkerson and others see plaguing the field evaporates. But as Fulkerson notes, the disagreement he describes also involves our students and their understandings about what ought to be happening in a writing course according to popular, intuitive notions that, I might add, owe a considerable debt to the color-blind rhetoric of current traditionalism that positions itself as apolitical. Citing Russell Durst's work, Fulkerson refers, in sympathetic lament it seems, to students who "resist politically, claiming 'they are being force-fed 'a liberal ideology'. . . . And they resist intellectually 'the work they are being asked to do in reading what seem to them unnecessarily abstruse essays and taking on the difficult task of forming and supporting interpretations of what they are finding out are surprisingly complex issues'" (664–65).

That anyone would argue against a pedagogy that stresses "complex issues" or see "the task of forming and supporting interpretations" as outside the province of writing instruction seems strange indeed—if anything, such a statement sounds like a ringing endorsement of writing methodology as successful pedagogy—but Fulkerson's attitude helps us understand the student resistance that confounds critical pedagogy and perhaps, in particular, writing instruction and that bears remarkable resemblance to a Platonic view of rhetoric as a "soft" study not able to meddle in anything so substantive—a view, as Bean characterizes it, that separates content from form. Despite Bean's eloquent defense, the academy's embracing of WAC pedagogy seems to parallel the interest composition showed in what Wendy Bishop identified as craft-based pedagogy. We continue to see a renewed interest in so-called genre approaches such as Fulkerson's or Gerald Graff and Cathy Birkenstein's "They say/I say" templates,[4] spawned perhaps by paranoia over the kind of criticism leveled by Fish. The "rhetorical turn" of composition studies, which as envisioned by such figures ranging from David Bartholomae to Susan Jarratt involved using writing to negotiate and confront difference, has taken a further turn in a spiraling inward move that sanitizes the messiness of discourse. We can, it seems, "retreat" behind rhetorical analysis and be completely removed from the substance of what we are analyzing. This trend of disengagement, in which rhetorical study threatens to collapse into itself, effectively ensures that an invisible whiteness remains firmly entrenched in writing pedagogy and consequently sabotages one of the best tools we have for interrogating whiteness: rhetoric.

Thus we have one perspective from which to understand my students' impatience with any attempt to peep underneath the skirts of a "100% Italian." (And the allusion to privacy violation is deliberate here, for I think we increasingly experience discussions of racism as intrusive probes into subjectivity just as Fulkerson and others see CCS exceeding the authority of the compositionist's charge to teach "writing.") And yet, as I said, I do believe my class needs to have a conversation. Just not the one they think I want to have. In my particular case, critics such as Fulkerson might not find my ways as remiss as the students, for the subject under discussion is undeniably a student text rather than some outside political tract that I am foisting upon them for analysis in the manner that Fulkerson decries. In other words, I'm not the one who brought it up. So perhaps even from a conservative standpoint the issue is fair game and is certainly part of what it means to engage in genre analysis for the purposes of helping students read and write personal essays: what effect/appeal is the author trying to achieve with the phrase? What reaction does it produce in his audience and why? What enthymeme is being deployed? In general, I think that craft-based pedagogy is one of the color-blind avoidance strategies we use to *discourage* critical discourse in the classroom to maintain white hegemony. (Such pedagogy relies on its own eviscerating aesthetic of kitsch, as I discuss below, where we seek to distance ourselves from unpleasant realities). That students perceive such rhetorical analysis of their essays as being inappropriately "political" and outside the subject of "writing" critique may be at least as much a testament to the pertinacity of traditional beliefs about the nature of writing instruction *as* it is a fierce defense of the inviolability of white subjectivity, what Keating refers to as the "denial . . . that is itself a crucial element of whiteness" (81). The latter view is how we might conceive of student reaction from the standpoint of critical pedagogy. That these two trajectories, however, intersect to mutually inform and reinforce each other is also not incidental. Even so, I would credit another important factor at work in this instance that goes beyond the general issues of what constitutes composition instruction or challenge to white privilege, and this factor concerns the larger, more complex discourse of kitsch that characterizes our *public* discussions of racism.

For the students are neither entirely right nor entirely wrong in their assumptions about where they think I am going with my questions, but in any event, they cannot hear what I am saying because the din of our public discourse on *race* is intruding and crowding out any other possibilities of, what I'll call for the moment, an "authentic" discussion on *racism*. Ed's essay is indeed steeped in multiple forms of invisible liberal whiteness: note for example that as he claims, through ethnic identification, his piece of the multicultural pie, he also uses his whiteness, via the incarnation of identity politics, to negate the significance of racism by claiming his status as a member of an injured (white but ethnic and perhaps working-class) group capable of surmounting the damage of racial epithets through sheer bravado. Color-blind rhetoric and neo-liberal whiteness have allowed him to appropriate (in what amounts to a parody of) the postcolonial strategy of using the master's tools to dismantle the master's house. That he does so with such ease and lack of consciousness is testament to the "success" of twenty-first-century whiteness. Indeed his strategic intervention of assuring the audience that he is "100% Italian" is designed to short-circuit any attempt by a critical audience to "see through" this white normativity that establishes its hegemony through injured ethnic status.

But this position, invoked reflexively and peremptorily to derail any potential interrogation of race, is not without justification—neither is the class's impatience with my attempts to "go there." It is my contention that this response of resistance, contrary to its characterization in critical pedagogy as merely territorial defensiveness, is rather a kind of intelligence, in so much as what we discuss in the name of confronting racism is as hollow as the whiteness we purport to be interrogating—and it amounts to a kitsch discourse of scripted obfuscation in which we all have our roles to play. For kitsch aptly characterizes not only the overt doctrines of white supremacy but also (perhaps especially) the more insidious reconstitutions of liberal whiteness's disguised hegemony in which racism often is ostensibly decried. Specifically, examining the media's liberal, multicultural rhetoric on race and racism through the lens of kitsch reveals an alienating and bankrupt discourse that refracts and prevents meaningful discussions of racism in the public sphere and in our classrooms and provides fodder for reactionary claims of postracism. This "false" rhetoric effectively shores up white privilege through a strategy of disaffiliation that focuses on trivial or sensationalized events of racism at the expense of the significant discursive and material manifestations of oppressive whiteness. By focusing on ephemera, it provides a rationale for white dismissal of racism's continued relevance in American society and serves as a locus of white identity formation. But as I discuss below, while a characterization of whiteness as kitsch, a dangerous and false discourse, describes quite fittingly the criticism that whiteness studies has leveled at white privilege in calls for its abolition, the attempt to describe whiteness in this manner—as false, empty, hollow, *inauthentic*— becomes its own variety of kitsch, essentialized and mired in melancholy, a self-conscious manifestation of its absent presence.[5]

KITSCH AND AUTHENTICITY: WHITENESS AS FALSENESS

In *Moby Dick*, Melville describes in "The Whiteness of the Whale" chapter, the color white as "palsied" and "a dumb blankness full of meaning . . . a colorless all-color of atheism . . . ," linking it to a "higher horror." Indeed, the nineteenth-century trope of whiteness in civilization discourse, in which both the color's attraction and evil are understood to reside in its blankness, its existential nothingness and all-pervasiveness, resonates remarkably well with twenty-/twenty-first-century critical understandings of racialized whiteness as omnipresent and unremarked, as "everything and nothing," and, perhaps most significantly, as false, "the fantasy of whiteness" (Seshadri-Crooks 60),[6] or what Kolchin says is characterized in the literature of whiteness studies as "the moral emptiness of whiteness." He points out that Ignatiev and Garvey, for example, argue that "there is no white culture" outside of a will-to-power variety of asserted privilege. But Roediger in particular characterizes whiteness as a false discourse: "whiteness is oppressive and false," and even though all racializations are constructions, whiteness "is infinitely more false, and precisely because of that falsity, more dangerous" (qtd. in Kolchin). Keating reports leading students through discussions where they arrive at the conclusions that whiteness "is an enormous vacuum or void, an anti-spirituality of sorts that promises fulfillment through a misguided (and perhaps deadly) faith in science, technology, and consumption of material goods" (99).

The question becomes: what precisely is the nature of this "falser falseness" that implies there is something "more true"? Roediger's use of the term suggests something beyond the notion of the constructed nature of race (as opposed to the discredited biological view) so foundational to critical race studies. In other words, maintaining here that whiteness is false is not merely to resist essentializing it but to assert a metaphysical judgment that reinscribes the nature of whiteness and links it to conceptions of a bankrupt discourse seen in the nineteenth-century constructions of Melville and Conrad—the "whited sepulchre" which describes inauthentic western civilization.[7] These attributes of falseness and danger, as they are held in the liberal imagination and proffered in critiques of whiteness, coincide with descriptions of kitsch—an aesthetic understood not merely as "fake" or inauthentic but dangerous in its suppression of "ugly" truths in favor of a type of beauty that abets totalitarianism and political control.

Kitsch, as an aesthetic category, in general parlance is often a synonym for "bad taste" and identifies such items as cheap art reproductions, plastic flowers, or tacky souvenirs along the lines of Statue of Liberty replicas and other key chain items, and so its applicability to whiteness and race as hegemonic discourses may not be immediately apparent. Indeed, much of kitsch theory seems to treat the status of materiality (Hoberman 78) or *objects*, as derived from Walter Benjamin's treatises on reproducibility in relation to art and modernity and capitalism. In this vein, kitsch can be defined as, for example, "mass produced objects of petit-bourgeois taste that attempt to ape the refinement of true art" (Westbrook 426–27) or "the banal by-products of mass culture resulting from eccentric, global circulation of *things*" (Mukhopadhyay 26, emphasis added) or "the attempt to repossess the experience of intensity and immediacy through an *object* (Olalquiaga 291, emphasis added).

But it is not just objects that can be reduced into "easily marketable forms" for consumption but *ideas* also (Banita 98), thus making kitsch a discursive phenomenon as well and connecting it to propaganda. Discussions of kitsch then typically contain tentacles of broader political and ethical implications that exceed narrow aesthetic configurations of art and value or taste and often stress what kitsch does *not* do: provoke critical thought. Definitions of aesthetic and political kitsch typically emphasize its saccharine emotionality as, in the case of Dorfles, art that "should produce pleasant, sugary feelings" or, in the case of Lugg, a hegemonic rhetoric evasive of "complex, painful realities" (106) in favor of "syrupy emotionalism" (119) that facilitates political control and manipulation. Deployment of kitsch as a theoretical lens typically focuses on a mass aesthetic experience promulgating a sense of belonging or distraction through sentimentality and nostalgia at the expense of criticality, where criticality is associated with an authenticity inimical to the artificiality of the kitsch discourse or experience. Both Hermann Broch and Milan Kundera locate kitsch in the sentimentality of nineteenth-century Romanticism and see it as a means of cultivating the superficial as well as manufacturing consent through promotion of idyllic beauty, or, frankly stated, an aesthetic based on "the absolute denial of shit" (Kundera, *Unbearable* 248), both literally and figuratively, an attempt to create a reality in which the excrement of the world is unacknowledged and hidden. Ironically, then, the idea of kitsch relies on a romantic/modern understanding of true and authentic: there is something true, something real (unpleasantly so) that kitsch seeks to suppress and deny. This protective psychology of kitsch is such that it appeals to collectivity, our desire to belong and be part of something greater than ourselves that facilitates the denial at the heart of the impulse toward kitsch. Thus appeals to patriotism, for example, are notoriously kitschy in both their evasion of complexity and their balm of inclusion.

I have described elsewhere how the general concept of kitsch as false or, more particularly, "bad or fake art that lacks a critical dimension" can be applied as a kind of Burkean "screen" to cultural discourse for the purposes of rhetorical analysis.[8] In this case, a review of kitsch theory reveals significant intersections with descriptions of and attitudes toward the discursive structures of whiteness, most conspicuously in terms of notions of falseness, as noted above, and more specifically repetition, sentimentality, nostalgia, and melancholy. Without necessarily using the term kitsch, theorists of whiteness have effectively described it as such by aligning it with falseness. My contention is, however, that ultimately whiteness's relationship to kitsch is an even more complicated one, since kitsch itself is a more complicated aesthetic with regard to authenticity than the term "fake art" implies. While, as I argue below, it makes sense in one regard to see whiteness as a false discourse based on sentimentality and nostalgia that impedes critical thought, politically correct discourses of "tolerance" and "sensitivity" also produce a public rhetoric of kitsch that allows whiteness to flourish and evade detection as it obscures more meaningful understandings of racism as particularized and embedded. Furthermore, the romantic desire for authenticity and to see whiteness as falseness becomes in itself a kitsch move steeped in melancholia that relies on the wounded status of white identity as a wholeness that doesn't deliver, a betrayal that is aligned with whiteness's "repressed promises of being" (Seshadri-Crooks 64).

NORMAL WHITENESS AND THE KITSCH OF THE ORDINARY

The post-structural perspective that differentiates whiteness studies from other antiracist efforts or inquiries into racism has produced one of the principal insights of the field: the relationship between whiteness's invisible status and its normative nature. In effect, white normativity is the insidious, passive racism that perpetuates post-civil-rights whiteness and functions analogously to heteronormativity as it contrasts with full-blown homophobia. The extent to which adherence to "the norm" is kitsch—and thus the extent to which modern whiteness perpetuates itself through kitsch—can be seen in the rhetoric of "normality" that pervades twentieth-century characterizations of sexuality and race as illustrated by Julian Carter. Carter brings to our attention two statues of nudes displayed at the 1939 World's Fair in New York that realistically depict in anatomically correct detail a young man and woman, robust and athletic, although not in any apparently indulgent or narcissistic way, what we might call "fit," as proud representatives of the modern, un-self-conscious notion of "normal." The statues were in fact named "Normman" and "Norma." The unremarked morphological white racing is of course an example, par excellence, of the invisible normativity of whiteness: there is no need to explain in the curatorial remarks—"the Average American Boy and Girl" (3)—that the norm is implicitly white. Nonetheless there is no doubt that "Norma and Normman should be understood as icons of a constitutively white kind of heterosexual eroticism" (2) meant to regulate discourse on both sexuality and race so that they "made it possible to talk about whiteness *indirectly*, in terms of the affectionate, reproductive heterosexuality of 'normal' married couples" (3, emphasis added). "Indirectly" here denotes invisibility. Importantly, Carter observes that the overall cultural effect in terms of the broader ideological landscape is one in which, rather than "facilitate political debate, . . . normality discourse generally worked to shut it down" (5).

This self-insulating effect of normal whiteness dampens any impulse toward examination, as we see in student writing and classroom discourse that resists such efforts. There is in the end very little for "normal" people to argue about as the status presupposes consent and agreement, precisely in the kitsch manner that Kundera and others describe. This depoliticizing feature (which is ultimately political or at least ideological), Westbrook tells us, is a function of kitsch as well as part of its appeal in that "The simple pleasures of kitsch fill in the empty signifying space previously occupied by the political" (430). Such "simplicity" produces a *jouissance* that defies analysis and presents itself as wholesome truth requiring no further explanation. This too resonates with Carter's observation that the nineteenth-century discourse surrounding "civilization" differed markedly in its policing effects from the twentieth-century normality discourse that replaced it, in that the former allowed for articulated (i.e., *visible*) political exchange in contrast to the apolitical presentation of normal. The phenomenon of modern whiteness, or white kitsch, perhaps with some predictability, begins what is a trajectory into banality, or at least begins to reproduce itself under this mantle with the notable, ongoing eruptions of white supremacy when normality proves insufficient to maintain white hegemony.

Thus what Carter is characterizing "normality discourse" is kitsch in its various strands that we have seen so far. Whiteness becomes a unifying discourse of idyllic consensus played out specifically here on white bodies that posture as pleasantly, reassuringly unremarkable in their ordinariness, an example of what Westbrook describes as the kitsch tendency to find "emotional communion in clichés and . . . our authenticity in the commonplace" (Westbrook 428). This observation about the construction of authenticity and ordinariness resonates with Strickland and Crawford's assessment of the authentic in relation to the normalizing effect of bourgeois orderliness and white subjectivity: "Taking on orderly . . . behavior and orderly . . . language helped Anglo Americans create an *authentic* racial identity as "white" people" (72, emphasis added). Carter, too, points out that "the 'polite' white speech" (5) that obfuscated the sexual *and* the racial was a key feature of this ordinary normality that instantiated and sustained the white subject via a seemingly effortless shorthand. The desire for the authentic generates, and is satisfied by, normality that produces a kitsch of nostalgia.[9]

At first glance, the notion of "idyllic ordinariness" might appear contradictory and that a celebration of the "averageness" that Normman and Norma represent is an antidote to glorifying kitsch rather than a promulgation of it. The idealized figure of the heroic statue epitomizing the Aryan ideal in Nazi kitsch seems a far cry from Normman and Norma's wholesome humility. And yet these sculptures capture the idyl of American whiteness, precisely as they embody the "ordinary." As art, the statues of Norma and Normman help establish the relationship between whiteness as political discourse and an aesthetic of kitsch and highlight a crux in kitsch theory regarding generality and particularity germane to the question of whiteness and other hegemonies.[10] In Musil's assessment, according to McBride, generality was the breeding ground of a kitsch that "shuns the task of presenting singular experience" (286) and was to be resisted through "the radically singular, non-systematizable" (285). This emphasis on the particular seems at odds with kitsch theorists who suggest kitsch lies precisely in the banal celebration of the quotidian and the unremarkable, "the smallness of the here and now" (Westbrook 430). Ironically, so connected with the inauthentic, kitsch becomes, through this lens, the means for constructions of authenticity as it sentimentalizes and revels in the redemptive powers of the ordinary against Modernist despair. This is the view espoused by both Hoberman and Binkley in their recuperation of kitsch (see note 11). Both approaches illuminate the phenomenon of white heterosexual normality, for the discourse of ordinariness systematizes the particularity of "average" experience into what Musil called the "formulaic abbreviation of the feelings" (qtd. in McBride 286) where the sentiment of lived experience is rendered normatively conceptual "to stabilize and sanitize emotional life" (291). Such a paradox is truly at the heart of twentieth-century American whiteness, to use Carter's phrase, for the fetishizing of ordinary, the normal, here is precisely the rhetorical short cut of "instant and effortless identifiability" (Kulka 29) so symptomatic of kitsch and, as we see, is so essential for the enthymeme of whiteness to function.

The realistic depiction of Norma and Normman as representative of white normality further resonates with Celebonovic's understanding of kitsch as "bourgeois realism," in which a conservative narcissism validates middle-class existence by providing a "clearly recognizable picture" (13) of "the ideal image conditioning public and private life" (46).[11] Celebonovic coined the term to describe, descriptively rather than pejoratively, the kitsch of popular nineteenth-century European genre painting that typically treated mythological or Orientalist themes. Celebonovic's characterization of such art is similar to what Westbrook sees in kitsch as a form of "self-delusion," in which, as he describes it, the function is to "project the viewers into a community imbued with meaning and in which they recognize their ideal selves" (Westbrook 426–29). In a consideration of whiteness and normality, kitsch as "bourgeois realism" is particularly helpful as it points to a bundling of class affiliation and racialized identity in which whiteness seems to promise implicit middle-class status that obscures actual class stratification. The suggestion here then is that twentieth-century whiteness and its trajectory position themselves differently than the nineteenth-century American whiteness that emerged out of white labor's compulsion to differentiate itself from blackness, as argued by Roediger. Thus the kitsch of normality creates an "ideal image" that is race-less, classless, and, as Carter reminds us, heterosexual.

The connection between kitsch and class in relation to the generative nature of whiteness is extended through Olalquiaga's analysis that differentiates between types of kitsch, which I see as connected to aesthetic judgments that are class based. While others, such as Nabokov, have also differentiated kitsch by category, they do so by identifying features or subjects of kitsch.[12] Olalquiaga, on the other hand, in her work *The Artificial Kingdom*, refines classification further by identifying two types of qualitatively different kitsch: nostalgic and melancholic, corresponding to Benjamin's distinction between the souvenir and the ruin. In this move, she lays the ground for effectively eliminating the related problems of elitism and authenticity in kitsch theory: kitsch is connected to both lowbrow and highbrow tastes but perhaps looks different in each case. As I will show, both types play a role in maintaining the discourses of whiteness.

Nostalgia for Olalquiaga, as epitomized in the souvenir, is a kind of low-brow schmaltz consistent with broader views of kitsch such as we see expressed in Kundera's idea of suppression of the messy and inconvenient and probably connected with Greenberg's "masses" who find kitsch "easier" than the avant-garde. Melancholia, on the other hand, that creates a fetish of the ruin, wallows in precisely the unpleasant truth that nostalgia hopes to efface—specifically, death and decline—and may be connected with a more elite aesthetic, as I have argued elsewhere.[13] Thus nostalgic kitsch is "better known" (Olalquiaga 292) in the plastic flower that cannot decay or the greeting card that joins us in celebration of perennial maternal love or the aphorisms of self-help and positive thinking. Such examples fit our various definitions of kitsch as syrupy, petrified, and simplistic. Laura Micciche describes nostalgia as "that most uncritical of indulgences" that "is . . . a product of universalizing discourses that project sameness and stability where there really is difference and uncertainty" (16–17). But kitsch is more comprehensive than this and sometimes, in its hyperseriousness, masquerades as criticality. This is melancholic kitsch in its antiludic strain, which elevates irony and wistfulness, so that not only does it not avoid difficult truths, it wallows in them—indeed makes an altar and bows down before them. The coming-of-age paradigm that generically charts an epiphanic movement from idealism or naive faith to "mature" irony might be an example of the melancholic aesthetic at work as a preferred "serious" literary taste. But if we take Olalquiaga's idea a step further, we will see that the fetish of such irony will (ironically) obviate the ironic mode and cross over into the realm of nostalgic kitsch in a systematization of "difficult" experience. Thus the "difficult," the "critical," and the "serious" run the risk of kitsch as much as the impossibly pleasant or "easy." We may even then end up with such a phenomenon as what Norman Finkelstein terms "holocaust kitsch" ("Daniel"), in which the atrocity of genocide is appropriated into an unassailable "industry" of propaganda (*Holocaust*).

As with Greenberg and others, Olalquiaga's notions of kitsch owe something in varying degrees to Benjamin's idea of mechanical reproduction and diminishment of the art object's authenticity (aura) through replication, but the identification of a melancholic kitsch resolves the problem of Romantic/Modernist presumptions of authenticity that haunt kitsch theory: there is "real," authentic art and then there is kitsch or "fake art"—the original object and the mass-produced replica. Adding the melancholic variety extends kitsch's reach to cover terrain that otherwise might be ceded to "genuine" art and indeed eliminates concern with that dichotomy altogether. This is an important move in understanding white kitsch. Thus the assertion of a revivified white ideal might be understood as nostalgia while the lamenting of its loss might be melancholic. But while white supremacist doctrine can be understood through the lens of kitsch, so too can liberal and progressive narratives that lament and condemn whiteness as impoverished ontology. Both are based on whiteness as loss of authenticity—whether through denial in the case of nostalgia or fetish in the case of melancholy—and the accompanying systematization of experience. As we have seen, normality discourse satisfies the craving for authenticity in what amounts to nostalgic kitsch, but critical whiteness studies, faced with the foundational premise of the "ruin" of whiteness, adopts a rhetoric of melancholy in which whiteness is invested with the burden of unattainable authenticity. Both pose obstructions to Leonardo's goal of going "*through* race in order to have any hopes of going *beyond* it" (125).

WASHING THE WHITE BLOOD FROM DON IMUS[14]: A STUDY IN RACIAL KITSCH

Katherine Lugg has pointed out how our political and educational rhetoric is steeped in a reactionary kitsch of sameness and banality that obviates critical thought and hampers the prospects of democracy. Surely we can say the same about the "public" discourse on race, which is neither populist nor democratic but rather corporatized and often organized around sensationalized media events focused on particular personalities. Such debates fall under the category of what Gurstein refers to as "commercial entertainment," which "is neither genuine nor popular . . . it is instead massproduced diversions meant to fill time that is not spent at work" (156). Such events are governed by the kitsch that arguably pervades all our entertainments and masquerades as serious treatment of news events. But my focus here is on the dampening effect such events have on developing a critical rhetoric of race, an effect that permeates the whiteness that reads and writes itself into the classroom. The scripted, homogeneous nature of these events, in which "sides" are ascribed particular language and roles, reflecting "a desire always to be able to identify the good guys and bad guys" (Awkward 148), bleeds into our attempts to discuss racism meaningfully. The complexity of lived experience becomes the compressed filler of white kitsch. And these kitsch discussions become an important means by which whiteness absorbs attempts to challenge it.

I consider here the case of Don Imus as one such event that sets the terms for how we look at racism in what passes for our public sphere. Imus, an entertainer in the shock jock tradition, became a center of "controversy" for racist remarks he made characterizing the members of the 2007 Rutgers women's basketball team as "nappy headed hos." His infamous statements were seen as the final straw in a career of performances that pandered to racist presumptions in his audience. As a result, the popular show was canceled only, however, eventually to rise, phoenix-like, in another incarnation, further underscoring the pyrrhic nature of this "victory" in the war on racism. When discussing this incident, commentators frequently begin with a disclaimer that they are not fans of Don Imus, find his humor nonexistent or sophomoric, and rarely listen to or watch the entertainer. I follow suit here. Unlike my students who develop an affinity with Joseph Conrad once they hear he was charged with racism (see Chapter 5), I have no such feelings of fondness for Don Imus. What interests me primarily here is the public response toward Imus and his utterances as it so seems to typify how we "do" debates on racism as spectacle.

Despite the public outcry overwhelmingly "against" Imus, many devout listeners were presumably distraught over losing their morning companion, although there seemed to be no liberal rhetoric that could craft an argument in support of the skit. Are white people protecting their investment in whiteness when they lamely defend what appears to be the indefensible? Was it a case of the rage and anger that often erupt as the emotional marker of white privilege coming under attack, as I discuss in Chapter 5? It seems legitimate to read such responses in this way, although notably few defended Imus outright, as most commentators attempted to put distance between themselves and the remarks in question either by taking the tack of a liberal "free speech" defense that tended to stipulate to Imus's racism, or a "condemn the words and not the man" approach that acknowledged Imus's "mistake" while citing the evidence of philanthropic actions as a better indication of his "true" and abiding character. As the *New York Daily News*'s Mike Lupica put it, "Nobody is defending what he said about these young women, starting with Don Imus himself. But do I think he is a racist? I do not." In either case, these responses avoided delving into what the remarks themselves might say about whiteness as people jockeyed for position within the allowable parameters of liberal response that, in the end, are the parameters of kitsch. We either condemn the remarks at face value as racist or attempt to rehabilitate the entertainer's ethos outside of irony while making a gesture toward a higher universalizing principle of First Amendment rights. There is little allowable room to understand the event in any other way, or, more importantly, to see beyond its apparent utility as a transparent barometer of whiteness and racism, which was the status granted to it in both new and old media. Such occasions as the Imus incident, however, ultimately do little to interrogate racism and end up providing a public space for liberal whiteness to "defend" itself by adopting a posture of disappointment over the alleged "insensitivity."

There is, I believe, something else besides affront to white privilege in an apostasy that begrudges acceptance of the above prescription and is unwilling to toss Don Imus unequivocally on the rubbish heap of discredited racists. That something else is akin to the glimmer of legitimacy I see in my students' desire to dismiss the classroom discussion of "100% Italian" that I mention earlier and all the classroom impatience with our civic discussions of racism. This "something else" can best be understood from the perspective of kitsch in terms of both Imus's performance as well as the subsequent closing of ranks that took place in the wake of his remarks. At the very least, we perhaps need to ask why this incident above any other would have resulted in his dismissal, as it was characteristic rather than aberrant in terms of the Imus repertoire. For the sacrifice of Don Imus on the altar of what passes for antiracist efforts bears all the marks of the kitsch move from particularity to systematized generality, a process that evinces little in the way of critical understanding. When viewing the events that produced the demise of Imus's show, we may view Imus as a racist entertainer who obfuscates and attempts to render palatable his racism through the liberal tradition of philanthropic gestures that produce temporary amelioration in the plight of the selected few. (We might, think, for example, of Ralph Ellison's description of rewarding the humiliated narrator of "Battle Royal" with his scholarship.) But another narrative is also possible, one that involves a more nuanced understanding of the relationship between racist kitsch and what I'll call "racial camp" and how the latter would only succeed in a "postracial" landscape. In other words, I'm suggesting that the Imus phenomenon can be understood in part as an impulse toward camp, that is to say, a parody of nostalgic racist kitsch, albeit a failed impulse that is reabsorbed through the kitsch response scripted in liberal whiteness, a response that may be both nostalgic and melancholic in its orientation as one variety morphs into the other.

Although often associated with gay culture, camp is not something only available to what Sontag, in her foundational essay on the subject, referred to as the "homosexual . . . vanguard" (117, 118). The aesthetic of camp is marked by "parody, exaggeration, mannerism and artifice" (LaGapa 92), and to distinguish between kitsch and camp, Sontag's observation that "Camp sees everything in quotation marks" (109) is very useful. One of the hallmarks of kitsch is that lack of irony or alternative frame of reference: "from a 'serious' point of view," much of camp is "either bad art or kitsch" (Sontag 108). Kitsch finds itself believing its artificiality, whether nostalgic or melancholic. Indeed one way to frame the distinction is that camp is kitsch plus irony, and one way to understand Don Imus is that he is a caricature of *himself*, a creation, indeed something like a hoax where the persona purports to be real. Whether he views himself this way is not certain, although in his first attempt to offer "context" for his remarks, he hints at such a possibility: the show, he explained, "makes fun of everybody. *It makes fun of me*, and it makes fun of everybody on the planet. And sometimes *it makes fun of me to a vicious standpoint*" (qtd. in Awkward 14, emphasis added). That Imus was not able to fully articulate the rationale of camp doesn't preclude its analytical validity, for as Sontag says, not all camp is "wholly conscious" (111). Anthony Asadullah Samad inadvertently supports this view of Imus as self-parody when he says "if I was to draw a picture of a 'nappy headed ho,' it would probably look more like Don Imus than any woman I know (you seen Imus' hair)."

As the above remark implies, Imus is a far cry from Sontag's "glamorous" (113) agent of camp, although he does seem to qualify here for the "epicene" (109) in his pathetic rendition of the "cowboy" figure.[15] Imus's "campiness" resides in his ridiculousness, a point underscored by Awkward when he asks us to consider an absurd Imus "aware of the irony" of an aging white man "using ghetto pejorative" (26). Indeed, Imus, famous for his sagging skin and collapsed lung, is as likely, in his remarks about the "toughness" of the champion-class athletes, to be parodying aging white masculinity as he is black femininity.[16] *USA Today* reported "The shaming of Imus was especially intense in part because his targets—winning teen athletes—are the antithesis of what he called them" (Puente). Setting aside the obvious problem with this statement—it implies there might be a group of women somewhere for whom such a description *would* be appropriate—an observation about the inapplicability of the remark to the subjects in question should have served to underscore rather than undermine the ironic nature of the performance. That it was not possible to be read this way tells us a great deal about the limits of discourse in our decidedly not "postracial" America.

Although Sontag offers, as one of her definitions, "a seriousness that fails" as a criterion for camp (112, see note 16), according to Nyong'o, Greenberg provides the same definition for *kitsch* as a "failed seriousness ... that attempts to say something profound, but can utter only clichés" (371). Sontag, however, also offers other (sometimes contradictory) attributes of camp, as we have seen, that would seem to distinguish the phenomenon from kitsch, suggesting that camp's relationship to seriousness is "complex": "One can be serious about the frivolous: frivolous about the serious" (116). Indeed, as we have seen, she says that some camp, were it taken seriously, would be misidentified as the "bad art" of kitsch (108). The dividing line here between camp and kitsch with regard to the perspective of seriousness is crucial in understanding the reception of the Imus performance. Although most people granted that Imus was attempting humor, his remarks, rather than seen as the camp "theatricalization of experience" (Sontag 114), were indeed read from the perspective of seriousness and understood as what Nyong'o has identified as the "failed humor" of the "racist kitsch" (371) found in Jim Crow caricature. According to Nyong'o, in order to maintain agency and not be engulfed by racist kitsch, "racialized others ... reassert our dignity and attain distance from the pleasure that the stereotype urges upon us. This oppositional discourse places the racist object in a new frame, one in which the object is resignified. From a token of mundane racist enjoyment, it becomes a totem of our racial survival" (371). This agentive response that transforms the kitsch object from a banal symbol of oppression into a rallying symbol of survival describes the scapegoating process whereby Imus becomes the embodiment of, in Awkward's phrase, "what evil look like," as African-Americans attempt to safeguard their "psychic health" (Awkward 19) in the face of the perceived onslaught of dehumanizing kitsch.

Perhaps, then, we cannot "afford" to read Imus as racial camp, only as racist kitsch—that is to say, not as parody of whiteness, but as a "serious" and "failed" attempt to imitate and thus impugn blackness through nostalgic representation that denies and promotes oppressive whiteness. The blogosphere was alive with comparisons to minstrel shows and a blackface Imus who idiotically imagined himself authentically representing and colonizing hip-hop idiom. Perhaps his white audience does read him "straight," an *Amos n Andy* knockoff intact in the twenty-first century perfectly preserved for the "pleasure," as Nyong'o says, that the racist stereotype provides. There is no doubt that such "uncomplicated" whiteness not only still exists but flourishes in the great "postracial" American society, albeit under the radar of public narrative. And yet, as we have seen, such "vulgar" whiteness is all too visible to maintain itself for long. Instead whiteness lives on intractably in the liberal *disavowal* of Imus that provides the opportunity for the disaffiliation from white supremacy so crucial to the "new" whiteness's invisibility. Thus it is "easy" for white liberalism to characterize the Imus performance as recidivism that warrants a scolding and a reaffirmation of philanthropic good intentions as remedy to racism.

The nostalgic narrative that played out in the aftermath of the incident illustrates this process perfectly. In response to a story that, according to journalism.org, was the "biggest" story of the year thus far, claiming more than sixty percent of all available "talk" minutes for that week and far outdistancing discussions of immigration or Iraq policy ("Imus Becomes"), the coach and players of Rutgers held a press conference devoted to what might be described as a defense of the women's honor and reputation, as though it were possible that Imus could be invested with the authority to tarnish either. The press conference was headlined as an occasion where the "face of grace outshines vile insult" (Lupica), and Christine Brennan of *USA Today*, wondering rhetorically how these women in their interview so "completely outclassed and outsmarted" Imus, asked "Just how out of touch is this man, to say the disgusting things he said about this group of young women, of all people"?

Outclassing and outsmarting the public buffoon known as Don Imus would seem to be no particularly tall order, and the low humor for which he is known an even less likely battleground for an epic struggle between grace and villainy, good and evil. These are the terms of nostalgic kitsch that insist on human triumph in heroic struggle, and this type of "emotional conclusion often functions not as a springboard for reflection but as closure, with a slight echo of moral righteousness haunting its presence: I am aghast" (Ratcliffe, "In Search" 285).[17] Coach Vivian Stringer reinforced this narrative when she compared the effects of Imus's remarks to the discrimination she experienced as a teenager. As reported by Kelly Whiteside, when Stringer first heard about the Imus remarks her thoughts rushed back to high school when she was cut from the cheerleading squad because of her race.

> In the mid-1960s, there were no girls sports teams at German Township (Pa.) High, so Stringer tried out for the cheerleading squad. She was the best at back flips and roundabouts, but that wasn't good enough.
>
> That night, a local NAACP leader stopped by her house in Edenborn, Pa., and persuaded her parents to let their daughter go before the school board. She was embarrassed and scared. Then her father, Buddy Stoner, a coal miner, told her something that is just as powerful today.
>
> He said, "It might not be about you but about future generations of young women. If you don't stand up for something, you'll fall for anything."
>
> And his daughter became the first black cheerleader at her high school.

The story in and of itself is its own testimony, a reminder of the lived experience of racism and discrimination, and as such bears witness to that history. But when set as the backdrop for the Imus incident, its meaning is sentimentalized and obscured, and the story becomes the basis of a logical fallacy that ultimately is less than useful in advancing understanding of racism. The implication seemingly is that the injustice to which Stringer was subjected serves as a lens to situate Imus's unsuccessful attempt at humor, a lens that will help us understand and make sense of what transpired. But what exactly is the relationship between the two stories? Imus's speech act, after all, could not prevent anyone from playing on a team. Is it possible to equate Imus's characterization of the players, even if we accept it as racist, with the denial of Stringer's civil rights? To use Stringer's story in this way obfuscates rather than elucidates our understanding of racism and occludes both incidents. For not only does Stringer's anecdote not shed light on the nature of Imus's offense but, positioned as it is, becomes tamed from its radical testimony on American racism into a heroic, "feel-good" narrative that celebrates triumph over adversity.

What's important about the sleight of hand here is the effect it has to bolster self-congratulatory liberal whiteness in much the same way civil rights history has been appropriated to foster American patriotism. Nicholas Guyatt calls this latter move an "integrationist version of American history," where Constitutional ideals have an "egalitarian inevitability" that culminated, for example, in the end of Jim Crow. "It is a story of reconciliation, not opposition or confrontation." Thus rather than a source of shame and a reminder of the utter disgrace which forms so much of the country's past, the civil rights struggle smoothly becomes a source of unified *American* pride and triumph that proceeded inevitably from common American values and legacy, despite the fact that a good number of the Americans in the drama were on the wrong side of the moral question. The same nostalgic impulse was at work in the January 2011 Republican orchestrated "read-in" of the Constitution on the House floor in an attempt to unify us and remind us of our roots. Key to this unification effort was the excision of references to the three-fifths compromise and the fugitive slave law even as the reading of the 13th Amendment was included in the celebration. Thus we laud the end of slavery while managing to avoid acknowledgment that it ever existed in the first place.

Despite the markers that reference community engagement and collective action, Stringer's story becomes absorbed into nostalgic kitsch as confrontation with racism is universalized into a celebratory "profile" of individual courage that inspires and unifies us all, an example of "subject matter with a clear emotional charge that triggers a ready emotional response" (Kulka 26). Initially, Stringer's testimony is positioned as an example of melancholic kitsch that fossilizes the narrative of struggle, made safe as a past moment functioning in the present to create a locus of consensus. This melancholy is the enthymeme that explains the connection between the civil rights era anecdote of discrimination and Imus's attempted twenty-first-century joke, two events that, on their face, are quite dissimilar. The cheerleading story is offered up as a weapon against the perceived insult, an unassailable credential that moves us from Imus's profane attempt at humor back to the realm of seriousness and reverence invoked by a past, venerable struggle. In this way, the melancholy is quickly transmuted into the nostalgia of triumph and an all-American, Algeresque narrative of success that is of little threat to institutionalized racism. It changes from radical testimony to become the kind of story of character that liberal whiteness can easily accommodate and contain.

CONCLUSION: TOWARD COMPLEXITY

So we banish Imus as though he were Falstaff: our clown has entertained us, and now by sending him away, we show how serious we are about this business of racism. It serves whiteness well to set Imus up as the straw man in a kitsch ritual of self-righteous indignation: progressive whites proclaim their support for Stringer and her athletes and in so doing reaffirm whiteness's liberal role in the amelioration of racial relations with the important effect of forestalling meaningful inquiry into passive racism and the current mechanisms of whiteness's sustainability. By taking Imus "seriously," he does indeed become the scapegoat that Awkward sees him as—a sacrifice for whiteness's "sins" whether he himself is a man to be cut loose or redeemed. Whiteness is self-correcting here, washing itself clean in the multicultural waters of tolerance and sensitivity, with perhaps something like a wink and a nod as the ritual is performed. We suppress the inklings that there is something less than honest in this rite, less than meaningful in this discussion as we assume the appropriate demeanor for the occasion—perhaps even holding "beer summits" that provide photo ops for the simulacrum of postracial harmony, while our popular discourse shuts down, through the extravaganza of media event, any worthwhile look at just how racism did and *didn't* affect the arrest of a Harvard professor.[18] But our students, like the children in the story of the emperor's new clothes, may not always be so polite and reverential—or perhaps they will be, while in their own minds further consigning our antiracist efforts to the bin of irrelevance and predictability as they lump our attempts in with our nation's sanctioned rhetoric. How then do we find ways to move toward more phenomenological analyses and discussions that students can respect; that will cut through the great predictable narrative of "diversity"?

The problem from the standpoint of critical pedagogy has always been how do we refrain from condemning students without "giving into" and thus supporting what appear to be racist predispositions? How do we help them (and ourselves) challenge the rhetorical constructions of whiteness that permeate their existences and their texts? One way perhaps is by resisting the kitsch of whiteness in its various permutations, with its imposition of narrative on experience, and by helping students understand those kitsch structures as well. As Hartigan writes, "As antiracism solidifies as a means of engaging racial inequality, it risks reifying both an object of investigation and a way of thinking about race that is inattentive to the dramatic ways racial identity is rapidly transforming" (*Odd* 231). Hartigan, while lauding the intentions of antiracist interventions, critiques the tendency to label, and thus dismiss, white behavior and rhetoric as simply racist without attending to the nuances that ethnographic study can reveal about such subject positioning. In effect, Hartigan is suggesting a means to move beyond the "pre-digested drip" (see note 11) of racial kitsch that "is unprepared to acknowledge the contradictions, inconsistencies, and ambivalences in white and nonwhite identities" (*Odd* 241). Rhetoric, of course, also offers a powerful means for aiding in this project.

One such example of this can be seen in Seibel-Trainor's classroom ethnography of an English high school teacher's efforts to enact antiracist pedagogy. A typical move in such classrooms is to expand the curricular readings to include the "multicultural" so that such texts can serve as an entrée into the workings and underpinnings of societal racism. These students, upon reading works by Maya Angelou and John Edgar Wideman, evinced the hostility and dismissive responses that critical pedagogues encounter all too frequently in the multicultural classroom and have come to associate with whiteness's implicit agenda. Remarks such as, "I liked how it [Wideman's work] wasn't all angry about racism and stuff, like Maya. That got really old" (*Rethinking* 81), are typically interpreted as manifestations of white privilege as well as whiteness's invisibility. And indeed they are, only as Seibel-Trainor's analysis shows, in far more complicated ways than we might imagine. A look at what she calls the "emotioned rules" of the high school's institutional discourse reveals that the students are framing their responses to the texts in terms of the governing rhetoric that comprised their high school experience: messages of self-reliance and staying positive, avoiding victimhood and dwelling on the negative, assuming individualistic personal responsibility and surmounting obstacles to achievement. These kitsch values and messages about what it means to be successful and mature were uncritically foisted on students constantly to the point where they came to understand critical thinking itself as an undesired response. Thus their racist statements were part of a bigger picture, as their teacher observed, where the rhetoric of the institution was interfering with their ability to engage with *any* text in a meaningful way when they perceived it to be about "complaining" (78). As one student writes, "I don't like people for having bad attitudes. . . . Who wants to read about that?" (90). The students' racist statements about the texts they were assigned are part of a larger institutionalized nostalgic whiteness that celebrates individual achievement and personal responsibility. To ask students under such circumstances to see white privilege is in effect placing them in a Laingian double-bind where they are told one thing is required to be "good" students but asked, in another context, to do something else. This is a good example of a defeating contradiction that undermines our educational efforts to probe racism. (For further exploration of such contradictions, see Ian's discussion in Chapter 6 of the cultural schizophrenia enacted through discourses of color blindness and multiculturalism.)

This type of insight into institutional culture has far-reaching implications. (Such an ethos as identified by Seibel-Trainor helps explain, for example, persistent misreadings of a story like Toni Cade Bambara's "The Lesson," when students, baffled by Bambara's critique of consumerism and capitalism, manage to find instead an endorsement of the work ethic and "a lesson" that anyone can transcend the limits of race if only they try hard enough.[19]) Thus reading whiteness through an ethnographic lens here and connecting it to specific and local cultures and politics is an example of refusing to apply a reified, monolithic narrative of whiteness that abets easy but ultimately unproductive rhetorical positioning of what constitutes the antiracist subject. Antiracist methodologies are prone to this rhetorical liability of kitsch when they do not allow for the overdetermination of subjectivities and experiences and seek instead to essentialize whiteness for the purposes of vilifying it rather than hearing what it has to "say." Critical whiteness studies, at its best, may offer us a way to navigate the kitsch of these efforts, whether we are considering the institutional context of our endeavors, our own subjectivities within our critical discourses, or the inflecting rhetoric of our public sphere.

4 Whiteness, Composition, and Enthymemes of Institutional Discourse

My first full-time college teaching job was at EC[1] in New Jersey. It was sixteen or so years ago, but it seems longer, maybe because of how much I've learned about the profession since those heady days. Like most people, I imagine, who have been on the job for that long I learned quite a bit by watching very good and maybe not so good teachers teach. What remains with me now is the emotion of having gone through those days rather than an extensive catalogue of actual events. I enjoyed my time there in lots of ways; I learned a lot, met lots of smart students and teachers—some of whom have become good friends over the years, and I'm sure they have had a significant influence on how I teach my classes and think of my role as Writing Program Administrator (WPA) at WU.[2]

My time at EC coincided with an important time for its writing program as it was addressing student demands for more inclusive reading materials, which mushroomed into the demand for more diversity in its faculty. I had the opportunity, then, to participate in the program's growth and development in ways I couldn't have imagined when I started there. I recall, for instance, how it felt to be acutely aware of being the only person of color in the room when the freshman writing faculty would hold its staff meetings. The college, which began as a small private seminary for German immigrants in the late 1800s, had become a school with a predominantly African-American and Latino student body of almost seventy-five percent by the time I had arrived in the mid-1990s. I remember thinking about the colonial nature of the Composition classes there for that reason and felt a bit uncomfortable about it, but these feelings were initially overshadowed by my excitement at landing my first full-time job in the profession as a coordinator of Basic Writing I and the workshops attached to the on-cycle Composition classes. Jobs like that were rare, and I knew plenty of smart MAs who graduated with me and were temps or secretaries. Actually, it occurs to me now that I've never *not* been aware of a shortage of full-time jobs in higher education; it was one of the subtexts all the way through graduate school, and it seems a perennial story these days that graduate programs are producing more students than the market can bear—a subject I'll say a good deal more about shortly as it has a direct bearing on how writing programs are structured, and how their function helps to reproduce racial and class-based inequalities I believe contribute to whiteness in composition studies.

I was also aware of the fact that all of the teachers on the EC writing faculty were women and, as I also figured out, predominantly middle-class. Those who were married with college-aged teens didn't have them enrolled in EC, and rarely missed an opportunity to share a story or two about their child's acceptance to Northwestern, their challenging Composition course at Boston College, or the resources they enjoy at Rutgers. Only one of them was male, and he was also the writing program administrator and a poet by training.

I recall one colleague of mine, the coordinator of Basic Writing II, the course above mine on the organizational chart, being impressed with his publications, and having great respect for his leadership of the adjunct faculty who comprised one-hundred percent of the teachers in the program besides himself, and I recall her giving me tips about how to win over the notoriously fickle group. My predecessor had irritated them with his disorganization, and my colleague made no secret of the fact that she was pleased I was on board. This is no doubt why she suggested that in my first meeting with the faculty in my role as the coordinator of the workshops attached to their courses I should bring a manila folder for each of them. She encouraged me to put my name, contact information, and my plans for the first workshop lesson for the first week of instruction in the folder so they'll have no questions about what their students would be doing in the workshops for the upcoming text—". . . that will impress them!" she assured me.

All the Composition classes followed a common syllabus, read exactly the same pages at exactly the same time, and all students wrote on exactly the same question, which was generated in the faculty meeting on a weekly basis. I remember being surprised by the books the faculty had chosen to read; *Five Lectures on Psycho-Analysis* by Sigmund Freud was among them. I thought it was an odd choice for lots of reasons, not least because it was extraordinarily difficult for students who, to begin with, were not traditional in terms of their academic preparedness, many of them being first-generation college students. In fact, most were English as second language learners. I found a memo that had obviously slipped behind the back of a drawer in my filing cabinet one day that explained the rationale. It was dated 1975 and was written by the freshman writing committee to the faculty senate. It argued that the then newly revised freshman writing course should include difficult texts (like Freud) in order to bring great works to the students and have them learn through the struggle involved in comprehending them. That is to say, difficult texts were sought precisely because they were difficult. If students could "get" material like Freud, they could "get" anything, so the rationale went on to explain. The memo exactly corresponds to the period of Open Admissions that had swept the entire country, and it was obviously part of EC's way of dealing with the mass of minority and otherwise underprepared students who were being admitted. As fresh-faced as I was just coming out of an MA program in English, I had no idea that my limited training in rhetoric and composition theory as part of a teaching practicum and few years interacting with other students and faculty in the field was more formal training in the discipline than many, if not all, of the adjuncts I worked with in the Freshman Composition program at EC may have had. WPAs know this is not unique to EC as most writing programs are staffed by adjunct faculty who are often very committed, and very good—just as the EC faculty were—but nevertheless have no special training in the theories that inform the discipline.

As it turns out, the difficult reading material necessitated the workshop component to the Composition course, and in my opinion then—as now— these workshops were highly advanced. They were, in effect, a built-in supplemental instruction period, capped at around twelve students, specifically designed to help them with reading comprehension, peer editing, and revision much like what might be expected in a present-day studio model of a Composition program. In my estimation, these workshops were critical to EC's program—as the memo also pointed out—not only because they were essential for helping students navigate the difficult material they were reading, but also because of their function as places for students to think about the course material in a way that was necessarily organized around their writing. I learned a great deal about writing pedagogy in those once-a-week workshops, and I credit them for honing much of what I understand in theory about how inexperienced writers develop and mature.

The workshops worked for students like Jose[3] who I remember because of his dramatic change over the course of one semester. I could tell he was looking for—and needed—attention by the way he walked into the room on the first day; bandana, baggy jeans, timberland boots, puffy-shelled jacket, and a swagger. He understood how to use the rhetoric of dissent. He was impatient. He wanted to know, but didn't have the time to learn. He always thought there was an angle, or shortcut to writing, and I assumed there and then that that was his M.O. in his other classes. He was frustrated with his Composition teacher, who he felt had something against him because he couldn't get better than a "D" in her class. It took him a long time—all semester and then some—to realize that writing took time, and was, to use a cliché, a process. He learned that, in large part, because of the workshops.

NEW CRITICISM AND A PEDAGOGY OF WHITENESS

My surprise at the choices of texts in the course when I first arrived turned to frustration within a few semesters. I remember in one staff meeting being struck by the tone of the discussion that the Composition faculty were having about their pedagogy and their overall approach to their students. There was a peculiar kind of "us" versus "them" about how they conducted themselves, which I never could quite figure out. Was it rooted in their status as faculty, contingent as it was, or was it a subtle kind of racism in the missionary, colonial sense? That is, to work at EC in their capacity as "gatekeepers," as one faculty member once said unironically, was a kind of moral duty, "so that our students could read and write well in order to be competitive in the marketplace." The commitment to the marketplace, shrouded as it was in a kind of "student need" discourse, was an overarching, ever-present theme that ran through almost everything that happened in the writing program at EC, and especially governed how a student would progress through it. In fact, this discourse was more powerful than almost anything else that came out of the faculty meetings or the lesson plans because it preceded the faculty meetings and the lesson plans since I believe the adjuncts brought it with them. In this sense, adjuncts and the institution had similar goals, objectives, and aims. Where the institution wished to prepare its students for jobs in the marketplace, adjuncts, it seemed, evaluated their student writing by asking, "Would I hire someone who writes—or speaks—like this?" To be fair, this description fits a general culture and was more typical of the faculty who had been there for many years—the more established, middle-class teachers. There were some who had not been there so long—younger, working-class—who, perhaps like me, had observed the practices and had become part of the culture by default rather than by way of a commitment to this de facto mission.

At the meeting, the book the faculty had uniformly assigned for their students to read, Toni Morrison's *Song of Solomon,* was discussed, and the instructors spent a good portion of the meeting complaining about the general quality of the students, "I cannot believe what this student has written and calls an essay!" one complained.

"What are they teaching in those high schools? My six year old writes better than he does!" another lamented.

"I had that student last semester. He really doesn't belong in college!"

The complaints rang out in familiar fashion, but in this particular meeting, they struck a deeper chord with me. This time, they centered on essays written by their students in response to the group question they had composed in the faculty meeting the week before. As with all of their other assignments, I was eager to hear their reports on how the students had done, but I was especially eager to hear how they had done with Morrison's book as I had constructed workshop activities for their students that I felt sure would help them do well with the question the faculty had posed for them.

While I do not remember the precise question, the formulation was always the same—"why does Darwin say human evolution is more like a bush than a ladder?" "Why does Freud use the term 'psychosomatic' to describe particular dreams?" "Why does Milkman feel such anger toward his mother?"

That is, the questions were very similar to the kinds of questions you might find at the end of commercial books and anthologies designed for freshman Composition classes which demanded a kind of New Critical response to a text, which I have come to view as a very white interpretive lens to use in such cases. Consider, for instance, Steven Lynn's description of New Criticism in his textbook on literary theory, *Texts and Contexts*:

> The odds. . .are excellent that some of your English teachers were trained in the methods of New Criticism, even if they never heard the term; and in surprisingly many classrooms today, even in the midst of a cornucopia of critical options, New Criticism is often essentially the only approach on the menu, its principles so pervasive that they seem natural and obvious—and therefore remain, often enough, unarticulated. (37–38)

To be trained in the principles of New Criticism, and to bring that training into the Composition classroom—as almost every adjunct I've ever worked with inevitably does—is no small matter. New Criticism teaches us that the "text" is a self contained entity with an internal unity. Conflict, ambiguity, and resolution all contribute to the meaning of the text which stands alone as its own universe, not so much in time as it is *through* time, as both the subject and object of study reveal the universality, we are to believe, of the human condition. These principles of New Criticism do not easily allow for students to engage their own experiences in the interpretive act, and so just as New Criticism was formulated in the 1920s and 30s as a reactionary response against liberal democratic progressive views at the time on the part of its architects[4] and became part of a kind of intellectual Jim Crow, so too does New Criticism serve as a kind of short circuit between students and their experiences and their intellectual academic pursuits when taught by most adjuncts who populate the vast majority of the Composition classes in places I have worked and most Composition programs nationally.

What makes the endeavor all the more problematic are the ways in which New Criticism as a pedagogy and an ideology masquerades as normative, "natural and obvious—and therefore . . . often enough, unarticulated." In this way, the adjunct population at EC was deploying a pedagogy of whiteness and was completely oblivious to it since in many ways they are positioned by their own academic training to do so and, crucially, *not* see that they are doing so. New Criticism, then, constituted one of the ways that whiteness functions in and through Composition programs and courses.

The teachers' responses to their student essays on Morrison's book, centering as they did on their assessment that students just didn't "get" the book, is perhaps more accurately described as the students' inability to make sense of the New Critical approach that was demanded of them when the text meant something far more personally complex than the teaching method could describe and account for.

It is the ways that the principles of New Criticism are situated in the course and considered, not just normative, but in opposition to the personal, subjective, and experiential, that I think whiteness informs pedagogy in composition studies. This opposition excludes certain languages, such as African-American Language, even as it valorizes the language of power—white middle-class English as normative. My argument, then, is not that teaching ideas of objectivity, and the analytical, is somehow bad or wrong; it's that these terms seem to have been co-opted by a particular kind of discourse and pedagogy, and they seem to fulfill a particular kind of function to the exclusion of other kinds of discourses and definitions of language. I question, then, the ways in which pedagogies informed by New Criticism and language are presented to students explicitly and implicitly and what that presentation comes to mean to them as learners, and what their subsequent understanding of language and education are when these terms become, as they inevitably do, material forces in their academic careers.

What was to me, then, a perplexing problem, namely, how the students who were overwhelmingly African-American and Latino were unable to "get" a book like Morrison's *Song of Solomon*, which appeared to me to be so central to African-American history and culture, had, it seemed, a tentative answer. The teachers would teach Morrison in precisely the same way that they would teach Freud in spite of Morrison's apparent invitation to do otherwise in everything her prose offers its readers.

There's a good example of this in Morrison's opening pages that's worth citing at some length because it illustrates how the African-American community of the novel takes control of their own reality through a skillful use of language which emerges out of their day-to-day cultural activity. "Mains Avenue" in the novel had, by the African-American community, been renamed "Dr. Street" since

> the only colored doctor in the city had lived and died on that street and when he moved there in 1896, his patients took to calling the street, which none of them lived on or near, Doctor Street. Later, when other Negroes moved there, and when the postal service became a popular means of transferring messages among them envelopes from Louisiana, Virginia, Alabama, and Georgia began to arrive addressed to people at house numbers on Doctor Street. . . . Then, in 1918, when colored men were being drafted a few gave their address at the recruitment office as Doctor Street. In that way, the name acquired a quasi-official status. But not for long. Some of the city legislators, whose concern for appropriate names and the maintenance of the city's landmarks was a principal part of their political life, saw that "Doctor Street" was never used in any official capacity. And since they knew that only Southside residents kept it up, they had notices posted in the stores, barbershops, and restaurant in that part of the city saying that the avenue running northerly and southerly from Shore Road fronting the

lake to the junction of routes 6 and 2 leading to Pennsylvania, and also running parallel to and between Rutherdford Avenue and Broadway, had always been and would always be known as Mains Avenue and not Doctor Street.

It was a genuinely clarifying public message because it gave Southside residents a way to keep their memories alive and please the city legislators as well. They called it Not Doctor Street. (4)

It's a funny story but one that serves a couple of purposes because it shows in one instance how Morrison illustrates the power of the African-American community in her novel: the idea that it controls its own reality as expressed through its own use of language. The excerpt also illustrates what Gayatri Spivak calls *catachresis*, which in the colonial context refers to the mapping of the exchange of concept-metaphors between the Western metropolis and its former territories or colonies (Spivak 60). In this case, "Mains Avenue" has no meaning in the black community that can compete with the concreteness of Dr. Street (or Not Dr. Street).

While I didn't see any of the student papers in their revised form, it seems plausible to me that the papers themselves may well have been a kind of catachrestic response to the essay question: one that the students attempted to understand through their own reality as expressed through their own language. The adjuncts I worked with at EC, then, were able to intellectualize Morrison using methods that didn't really account for what she was actually doing. From this point of view, it's not unreasonable to argue that the teachers themselves appeared to be *in the way* of the most effective pedagogy for these students. The irony of the students' apparent incapacity to see the text as an important cultural document of their own is redoubled in that their abilities to read and interpret the text might actually exceed those of their teachers. Put another way, the teachers might actually be entrapped in their New Critical (white) way of reading both Morrison and their student essays.

The irony—itself such an important concept in New Criticism—does not end there, because the presence of Morrison's text in the course in the first place was an attempt on the part of the writing program to be "inclusive." Also tentatively answered, then, was why I heard such frustration from students like Jose when he walked into workshop: their teachers don't assign books they are interested in, and the curriculum is not "diverse" enough. Both appeared to have their roots not in the choice of texts in the case of Morrison, but rather in how the texts themselves were being taught and interpreted by an adjunct faculty whose training had prepared them to expect a particular kind of reading and writing from students that did not connect the primary text with the students lived experiences in meaningful ways. That is to say, students were not encouraged to see the connections between their cultures and experiences and those of greater U.S. society since their responses to texts and their teachers may be formulated in ways unfamiliar to formal academic discourse. Morrison's text, then, becomes a kind of "classroomspeak" ostensibly there to demonstrate the absence of whiteness in its attempt to represent inclusiveness, but in effect demonstrating the ubiquitous presence of whiteness in the course through the classroom pedagogy deployed to teach it.

A similar form of classroomspeak multiculturalism is addressed by bell hooks in *Teaching to Transgress: Education as the Practice of Freedom*, where she outlines some elements of this pedagogy. She says:

> All too often [I] found a will to include those [texts] considered "marginal" without a willingness to accord their work the same respect and consideration given other work. . . . Individuals will often focus on women of color at the very end of the semester or lump everything about race and difference together in one section. This kind of tokenism is not multicultural transformation, but it is familiar to us as the change individuals are most likely to make. (38)

The form of multiculturalism suggested above involves race, class, and the institution's function to make middle-class citizens and has the compounding effect of making teachers miss key cultural referents that might make the text a more valuable learning instrument for students. Indeed, I think hooks' description is a corollary of the inability on the part of faculty to interrogate their pedagogical practice.

A CRISIS OF OVERPRODUCTION AND UNDERPREPAREDNESS IN ADJUNCT LABOR

Looking back at my discussion of the EC adjunct faculty, it may seem as if I didn't appreciate their efforts as teachers doing a difficult job. I did. I know many of them were committed and no doubt helped many students write better. But I see their position on campus as highly problematic not only because they had a difficult job, but also because I think it's symptomatic of larger structural issues having to do with the inability of rhetoric and composition to ever have really had a practical presence on college campuses for any sustained period of time. That is: when was the rhetoric and composition moment on college campuses? When, outside of the Ivy League—perhaps even including there—was a writing program ever fully staffed with formally trained rhetoric and composition writing teachers, not adjuncts who may have years of training in related fields, but are nevertheless not specialists?

Central to this question of rhetoric and composition specialists teaching in large enough numbers in writing programs is the crisis of the overproduction of PhDs generally, but especially in areas outside of rhetoric and composition. In the fall of 2010, I hired four PhDs and two ABDs in English to teach as adjuncts in the First-Year English program. None of them had a specialty in rhetoric and composition. All of them wanted full-time work but couldn't find any job openings in their specialties, which ranged from Victorian to Modern American literature. I believe this crisis is part and parcel of the economic structure of rhetoric and composition programs and represents a significant source of income for English departments and institutions of higher education generally as the demand for apparently qualified applicants to teach writing is kept low by the vast numbers of adjuncts there are to choose from.[5] From what I can tell, students suffer not because they don't have a trained English professor in the room, but because they don't have a trained English professor who understands the nature of writing as most rhetoric and composition specialists do. This is certainly the case at WU where about eighty percent of our First-Year Composition courses are taught by adjuncts in any given semester—not a rare occurrence at most institutions of higher education I'm aware of.

The lack of specialization in rhetoric and composition among the vast adjunct pool who teach in composition programs underscores the pedagogical and intellectual problems that suggest a kind of miscommunication between adjunct faculty, students, and the administration of the school. While these problems are centered on texts and pedagogy, they have implications that reach farther because of how they affect what students learn, how they learn it, and how the business and economics of learning reinforces a culture of whiteness.

WPAS, FRESHMAN COMPOSITION, AND THE WHITENING OF LANGUAGE

In my role as the Writing Program Administrator at WU, I am often surprised by the ironic similarity to conditions I left at EC. At WU, though, my location in the institution not only allows me to see the pedagogical contentions in the classroom, but also the administrative ones over the role, purposes, and uses of language in and around the writing program and the university. That is to say, the question isn't just what kind of language will be considered legitimate currency in the program and in the university, but also how that language should function to deliver education through writing instruction to students. Consider my thought process as I redesigned our first-semester freshman writing course for inclusion in our new university core curriculum recently in consultation with a colleague:

> *Course Description:* Students will produce essays in a variety of genres (such as autobiography or creative nonfiction) and rhetorical modes (such as argumentation or exposition) using writing to explore their personal experiences, observations, and ideas. Students will share their writing with their peers, receive

feedback on drafts, and revise as they progress through process-driven writing. This course may be organized thematically or rhetorically.

Course Objective: to enable students to develop expository essays exhibiting a coherent structure and, as appropriate, integrating research.

Course Outcome: Students develop pieces of expository writing that renders clearly the writer's experiences and observations, constructing logical arguments supported by secondary sources such as cited material obtained through research where appropriate.

This won't work! I don't want to antagonize the people who sit on the university core curriculum committees. I'll have to change this course outline... In the Course Description perhaps I can put the idea of argumentation and exposition *before* the mention of "autobiography and creative nonfiction" so as to minimize them as the committees read the proposal, and I can simply remove "personal experiences" and keep only "observations".

The outcome is too subjective as well...focuses too much on the students' experiences.... I need to frontload the idea of research so this outcome will appear more academic to the committees: less personal and about the student. So let's see...

Course Description: Students will produce essays in a variety of rhetorical modes (such as argumentation or exposition) and genres (such as autobiography or creative nonfiction) using writing to explore ideas, observations, and experiences. Students will share their writing with their peers, receive feedback on drafts, and revise as they progress through process-driven writing. This course may be organized either thematically or rhetorically.

Course Objective: to enable students to develop expository essays exhibiting a coherent structure and, as appropriate, integrating research.

Course Outcome: Students consult various sources presented in class to support their assertions or otherwise rigorously engage alternative arguments in their essays.

Writing this course description reminded me how conservative institutions of higher education in the U.S. actually are where language use is concerned, given their reputation in wider U.S. culture—and on university campuses themselves—as bastions of liberalism. This conservatism is mirrored in the gulf that I perceive to exist between teachers in disciplines outside of composition and rhetoric—and many situated awkwardly inside of it—over the nature of English composition: what it is, what it is supposed to do, or even what it is capable of doing, in a fifteen-week semester. What I hope is clear from the demonstration of the thinking process I went through to submit the English Composition course proposal to the various committees that will oversee the adoption of writing courses for the University Core Curriculum is that a significant amount of time was spent concerned with making sure the proposal got through their vetting processes, not because the course wasn't written with care, or because it's not of high quality, but rather because of my concern that they may not consider it academically rigorous enough. This concern with academic rigor is one of many complaints about First-Year English that's been consistent in the various schools where I have taught, and no doubt it's a complaint rhetoric and composition people hear in colleges and universities across the U.S. when there is concern that freshman English has not taught students how to write.

Working with adjuncts, talking to faculty members outside of the discipline of rhetoric and composition, and running a writing program have actually taught me to associate this criticism with the kinds of activities I see as vital in a freshman English writing course, namely the development of the students' own voices using their own, often nonstandard languages, and their ability to see their rhetoric as both academically significant and a material force that, with time, can actually be important to their academic and intellectual growth in whatever discipline they choose to study.

It was, in fact, refreshing to rethink First-Year Writing to fit the goals and objectives of the new core curriculum; revising the course reminded me of what these courses are capable of doing. This is especially true given the new curriculum's commitment to having students write at all levels of their involvement with it and in a variety of settings and genres that are both discipline and area based—the school's core curriculum is better and more rigorous because of this commitment, and the responsibility of writing will now be spread across all disciplines once a course proposal meets the requirements of a "Writing Intensive" course. However, I found the process of revising the proposal, as I describe above, troubling since I had to account for things that didn't have much to do with teaching students how to use language or writing in ways I thought were most effective, but was rather an exercise in how I could appease people who, as a set of committees, have a very different philosophy of writing, writing pedagogy, and language than I do. The changes that are detailed above, while they may appear minor—may in fact be minor—are nonetheless changes I felt compelled to make to satisfy my concern that I was giving voice to student language, and to satisfy what I perceived to be my audience's expectations. These changes, then, are indicative of the various roles English composition has come to play on the campus where I work and teach.

On the one hand, it is a course that is there to help prepare students for the rigorous academic writing they are expected to do in upper-level courses by foregrounding principles of New Criticism as I discuss earlier. Connected to this interpretive lens students are expected to adopt is the focus on direct grammar instruction, attention to form, convention, formal rhetorical modes, and the explicit use of a particular dialect: the white, middle-class English of the Northeast where I live. The pedagogy, which is most consistent with a current-traditionalist approach, as Lynn Bloom suggests in her essay "Freshman Composition as a Middle-Class Enterprise," is driven by the middle-class experiences of the teachers, and the mission of the institution to reproduce middle-class values (Bloom 656). The impulse toward middle-class values and writing instruction seems to make sense if we think about it in terms of the mostly middle-class faculty at EC and the suspicion of a colonial enterprise I had about the program. Successful completion of the program means successfully mimicking those who have mastered it. In the wholly racialized culture we live in, this means mimicking the mostly white middle-class values of the adjuncts, even if they themselves are not middle-class as is often the case with the adjunct pool at WU and elsewhere. It means, as David Bartholomae says in his essay, "The Tidy House: Basic Writing in the American Curriculum," imagining and re-creating the student as an incomplete version of ourselves and reconfirming existing patterns of power and authority, reproducing prevailing hierarchies (18).[6]

It also suggests a Platonic view of language similar to what Sharon Crowley and Debra Hawhee describe in their textbook, *Ancient Rhetorics for Contemporary Students*. Attributing this view to the influence of John Locke in Western thought, they identify it as a representative theory of language where, ". . . words represent thoughts and . . . the function of words [is] to convey the thinking of one person to another as clearly as possible" (22). They go on to point out that in this theory, "language is transparent . . . it lets meaning shine through it . . . [and] it assumes that language represents meaning, that it hands meaning over to listeners or readers, clear and intact" (22).

When I talk with people across my campus about writing, I am often confronted with this Platonic view of language that seems to insist on its essential ideological neutrality. Language, for instance, cannot be raced or classed; it is merely *there* available for students to learn if we in the writing program would only teach it. I believe that those current traditionalists among us in rhetoric and composition share this view of language explicitly or implicitly precisely because of this pedagogical model's focus on form at the expense of content. Such rhetoric in combination with the stranglehold of New Criticism is an important means through which "color-blind" whiteness maintains itself at the institutional level as I discuss in Chapter 6.

In this Platonic, current-traditionalist way of teaching, I see an uncanny alliance between the adjuncts that I have worked with and the power structure that exists on my university campus today. Both tacitly endorse an approach to writing pedagogy that seems unduly influenced by New Criticism's insistence on the objectivity of texts, and by extension, language.

On the other hand, as I imagine the course, it too prepares students for the rigorous academic writing they will do in upper-level courses and in other disciplines, but it does so through what might be called a sophist view of language where language is treated as the source of knowledge (Crowley and Hawee 23). In this view of language, as Crowley and Hawhee argue,

> . . . there is no absolute truth that exists separately from human knowledge. . . . contradictory truths will appear since everyone's knowledge differs slightly from everyone else's, depending on one's perspective and one's language. (23)

I believe the view of language I have adopted differs from my colleagues' in that in my approach students see language itself as a way of knowing: a place where they meet other languages of all kinds and begin to understand how flexible and useful the very notion of language can be for all kinds of learning. The notion of language as an ideological force is implicit in most things my students write, and I invite them to see their writing this way; as reflections of themselves and their experiences—personal and academic.

In Chapter 2 I discuss the ways in which the Basic Writing student is permitted a seat at the table of higher education in a mix of motives. Part of this mix has to do with the historical and present purposes of Basic Writing as a discipline and a project on college campuses. That is to say, in that chapter I begin a questioning of what, exactly, Basic Writing is supposed to do. I argue there that its ostensible purpose to teach underprepared students "how to write" is compromised by the class-based and racialized hierarchy of language that is endemic to academia.

Part of my objective in this chapter is to extend that discussion to comment on a series of fundamental miscommunications I believe exists among students, Writing Program Administrators, administrators of the institution, faculty, adjunct and otherwise, both inside and outside of rhetoric and composition, about what the course is and how it should be structured. If my previous chapter argued for a seat at the table of higher education for those who come to it with nonstandard dialects, then this chapter begins to question what happens to such students as they move through their writing course work.

SUBJECTIVITY, AND THE IRONY OF "PLACE" IN INSTITUTIONS OF HIGHER EDUCATION

My experiences at EC and at WU reveal my own ironic relationship to writing program administration even as it points to how these programs can get in the way of the most effective learning for students. For example, my critique of the adjunct faculty at EC who did not question their own pedagogy or why, exactly, their students might not be able to understand something like Morrison's *Song of Solomon* may seem to the casual observer equally applicable to the adjuncts who work with me in the writing program I direct at WU. My nuanced attempt to provide a place for student language in the course outlines, and the pedagogy I use in my own writing classrooms, may seem trivial compared to my paradoxical role as an architect and administrator of courses that are arguably unduly influenced by "the market". The paradox has allowed me to see the role of all the players in an institution more sympathetically, and I spend most of the space in the rest of this chapter contemplating how to make sense of the paradoxes.

Interpellation and "Place" in Writing Instruction

Luis Althusser identifies education as the most powerful ideological state apparatus (ISA) in practice and this may be one way of accounting for my own ironic place and, perhaps, the philosophical differences I see between me and some of the teachers I have worked with over the years.

For Althusser, "practice" has special significance since it is the process by which an ideology involves people—or subjects—in its reproduction. According to Althusser, subjectivities—the teacher, the student, or the WPA, are "always already" overdetermined and interpellated such that individual agency is practically impossible as it conforms to prevailing ideological dictates. This is certainly the case for adjunct faculty whose own position on college campuses as contingent labor must conform to what they perceive the wishes of the institution to be. The institution as rhetor, I would argue, is the most powerful "voice" the adjunct hears, and it is in this way that they and university administrators have common objectives which are often inconsistent with those of the WPA. Both endorse a pedagogy and a rhetoric that are in fact consistent with the dictates of the market and, as Althusser implies, ideological capitalism; the very system which has positioned both the administrators and the adjunct faculty as "subjects," and in the case of the adjunct, as specifically *contingent labor*. In the subject of the adjunct, then, we have a person who is quite often trained in the principles of New Criticism, frequently practices current-traditionalist writing pedagogy, and a person who *wants* to prepare students for "the market," if for no other reason but to ensure that they are hired again for the upcoming semester. We also have someone who, ironically, has been extraordinarily exploited by that very market-driven system their pedagogy appears to have so much faith in.

We might then identify what we do in higher education where minority students are concerned as getting them to "write white," and I suppose in some ways that is what I am implicitly arguing throughout this essay, but not because the writing itself—the particular form, rhetoric or structure—is essentially "white," it's because the political and ideological context that students are asked to produce this writing in is always already interpellated as white since this context historically privileges white cultural norms to the exclusion of, and in opposition to, the written and linguistic norms of racialized others. When black students mimic the kinds of writing we ask of them in these writing courses, they see it, I argue, as white and identify with it as such. They wittingly become part of a cultural system that pits their one subject position (whitened) against their other subject position (black) as might be exhibited in their nonstandard dialects.

In a sense, the revision of the Writing Program's course outline that I cite earlier, and even such things as the choice of texts that the program endorses, and the statement of our pedagogical philosophy are subsumed under the official discourse of the university, which pays very little attention to such matters in practice, unless they are grossly out of step with the institution's mission to reproduce white middle-class values. For example, the way my writing program is positioned in my institution permits me to hire highly educated individuals, often with degrees in English, but rarely with a specialization in rhetoric and composition as I discuss earlier. These hires often take place within the last week or so of the summer, just before the beginning of the new semester. I will hand the new hire a copy of our First-Year English Handbook, but I am by no means certain that they will read it, and if they've had experience teaching at other colleges or universities, I can be virtually certain that the syllabus they use at WU will be identical to the one they use at their other school. The practical aspects of adjunct work where they are often juggling six or seven courses at three or four institutions means that this kind of syllabus sharing is more often the case than not.

The vast numbers of adjuncts who teach in any particular program mean that they may be observed once in their first semester, and perhaps again in their second, but the labor-intensive work of observing all of them over the course of an academic year makes it likely that a particular adjunct may not be observed again for another year or two. Their task, then, is to ensure that their students *appear* to know how to write, and that they do not generate student complaints or bad evaluations. I say "appear to know how to write", because their pedagogy, which is often New Critical and current-traditionalist in its approach, as I have said, pays special attention to surface-level errors without necessarily addressing the notion of language in a deeply complex way. The effect is that the demand that students learn how to write from the institution is read by the adjunct as this New Critical current-traditionalist pedagogy, and they almost completely ignore the specialization in rhetoric and composition the WPA may have. The adjunct and the administration are of one accord, and the students' writing is never really addressed by those who have training in writing pedagogy.

In this way my place as a WPA is short-circuited by the structure of the writing program and how people come to work in it. My position as an administrator is an interpellated one where I appear to run the program, but where it is extraordinarily difficult to actually establish a coherent consistent philosophy that would govern it, the courses, and the adjuncts who teach in it. I become a function—a manager of teacher-student conflicts, grade disputes, and schedules. Ironically, I am often seen by adjuncts as a function of the institution, and by definition of the market. That is to say, it would not surprise me if many of the adjuncts who work for me see me in very similar ways as I see them in relation to the institution and the market. In a very real sense, then, adjuncts, WPAs, students, and institution administrators are always each other's audience and rhetor: always talking to each other, or should I say talking past each other?

WHITENESS, COMPOSITION, AND ARISTOTLE'S ENTHYMEME

I'd like to introduce Aristotle's enthymeme here for a couple of reasons. First, I want to take seriously the idea that the relevant players in an institution—students, teachers, administrators—actually do, to some extent, talk past each other and that this miscommunication has consequences. Second, and perhaps more importantly, I think the enthymeme provides a useful way of seeing how subject positionality is connected to whiteness in institutional practice as I argue throughout this essay, because it allows us to think of the various players or subjects in an institution rhetorically. That is to say, we can think of them in terms of rhetor, audience, language and power; we can probe how whiteness works to exploit gaps in communication.

The Enthymeme in Historical Context

Aristotle's enthymeme has, historically, been the subject of considerable debate. This is true not only for interpretations of his intent for the enthymeme, but also because of the way that it has come to be defined since his theorizing of it. The recent history of the enthymeme, and by recent I mean that occurring within the last half century or so, has seen its own interpretive complexities. These have been studied (or further complicated) by the likes of James C. Raymond, Lloyd Bitzer, Grimaldi, Walzer, P. J. Corbett, and others who struggle—often with each other—over the precise definition and meaning of the enthymeme and how best to assess its uses. Corbett, for instance, in his book, *Classical Rhetoric for the Modern Student*, argues that Aristotle intended the enthymeme to be the rhetorical equivalent of the syllogism where the conclusion and one of the premises are stated, while the other premise is assumed to be understood by the audience.[7]

I used a kind of enthymeme as described by Corbett in the revision of the course description I discuss earlier. In this case, the tentative conclusion is the belief that students will acquire college writing skills based on the probable premise of a current-traditionalist model of writing pedagogy. My understanding of the group of committees and the academic culture from which we all come prepared me to account for their biases and beliefs which, as I have argued, are connected to the economic market in complex and pedagogically problematic ways. I therefore used words that I thought might appeal to those people who may share those beliefs. I didn't say I wouldn't teach critical autobiography, I simply reversed the order that it appears in the course proposal. Also, I didn't say I wouldn't use students' autobiographical material as an important teaching tool, I simply omitted it. In this sense, I present enough material so as to imply a premise I know my audience (the committee members) wants to see, even though I know that it is not, perhaps, everything I intend for the course. The fact that the course in practice is likely to be taught by an overwhelming number of adjuncts and others who will share the committee's views on language aside, I've at least, in my limited way, provided an opportunity for an alternative interpretation of the course outline—or so I'd like to believe.

Corbett's view of the enthymeme competes with others. Raymond, for instance, in his essay, "Enthymemes, Examples, and Rhetorical Method," argues that the enthymeme, like the example, is fundamental to that part of rhetoric that treats demonstration, and he distinguishes it from other kinds of rhetoric accordingly. His essay points out that the two competing schools of thought on what the enthymeme is are inaccurate. Drawing on Lloyd Bitzer's work Raymond concludes that enthymemes are not syllogisms with a suppressed premise as some have argued, or a syllogism with a debatable premise as others have argued, but rather, Raymond suggests, its essence is its dependence upon premises drawn from the audience's presuppositions (Raymond 141). I read Raymond here approaching a definition of the enthymeme that seems consistent with the etymological roots of the word en (in) thymus (the mind, spirit, or body) because on the one hand his definition invites us to read the relationship between the audience and the rhetor as dialectical, and on the other he seems to account for the audience's ideological disposition.

Going back to my course description for a moment, it is clear that the changes I made were far from dramatic. In fact, the changes were more about what I didn't say than what I did. In omitting mention of practices that are more centered on student writing and language than on format and notions of correctness, I relied upon my audience's presuppositions: their desire to want to see our institution's writing courses functioning in a particular way with a particular writing pedagogy. It is therefore the role of the unstated premise as a stand-in for the audience's presuppositions that is most relevant to us in Raymond's formulation of the enthymeme because it is at this point that the rhetor's knowledge of his/her audience is tested and meaning is made.

If Raymond questions the long-standing competing definitions of the enthymeme to posit his own, Carol Poster, in her essay, "A Historicist Reconceptualization of the Enthymeme," moves the debate over the nature of the enthymeme a considerable distance further when she posits the notion that, in fact, we're asking the wrong kinds of questions when we seek to define the enthymeme.[8]

Poster's work on the enthymeme is important because it creates the possibility of a postmodern application of its uses: one that removes the need for a singular definition. If a singular definition is not at issue, then we are concerned not only with how the enthymeme may be the subject of subtle ideological shifts in meaning over time and through language as Poster suggests, but also the term's ability to describe how these shifts occur, embedded as they are in language, culture, history and inequality. Aristotle seemed to be pointing to this kind of complex understanding of the enthymeme when he called it "the substance of rhetorical persuasion," "the very body of proof" (*Rhetoric*, Book I, 1354a; Bizzell and Herzberg 179), and referred to it as the very mechanism by which to "address popular audiences" and "make the uneducated more effective [at charm[ing] the crowd's ears more finely (*Rhetoric*, Book II, 1395a xxii; Bizzell and Herzberg 225). The enthymeme, then, does double duty as both a subject that embodies the complexity of language and ideology, and a method of unraveling the complexities of language and ideology.

Building on Poster's work in his essay, "The Enthymematic Hegemony of Whiteness: The Enthymeme as Antiracist Rhetorical Strategy," Matthew Jackson posits a postmodern notion of the enthymeme where he argues that our culture supports a structure of white supremacy, in part, through many small but ideologically significant enthymemes that underscore an inherently racist social fabric. One example of this that he draws our attention to is as follows:

> I recently heard [Jack] Cafferty on CNN. . .asking viewers, 'Should Phoenix, Arizona police be able to enforce federal immigration laws?' In what Cafferty sees as 'another example of local governments getting serious about illegal aliens, while our so-called leaders in Washington continue to do nothing and in the process *compromise the nation's security*,' he has embedded a racist enthymeme wherein people of color are associated with a breach in national security (emphasis in reading of his delivery).
>
> I am not saying that a particular individual such as Cafferty or organization such as CNN is being intentionally racist. The point is that racist enthymemes can function to support arguments for white supremacy inconspicuously and indirectly. Such phrases, or 'fragments of discourse,' are examples of unfinished and under-examined arguments that we might hear on the radio, see on the television, read in the newspaper or on the internet. . . (606)

He goes on to argue for a postmodern understanding of the enthymeme that is adaptable for critical rhetorical and pedagogical strategies, informed by whiteness theory, to contest elusive arguments of white supremacy—arguments that are not always clear, logical, or syllogistic, but are yet persuasive. He continues, 'We the people' as an audience—especially whites and those invested in the privileges of whiteness—are in an enthymematic relationship with the hegemonic premises and claims of white supremacy where the unspoken goal is to maintain the structures of privilege (607–08). He concludes his piece by suggesting that as long as he remains silent he effectively gives tacit support and de facto consent to arguments for white supremacy (630).

When institutions of higher education and faculty who populate them argue for a writing pedagogy that marginalizes students' language, or otherwise positions it in opposition to dominant forms of pedagogical practice, they too participate in enthymemes of white supremacy. Just as Jackson did not argue that Cafferty was a racist, I am not arguing that these individual faculty members are intentionally racists, but I am suggesting that their stance on the role of language, and their use of New Criticism and current-traditionalist pedagogies in institutions of higher education, often participates in an enthymematic relationship with the hegemonic premises and claims of white supremacy where the unspoken goal is to maintain the unspoken structures of power and privilege.

COMPOSITION'S RACIALIZED ENTHYMEMES: WHITENESS, PEDAGOGY, AND PRACTICE

Institution as Rhetor

In many ways in the discussion above I've been describing how institutions speak to students. That is, how they are rhetors for students conceived as an audience in a particular way. In his famous essay, "The Writer's Audience Is Always a Fiction," Walter Ong begins by pointing out the important distinctions between audiences conceived by oral rhetors, and those conceived by writers showing that a writer's audience is necessarily fictionalized in ways a speaker's audience is not. Ong asks, "What do we mean when we say the writer's audience is always a fiction?" He suggests there are a least two responses to the question, but we are, for the moment, only concerned with the first. He says, "First, that the writer must construct in his imagination, clearly or vaguely, an audience cast in some sort of role . . ." (12).

While Ong here refers specifically to the relationship between a writer and his audience, it seems to me that the way an institution constructs its audience bears a similarity to both a speaker who has the immediacy of the audience's presence, and a writer who must contend with an audience that is distant both in time and space. That is, the nature of an institution's rhetoric exists between the two notions of audience Ong discusses. A practical example of this is that on occasion, the institution may write to its student body as a class or category of people, or may act in a particular way—priorities that make parking difficult for students, or a lack of dorm rooms, or administrative decisions about the quality of dining hall food—demonstrating action as symbolic language. Alternatively, the institution may speak specifically to a student—a professor who advises a specific student on what graduate program to attend or a reminder that a particular course requirement needs to be fulfilled. So the similarity between Ong's notion of audience for a writer and the notion of audience concerning the relationships between academic institutions, students, teachers, and administrators seem applicable at least some of the time. This is generally true beginning with the notion of "student as customer," but equally true in classroom pedagogy as I've attempted to demonstrate in this essay. Even when students are asked to write autobiographical essays, or opinion papers, for instance, these assignments are not unmitigated by the institution—as represented by the teachers who have imagined constructions of who the students are, what the objective should be with respect to how they need to be changed, and what to expect from their work.[9] That is to say, the institution as speaker or rhetor constructs an image of its audience—the student—to suit its needs, sometimes at the expense of the needs of the students themselves. This is consistent with an enthymeme where the audience's presuppositions stands in for the unstated premise as described by Raymond.

For example, the institution must be committed to market-driven forces since it is, in many respects, subject to the market, and to preparing students to function in that market. In a sense, the institution must help to change students into what the market requires regardless of what the student may want or need, which is arguably an institution that will help in the fulfillment of ideological, political, and intellectual freedom, no less than economic freedom. The act of educating the student itself becomes one of submission to a market that cannot guarantee any of these.

Rather than bridge race and class gaps, then, institutions are often disposed to exploiting them. For example, not only is Basic Writing an apartheid formulation as I've discussed in Chapter 2, it is also an extremely profitable one populated primarily with minority students and taught overwhelmingly by adjunct faculty. Similarly, not only is passing the "gate" of freshman Composition a requirement for all college freshman in accredited institutions of higher education today, it is also raced and classed in particular ways as this essay demonstrates. There is a parallel to the institution's rhetoric. What happens when students talk back to the institutions and their teachers? How might they do this?

Engaging Whiteness: Students as Rhetors

My students have produced some remarkable writing that comments directly on the role and uses of writing instruction in higher education, and the ways in which it often reinforces dominant practices, that exposes whiteness in composition. I have written elsewhere of Hykine Johnson,[10] a student of mine some years ago who wrote the poem which appears below. The poem was sent out to the entire college community, including the board of governors, faculty, staff, and administration. He was subsequently reprimanded and eventually asked not to return to campus not least because of the distribution of his poem. In my view the poem represents a "talking back" to the rhetoric of the institution. He is responding to his experience of two semesters in school where he was largely unsuccessful in his academic pursuits and is now, through the poem, expressing his gratitude for being allowed to remain in school, though on a provisional basis. The poem is also both an explicit and implicit expression of how frustrating and difficult life on the streets and life in school are and, in particular, the poem is an expression of how frustrating navigating these two worlds is for him. Walter Ong suggests in his second point regarding the fictionalized nature of the audience that it must not only be fictionalized by the author, but "[it] . . . must correspondingly fictionalize itself". He continues, "A reader has to play the role in which the author has cast him, which seldom coincides with his role in the rest of his actual life" (12). It is this recasting which is evidenced and struggled with in Hykine's poem. He is, in many respects, attempting to re-create himself in the role the institution has cast for him: a role that is raced in that he must mimic whiteness, and classed in that he must mimic middle-classness. Here's what he says:

SHIT IS HARD. . . . .
MY LIFE IS HARD,
YOU WILL NEVER FIND A NIGGA THAT WILL SAY THAT
    HE PULLED MY CARD, I WISH THAT I COULD FIND
    ANOTHER WAY,
THAT IS HOW I GREW UP WHAT CAN I SAY, FUCK THE
    STREETS NOW I'M TRYING SCHOOL, IF I FUCK WITH
    THE STREETS I WILL BE A FOOL,
PEOPLE SAYING BLACK POWER , BLACK POWER ,
IF WE DON'T PULL TOGETHER OUR DREAMS OF BLACK
    POWER WILL BE SOUR,
TAKE IT FROM SOMEBODY FROM THE STREETS,
SOME PEOPLE IS NOT FEELING ME THIS SHIT IS DEEP,

Hykine's poem uses racialized enthymemes which reveal how whiteness functions and shapes student discourse in institutions. His unmistakable message in the poem is his willingness to try school though he still seems torn between it and his street life, as indicated by "I'm trying school" and its tone which seems both conciliatory and knowing. He is *for* the academy, *for* school, and anti-street life because he knows what street life holds for him. He recognizes urban street life and life in school as two very different things, and in this respect his poem represents a cross-cultural document where he tries to communicate to the campus community, which he sees as alien to him and his experiences.

Also significant here, however, is Hykine's knowledge of himself as an 'Other.' I understand his poem as an example of what Mary Louise Pratt has called autoethnographic writing: writing in which "people undertake to describe themselves in ways that engage with representations others have made of them" (35). In this way, Hykine is participating in the Du-Boisian notion of "double-consciousness" which Catherine Prendergast suggests, because of its specifically racialized history, "should not be manufactured in the composition classroom" (46). This is perhaps because there are limits to what we can expect to happen in terms of "white awareness" in our institutions. Still, it seems to me that Hykine recognizes this cultural two-ness, and uses the enthymeme, along with other rhetorical devices, to begin his relationship with academia anew. Hykine was indeed on the borderland between school life and street life, and he no doubt saw the stark contrasts between the two; his poem reflects a certain kind of knowledge he knows his audience has of street life. He enacts the pathos embedded in the essence of the enthymeme as a rhetorical strategy to pull his audience in. This is most obviously established by his unqualified use of the phrase *the streets*, but particularly his use of it in the last two lines "Take it from somebody from the streets, some people is not feeling me this shit is deep." The key here is that his audience *is* "feeling" him, and they do know what the streets represent precisely because of the way the enthymeme works through dependence upon a suppressed premise. In this case that premise is the social consciousness of anyone familiar with northwestern New Jersey and its proximal relationship to Newark as a specifically African-American place, and Hykine's hometown.

Pratt's essay is also useful because while the poem itself boldly displays the language of "street life," the form and theme demonstrate a preference for school life. It is an attempt on his part to reach out to the college on its own terms or what he sees as its own terms. Just as the institution and the pedagogy of the faculty rely on assumptions about what its audience, the students, need so too does Hykine make assumptions about his audience, the entire college community, regarding his poem. The college community does not focus attention on the element of his poem that demonstrates he is anti-street life and pro-school life, though parts of the poem explicitly state just that. He depends on us paying attention to these facts for his poem to have the desired effect of allowing people to see that he has made a commitment to school and he sees himself as an artist, an author and a poet. His *language* instead took center stage in the poem which called the wrath of the administration down upon him. In a sense, Hykine invoked an enthymeme that was both beyond his control and one that was racially charged. He did not know enough about the academic community that he was communicating with and therefore committed the *faux pas* that was his poem.

From the next e-mail he sent out we might be able to assess the institution's response to him. He says:

> This Hykine Johnson I'm sorry if my poem caused any problems I shouldn't have used the word that I did. And I'm sorry, and it will not happen again. I just was expressing myself I didn't want to cause problems Hykine Johnson (Johnson).

Someone obviously made him write this retraction and in so doing attempted to overlay the institution's values on Hykine and his language. He was censored because he did not approach the institution in a manner it could process into white middle-class discourse. In an interview I had with him he says as much. When asked why he thought he was reprimanded he said, "I wrote from my heart, and from what I feel, and I guess it just was not good enough for them" (phone interview).

"White" Student as Rhetor

If market-driven forces implicitly expressed in institutional rhetoric have an effect on African-American students like Hykine that is visible because of his language and experiences, they have an equally powerful effect on white working-class students who are invisible for the same reason. That is to say, white—particularly working-class—students are often invisible in large measure because of their ability to better approximate middle-class language and culture, but they're no less vulnerable because of these same forces. Just as the white working-class students were made invisible by the media coverage of the crises surrounding Open Admissions at CUNY,[11] so too are they made invisible—constructed and spoken to as "normal," middle-class students by the institution.[12] Consider, for instance, the following essay written by a third-year writing student in my critical writing class in the fall of 2010. She is white, and in many respects the position she articulates is invisible to the institution precisely because of her working-class identity as her essay makes abundantly clear. Here's her essay in full:

Inferiority in the Lower Class: Maintaining a Contrivance
By Amanda

I was born into a working-class family. My mother grew up in Passaic, New Jersey, and my father had his roots in Union City, New Jersey. They were both the product of low-income families, my mother and her three siblings crammed into a small apartment with her mother and father and my father residing in one equally small with his four siblings and their parents. Neither were educated much past high school: my father graduated in 1964 and was an electrician by trade, my mother dropped out at the age of sixteen, later receiving her GED and getting a certificate in computer software training. They both struggled to scrape up enough money to pay for a house, food and utilities. In a period that happens some time before my memories formed, my father was forced to stop working due to disabilities. Our family depended on my mother to make the money that would support us, a difficult feat as she was continually cycling through jobs. Just when it appeared she had secured a decent job with benefits and a living wage, there would be problems within the company and she would be laid off.

Eventually, my parents could no longer afford the house our family lived in. They fell behind in payments and the bank foreclosed on their mortgage. My parents, my brother and I were effectively homeless. Despite our economic troubles, the words "you have to go to college" were a constant refrain throughout my childhood. My parents had me thinking about Ivy League universities before I graduated from elementary school. They both keenly felt that their lack of higher education was what kept our family from economic success and were convinced that I had to be the one rescuing my family: the first to graduate from college, the first to live comfortably without worrying about money. Unfortunately, having grown up in a lower social class ensured that I will probably worry about money and employment to some degree for my entire working career, regardless of the education I am receiving. A distrust of the American economy and educational system has marked me as different than many of my peers. I take my part time job far more seriously than the people I work alongside. I put up with inequity because I am frozen by the awareness that I need a paycheck combined with the learned belief that few jobs, or perhaps just no job that I could procure, will prove to be a stable source of employment or income.

In Studs Terkel's recording of C.P. Ellis, a lower-class ex Ku Klux Klan member, Ellis notes "I always left school with a sense of inferiority. The other kids had nice clothes. I just had what my Daddy could buy. I still got some of those inferiority feelin's now that I have to overcome once in awhile" (389). For Ellis, the shame of being poor and belonging to a lower socio-economic class than his peers has translated into adulthood. While he is no longer the child on the playground wearing the worn-out clothing, he recognizes that these instances of feeling different from his peers has shaped his continuing feelings that he is somehow worth less than his current, adult peers. This same inferiority is consistently bred in people belonging to the lower classes. The consumerist values in American society have increasingly set up the understanding that to be of worth, one must own nice clothes, a beautiful dwelling, an expensive and a flashy car. It goes without saying that citizens with low paying jobs cannot afford many luxuries, and therefore understand themselves to be of less worth than citizens of a higher economic class. Naturally, these feelings of inferiority translate from dismay over a lack of buying power into feelings of inferiority over educational level, job skills and job prospects. My parents could not hold down jobs, so it now stands to reason that my own ability to hold down a steady job is in jeopardy. It matters little how much effort I put into my dead-end job; how reliable I am or how seriously I take company policy. While I am not consciously thinking that my roots in the lower class make me inferior to my middle and wealthy class peers, my actions and other thought patterns suggest that I do believe in this innate inferiority to some extent. My mother was laid off from several jobs through no fault of her own so I have internalized the fear that our family is expendable. Now that I have a job of my own, I am fastidious about being on time, working hard, and never calling out on a shift even when I am sick. These sound like all the traits of a good employee, but they are the result of my constant worry that I will lose my job if I do not do everything perfectly.

This worry is not assuaged by the thought that I will get a "real" job after college, a sentiment expressed by many of my friends. When I contemplate it, I worry that I will not get a "real" job. I worry that retail work will become my "real" job despite a college education. Spoken from the mouths of my parents, college was inevitable. Having a college degree meant that you were worthwhile. There were no other options, no skilled trades. I would go, and there would be no talk of financial aid, or how many thousands of dollars in loans I would accrue before I graduate. However, I do not share their faith in education, especially in the faltering economy. I am close to graduating college now, the first in my family to do so, yet this achievement seems to amount to nothing but a massive debt. This sense of powerlessness over my economic situation is commonly shared by lower class citizens. It is the same powerlessness that prompted C.P. Ellis to join the Ku Klux Klan. He notes 'I can understand why people join extreme right-wing or left-wing groups. They're in the same boat I was. Shut out. Deep down inside, we want to be part of this great society. Nobody listens, so we join these groups' (391). Not every person of a low socio-economic status seeks such an extreme outlet to gain power and vent their frustration, but there is always that lingering feeling that, as individuals, they do not matter in society. The belief that one has no control over the ability to improve their circumstances is prevalent, resulting in new generations of Americans who perpetuate the same cycle of poverty as their parents because they do not have hope for a better future. They do not believe, as I scarcely believe, that education will grant them access to better jobs and greater job security. Even more insidiously, people of the lower classes have been convinced that they are not deserving of better jobs; that they must be lacking in some essential quality that their wealthier counterparts possess.

I relate to my social class through a shared sense of general discouragement. I am well educated and intelligent but I hold little hope for my economic prospects after college. I dread retail work, yet feel resigned to it. These feelings have been fostered in an entire group of people by those who stand to benefit from maintaining the poor economic, educational and health standards of the lower class. They were created by wealthy business owners who rely on feelings of inferiority to ensure that they will always have workers that will tolerate jobs with unlivable wages and no benefits. As long as the lower class continues to operate under the assumption that they cannot achieve or do not deserve a better life, the higher classes will be able to maintain their wealth by profiting from poverty. C.P. Ellis ended up going back to school, furthering his education, overcoming racism, and becoming a union leader. Unfortunately, not every person of the lower class is able to see past the constraints of the social structure into which they were born. Everything seems rigid and predetermined though the feelings of inferiority experienced by people like C.P. Ellis, like myself, have been synthesized by outside forces. We are all operating under a world view created solely for the advantage of the wealthy elite.

If Hykine deploys enthymemes to expose the stark contrasts between his two lives for his audience, which is his institution of higher education, Amanda exposes the enthymemes of unfulfilled settled expectations for the audience of hers. That is to say, one way of reading Amanda's essay is to argue that if you are white, go to school, get good grades, and master a particular dialect as she has pretty much done, then, the syllogism goes, you'll be competitive in the market place and get a job. Amanda's essay, then, exposes not just the whiteness embedded in enthymemes deployed by academic institutions, but also the whiteness that is embedded in an economic system that these institutions participate in. In this way Amanda's essay may be seen as an example of an "injured whiteness" as discussed in Robyn Wiegman's essay, "Whiteness Studies and the Paradox of Particularity"[13] where the economic system is unable to meet the settled expectations of white identity.[14]

Amanda wrote this essay in response to a unit organized around the idea of social class. My objective in selecting the readings for the unit was to establish a way for the group to talk about what social class is, how we as a group might experience it, and how we might want to relate it to aspects of our lives. The students generated the questions for the writing assignments, and Amanda chose to write on the question "Discuss your understanding of your social class in relation to one of the readings we've discussed so far this semester." Amanda chose to use, as a touchstone for her essay, Studs Terkel's "C.P. Ellis," a personal interview conducted by Terkel of Ellis, an ex-Klan member who becomes a social activist through his relationship with Ann Atwater, an African-American he met and worked with on a community project.

Her use of Ellis is significant because in many ways she models her essay on Ellis, who plays out the characteristics of an injured white identity that is rehabilitated through class solidarity, and through an invocation of the rhetoric of the civil rights movement of the 1960s, as Wiegman suggests is one of the rhetorical maneuvers available to whites who wish to reclaim, or otherwise make whole, their whiteness (Wiegman 146). Like Ellis, Amanda identifies herself as specifically working-class—which is an implicit rejection of the interpellated version of herself as middle-class that the rhetoric of the institution in its policies endorses—and she is injured by a faltering economy and the breach of the promises higher education was supposed to provide, which is, paradoxically, middle-class security. That is, she enunciates a clearly defined sense of exploitation on the basis of her class identity. She is a working-class woman, and she is coming to realize (like millions of others just like her around the U.S.) that no matter how well she prepares herself via schooling/education, the job(s) she imagined for herself may not be there for her. Her middle-class aspirations (beyond mere social climbing) may be out of her grasp for the long run as a result of regional and national developments outside her control.

History tells us that Ellis apparently rejected his white identity through praxis. What happens to him can't happen just from going to college; there was a sustained commitment to community action which seems to repudiate differential treatment in favor of equality and universal class advancement—an extraordinarily difficult and risky achievement for someone who lived in the deep South proclaiming allegiances with antiracist, pro-union political agendas. I wonder what Amanda might do since, in some ways, her essay ends at a time—her junior year and place—she's still in school—that does not afford us clear answers.

I use Amanda's essay here not to expose her as someone who somehow craves white identity at all costs. I know her well enough to know better. Rather, I wish to demonstrate the irony embedded in whiteness because of a failure of rhetoric in this culture as presently organized to clearly articulate positions outside of it. I was initially drawn to Amanda's essay because I saw it first and foremost as a "talking back" to an institution that had made implicit promises to her that it cannot fulfill. In this way, I see her text as a kind of complement to Hykine's poem where between them the complex and messy business of race and class are made more complicated by the way each of them engage institutional whiteness.

If I had the opportunity to work with Hykine again, I might introduce him to the work of people like Victor Villanueva, Gloria Anzaldua, and Keith Gilyard—all of whom had to reclaim their marginalized identity by writing personal biographies, which they made public. The act of writing in mixed dialects as they do (and making that writing public) freed them to write and present selves that were acts of resistance by definition. There's a limit to how critical institutional literacy can be, but these scholars show the way for people like Hykine, where the clash between "street and academy" has potential for being transformational in ways they do not for people like Amanda.

Amanda's essay presents a different set of problems, far more difficult to contend with in many ways. Her legitimate claim to the security she craves seems most easily secured through her appeal to whiteness as an injured identity, which, it seems to me, implicates people like Hykine because of its inherently exclusionary nature. That is to say, there's a certain kind of strength in seeing the two texts as a "talking back" to institutions they are each alienated from. This extends to life outside of school, in the economic market, where Amanda, despite her pessimism nevertheless has better job prospects than Hykine because of her language and proximity to middle-class cultural capital. The task would be to find a language—a rhetoric—for Amanda that successfully confronts this irony in whiteness.

5 Moving Whiteness
Rhetoric and Political Emotion[1]

> The emotional struggles against injustice are not about finding good or bad feelings, and then expressing them. Rather, they are about how we are moved by feelings into a different relation to the norms that we wish to contest, or the wounds we wish to heal. Moving here is not about "moving on," or about "using" emotions to move away, but moving and being moved as a form of labour or work, which opens up different kinds of attachments to others, in part through the recognition of this work *as* work.
>
> Sara Ahmed (201)

When I teach *Heart of Darkness*, I often introduce students to Chinua Achebe's well-known "An Image of Africa," an essay in which Achebe denounces Conrad as a "thorough-going racist" and dismisses his liberal ideology with its effective erasure of Africa. Upon reading Achebe's argument, many white students will invariably try to undermine his indictment by claiming he is applying later moral standards to earlier work or that Conrad's intentions were not to write a racist book (even if he ended up doing so). All of these arguments, which indeed have intellectual merit, can be engaged and countered—as Achebe does—and I ask students to read this essay precisely because of the questions his critique raises about liberalism as well as narrative theory. But what strikes me is how fervent and invested students become in defending a book that, prior to seeing Achebe's essay, many of them read with thinly veiled indifference. As I remind them of their earlier disinterest in Conrad, I ask them how they account for so impassioned a defense of a work they didn't even like. The question, unanswerable it seems, often draws embarrassed smiles and shrugged shoulders.

What occurs to me is that such intellectual sparring, the very stuff of academic exchange, may be beside the point. For to ignore the emotional dimensions of this discussion, I think, is certainly to miss a good portion of what the argument may really be about: the *emotional stake* that these students have in their whiteness. But ignore it is precisely what pedagogical propriety will push us to do: circumvent the emotion and focus on reason-ableness of argument. To do otherwise would seem to take us into an area that is off-limits—the realm of affect, which, as we all know, is present in the college classroom even as we avoid acknowledging it, almost as assidu-ously as we might avoid the mention of bodily functions. To transgress that boundary would produce, both in students and teacher, a sense of embarrassment and a feeling of privacy violation. We have a certain right to meddle with each other's intellects but not our emotions or bodies, the professional rights to which are owned by psychotherapeutic and medical discourses, respectively.[2] Thus whiteness too comes to enjoy a right to privacy in our classrooms, tied as it is to emotional being and even *bodily* integrity when that whiteness serves as a fundamental source of identity, whether acknowledged or not. To disrupt whiteness will necessarily mean to interfere with its emotional sovereignty.

The spirited emotional response that the students have to Conrad and Achebe is of a different order than the disengaged one that I describe in Chapter 3, in which students practice a passive withdrawal from what they think will be hackneyed recitations of liberal whiteness's obligatory disavowal of racism. Here we see what might be the flip side of that coin. Instead of dismissal, the opposite reaction is provoked in students who might otherwise be content in a protective armor of apathy. Perhaps, however, the responses are not mutually exclusive. In a recent classroom discussion of Alan Gribben's proposed edition of *Huck Finn* and the controversy surrounding the replacement of the word "nigger" with "slave," I observed what seemed like an alternating mixture of indifference and passion as students, in a threaded discussion, defended Twain's book against censorship and bowdlerization (a book most of them hadn't read) even as they wanted to move away from having the discussion at all, proclaiming the very existence of such a controversy "ridiculous."[3] From what perspective, I wonder, is it ridiculous to consider this question? What is "ridiculous" shorthand for? Is ridiculousness here dismissal of yet another scripted speech on race, or is it a vehemence that defends intractable whiteness? (And I'm aware of my own emotional response here—my impatience with their impatience; my trepidation over the looming encounter with whiteness.) Is it the general cultural presumption at work here that debate, controversy are bad things that the good manners of whiteness bid we avoid? Is it a silent, invisible whiteness I'm encountering, normalized and blind to its entitlement? Is it a bored disengaged whiteness that senses and recoils from political correctness? How invested are the students in that "ridiculous"? Is it provocation or retreat? One woman who argued against teaching the edited version invoked arguments about authenticity and said the original book provided the occasion to teach us about the history that we had progressed and moved on from. As it turned out, she was one of the few who had read the book and had done so in seventh-grade English. Had the class discussed the book in the context of that history that she mentioned? I asked. No, she said. I asked her what she had thought about the ubiquitous word "nigger" in the text. Her reply: she hadn't noticed it.

I wonder how it is possible that a twenty-first-century reader doesn't notice a text replete with racial epithets. Is it a sign of racist kitsch or racialized camp: the obliviousness of white entitlement or the postironic acceptance of the word in a hip-hop saturated youth climate? But I wonder also what motivates this wide swing from "not noticing" to a strong defense of "history." The learned dynamics of classroom debate itself may tend to produce such stilted rhetoric where "to discuss" means to find a position, occupy, and defend it. (Even my presenting the "debate" to the class in this way—as something that requires taking a side—contributes to this phenomenon, so that whiteness piggybacks on a larger cultural framework.) The intellectual arguments themselves about Gribben's book seem circular and, in the end, unimportant, in both the blogosphere and the classroom as various "sides" martial evidence and rationales. It's easy enough, after all, to assert the inviolability of authenticity and authorial intention—and white people are by no means alone in laying claim to these positions. At the end of the day, those may in fact be the correct arguments. But such debating logic doesn't tell us enough about why we bother to debate at all, the complicated amalgam of emotions and affect that attach to and drive the exchanges, that make us care—or not care. What I wish to discuss here are not the relevant intellectual merits of such discussions but rather the nature of their emotional valences in relation to whiteness. The question becomes not who is right or wrong in terms of literary theory, but rather why the answers matter—or don't matter—to us. "By attempting to state that which was formerly unstated" (Ratcliffe, "In Search" 284) in such exchanges we reveal for ourselves and our students the "emotioned rules" (Seibel-Trainor, *Rethinking*) of normative whiteness and open up the potential for confronting them.

In the last decades, an efflorescence of whiteness studies has "focused on race by uncovering, interrogating, and theorizing whiteness as a largely unacknowledged but . . . vastly important rhetorical and epistemological system" (Miller 199), a system which needs to be interrogated lest, as Coco Fusco says, its invisible normativity "redouble its hegemony by naturalizing it."[4] The underlying rationale of much of this work is the belief, "a premise of 'first-wave' white critique" (Hill 243), that turning the gaze of critical race theory toward this previously unacknowledged racialized identity of whiteness can produce better understanding of its oppressive and insidious construction. The hope is that whiteness studies can help move us through a morass of liberal multiculturalism—politically correct and toothless— toward a more radical, more "disturbed" understanding of the ontology[5] of race and its relation to lived experience by implicitly requiring a recognition and moral accounting from those whose existence is steeped in the phenomenon of whiteness. But how has and how will such a project proceed? Specifically, how will we move from acknowledgment or visibility to praxis and change? For as we saw in Chapter 1, the well-meaning efforts of white people to interrogate their whiteness as often as not have become complicit in that whiteness despite an aim toward revealing and dismantling the normative grip of whiteness and racism.[6] Likewise antiracist educators, as discussed in Chapter 3, continue to be frustrated in their attempts to move students out of whiteness. If whiteness studies and their contribution to critical pedagogy's antiracist agenda have not lived up to expectations, what exactly has gone wrong? More specifically, what is the nature of the gap that exists between awareness and change?

Jessie Daniels implicitly poses such questions about whiteness studies and the scholars and writers who produce it when she observes that "The difficulty I see with what the authors offer in terms of praxis is that they rely on an appeal to the reasonableness and well-intentioned nature of whites—who will see that this [whiteness] is a waste and stop. . . . *Their* [the authors'] *own evidence, however, contradicts this. . .*" (203, emphasis added).[7] The appeal to reason and good intentions that Daniels so skeptically wonders about may well be said to be problematic not only for discussions of racism but, in general, for the approach that critical pedagogy has adopted in its efforts to focus education on social change. Starting from the assumption that the classroom is never an ideologically neutral space, the critical or radical pedagogue seeks to disrupt hegemonic discourses precisely by drawing attention to their potent normativity, a goal in common with critical race theorists' insistence on race-conscious intervention. As such, the critical study of whiteness is not only an inevitable outgrowth of CRT but also an essential component of liberatory education's attempt to reveal to students how whiteness looms large in the worlds they inhabit.[8] But too often the tacit operative assumption is that arming students with the "facts" about the inequities of their societies will give them the necessary motive to become critical social agents. This assumption is consistent with a view of political theory whose "proponents seek to persuade by argument directed at rational beings and see political actors as driven chiefly by rational motives such as norms of justice or economic self-interests" (Koziak 4). In effect, North American traditions of critical/radical pedagogy have privileged a rhetoric of *logos* (and, to some extent, *ethos*) while giving short-shrift to what Aristotle referred to as "those feelings which so change men as to affect their judgments": emotions. Take, for example, Julie Lindquist's characterization of critical treatments of class in composition pedagogy where instructors

> urge students to see how cultural products participate in processes of social saturation and train them to be skeptical of the apparent naturalness of everyday life. In general, pedagogies informed by critical and cultural theory have treated class less as a complex affective experience than as a set of social issues to be addressed through systematic analysis. . . . [Such] approaches work by attempting to change students' understanding of how class operates . . . (190)

In their discussion of critical pedagogy's neglect of the affective dimension of education, Dale Jacobs and Laura Micciche, editors of the collection *A Way to Move: Rhetorics of Emotion*, contrast this omission with the emphasis Paulo Freire, ironically a strong influence on North American pedagogy, places on emotion in the critical process: "Knowing for me is not a neutral act, not only from the political point of view, but from the point of view of my body, my sensual body. It is full of feelings, of *emotions* . . ." (6, emphasis added). As suggested in Jesse Daniels' observation about the difficulty of disrupting whiteness, attempts to confront white racism often evolve around a *logos*-centered epistemology devoid of the emotional considerations that Aristotle and Freire appear to identify as essential to the project of human knowing. Christine Sleeter sums up this approach as one where: "Prejudice and misperception can be corrected by providing information. With more information, white people will abandon racist ideas and behaviors and (presumably) work to eliminate racism" (158). According to Sleeter, such "psychological" conceptions are flawed because, lacking in structural analysis, they stem from a liberal premise that assumes racism is an illogical discourse fixable through the rationality of individuals. Such approaches do not recognize that "White people's commonsense understandings of race" represent their group's "vested interest in justifying their power and privileges" (158).

Many researchers and theorists such as Sleeter point to the inability of white people to interrogate the racism inherent in whiteness or to effect any change in white hegemony. Sleeter concludes, and perhaps quite rightly, that little can come from this line of endeavor, for she sees the supposed irrationality of whiteness as being, on the contrary, what Seibel-Trainor describes as white people's very "rational understanding of their socioeconomic interests" ("Critical" 632). Janine Jones also acknowledges the rationality of whiteness: "If a white person applies rules in some special way when it comes to blacks it is because his reason *is* well intact. For his way of reasoning may help him achieve his practical goals, which are of primary interest to him, even if it falls short of his ideals" (65). Thus the invisibility of whiteness is no mere oversight but instead a hegemonic technology of "ignorance" where "white discourse," in "refusing to name and undo its own innocence, . . . silently screams its collusion in perpetuating racist discourse" (Curry 15). But despite its "rationality," whiteness does indeed contain an affective dimension, apparent and often remarked, but perhaps insufficiently theorized. bell hooks, for example, mentions the "disbelief, shock, and rage" (*Essential* 20) and the "amazement" (21) white people evince when their whiteness is critically scrutinized. She uses the phrase "deep emotional investment" to describe the attitude of whites toward maintaining the "mystery" of whiteness.

A view of whiteness as "rationally emotional" is consistent with ongoing scholarship that refigures emotion—from private, isolated, internal event to, instead, cultural discourse that is normative and that yields itself up to rhetorical analysis, what Ahmed refers to as the "sociality" of emotion, in which we see "emotion as social form, rather than individual self-expression" (9). Although often popularly regarded as solely an idiosyncratic or personal physiological response, emotion and affect in contemporary scholarship have been understood as "social, cultural, political and historical" (Abu-Lughod and Lutz 18), conceivable not only in terms of interiority but "as a form of social action that creates effects in the world, effects that are read in a culturally informed way by the audience for emotion talk" (12) and that contain "power relationships otherwise partially concealed" (Stearns and Stearns 14) when the social aspects of emotion are unexamined. Emotions are a language through which we communicate and make meaning—with ourselves and with others; emotions are products and vehicles of culture. Understandable as social and discursive phenomena, they are very much part of the domain of rhetoric, and not merely as poor adjuncts to reason. Indeed, reexamination of classical conceptions of emotion, such as Aristotle's theory of emotional rhetoric, suggests a blurring of boundaries between *logos* and *pathos* where the latter "has a sort of rationality" (Walker 81) and that "the moods of rational assent and dissent . . . emerge from within existing affects" (83). Thus rhetoric laid an early claim to the now popular notion of "emotional intelligence."

In failing to account adequately for emotion and affect, "antiracist educators have misplaced their energy" (Seibel-Trainor, *Rethinking* 3) into rational analysis and persuasion, and a rhetorical study of emotion is integral to critical pedagogy's efforts to disrupt "the vastly important rhetorical and epistemological system" that critical race theory has shown whiteness to be. Coupling the emerging rhetorics of emotion with whiteness studies' insights into racism can help us map the "mystery" of whiteness as it structures social consciousness and perhaps, ultimately, provide a means for rhetorical "restructuring," as we take into account the political dimension of our emotional responses. As Lynn Worsham has argued, "the work of decolonization must occur at the affective level, not only to reconstitute the emotional life of the individual but also, and more importantly, to restructure the feeling or mood that characterizes an age" ("Postal" 216). Here she is effectively calling for what Aaron David Gresson continues to refer to as "emotion work" (98). A look at what Henry Giroux has called a "pedagogy of whiteness" will demonstrate how a study of emotion as rhetorical system can abet the efforts of critical pedagogues such as Giroux by taking on the "emotion work" of whiteness.

In his promotion of "a pedagogy of bafflement that takes whiteness and race as an object of serious debate and analysis," Giroux acknowledges the reluctance of white students to engage in such processes and advocates an examination of resistance "for the knowledge it yields, the possibilities for exploring its silences and refusals" (308) and further suggests that students "be offered a space marked by dialogue and critique in which they can engage, challenge, and rearticulate their positions by analyzing the material realities and social relations of racism" (309). His last remarks epitomize the important and laudable goals and methodologies of the radical educator. And Giroux acknowledges the emotional dimension of the task: "making white students responsive to politics of racial privilege is fraught with the fear and anger that accompany having to rethink one's identity" and that we need to engage students in "fostering less a sullen silence or paralyzing guilt and more a sense of outrage" (309). Despite this acknowledgment of the crucial role of emotion in political and ethical development, Giroux's pedagogy implicitly steers us away from attention to affective response when he suggests that the way to navigate this emotional minefield is by "Making whiteness rather than white racism the focus of study" in order to handle the outpouring of emotion that ensues when white privilege is confronted. What he calls "an important pedagogical strategy" is for all intents and purposes a strategy of emotional diffusing in favor of logos-based analysis where the emotions of whiteness are sidestepped through seemingly objective intellectual engagement. In other words, a rational study of whiteness will lead to the dismantlement of this irrational discourse. Despite deeming it important, Giroux intuits the limitations of this strategy when he calls for "more theoretical work . . . to be done to enable students to appropriate the tools necessary for them to politicize whiteness as a racial category without closing down their own sense of identity and political agency" (310). My argument is that studying emotional discourses and equipping students with a rhetoric of emotion may be an important step in helping them acquire those "tools" to which Giroux refers.

Emotional Rhetoric

The reassessment of classical rhetoric that has expanded our understanding of the rational and its relation to affect draws into question the validity of the academic tendency to ignore the role of emotion in intellectual formation and exchange. In the ancient rhetorical traditions, *pathos* was considered a crucial area of study, although, as Richard Katula acknowledges in his discussion of Quintilian, "Modern readers may raise a question regarding the 'ethics' of emotional appeal" (12) when it is seen as a means of manipulation to distract from logos-based truths.[9] The question (which may be asked of persuasion in general) is how the role of emotions is conceived in rhetoric. When Cicero, for example, states in *De Oratore* that "it is impossible for the listener to feel indignation, hatred or ill-will, to be terrified of anything, or reduced to tears of compassion unless all those emotions . . . are visibly stamped or rather branded on the advocate himself" (II, 189), he might be promoting a practical but superficial emotional rhetoric, in which rhetors opportunistically acquire emotional literacy for the sake of persuading others. But when Cicero adds that "I give you my word that I never tried . . . to arouse indignation or compassion, either ill-will or hatred . . . without being really stirred myself," he begins to ascribe a more profound role to emotions. Instead of mere trickery or deception, we have instead the beginnings of a theory of deep empathy akin to method acting that provides the basis for humanistic growth through role playing: "I did those things approved by yourself, Crassus—not by way of technique, as to which I know not what to say, but under stress of deep emotion and indignation . . ." (II, 195). Not merely a vehicle for winning cases, feeling in this construction becomes a significant way of being in and understanding the world.

As mentioned above, recent scholarship on Aristotle also helps us reconfigure the rhetorical significance of emotion. Rather than merely a necessary evil in the art of persuasion, the study of pathetic appeal had larger implications for Aristotle, according to Ellen Quandhal. Building on the work of other scholars in this area, Quandhal asserts that "Aristotle is an indispensable predecessor for acknowledging and working with . . . emotion in rhetorical education" (11). She further derives from Aristotle's rhetorical treatment of emotions that they "have their vitality in an ethical sphere" (19). Indeed "emotions play a necessary role in good moral judgment" (Koziak 15). This last idea concerning the ethical nature of emotions, as well as Stearns' and Stearns' insight into the power relations that are embedded in emotional discourse, provides a basis for analyzing the emotions of whiteness and their significance to the discursive structures of racism. From this perspective, rather than merely "private" and therefore unchartable and irrelevant, the emotional experience of whiteness is, on the contrary, socially shaped and experienced. These emotions, I suggest, can help us "find," in our so deemed "postracial" era, those structures of whiteness and examine the way we perpetuate them rhetorically. Furthermore, a consideration of emotional ethics may offer alternatives to *logos*-based strategies for de-investment from whiteness.

Tracing Emotional Whiteness

In the preface to *Playing in the Dark*, Toni Morrison's meditation on whiteness in literature, she conjectures about French writer Marie Cardinal's literary treatment of her mental breakdown in the book *Les Mots Pour Le Dire*. Morrison notes that, according to Cardinal, her first panic attack was precipitated by a Louis Armstrong concert, an experience that "tore at the nerves" (viii). Morrison theorizes that for Cardinal the feeling that she is going to die is uncannily related to Armstrong's blackness and the jazz that he performs that evening; that Armstrong and his music as Other become the projected repository of darkness necessary for Cardinal's whiteness. The confrontation with her inability to recognize this construction, Morrison muses, in part produces the emotional response of terror. In Morrison's analysis, then, whiteness and emotion are inextricably linked even though the link goes unanalyzed in the account that Cardinal offers in her autobiographical narrative.

While Morrison is frankly speculative here, her ponderings are, as they are intended, heuristically useful, especially in suggesting the way emotions can point us to invisible power structures of whiteness embedded in the emotional responses of individuals performing as social agents. For example, consider the following scenario where emotional whiteness manifests itself: an episode from the TV show *COPS* features an unruly, drunk white man being arrested. During the course of the arrest, the man becomes increasingly angry at what he perceives to be rude treatment by his captors, and he utters the phrase, over and over, "but I'm a white man; I'm a white man." Implied in the proclamation, of course, is the idea that his whiteness should preclude the abuse he is receiving at the hands of the authorities. He exhibits the amazement and rage that hooks reminds us occurs when white privilege is challenged. His emotional response, his shocked disbelief, points us to the invisible privilege of whiteness, which the man (who could not count on the privilege of being middle-class) was assuming as his due. In this case, whiteness fails to grant him the protection he expects it to carry, and, as a result, this usually unarticulated (and perhaps inarticulable) privilege *had* to be articulated and thus made visible in a way that it often is not, precisely and ironically because the privilege turns out to be a chimera. The comic absurdity of his utterances becomes understandable when we consider that the failure of the assumed privilege and the crisis it produced culminated in an outrage that is not unlike the anger members of any dominant group may experience when a tension is created in their own sense of entitlement, a situation which often occurs in our college classrooms when students encounter texts that call into question the unexplored status quo.

Indeed this notion of privilege is a stumbling block in the classroom, when working-class white students become resentful at hearing about the supposed benefits of their whiteness as, for example, Charles Gallagher describes in his study of white students who assert their whiteness in reactionary ways when confronted with other ethnic groups in multicultural educational institutions. Often such students perceive themselves as struggling and economically disadvantaged (and indeed they are), and they respond to the suggestion that they are privileged with skepticism and anger, an emotion that can be understood as being about the *failure* of the *expected* privilege which whiteness promises as its entitlement but does not always deliver. White people, resistant to and untrained in materialist, class-based understandings of their society, see themselves as the rightful beneficiaries of an American system of meritocracy. In other words, as white people, they fully expect to achieve social-economic stability when they follow the "rules" of earnest industriousness; the unwritten, unspoken, unacknowledged—the "invisible"—expectation is that they should succeed in a way that those who are not white should not. The outrage and racist resentment they feel when confronted with meritocracy's failure is a measure of their investment in whiteness and the protection they expect it to afford—their belief in their own white superiority. In his discussion of anger in Book II of the *Rhetoric*, Aristotle asserted that "A man expects to be specially respected by his inferiors in birth, in capacity, in goodness, and generally in anything in which he is much their superior" [1378b–79a], implying that anger increases against those we perceive as below us in the social order. If Aristotle is correct, then anger will function as an important marker of whiteness, as the emotion can be linked to the feelings of entitlement and superiority that whiteness engenders.

Critical pedagogues are familiar with the emotional classroom "crises" that can ensue when privilege is confronted, and we often find these situations as difficult and as uncomfortable as our students do. As highly emotionally charged as these moments are, we perhaps pay less attention to the affective aspects than we should, seeking instead to navigate *around* rather than *through* the emotional discourse as though it were the unfortunate side effect of our inquiry rather than part of the inquiry itself. Zeus Leonardo highlights the need for this transparency when he observes that "In order to transcend current race relations, which is a concrete possibility, we must first go *through* race in order to have any hopes of going *beyond* it" (125). My contention is that charting emotions can help make visible cultural investments in whiteness and that such work is fundamental to equipping our students with the rhetorical tools they need to understand the discourses that interpellate them. I am arguing here for a political conception of emotion that "should address how to incorporate and educate the emotional capacities of citizens" (Koziak 5). Indeed Janine Jones argues that "goodwill whites" may be deficient in "Their capacity for a certain type of understanding . . . the type of understanding necessary for navigating a world that includes more members than one's self" (66). Certainly a crucial first step in such a project of remediation would be the identification of those "capacities"; to become aware of how emotion shapes and is shaped through the public sphere and how, through emotion, we effect social participation in "common" discourses.

In part such a politics would entail analyses of what Koziak calls "scenarios of emotion" (27) that trigger particular cultural responses of emotion. If, for example, we accept Toni Morrison's interpretation of Cardinal's breakdown as projection of unnamed whiteness, our understanding of the episode then is in keeping with contemporary understandings of trauma where an event such as the Holocaust is not merely psychological and private, an individual's own personal affair, but social and historical and locatable in a larger cultural landscape.[10] From this perspective, learning to "read" emotional whiteness can bring us to whiteness's often disguised discursive social constructions and help us understand the ways in which our emotional responses are imbricated in those constructions. In order to demonstrate the implications of this idea, I offer a reading of an excerpt from an electronic threaded discussion held by students in a first-year writing class. In my reading, I suggest that we can see the emotions of whiteness at work in shaping a student's political analysis. While the scenario here is clearly more mundane than Marie Cardinal's dramatic breakdown, the emotions exhibited are, I believe, nonetheless reliable indicators of the role that the rhetoric of whiteness plays in determining the student's response.

The electronic discussion was given as an assignment to probe a *New York Times* piece (Verhovek) that described the firing of two women at a small Texas insurance agency for refusing to sign a pledge to speak English only at the office. Ironically, the women had been hired for their bilingual abilities to serve Spanish-speaking customers. The women were Chicanas, and the owner of the agency, who took the extreme measure of drawing up the pledge, was Anglo. He wanted them to speak Spanish only to Spanish-speaking customers but otherwise use English when conversing with each other, since he and most of the employees only spoke English. The agency owner is depicted as something of an anachronistic buffoon. He is quoted as saying he took two years of Spanish in high school but doesn't remember any of it, and he makes statements such as "That's one smart Mexican gal" in reference to a Chicana worker who agreed to his terms and signed his pledge.

I asked students to identify and discuss what they thought were the important issues raised in the scenario as described in the news article. Many of them, including the student Joe, whose response appears below, configured the controversy in terms of an employer's rights, choosing to ignore the political discussion of linguistic hegemony that the author of the article raised as he included opinions from local residents suggesting the owner of the insurance agency should learn Spanish. Joe references that section of the article in his contribution to the discussion:

> I also agree with the boss. If it is his business and he asks a simple request to speak english on the job, unless it's necessary to speak spanish with a customer, then i think there is nothing wrong with that. It is his place of business and that is how he wants it to be run. By simply asking them to not speak Spanish on the job he isn't violating any rights of their's, especially if they know how to speak English fluently. They are making it as if he said they cant speak Spanish EVER AGAIN NO MATTER WHERE THEY ARE! But no, he just asked them for HIS business, when they are working. Also, what really made me mad was at the end of the article when her fiancé Wayne Collins said, "It's a free country, so i think they should be able to speak whatever language they want. And if it really bothers the guy that much that he doesn't understand it, then maybe he should learn Spanish. I mean he could take a class or something." What the hell is that. I'm sorry but we are in America, and it's HIS business! Why should he have to learn a second language to suite his employees when they are more than able to ablige his request. God forbid that if they didnt know English fluently and he asked them to take english classes, this whole situation would be ten times worse!

Although couched in what might be called a race or ethnic "neutral" argument about an employer's right to run his own business as he sees fit, the emotions that the student feels and expresses point to a submerged discourse of whiteness that the student rightly perceives, at least on an emotional level, as being under attack. I am not suggesting that Joe's argument about the owner's rights is a dodge. Indeed, the rhetoric of color-blind rights itself is often strongly linked to white privilege. But the student's anger and indignation may exceed the issue he is able to name. After all, Joe, who was not a contentious person but fairly mild mannered, had heard other opinions that he didn't necessarily agree with throughout the course of the semester, but none had produced such a strong response in him. His vehemence continued during class discussion, and when I asked him why this issue made him so angry when others had not, he expressed confusion over his feelings, acknowledging that he didn't quite understand the strength of his reaction.

It's certainly possible that Joe could be feigning ignorance of his affective capacities—that is to say he knows, or rather he is aware of, the cognitive dimension of his emotional response that underscores, as Seibel-Trainor puts it, the investment he has in protecting his socioeconomic interest through the discourse of whiteness ("Critical"). Nussbaum, for example, tells us that Aristotle's conception of anger, and emotion in general, contains this cognitive dimension—in order to *feel* anger one must *think* a wrong has occurred (*Therapy* 80). But it seems to me equally possible that Joe doesn't understand the emotions that link his indignation with what he sees as an affront to the boss's authority and to Joe's statement: "this is America." From a rhetoric of logic this statement would seem out of place in an argument defending the employer's demands; we might expect to see such a statement invoked to defend employees' rights to free speech rather than to justify an employer's rights to curtail expression. But of course rhetorically the statement *is* understandable, and it becomes so when we factor in the "emotional logic" that erupts when white privilege is questioned, that is to say when we understand whiteness from Aristotle's "recognition that all practical reasoning is pathetic reasoning" (Walker 91).

Joe's rhetoric is what Ahmed describes as an emotioned narrative that "works through othering" (1). The statement "This is America" functions here as an enthymeme of whiteness in its reliance on an audience's understanding of the phrase's cultural resonance. As Walker points out, the shared premises in the Aristotelian enthymeme are inherently pathos-based (91).[11] In this instance, the line "This is America" is not shorthand for liberty and freedom but rather Anglo hegemony in the expectation that English is the language of a white America. "This is America" means this is the Anglo America that the insurance agency owner—and Joe—have come to rely on. Any analysis of Joe's statement must take into account its emotional rhetoric—and not because one couldn't make the argument that there is something efficacious in people speaking a common public language. Certainly one could. But the trail of emotion is pivotal here in understanding the rhetorical situation. Joe's anger shows that he is not so much arguing efficacy as his investment in the notion that the English he speaks as a white American cannot, from his point of interest, be marginalized. This is an emotional cultural rhetoric that he understands and in which he can participate. In turn, this rhetoric shapes what is possible in his political assessment. So while the emotional scenario *reveals* to us an episode of whiteness, importantly we find also a complex interweaving of thought and emotion that *produces* whiteness and allows for the agent's participation through it, and maintenance of it, in emotional discourse. Such a process, similarly, can account for students' rallying to the defense of Conrad's *Heart of Darkness* against Achebe's claim that the book cannot, because of its racism, be considered a great work of art. Responding to the logic of whiteness's "emotionology,"[12] these students are unable to "hear" Achebe's argument, for as Aristotle understood, albeit begrudgingly according to Jeffrey Walker, "logos cannot 'command' or compel emotion . . . a state of emotion once aroused will strongly determine how [the mind] perceives and interprets any 'premises' presented to it" (81).[13]

Emotion as Ethics and a Theory of Recognition

In the above-mentioned essay, "An Image of Africa," Achebe focuses our attention on the scene where Conrad's Marlow looks at the dead helmsman and sees in him the "claim of distant kinship" (1451). For Achebe this is a pivotal scene and damning example of the ethical failure of the political liberalism that disallows the equality between European and African. Instead such a worldview weakly posits the possibility of a nebulous *connection* derived from notions of nineteenth-century Primitivism. The "kinship" that Conrad's prose references here then is mere euphemism from Achebe's perspective. But is the idea of kinship and its possibility more powerful than Achebe, or Conrad for that matter, credits? For Achebe's argument highlights the uncanny reaction that Marlow has to the helmsman's gaze, as Marlow retains it in his memory: a haunting reminder of some connection he is unwilling and unable to understand. Really, then, the helmsman's death is not for Marlow, who remains steeped in his whiteness here, a moment of true "kinship" recognition but rather a distinct and persistent failure of that recognition. He cannot find kinship in the Other, so Marlow, if not Conrad too, fails—emotionally and thus, importantly, ethically.

I use this scene, which is steeped in images of kinship and recognition, to introduce a discussion of the ethical dimension of emotional rhetoric and to suggest a possible paradigm for thinking about the cultivation of emotional capacities for the purposes of creating social change. To do so, I rely here on Barbara Koziak's work with what she calls the retrieval of a political model of emotion as a corrective to political theories where "The disregard of emotion has perpetuated certain strands of liberal theory and explanatory political science that rely on the universality of [mere] self-interest" (4). According to Koziak "the issue of political emotion has been least conceptualized and analyzed" (123–24), and she asks the question, "Is there any account of political life that pays equal respect to reason and emotion and reconsiders the idea of a strict dichotomy between the two?" (2).[14] Aristotle, she tells us, provides the basis for such an account to move beyond rational "self-interest"-based models, those same models that Sleeter sees at work in the perpetuation of whiteness where white people reveal their rational investments in maintaining the status quo and thus have no incentive to change. Does factoring emotion into our political rendering of whiteness make the possibility for change any less bleak than Sleeter implies?

Building on Nussbaum's work regarding the cognitive and rational dimensions of emotion, Koziak asserts that for Aristotle "The acceptance of a moral idea requires both our rational and our emotional faculties" (105). By considering Aristotle's body of work (as well as non-Aristotelian occurrences of the word), Koziak arrives at an expanded understanding of the Greek concept of *thumos*, which has often been associated with notions of anger, spiritedness, and masculinity. She argues to broaden *thumos* to be "a name for the characteristic emotional response of citizens for one another, one that is inculcated by laws, by the way of life of the regime, and by the regime's cultural production" (127) or, more succinctly, "the name for the capacity to feel emotion" (100). She concludes from this that "Aristotle . . . contends that both *thumos* and *logos* are necessary to political activity" (31). Thus emotions are a key component in the political and social life of the citizenry and must be accordingly attended to in any political or rhetorical theory.

This idea suggests that whiteness, or any inherently unethical discourse, is not reducible to an "irrationality" that can be fixed with logic, nor is it simply a rational investment in a group's socioeconomic interests. As a political response, it involves a more complicated amalgamation of emotions that then must be understood and addressed from a perspective that accounts for rather than dismisses this complexity. Koziak's attempt to retrieve a politics of emotion takes her to a reconsideration of Aristotle's tragedy theory, specifically the concept of recognition, the dilemma of which I see illustrated in the "scenario of emotion" replicated in the helmsman scene of *Heart of Darkness*. In the tragedy theory, Koziak sees Aristotle establishing a salient model for locating the political in the emotional sphere and inculcating what she understands to be one of Aristotle's goals: the cultivation of moral emotional dispositions that help inform rational thought.

Rather than focusing on *Oedipus*, Koziak draws out the moral implications of recognition as it is linked to pity by turning to Aristotle's discussion of *Iphigenia*, where Orestes and his sister must struggle to transcend their self-absorption and recognize their kinship. She claims that the *hamartia* in this case is "the failure to recognize the kin in the stranger" (149). But the

characters 'undergo' a recognition. . . . They are seized by events, seized in a moment of shock when they suddenly know their relation to a stranger, know the story of their own lives. Characters become spectators, seeing the life they have led for the first time. The former story of their lives is revealed as false; now they can proceed on the truth of their relationships, their acknowledgement of kinship. (140)

Thus she concludes that "the *thumos* of good Aristotelian citizens, that is, their emotional capacities, should be shaped to feel pity, meaning specifically to feel a kinship with citizens and strangers" (149–50). Koziak's take on Aristotle is that the citizenry's moral disposition is in its very nature deeply emotional and, importantly, educable.

While Koziak's treatment of tragedy focuses on recognition, Jeffrey Walker's explanation of Aristotle's *katharsis* in relation to emotional rhetoric lends further credence to Koziak's understanding of Aristotle's moral project. Walker notes that in *Politics* 8.7 Aristotle makes clear that "he is using the term *katharsis* in a special, unusual way" (77) and argues that emotional *katharsis*, differing from the medical model of purging, is better understood as being "put into a state" and that "this 'state' is expressed behaviorally and physically as a particular type of *pathos*" (78). This idea of *katharsis* as an *evoking* (rather than expurgation) of a particular emotional state implies an ethics of emotion where "we begin to think of rhetoric as an art of shaping and guiding an audience's *pathe* toward a *katharsis* of particular moods/intentionalities in practical judgments/actions" (85) and to "promote *katharsis* of more reasonable, 'ethical' moods more suitable to prudent choice and action" (91).

Meeting the objections that Jessie Daniels made to *logos*-based models of eradicating whiteness would seem to require us to move in the direction of Aristotelian-conceived emotion that Koziak and Walker envision. In order to transcend their whiteness, white people cannot merely be "told" about their whiteness; that is, "it will never be sufficient for the rhetor merely to *declare* the premises" (Walker 85, emphasis added). Rather we must be "seized by events." At first glance, such a theory of political emotion might appear to move us in the direction of the liberal sympathy (what Megan Boler has criticized as "passive empathy" [156]) and the rhetoric of "tolerance" that have so paralyzed the political project of multiculturalism: the kind of sympathy that Achebe derides, as it produces little more than the condescension of uninterrogated white man's burden while failing to pose any significant challenge to whiteness's oppressive "mystery." Indeed, it seems to preserve the privileged subject position of whiteness where one has the luxury or choice of feeling empathy and bestowing recognition.[15]

But recognition, as Koziak has explicated it, is quite different from this sort of sympathy. Koziak, echoing the dire *empathy*[16] of Cicero's "stress of deep emotion and indignation," uses the words "seize" and "shock" to describe what amounts to an epiphanic insight where participants achieve an ironic distance from their own lives, forever altering their ontological relationships. Such a description suggests a crisis model of political emotion that relies on inducing the desired recognition, similar to what Shoshana Felman describes, in her teaching of Holocaust narratives, as the movement from "cognition" to "performative" understanding (56). What would constitute such crisis is an important issue for emotional education to address. If we accept Achebe's argument regarding the helmsman scene in *Heart of Darkness*, not even the dead man beside Marlow can cause this character to be "seized by events" in order to "undergo" recognition of kinship. But perhaps it can be argued that there is the beginning of "crisis" for Marlow in this scene. Certainly it is in this moment that Conrad has Marlow coming the closest to achieving emotional, and thus political, understanding of, and change in, his white identity.

Importantly the main thrust of Achebe's critique is to point out just how easily narratives of whiteness end up recentering themselves at the expense of marginalizing the Other, even as they may attempt to indict that very whiteness. This danger is quite real, as I discussed in Chapter 1, with regard to the awareness narratives that we find in critical whiteness scholarship, in which white people, through autobiographical storytelling, purport to achieve critical recognition of their whiteness with life-changing consequences. When, to use Swiencicki's distinction, do narratives of *guilt* become the worldview altering narratives of *shame* that move beyond liberal sympathy to achieve, what is by definition, the radical recognition that Koziak sees Aristotle modeling for us as the basis for political emotion? For as Swiencicki reminds us in her exploration of the critical potential of narrative to disrupt whiteness, guilt may be uselessly paralyzing to the agent, but shame can produce the existential self-consciousness necessary for the development of a renewed ethical relationship to the world. I have already indicated my reservations with respect to the disruptive potential of such narratives, claiming that their transformative possibilities can become submerged in the generic demands of the performance of confession. The question is not whether white people should have epiphanies about their whiteness—clearly they should—but whether narrative performance in the form of published writing is the vehicle that can produce them. In chapter one, I raised questions about the usefulness of such narratives in the scholarship of whiteness studies, but here we may raise the question with regard to pedagogy, for rhetoric and composition scholars, myself included, have often attributed a transformative function to student narrative. Is narrative the rhetoric that will produce cathartic epiphany and disruption? And how do we know when it has? For student texts are no more transparent than others, although we sometimes read them as though they are.

Toward Dialogue and a Pedagogy of Empathy and Recognition

To confront the previous question, I begin with another: can crisis be used productively without alienating those very citizens in whom we wish to cultivate moral emotional capacities? This is an important question with regard to implementing a rhetoric of political emotion and one which teachers of critical pedagogy must attend to and frequently negotiate. As Fishman and McCarthy have noted, a case can be made as well for nonconfrontational pedagogical models that work toward psychological and political transformation. Alcorn maintains that "true learning—the kind that changes subjectivity—hurts. But we can help students with this learning, only if we try not to hurt them. We must respect in learning the time of anxiety and the time of suffering" (176). Alcorn addresses the failure of critical pedagogy "to advance political progress in the body politic" (172), and he attributes this to the failure to recognize the emotional process of grief that accompanies shifts in subjectivity for "beliefs are not simple signifiers, but part of a network of signifiers, images, and affects that form a system that supports the sense of self" (177).

The emotions that produce pleasure no doubt must be considered alongside those that produce pain as we explore what constitutes "the emotional repertoire of citizens" (Koziak 149). Seibel-Trainor observes that critical pedagogues' efforts to effect social change through teaching, particularly with respect to whiteness, "are compromised by (in part because they are predicated on) the moral necessity of excluding the very [white] students whom, arguably, we most need to reach" ("Critical" 636). This tendency toward exclusion can be linked to critical pedagogy's overreliance on a persuasion of logos, and perhaps a fear of "personalizing" the politics necessary for social transformation, as we find our attempts to reason students out of their whiteness frustrated again and again. In her call to move "from liberation to *love*" ("Critical" 647, emphasis added) of such students who have become "unlovable" to us because of their political views and moral positions, Seibel-Trainor is in essence arguing for an affective correction to logocentric epistemologies as well as pointing us toward other emotions that need to be studied and considered to develop a rhetoric of political emotion. No doubt we must also recognize the "kin in the stranger" of our students if we are to be effective in helping them through a process of recognition. Composition and rhetoric's answer to critical pedagogy's crisis of alienation and passivity has been writing, especially politically inflected narratives, in which students use literacy to confront and refashion identities. But process writing methodology, in which the goal is to produce a final "acceptable" text and, in the case of narrative, a revised subjectivity, may be counterproductive to critical pedagogy's antiracist goals that instead require less static rhetorical paradigms in favor of messier, less quantifiable dialogue and listening (see Ratcliffe, "Rhetorical") in order to achieve cathartic recognition that goes beyond disposable empathy and narrative performance. Rather than school essays and literacy narratives in which students proclaim their performed identity, we perhaps should look toward more dynamic, interactive forms of literacy that focus less on performing subjectivity and more on the "to-ing and fro-ing" of sustained interaction *between* and *among* subjects.

The broader questions we might ask are: what emotional responses are necessary to produce the radical recognition required for meaningful transformation and social change, and what might a pedagogy that fosters such emotions for this purpose look like? In her discussion of the jurors in the Rodney King case and other public responses to that defining cultural event, Janine Jones attributes the jurors' verdict (as well as larger public response from the white-identified community) to a failure of empathy (see note 16), a failure that resulted from an inability or unwillingness to form an emotional response to the beating and instead to rely "on the physical evidence" (77). Jones asks whether the lack of affect in such objective, "rational" responses doesn't constitute "a kind of irrationality" (66), albeit one with its own logic that shields the white person from "the considerable pain, guilt, and shame that might be elicited" when she sees "how she benefits from racism and perhaps serves as an active, intentional, though unconscious, participant in it" (69). In Jones's analysis, which rests on the complex interdependence of emotion and reason, the failure to empathize precludes the possibility of recognition that would produce ethical responses. The tragedy of Rodney King then becomes one of failed emotional education; the *hamartia*, as Koziak might put it, was the failure to cultivate an emotional capacity that would allow for the ethical recognition of kinship on the part of the white jurors. This idea suggests that we cannot afford to shield either ourselves or our students from the emotional responses necessary to produce fully educated citizens. If recognition is to occur—finding the kin in the stranger—it must happen *through* emotional response rather than by the intellectual evisceration of it.

Jones's explanation of how critical empathy happens is again instructive in this regard as she cites scholarship that explains the achievement of such empathy as a process of "mapping the structure of an experience (where specific emotional content is part of the structure) onto the structure of an experience of the individual with whom we seek to empathize" (71). Among the reasons such mapping may fail to occur is the question of motive, the question with which this chapter began. White people cannot achieve empathy and thus recognition because they do not wish to when the change that such recognition produces works against the maintenance of their own hegemonic interests. But a rhetoric and pedagogy of emotion might lead us to ask, as Jones does, not just about the cognitive, or "rational," dimension of emotion that Nussbaum attributes to Aristotle, where every emotion requires a belief, but rather the reverse. Thus "instead of asking what happens to an emotion if you remove the belief that caused it . . . , we might ask what happens to a belief when you remove the emotion that caused it or is a component of it" (Jones 76–77). If we address the emotional dimension of whiteness—that is to say, if we view whiteness as a "problem" of emotional rhetoric—what happens to the *belief* in whiteness? The approach of inducing empathy-based recognition as a strategy for dismantling whiteness is one that poses the question in this way. And such strategies may help move the transformative potential of critical whiteness studies beyond the limitations of a rhetoric of rationality.

6 Encountering Whiteness as Resistance
Dialogue and Authority in the Composition Classroom

In Chapter 4 I discuss the ways in which Aristotle's enthymeme is a useful theoretical frame for understanding the various ways in which players in higher education—students, full-time professors, adjunct professors, and administrators, are often at cross purposes with respect to the goals and objectives of freshman English and language use on college campuses generally; how, for instance, institutions as rhetors speak to students as their audience. I end that essay with a discussion of two student texts which "talk back" to the institution. In this essay, I want to talk about how students talk back to me, as a specifically black professor, in various ways. I am especially interested in the ways white students use forms of resistance through a mix of discourses—multiculturalism, color-blindness, political correctness—which protects and reproduces an embedded whiteness. This whiteness, I argue, subverts the very dialogue upon which progressive pedagogies, such as those I try to employ in my classroom, depends.

THE SHOCK OF ARRIVAL

I was hired as a one-year, non-tenure-track faculty appointment at WU in 2003, and I had taken something of a risk leaving the job security I had as the coordinator of Basic Writing I at my prior institution. I had held that position for eight years after completing my MA, and it was comfortable, if limiting, since there was no real possibility of promotion. I had worked on my PhD, mostly at night, and was now ABD. The WU post offered the possibility of advancement and a tenure-track job after the completion of the one-year appointment, provided I could make satisfactory progress on my dissertation, which I took to mean that I had better finish it.

On my first day of class I was surprised at how surprised I was by the number of white students in the classroom; there were two or three black students—all women—but the sea of white faces staring back at me initially startled me, and I hadn't accounted for this feeling in my preparation for class. It appeared to be a very different place to the school I had left a few days earlier. That school's student population was predominantly black and Latino, and was mostly drawn from the surrounding neighborhoods of Orange, East Orange, Newark, and Irvington. They were solidly working-class, and largely considered, black towns made up of African-Americans, Haitians, Jamaicans, Trinidadians, Guyanese, and other Caribbean or otherwise African families that had changed the communities significantly since my family had immigrated to East Orange in the early 1980s. My prior institution, EC, reflected this change and mixture, and in many ways contributed to my comfort level there as these students were from the very neighborhoods where I had spent the last twenty years of my life; they were me in concrete ways. My parents were Jamaican and living in East Orange, I had married a Trinidadian woman who had lived in Irvington, and I had students who knew me as a neighbor. The irony strikes me now that I would register some discomfort at not seeing more black faces in that first class at WU, since it reminds me of those early days after my immigration. On that occasion, as I discuss in Chapter 2, I was surprised by the sea of black faces I saw in the hallways of Clifford Scott High, which was very different from the working-class school I had then just left in England where I was one of three or four black students in my classroom. I suppose I had changed some.

I don't mind admitting a certain degree of anxiety and intimidation that first day at WU, partly due to being in a new environment, I'm sure, but also because of the number of white students before me. I suspect that they felt the same way since it was their first day in freshman writing. Many of them coming from the middle and upper middle classes of New Jersey's suburbs had likely never had a black teacher before or sat next to a black student because of New Jersey's de facto segregated school systems. Their anxieties, then, like mine, were no doubt inflected by the racialization of the classroom as well as being in a new place.

I see EC as unusual in many ways now, because it gave black and Latino students a chance at something greater than the working-class lives they would no doubt have been consigned to without the benefit of the four-year degree the school provides. In this way it's positioned between community college, in that it tends to draw similar students, and the surrounding universities of Rutgers-Newark, Seton Hall, and WU. The school, then, functioned as a kind of safe house: a place that served an important need and function in the communities from which the students and I lived and worked.

Going to graduate school in the evenings and teaching during the days provided me with a ready-made opportunity to practice what I was learning, such as the principles of critical pedagogy, as I had understood them and studied them with Ira Shor at the CUNY Graduate Center, particularly the idea of power sharing. I had run into many of the problems Shor outlines in *When Students Have Power*, and much of my practice was still a "work-in-progress." For example, I ran into the problems that Shor describes of students not wanting to power share, not understanding the explanatory discourse I used to introduce power-sharing, and reluctance on their part to take public risks (Shor, *Power* 18–19). I was experimenting in my classes, with varying results ranging from minor interruptions to the rhetoric of the classroom they were used to, to complete confusion in some students leading to a drop in attendance. That is to say, I nearly lost the class as Shor did (*Power* 4). In my home community of EC, I had a sense of security in that I knew these students very well; I could adjust to address their particular needs. There was a constant dialogue between us, even those who didn't always show up for class. These experiences taught me that it is extraordinarily difficult to practice a theory of pedagogy well under the best of circumstances—I would even add that there is no such thing as a pure praxis for a given pedagogy, critical or otherwise, as Shor himself implies in his book, and that the individual human beings before you must always be a primary concern; something I knew intellectually, and had thought a great deal about in the courses I had taken with Sondra Perl at the Graduate Center, but nevertheless had to experience to understand completely.

On that first day at WU, I had not taken the risk of beginning with a syllabus-less class and the idea of power-sharing. While appealing in many ways, it was not something I was willing to try in this new place with these new students; I didn't think I knew them, or the institution, well enough to risk seeming incompetent, and I was acutely aware of how my racial identity as black and male might underscore negative stereotypes. I would use texts to raise probative critical issues, front-loading the dreaded teacher commentary, but do so in a way that invited students to see and make connections to their own lives and to the world around them through a critique of our society if these students were open to the idea.

I was at a familiar point in that first discussion, using an excerpt from David Bohm and F. David Peat's discussion on dialogue from their *Science, Order, and Creativity*. In the piece they talk about the difference between an argument and a dialogue. They assert that in an argument people hold relatively fixed positions, and the objective is to win the argument by persuading the listener to adopt the position they are competing against. In a dialogue, however, the objective is to tend toward a particular point of view, but not hold that position nonnegotiably. Indeed, the idea is to hold one's beliefs in suspension and actually entertain the opposing position without thinking of it as untenably out of hand. This in fact speaks to a criticism of whiteness studies and discussions of race and racism generally: that too often they are centered on winning arguments, instead of engaging in dialogue, not allowing for the misinformed, especially in young people such as the students we encounter.

I was preparing them, I thought, with this piece, to contextualize the first unit of readings organized around "Language and Power." Then a student, James,[1] sitting near the front, white, male, a little taller than me, and dressed in ripped jeans and a hoody that on a black student may have been taken for old, shoddy clothes, asked a question—one that challenged my assertion and interpretation of the short piece we had just read. "I'm confused," he said. "Are you saying that dialogue can solve all our problems as a people? "What if," he continued quizzically, "dialogue won't work?" I was taken by surprise, shocked, initially by the question being asked, but then the question itself was a remarkable one for a freshman I thought. My initial response—the response that carries the deepest emotional content now, was that this was an affront. Was he challenging me because I'm black? Was the challenge because I'm small in stature, or because I look too young to be at the front of the classroom? Was he, in short, questioning my authority? And what should I do about it? In some ways, this moment had underscored some of my fears—that perhaps I wasn't quite ready to step into the role of a university professor. Perhaps these students were just not particularly accepting of black English professors. After a moment, the student's expectant gaze, inviting a response from me reassured me. As I later learned, James was an exceptional student in many ways. He wanted to engage in a *dialogue*—he was enacting what I was professing, and I hadn't accounted for that. It seemed I would have to adjust.

RACIALIZED AUTHORITY IN THE WRITING CLASSROOM

I know there's a rhetoric in the classroom that settles power and authority on the teacher, but when the teacher is racialized in a place like a writing classroom, particularly when the students are predominantly white, the function of power has the potential to be particularly complex. My idea of critical pedagogy had now been complicated by my arrival at WU, and the issues of racialized authority in that classroom. As Wendy discusses in Chapter 3, we tend to have scripts about how we are supposed to talk about race that make it difficult to engage in real dialogue on the subject even in the best of circumstances. I want to argue here that when the teacher is black, and the students are not, there are dynamics of power that threaten the very processes of teaching and learning that our pedagogies must account for. That is to say, the scripts Wendy talks about may not even see the light of day when race and power are conflated.

For instance, I know that some of the notions I had, and the differences I perceived about the students at WU and those I worked with at my prior institution can be explained by my submersion in the one community and my relative ignorance of the other. But my experiences in the insularity of my community, I would argue, are not unusual, and are directly related to the ways in which whiteness is maintained in a "color-blind" U.S. Indeed, my arrival in East Orange was not an accident, but was the result of the redlining that was in place when my aunt on my mother's side had saved up enough money to buy a house and move from the apartment she and her husband had rented in Orange, New Jersey, after emigrating from

Jamaica in the late 1970s. They were shown homes in East Orange, but not in the white neighboring towns of Montclair, West Orange, South Orange, Caldwell, and Livingston.

My mother's visit to her sister in 1979 after being laid off during the unemployment crisis in England brought on by the Thatcher years, and her subsequent immigration to the U.S. through sponsorship, meant that East Orange would be our new hometown when my brother and I arrived in 1983, and not somewhere else. It further meant that Clifford Scott High School would administer my schooling for the next three years, and not the better resourced Caldwell High, which I remember so well because their soccer team would come to play Clifford Scott and find it increasingly more difficult to beat us as we got more and more students from the Caribbean whose families, like mine, were similarly redlined.

These incidents of redlining remind me of New Jersey's governor, Chris Christie, on the night of the election that propelled him to the governorship, and national prominence. In his victory speech he says:

> New Jersey is an extraordinary place. Here I am, a guy who was born in Newark 47 years ago. Two parents struggled to make ends meet, brought me home to a fourth floor walk up apartment on the corner of South Orange Avenue and 14th street. Then five years later they moved us to Livingston because they wanted our family to have the best public education we could possibly have. And everything I've been lucky enough to become, the foundation was laid for that in those schools, in those years, by great teachers and by my great parents that gave us the values that allowed me to be standing in front of you tonight as the 55th governor of the state of New Jersey. . . (Christie)

I find this speech striking because Christie, who is a few years older than I, juxtaposes his early years in Newark with those in Livingston, some eight miles west of Newark, and one of the wealthiest towns in the state. Christie clearly indicates that he got to Livingston in ways not dissimilar to how my aunt got to East Orange, and he indicates, by way of an enthymeme centered on education, that his family was running from the poor schools in Newark, which also happened to be populated with minority children, to the better schools in Livingston, which happened to be populated with whiter children like himself. Indeed, he credits his very success, "everything [he] has been lucky enough to become" to the foundation those schools laid for him. The opportunities open for Christie were not, apparently, open to me or the children I went to school with in East Orange, and an army of realtors protected—quite literally—his property interests in whiteness[2] and also, apparently, protected him from people like me.

Christie goes on in the speech to claim that he wishes for all of the children of New Jersey to have the same opportunities he had. But his first year and few months in office make this claim dubious since his attacks on teachers' unions and his corporate model of education supporting charter schools have worked to divide communities like the ones I live in by siphoning off tax dollars that would support the public education system instead of aggressively reforming those systems. The reality that today we can still point to many towns in New Jersey as "black" or "white" is testimony to the fact that what Christie and I experienced is still prevalent today. As Jonathon Kozol points out, our communities are roughly as racially divided today as they were before the Brown vs. Board of Education decision in 1954. [3]

I also understand that the difference I perceived between the students I worked with at EC and those I encountered at WU may be described through a study of social class formation and class analysis. That is, I understand that while whiteness can be said to exist in the material world, it does so purely on the basis of an unjustifiable political identity. It is unjustifiable for at least two reasons. First it is taken as natural, as a backdrop against which all other identities must be evaluated. Second, it implies racial divisions are primary over those of social class, and I'm not sure they always are. But the temptation to read "race" as primary over all else, I remember, was very powerful in that first class at WU. It required all of my academic and intellectual training *not* to see this episode in that way.

I raise the incident of James's question, my response to it, and these anecdotes to point out that no one is immune from the racial discourse that constitutes, as Toni Morrison and others have argued, "our wholly racialized society" (Morrison, *Playing* 12–13) today. The example I offer of my mother's experiences and Governor Christie's, juxtaposed to mine, serves as evidence that while in a truly color-blind society, my response would be irrational. In the version of color blindness currently in vogue in the U.S., it is not only rational, but also quite necessary.

MY RACE PRECEDES ME

A white colleague of mine and I often talk about the various responses we get from students regarding race and racism when they are raised in our respective classes. He has a whole unit on it, which covers more than a week of class time, and I explicitly cover race and racism for about a week. Yet my students, on the whole, see my examination of race and racism as already implied in everything I say even when the lines of discussion I invite them to pursue do *not* specifically include race. For instance, I frequently ask students to write anonymous "note to me" on index cards throughout the semester to share their thoughts and feelings about the direction of the class, and what we should do more of, or less of. An inordinate number of them will typically say a version of "class is going well, but we should talk less about slavery and race." So when I actually open my mouth and talk about it, it's as if it was something the class expected me to do anyway, and once it's raised as a topic, their expectations are met. In this sense, my white colleague has a power I do not. He may engage in forms of dialogue that I cannot. Because he is white, he can occupy a neutral, invisible position with regard to race that I simply cannot. When he talks about race, it's not assumed that it is from a position of self-interest, but when I talk, my subjectivity as black and male make me biased—or so our student responses would seem to suggest.

My colleague specifically discusses whiteness in his class by first making light of it. He'll say things like, "In case you haven't noticed by now I am white—but that could change, you never know. I'm working on it." It's an interesting tack to take, and when his students see behind the humor, he says, he hopes they'll begin to understand the mutability of whiteness: the ways in which it really is a very slippery identity, even as it is one, according to Toni Morrison, that is essential for white America's sense of self. [4] My colleague explicitly talks about whiteness being a color so as to engage the discourse of color blindness, which often leaves it out. This is something I rarely do unless prompted by the class; the closest I've come is when students are curious why I speak the way I do. Since I speak with an inflected British accent, and I'm very dark, they wonder about my background. It's only in cases like these, rare as they are in my second-semester composition course on literature, that I will raise the idea that my speech might be considered "white," and I'll often get a nod of recognition from them. I'll invite them to think about what that means. In situations when my subjectivity is being explored in class like that, I'm always quick to point out that my parents spoke with unmistakable Jamaican accents, because I want to show the mutability of racial identity generally as well.

CULTURAL SCHIZOPHRENIA: MULTICULTURALISM, COLOR BLINDNESS, AND POLITICAL CORRECTNESS

Somewhere between the discourse of color blindness and the discourse of multiculturalism, lies the rarely acknowledged discourse of schizophrenia in the U.S. today. Eduardo Bonilla-Silva points to aspects of it in his book, *Racism Without Racists,* when, in his chapter 3 interviews, he analyzes "rhetorical incoherence" (68). Bonilla-Silva's objective in that chapter is to record "styles of color-blindness," but his findings are equally indicative, I think, of a discourse of color blindness where we are not to see color, as he points out, and multiculturalism, where we are supposed to celebrate color and cultural diversity. Bonilla-Silva does an excellent job of pointing out how racism and whiteness have survived, and indeed thrive in a color-blind U.S., and multiculturalism is most closely linked to the idea of the elasticity of whiteness Robyn Wiegman articulates since the point is to celebrate the cultural diversity of all Americans. [5] In fact, Martin E. Spencer points out that it was in response to an emerging form of multiculturalism that

Jesse Jackson launched the movement to designate "Black Americans" as "African Americans" (548).

Perhaps the two competing ideas are nowhere more prevalent, or confused, than on college and university campuses where students, and teachers, are asked to see each other as both assimilated Americans (read color blindness) and as unique cultural "Others" (read multiculturalism). The net effect, I argue, is the reproduction of the racism embedded in both policies and, worse yet, the short-circuiting of the learning experience through the paucity of student dialogue in the classroom.

An experience I had in a staff meeting at a previous institution some years ago serves as a useful example of how this plays out with teachers. In the meeting, one of my colleagues brought up the issue of classroom practice. She suggested that the school, and by implication those in the meeting, not be so single-minded in its approach to teaching. Instead of teaching about race or class or some such thing *all* the time, we should, she suggested, teach a broad and wide range of subjects and topics that will make our students "well-rounded individuals" and able to compete in the new millennium. She made reference to an essay in Ralph Ellison's book, *Shadow and Act*, to illustrate her point that Ellison in the essay had moved (intellectually and artistically) away from the blacks in his home state of Oklahoma because, as the essay seemed to indicate, their art centered only on issues of race.

Her use of Ralph Ellison to make her point was a shrewd move. She was gathering ethical authority for her rhetorical move to whiten black literature using a black author; it was particularly powerful, not only because I was the only black person in the room, but also because of Ellison's prominence. This feeds into the schizophrenia I refer to because it's an attempt to promote a color-blind pedagogy through the ethical authority of multiculturalism, and it clearly contributes to the reproduction of whiteness through the use of a black author. I was therefore beginning to see that her implicit argument was that we can and should emulate Ellison at the school.

In my response to her I illustrated three things. First, that I agreed with her in principle: we should develop curricula that expose a wide variety of ideas. But to do so at the expense of our students' awareness of the function they and the cultures they are connected to have played—and continue to play—in our society would be problematic. Next, I suggested that Ellison had his own agenda. He said and did various things for specific political reasons and he made conscious decisions about the lens he would use to interpret the world.[6] Finally, I suggested that we think about what lens our students are using to interpret the world, and part of our job is to help them see and evaluate both the consistencies and the inconsistencies of that lens. I felt somewhat defensive when another staff member chose this opportunity to tell me that they had always wanted to ask me a question. "Do you", she said, "push your opinions on your students?" I replied that

I very often introduce ideas which students have had little exposure to, and in my classroom, political, economic, and social issues connected to students' lives are frequently raised through texts and discussions. Politics, I explained, is always in the classroom, and moreover, it is always at work in the consciousness of the students. I was stunned by the response of the room to this. Comments ranged from "Shouldn't you be most concerned with teaching our students to write" to "I don't consider myself political in the classroom, I rather consider myself an English teacher, and I think I assume a position that allows my students choice about what they want to write and what they want to say."

As we walked out of that meeting, the director of the department congratulated us all on our openness. She, in essence, praised our diverse outlooks and herself for hiring people who represented so well the "free marketplace of ideas." I left the room, however, rather frustrated and wondered how I should make sense of where my colleagues stood and what they stood for. What implications would their positions have on their students? In other meetings I had been impressed by much of what they said about their classroom practice, but what should I make of their impulse toward a neutral, apolitical stance as if such a position could really exist, or their ability to be sporadically progressive without a consistent recognition of the ever-present role of ideology? In a sense the director had overlaid a particular discourse of multiculturalism which camouflaged the problem, which I perceived to be the support of a kind of color-blind pedagogy, but didn't do anything to really resolve it.

How do current notions of multiculturalism, and color blindness, coupled as they are to notions of political correctness, affect white students, particularly in a classroom where the teacher is black, like in my classroom? We might, for instance, interpret Amanda, the student I discuss in Chapter 4, as invisible to both discourses of multiculturalism and color blindness in the sense that she is white *and* working-class. Her working-classness works against her in a multicultural society since what is celebrated is ethnic identity, not social class, and certainly not the working class, and her whiteness elides important differences between her and the middle-class "normal" of the institution as suggested by Robyn Wiegman's rhetorical mapping of the elasticity of whiteness, particularly the strategy of "injured whiteness." The use of the word "white," then, in Amanda's case is a problematic one. What the word is in danger of achieving where she is concerned is an interpellation of her as "middle-class white" such that her social class is completely elided. This reading of Amanda helps to explain Bonilla-Silva's findings that working class women are more likely to express progressive beliefs than other segments of the white community (144). While skin color is a mark of difference, it is not necessarily an accurate description of social consciousness, or, more importantly perhaps, economic status, though especially in the area of social consciousness the temptation to think "white middle class" is tremendously powerful as I suggest in my discussion of Amanda in Chapter 4. Amanda's material reality may require her to appeal to an injured white self, which is one possible reading of her essay; one which allows her to circumvent the language of political correctness since she can appropriate the language of protest instead. This, too, is supported by Bonilla-Silva's findings when he points out that "many [white working-class women] had problems with Affirmative Action, residency concerns, and school choice, just like other segments of the white community (145).

Another way that multiculturalism and color blindness affect white students is that they prevent them from having to engage in precisely the kinds of meaningful conversations and learning experiences progressive teachers in composition should welcome if we are to confront the ways in which their identities are implicated in the development of their writing and thinking skills. Multiculturalism does not implicate white, middle-class "normal" American culture because that is not said to be a culture, as such, in popular discourse. Similarly, color blindness does not implicate whiteness, because, again, it is not thought of as a color in popular discourse. Both multiculturalism and color blindness seem to contribute to a general culture of political correctness in my classroom, I believe, that make it extraordinarily difficult to teach in ways I think would be most meaningful and useful.

I want, then, to discuss the various forms of resistance I encounter as a specifically black professor working with a predominantly white student population, and how that necessarily shapes how I'm able to teach, what I'm able to teach, and what these students are able to learn from me. It is important for me, then, to pay careful attention to how I teach white students— an ironic reversal of so much of the scholarship in composition today, which is about how white teachers think about how to teach black students. That is to say, the notions of multiculturalism and color blindness as aspects of political correctness often provide white students with strategies to avoid engaging in classroom activities that are likely to have the most impact on their learning and development as writers, and this is rarely considered in the literature of composition studies, perhaps because so few compositionists are black or of a racial minority in comparison to our white counterparts.

SCHIZOPHRENIA AS WHITE RESISTANCE

Consider the following experience, which I had in a second-semester Introduction to Literature composition course some years ago. In this course, students worked in group clusters of four or five and shared questions about the literature they read, drafts of their essays, and frequently their journal entries. Jody, a white female student in the class is responding to the essay question: "Discuss the ways in which your identity may be reflected in at least one of the characters we have studied in this unit." After the peer-review session had ended, Jody approached me. She was visibly upset. Other students were bustling around the desk, and she wanted to speak to me there and then, but didn't seem to know how to say what she was thinking. The attention she had begun to attract from other students because of her demeanor prompted me to suggest she speak to me in my office, or send me an e-mail. Jody's e-mail, which I've reproduced below, references two of the texts we were reading at the time, "Girl" by Jamaica Kincaid and "The Wife of His Youth" by Charles Chesnutt. Here's what she says:

> The two characters I compared myself with was "girl" and Mr. Ryder, saying they both sought "social acceptance". Towards the end of my essay I told a story that I saw as being similar to the one in "The Wife of His Youth". I said my mother had found out that I was interested in a male who happened to be Hispanic. I was very surprised at her reaction to it when she found out. She told me she felt that if I were to ever get married to a Hispanic male, she feels that they don't become as successful as "others". I wasn't too sure what that meant. Especially coming from a person I always saw as so accepting. When it came down to it, though, she acted just like the rest of society and objected. I actually reconsidered what I was doing and thought, "Would dating a Hispanic guy bring me down in any way?" After giving it some thought, it didn't take me long to realize whatever makes me happy is most important. Society told Mr. Ryder and me that in order to be successful, you must stick with your own race. To me though it came down to more than the race or gender you are. "To thine own self be true." After getting reactions from my group, I was very surprised when they told me to consider re-writing my essay. I didn't mean to offend anyone in any way, and I thought I made it clear in my essay that it wasn't what I THOUGHT, just what "others" thought like in society, and how I was GOING AGAINST it, like Mr. Ryder. I will definitely re-write it or take it out completely, if you too find it controversial. But like many of the stories we read this semester it deals with serious issues, like race and gender oppression, and I thought I was just comparing my experience to one similar in the literature.

Unfortunately, the draft Jody wrote that her cluster group read, and the revised essay I encouraged her to write, are lost, but I like to think of this e-mail as illustrating the kind of writing, thinking, and issues one would want to see in our composition classes because there is a certain sincerity—if naiveté—about Jody's situation that seems primed for dialogue and engagement.

I see the e-mail as significant for these reasons, but also because it is written from the point of view of someone who, apparently, has yet to learn the language and strategies of color blindness and multiculturalism—she is very clear about her perception of people and the world before she spoke to her mother and before she wrote the draft for her cluster group. That is, her e-mail does not invoke the language of political correctness that is embedded in the discourse of the college community. It is this candidness that the students in her cluster group likely responded to, and it is because of their submersion in the discourse of multiculturalism and political correctness—the schizophrenia of the discourse surrounding race and racism—that causes them to register such shock that she would write the draft essay in the first place, and that she would consider handing it in to me, as a black professor, in the second place. In their act to maintain color blindness, they actually invoke a form of whiteness, which they simultaneously encourage Jody to participate in by encouraging her to leave important questions unanswered.

I do not assign blame to the students in Jody's cluster group for their actions; rather I see them as symptomatic of a general state of affairs where white students and black professors are concerned. I nevertheless see these actions as having the effect of potentially cutting off dialogue between me, and Jody, and perhaps more importantly, between me, them, and the rest of the class. This is perhaps because they misread "race talk" for offensive talk, and perhaps find it difficult to find a position from which to speak where race and racism are concerned. They also misread what the objectives of the class are; that is, they misread the classroom space I attempt to create where I want to encourage dialogue on issues such as racism and gender oppression. This may well be another way that my race, and their preconceived notions of what I represent, precede me.

They also misread the nuances in Jody's text—particularly the part that she has in block capitals in her email, that she was going *against* the racism she has discovered in society and, to her surprise, in her mother. They further misread Chesnutt's piece in that they fail to see and comment on, as Jody does, the moral center of the story, which is whether or not Ryder should accept the wife of his youth. More powerful than all of these concerns, perhaps, are the many questions that go unanswered. For instance, why shouldn't an audience of her peers, the audience I encourage them to write for, read such an essay? Why shouldn't we engage in a dialogue about what the essay should mean to us as a class and as a community of learners and citizens at WU and beyond? Why was Jody given the advice to *rewrite* her essay so as not to offend me?

In asking these questions I do not discount the difficulty of raising candid questions about race and racism to a black professor; the tension associated with "race talk" make this extremely difficult and may explain why Jody was so upset. No one wants to land in the minefield of being accused of racism—being controversial is a bad thing because it puts you in league with racists. Therefore, students tend to avoid the subject, thereby reproducing it in the form of cutting off dialogue and doing nothing to disrupt the status quo. We generally don't allow people to make mistakes when it comes to this kind of thing, which brings us back to the notion of dialogue. That is to say, the cluster group functioned in a way that clearly protected whiteness by maintaining a certain status quo in the classroom that would have left questions about racism, identity, affiliations, and power inconspicuously unanswered, had it not been for Jody's essay, and her willingness to see me as open enough to be approached.

Jody's work is connected to other students' writing which I am tempted to see as more informed by the schizophrenia of multiculturalism and color blindness than hers. For example, in the anonymous "Notes to me" that I invite students to write throughout the semester to critique and influence the direction of the course, a significant number of them say in various ways "I like class, and you are a good teacher, but we should talk about something other than slavery and race all the time," as I explained earlier in this essay. I got these specific responses back after the class had read Kate Chopin's "Story of an Hour" and "Desiree's Baby"; Jamaica Kincaid's "Girl"; William Faulkner's "A Rose for Emily"; and Charles Chesnutt's "The Wife of His Youth," and while I was endeavoring to illustrate the ways in which gender, specifically, is a key construct in social class generally, but also as it relates to present-day oppression of women. This in fact, is a point Jody makes in her e-mail though she herself did not seem to be aware of it when she suggested that Mr. Ryder was being forced by society to stick with his own "race." Anyone familiar with Chesnutt's short story knows both Liza Jane and Mrs. Dixon are black. However, Mrs. Dixon is light-skinned and a member of the Blue Veins Society, which is a middle-class and upwardly mobile black "club."

There are other important aspects of Jody's e-mail which reveal how whiteness functions through the schizophrenia of the color-blind-multicultural-political correctness mix, and how the short-circuiting of dialogue in the classroom makes it impossible for a coherent pedagogy, such as critical pedagogy, for example, to have the kind of impact we would want in our students. Certainly Jody's discovery about her mother's contradictory stance on social acceptance of "Hispanics" is revealing and an important learning experience for her. Her mother is exhibiting color-blindness in that she, according to Jody, is "so accepting of others," and a form of whiteness when the practical implications of this professed belief have to be confronted, namely, the idea that "if [Jody] were to ever get married to a Hispanic male, she feels that they don't become as successful as 'others'" where "others" seems to stand in for "white men". I recognize, then, the "play" that this schizophrenia creates between what we profess, and what we're actually willing to accept as Jody herself points to when she registers surprise at her mother's position given her apparent open acceptance of "others."

It is significant that Jody's mother should couch her reservations about Hispanic men in material terms since the recourse to materiality is an important way that whiteness constitutes itself. Jody's mother expects her daughter to marry a white man, because white men signify material wealth to her. The thought of Jody marrying someone else unsettles the settled expectations of whiteness[7] Jody's mother has for her daughter.

I had chosen this assignment recognizing that for many students Composition II would be their last opportunity to read and write about literature and have someone help them do it in a college setting, since the course was required for all majors. I felt that these texts, particularly "The Wife of His Youth," allowed students to use literature to interpret, analyze, and reflect about who they are, and how they are socially constructed in our society. The text, "The Wife of His Youth," actually did its job in some ways, because it helped Jody find a language to articulate her experiences and her feelings.

I also realize that Jody's experiences provided an excellent opportunity for her, and perhaps the class, to discuss the significant differences between her and Mr. Ryder on the one hand, and her Hispanic friend and Liza Jane on the other; differences which are at least as important as the similarities she sees, and ones which would add important nuances to her essay and her experiences reading literature. For instance, Jody has used the word "race" to illustrate the difference between Mr. Ryder and Liza Jane. It's a misreading, to be sure, but a significant one because it again illustrates the materiality that students see as constituting race. Jody sees Mr. Ryder's light skin, refined manner, and fine clothes as a marker of whiteness.

Jody's recourse to Shakespeare toward the end of her e-mail is also significant since it steers her conversation in the e-mail away from a politicized discussion with the possibility of further dialogue—or even open-ended questions—toward a kind of humanistic, liberal individuality that anticipates, in some ways, the discourse of schizophrenia connected to color blindness, multiculturalism, and political correctness.

I wanted to know more about Jody's thoughts. She was unusual in that she seemed candid and open enough—perhaps confused enough—to want or need help sorting out what she was feeling. I invited her to use the journal writing in the course as a space to explore these experiences. What follows is one of her journals:

On Mondays and Wednesdays I have "Intro to Literature" and "Racism and Sexism" one right after another. Between reading literature in English and articles in my racism and sexism class, issues became very overwhelming to me. I grew up eighteen years of my life in a small suburban town, predominantly white. I am expected to know about controversies in society dealing with race that supposedly are normal in everyday life. I can't believe how unaware I've been all these years living in my little bubble of a town.

Now, I feel as an eighteen year old white female I have to be careful of the things I say, in fear I may offend someone. I hope that I can take these experiences and learn from them in the future. In my classes I want to see things from other point of views, but at the same time still stick to my beliefs. The problem now becomes, do I have a right to say my opinion even though I have dealt with little prejudice? I am really confused in this environment I was recently thrown into, but hopefully it can help me grow as a person.

While illustrating how overwhelmed she is by her new environment, which is not necessarily a bad thing, Jody's journal also seems to indicate that she is developing a response to the university community which reproduces an insular identity for her with a developing sense of her whiteness to contend with; an identity implicitly encouraged by her group cluster. This developing identity is suggested by the following, "As an 18 year old white female, I have to be careful of the things I say in fear I offend someone . . . In my classes I want to see it from other point of views, but at the same time still stick to my beliefs." One way of reading this statement is to suggest that there is guilt associated with her subject position, though she does not appear to be fully aware of why she should feel it. If Jody was unfamiliar with the nuances of schizophrenia associated with color blindness and multiculturalism clearly her classmates responses—and her mother's—now make this unlikely. Another way of thinking about her assertion implicates "emotion." That is to say, there is not only an intellectual element to the issue of how she relates to racialized others, which she can begin to resolve through her interpretation of Chesnutt's "The Wife of His Youth," but there is also the role of emotion vis-à-vis intellectual and academic development, particularly as it is connected to her mother, and her developing identity as a student. On the one hand, she really does not want to offend anyone, as she says, and I imagine, least of all me in the context of the classroom, yet she wants to have a sense of herself as expressed in her desire to "stick to her beliefs."

The willingness to communicate with me, however, in the midst of her confusion, presents an opportunity for dialogue, and the potential to engage a meaningful pedagogy that addresses the student phenomenologically, along the lines that Max van Manen[8] advocates rather than the prepackaged assignments that we, teachers, sometimes share with each other because they happened to "work" with one set of students. Van Manen suggests a pedagogical strategy that invites and creates a space in the classroom for a host of varied lived human experiences with the fundamental premise that we are, after all, all human, and I would add, equally unfit for opppression.

*   *   *

It's unclear to me what role the institution, and society at large, played in Jody's life, or how other students like her may respond in situations similar to hers. I wonder about the effect her college education has had on who she has become. She is no longer a student at WU, but I had an opportunity to talk with after tracking her down to get permission to use her writing. She graduated several years ago with a degree in business and is now enjoying a career as an executive for a major corporation. She has bought a house in northern New Jersey, and says she often thinks about our class. In fact, when I called her she had recently reminded her mother of the episode involving her Hispanic friend and recalled for her that she had written about it in school. Her mother doesn't remember the incident at all, and is happy with Jody's choice—Jody and her friend are still a couple. I'd like to think that her Composition II course helped her sort through the complex business of race, racism, and whiteness in some small way.

Afterword
"Washing the White Blood from Daniel Boone"

Wendy: I remember coming across this painting by Jared French, *Washing the White Blood from Daniel Boone,* and thinking how incredible an illustration this is of some of the things that have come up in our thinking about whiteness studies. I'm struck by how the Boone figure is centralized, even though the project here is to wash away the whiteness. He's the focus, and it's almost like the Native American figures are "servicing" him and taking up the burden of his whiteness. Boone declares his need to be free of his whiteness in order to join the human race. It reveals the melancholia of loss and longing that seems so much a part of the ironic position whiteness sees itself occupying.

Ian: You say even though his white blood is being washed, it's almost like the Native Americans are servicing him. This caught my attention because I, too, think there are several things going on in the painting and also in your response to it. First, you point out that the ostensible reason for the gathering is to wash the white blood off of Boone. It's in this sense that the painting speaks in Jungian terms; the notion that Boone will become one with the Native Americans. But what's the nature of that oneness? As you point out, the Boone figure is centered, and the Native Americans are servicing him. If he's a representation of whiteness, as I think you're inviting me to see him, then the oneness is on Boone's term—as outnumbered as he is by the muscular, sexualized men surrounding him. What you also seem to be suggesting is that the recentering of Boone's whiteness represents a kind of unwitting and ironic naiveté on the part of the Native Americans. Their attempt to draw Boone into their cultural unconscious makes them part of the project of whiteness; reinscribing as it attempts to wash it away. I'm particularly sensitive to this interpretation of the painting as it's a potential criticism I'm sure some may have of this very book.

I'm also sensitive to a critique of the book that might argue with our definitions of whiteness. I'm aware, for instance, of

Washing the White Blood from Daniel Boone. By Jared French (American, 1939).

Bartholomae's epitaph in his essay "The Tidy House: Basic Writing in the American Curriculum," where he quotes Spivak who in turn comments using Foucault. She says, "Remember, in Foucault's passage in his History of Sexuality: One must be a nominalist. Power is not this, power is not that. Power is the name one must lend to a complex structure of relationships" (4). Some might argue that what we've done is name power "whiteness." But I hope that readers will also see that we've done so with a purpose of exploring that complex system of relationships that she speaks of. For example, I've been reminded of Frank Norris's book, *The Octopus*, quite a bit as I've been working on this book. Whiteness seems to me to be a kind of octopus in the sense that I think Norris was after when he uses it as a metaphor for the rapid industrial and mechanized expansion westward, and where no one human subject appears to be in control—sort of like the financial crash we've just experienced in this country.

Spivak goes on to say "the subaltern is the name of the place which is so displaced from what made me and the organized resister, that to have it speak is like Godot arriving on a bus. We want it to disappear as a name so that we can all speak" (quoted in Bartholomae 5). Bartholomae includes this quote from Spivak because I think he wants to posit the basic writer in terms of the subaltern—colonized. Once they are named as the counterpart to the occident, or the colonizer, they become their nominal function. I hope readers will not read our book this way: where "whiteness" is like a distorted Godot preventing dialogue.

Shifting back to the notion of oneness and how it might apply to whiteness in the context of composition, I'm reminded of something you once said to me. You said that institutions want to change students, but they don't in turn expect to be changed in any significant way by them. For some reason French's painting reminds me of that comment, and I think it's because what gets valued, in an uncanny way in both, is an embedded whiteness. Just as the Natives enshrine whiteness in an attempt to wash it away, so too do institutions enshrine whiteness in projects like multiculturalism, or as I point out in Chapter 4, the deployment of texts by nonwhite writers that invariably get read in precisely the same ways as all other texts get read. I'm aware as well of the ironic use of the word "nonwhite," which in some ways illustrates the point I'm making.

I want to go back to something else we've covered in conversation, and I'm hoping that we can include it here. That is, the discussion of your father and how you recognize how his life, and by implication your own life, has been shaped by benefits you see he accrued as a direct consequence of his white identity. Can you comment on that? I'd especially be interested in you connecting it to our discussion of this painting because in some ways I think I (we?) are being asked to see the Boone figure as representative of white identity. It's highly sexualized presentation—almost androgynous-like—causes me to suspect that it may even be an attempt on French's part to capture male and female white identity. Here then the visually feminized Boone masks the ruthless masculinity that the whites who followed his pioneering trail would bring to the Native American. How, then, might your father (and you?) as whites be implicated in the painting?

Wendy: The thing is it's not just Boone that represents whiteness but that the whole painting represents how whiteness, progressive liberal whiteness, too often sees itself as it struggles to come to terms with racism through the rhetoric of multiculturalism and inclusion. In fact it seems to me that the "collective unconscious" is not there for the Native Americans to own as you suggest when you say they are absorbing Boone into it, but, like concepts of universalism in general, is really an avatar of whiteness. I suppose what I'm saying about *Washing the White Blood from Daniel Boone* is that it illustrates the pitfalls of whiteness scholarship. In some ways it seems like that's what critical whiteness studies wanted to do—wash away the white blood—in the sense that we wanted to remove the insidiousness of whiteness by eliminating the essentialism of race—race as "blood." Which isn't a bad thing to want to do, I suppose. And it also suggests that our idea of "blood" is really cosmetic, something that actually *can* be washed away. But when we look at how it plays out in the painting, we see all the unforeseen consequences of this methodology: the recentering of whiteness, as we've noted, as whites attempt to "save" themselves by relinquishing their whiteness in order to join humanity. The iconography of Boon is ambiguous: in one way as a frontiersman he epitomizes the racism of Westward Expansion and the subduing of the Indians, so he must be rendered harmless—we must find a way to disarm him—and that "way" seems to be implicated in his relationship to the Native Americans who adopted and befriended him—something the painting gestures toward. Whiteness here imagines itself as seeking forgiveness so that it might find a way to go on, absorbed into and reinvigorated by a postracial ideal. And I suppose it's no accident that his loss of whiteness here, as you note, feminizes him as he wears his nice pink and ribboned skivvies—an interesting evocation of civilization discourse, in which whiteness presents itself as anemic and a contrast to the contemporaneously circulating image of the muscular, "All-American" Normman statue that I discuss in Chapter 3. But it's worth noting that Boone might also be seen as some kind of victim—abducted by the Other—and his rehabilitation is a failure in that he will take the first chance he gets to escape. So does liberal whiteness oscillate between wanting to absolve itself and wanting to claim its perceived privilege? But we strip him naked and scrub away all that whiteness, almost as though it's a sacrificial rite, so he is prepared for something, but what? And in many ways, that's the question that whiteness studies leaves us with—now what? I think this is the question which you've been responding to throughout this book and our discussions about "white irony." So as I point out about narrative performance of whiteness, once we confess our whiteness, where does that leave us? Clean and ready to be absorbed? Or does it really leave us nowhere at all? Or worse yet, ready to reassert whiteness when it is no longer convenient to be washed clean?

I suppose that's how I would answer your question about my father and me. It doesn't matter maybe whether I confess my racist childhood or "out" my father as a racist, although I imagine, like the Daniel Boone in French's painting, this is something necessary for my own psychic health—dealing with my whiteness is rendered a step in some kind of psychic integration or self-actualizing project. What probably does matter, a lot, is that the modest house he built in a white neighborhood in 1950 appreciated in value as the neighborhood became even more white and middle-class, and it appreciated, as we know, because of larger economic forces of deregulation and speculation that fueled, in an ultimately very detrimental way, the late-twentieth-century American economy. When he died, the money in his estate that came largely from that appreciating house allowed me to have enough money to make a down payment on my own house. That transgenerational transference of wealth, that's perhaps truly the heart of whiteness—that's how I'm very implicated and end up asserting my whiteness.

Ian: I like the way you use the painting to illustrate how we've discussed the complexities of whiteness. I wonder about how Daniel Boone is being deployed though. There's a point at which he becomes a metaphor that, to me, begins to break down. I understand him as a pioneer of the American West in many ways, and a legend/myth in his own lifetime. But Boone may well signify a whole host of things having to do with the extermination of Indians, the stealing of land, and U.S. expansionism generally that doesn't have much to do with the historical figure at all. Again, I'm reminded of Norris's book where Boone might be a convenient stand-in for the railway, but perhaps not big enough. Or should I say, the historical Boone may not be big enough, but the mythical Boone is—a kind of symbol of white masculinity mythical and, as it plays out in the painting and in fact, ironic.

From what you say, I see your father in similar ways. I didn't know him personally, but from your description I imagine a man of modest means, who was wise enough (and white enough?) to make decisions for his family that left you with a modest legacy—a down payment on a home. I think it would be a mistake to see these things as a privilege though, as you implicitly do. To do so would be confusing, I think, the mythology of white identity with the reality of your father's actual lived experiences. That is to say, I doubt that your father enjoyed many luxuries that would be considered extravagant because he happened to have white skin, and so even if we have to remain cognizant of individual acts of racism, and the enormously seductive pull of majority group identity that is whiteness, we must also recognize that your father was not extraordinarily wealthy. There's nothing he had that I would begrudge him. This may be another way of describing the irony of whiteness: that people are drawn to it in spite of the ways in which it does not serve their best economic interests.

Wendy: Luxuries, no, and if we want to say that in a country—or world for that matter—where the concentration of wealth is so extreme that very few people are "winning," I think that's fair enough. But in this very specific way, my father's whiteness afforded me a *stability* that I might come to take for granted, to expect as my due, and it's accomplished in the manner I describe so that we can have racism without racists, by which I mean the enormous, demonstrable inequity that continues to exist and that seemingly can't be addressed by rhetorics of tolerance and inclusion. So the image we have of washing away whiteness through moral accounting—or in the case of the Daniel Boone painting, through desire, I suppose—remains the kind of romantic chimera we see in French's painting.

Ian: To your comment ". . . my father's whiteness afforded me a *stability* that I might come to take for granted, to expect as my due, and it's accomplished in the manner I describe so that we can have racism without racists . . ." might I also add, as enshrined in the narrative of U.S. law? This, in fact, is one of the most important insights of Cheryl Harris's "Whiteness as Property": the idea of "settled expectations"—that somehow your stability and happiness as a specifically *white* citizen is a property right protected by U.S. law, as the history of the narrative of U.S. law has ably demonstrated. But at what point does my humanity, speaking as a black person, trump your right to have expectations built on your father's legacy or pursuit of happiness? I think that's one of the questions your analysis invites, and something Critical Race Theorists, such as Harris, studied. How does one square the legal decision of something like Plessey vs. Ferguson, which argued among other things that there is no right that a black person has that a white person is bound to respect, with the failure of the remedy, Brown vs. Board of Education, as Jonathan Kozol points out as discussed in our Introduction? There's a long history of legal ruling, civil life, accumulated wealth, and the fulfillment of settled expectations that occurs between these two rulings, which suggests black folk in the U.S. don't have to go back to slavery to talk about reparations. There are reparations to be had for things occurring now as Michelle Alexander's book, *The New Jim Crow: Mass Incarceration in the Age of Colorblindness*, seems to suggest when she argues that while Jim Crow laws are no longer on the books, the racial caste system it produced remains firmly entrenched most evidently in the prison system. I see that book as just one recent appeal to us to pay attention to how U.S. law continues to have a paradoxical relationship toward black people.

Wendy: So are we no better off than we started? Are we trapped in white irony? That's the cynical view, and despite what we've pointed out here, I actually don't believe that. You and I are teaching writing and rhetoric to very different student populations, as we've discussed. My institution has historically been very white and tending toward middle-class. In fact, I remember when I interviewed for the position. I was taking a cab on the way from the train station and making small talk with the cabdriver. He asks my business, and when I tell him I am interviewing for a job at the university he is driving me to, he treats me to his views on what's wrong with higher education: "It's awful," he said, "the way they give all the money for college to the foreigners and minorities and it's gotten now so that, you know . . . the regular people can't afford to go." I think his blunt introduction into this community I was entering was apt and telling, although by no means exclusive. A few weeks later at another job interview in California, I did a presentation for the faculty on the rhetoric of whiteness—tracing moments of "invisible" whiteness as they occur in student writing to help us, I believe, better understand what we are reading when we look at student texts. I remember my presentation generating very little response, but there seemed to be a vague sense of confusion about what such work has to do with teaching students how to write academic essays. I remember one of the few questions, asked in puzzlement: "Do you think someone who has a conservative ideology can write well?"

So I think in our collaborative inquiry perhaps we've gotten somewhere after all, at least by changing the terms of the debate, or at least I hope so. Our essays are very different, and maybe are attempting to do different things, but they "speak" to each other, in the spirit of open-ended dialogue that we've been so bold, or naive, to place our faith in.

Ian: No, we're not where we started, and I don't believe we're trapped in white irony. I think that the essays here present the palimpsest that we were after when we said, in the Introduction, that we wanted to create an epistemology of whiteness in composition studies. But it's not just the essays themselves that contribute to that epistemology, but also the practice of dialogue that they together represent, and what I've come to learn about how whiteness works through race and racism in the U.S. by talking candidly with you as one who signifies as both white and female. Subjectively I know my teaching has changed for the better as a result of the thinking and learning I've done moving through this project, and I hope some of that will come through for others as they read the book. I'm reminded of James C. Scott's *Domination and the Arts of Resistance*, in particular his chapter 7, "The Infrapolitics of Subordinate Groups," where he defines *infrapolitics* as the little acts of daily struggle waged by subordinate groups, like infrared rays which are beyond the visible end of the color spectrum, but nevertheless have an impact on power. He also argues convincingly that systematic subordination generates pressure of some kind "from below" (186). While this book is not exactly infrapolitical as he discusses because it is not under the radar, so to speak, it does, I think, contribute to the "infrastructure" of resistance against oppressive systems he invites us to consider. It is, at the very least, a demonstrable act of resistance, and a contribution to the struggle against racism.

Notes

NOTES TO THE INTRODUCTION

1. Throughout this book, we question the assumptions of what Chris Hedges has defined as "Modern liberalism" and its faith that "Human institutions and governments . . . inevitably better mankind" (84). We use liberal here, with its emphasis on individualism and progress, not as a counter to conservative, but rather as that which undercuts the radical, what Fergus has equated with "soft power." According to Fergus, Malcolm X understood "soft power" as "friendly" hegemony that was "benevolent" and "philanthropic." This contrasts with "hard power," which seeks overtly to eliminate and deny rights (9).

2. Aronowitz cites an increase in the middle-class from twelve to fifteen percent of the total African-American population for this time period, but he also points out that as the middle-class percentage increased, the income for African-American poor decreased by twenty-five percent so that "for most Black women and men, the last decade has been an unmitigated disaster" (189).

3. Just as Keith Miller has argued that the rhetoric of Malcolm X engaged critical whiteness theory before it was so named, we note too that these writers also anticipated the trajectories of contemporary whiteness theory. Du Bois, for example, writes in a similar vein to Bennett, Allen, and Ignatiev with regard to the invention of whiteness and its relationship to labor and social class (see note 5). In *Black Reconstruction in America 1860 to 1880,* Du Bois argues convincingly that whites immigrating from central and western Europe to the New World were unwilling to regard themselves as a permanent laboring class, and he concludes, "it is in this light that the labor movement among white Americans must be studied" (17).

4. How and why racism began to take shape in America are still very much in question among historians, and the debate is best articulated by Theodore Allen in his book *The Invention of the White Race.* Here Allen argues that the split between historians falls along two lines, the psychocultural and socioeconomic. The psychoculturalists, such as David Roediger in *Wages of Whiteness* and Winthrop Jordan in *White over Black,* suggest that racism stems from the observation of "natural" cultural biases and emanates from the working class as immigrant workers attempt to distinguish themselves from slave laborers. The socioeconomic argument, as predictably asserted by Allen himself along with Bennett as well as Du Bois, suggests that institutional racism, as a strategy created and deployed by ruling classes to maintain oppression, is the principle cause of the racial disparities we see in society generally.

5. Bennett and Allen trace the roots of American racism, and indeed the invention of the white race itself, to the plantation aristocracy's need for a "buffer

class" of erstwhile poor whites between themselves and the black slave, while Ignatiev shows how in Philadelphia's Walnut Street Jail in the 1820s racial division was subordinate to the prison culture, which the prisoners themselves controlled. Both Bennett and Allen point out that the social position of the "buffer class," while providing relative privilege for poor whites in relation to blacks, made class-based revolt in the seventeenth century increasingly unlikely and allegiances based on the notion of race increasingly more likely. Indeed, whites in the buffer class helped to support a social and economic system that was at fundamental odds with its own best economic interests. This unwillingness to find common cause with what was considered a permanent laboring class—blacks—signaled the division of the working class along specifically racial lines.

6. Aronowitz sees the reliance on ethnicity as a kind of anemic political "strategy" of social and personal identity that takes place in response to a climate of antiradical rhetoric so that the hyphenated identity of ethnicity is a palatable, more polite alternative to radical race-, gender- or class-based identity:

> Among the entailments of this strategic identity was the reintroduction of the hyphen into cultural identity. . . . By the self-designation of "African American," "Mexican American," or "Chinese American" rather than the more radical terms Black, Latino, Asian, which were distinctly diasporic terms, this fraction of racialized communities announced its primary identification with the nation in which ethnicity was situated as a plural modifier. (206)

We note here that the concept of the "national identity" is itself a coded whiteness that is the center of the universe of these satellite identities, which thus are defined and brought into being by whiteness.

7. See, for example, Janet Zandy's *Liberating Memory* and Dews and Law's *This Fine Place So Far from Home*, volumes that problematize the presumed middle-class orientation of academia through the narratives of working-class academics, many of which ethnicize the white working-class experience.

8. We quote here at length from a transcription of an American Studies workshop published in *Radical Teacher* ("Class in the Classroom") about the significance of making class "visible" in the academy and how that contributes to a multicultural project. One of the effects of this visibility is to restore significance to the white subject as suggested in the professor's anecdote below.

She describes three students, Margaret, Darrell, and Zulan and their interactions. Margaret is characterized as working-class white, although the teacher did not know this as the student did not self-identify, which, as the instructor points out, is typical of working-class students. Darrell is described as African-American and taciturn while Zulan is African-American and well spoken and insightful. The professor describes the introduction of the course and how she asks students to read from a multicultural reader to solicit written responses or group oral presentations. The teacher was astounded by the vitriolic attack that working-class Margaret mounted against multiculturalism when she brought to class a copy of *Cosmo* and asked the males in the class whether or not they found the white model featured on the cover desirable. Apparently the quiet Darrell raised objections to Margaret's assumptions, but was not able to quell Margaret's "rap" against multiculturalism. The teacher describes her own anger at Margaret as well as Margaret's mounting impatience and hostility toward the teacher's multicultural agenda.

The instructor then describes class response to a novel, *Storming Heaven* by Denise Giardina, which describes union organizing in 1920s West Virginia and the novelist's family involvement in the enterprise. This novel had a profound effect on the rabid antimulticultural Margaret, who approached the teacher after class to further discuss her response to the story:

Zulan listened attentively to Margaret's rap: "This was the story of my grandfather. I never expected to see my grandfather's story in print. I grew up hearing the story from my mother of the mine operators' brutality. I heard the story of my grandfather making, painstakingly making, blueprints of the mine shafts and where the supports were going to collapse and kill miners. He took those to the mine owners and he showed them, assuming they would do something. Of course, these supports collapsed right at the points my grandfather predicted they would, killing miner, after miner, after miner. But I couldn't repeat those stories my mother told me because I feared no one would believe me. And now, finally, I have read those stories in a required text for an English literature class." Margaret asked, "Is this what multiculturalism is all about?" and I answered, "Yes." And she said, "Well, I'm going to have to reconsider this whole thing." As Margaret left the room, Zulan commented dryly, "You can't see the puzzle until you see your own piece."

What is obvious here is that Margaret needs to learn about her heritage as much as Darrell needs to learn about his, as much as Zulan needs to learn about hers. And Margaret needs to find that heritage in literary texts, just as Darrell and Zulan need to find their heritage in literary texts. ("Class in the Classroom" 46)

The implication is that cross-racial alliances can be formed by the study of class, but this alliance is, as constructed here, dependent on the white working-class students' perception of inclusion established through injured status.

9. In her study of student autobiography, sociologist Karyn D. McKinney finds that despite the complexity of racialization in twenty-first-century America, the black/white opposition remains a powerful trope in the construction of identity:

Although other groups are growing, with racism directed at them as well, one can argue that a black/white paradigm still holds for U.S. racism, for several reasons. The modern idea of "race" was constructed in response to the relationship between whites and African-Americans. Other groups who have entered the United States have had to contend with this system and be judged by its standards. . . . Further, African Americans were the only group ever held in long-term legal servitude in this country, and the only group whose enslavement was legitimized by the Constitution. For these reasons and others, the black experience in the United States has been so unique that racism to some extent persists and operates according to a black/white paradigm. (101)

NOTES TO CHAPTER 1

1. After making this observation, Carter goes on to say that "It is much less common for scholars to ask *how* whiteness became 'invisible,' or to connect that transparency to whiteness's historically specific cultural contents and meanings" (28). She does so by arguing that whiteness's uncontested hegemony, achieved through its instantiation in heterosexuality and the ideal of modern marriage, rendered it "normal" in the twentieth century. She specifically questions Roediger's assertion that whiteness is "empty" rather than

productive: "In such analyses, whiteness appears to be 'normal' because it is powerful enough to 'hold back,' that is, silence or marginalize, the voices of those who might testify to its specificity and its violence. . . . though most whiteness studies are motivated by a desire to reveal the political contents and consequences of whiteness, I am concerned that assertions of its emptiness may actually work to renaturalize the category in ways that produce political stasis rather than transformation" (29).

2. Thandeka, in her examination of such narratives as recounted to her orally, has questioned the white subject's move to classify his/her behavior/attitude as racist, claiming that the white person incorrectly dubs the racialized wound of whiteness as racism because it is the only rhetorical position available to describe the experience (see above). "The [feared] charge of racism" can, for the white liberal subject, "act like a prisoner's stun belt used to exact a confession" (9).

   Hartigan, too, has questioned the way racism is read into the white subject's narrative by researchers, claiming that the lens of antiracism obscures important ambiguities in an unproductive way. See chapter 9, "Object lessons in Whiteness: Antiracism and the Study of White Folks," in *Odd Tribes: Toward a Cultural Analysis of White People.*

3. See Krista Ratcliffe's comment about self-actualization with regard to her work in whiteness: "I offer this book . . . not as a final stage of self-actualization about identifications with gender and whiteness. (I happen to think that self-actualization is one of our more insidious cultural myths. . . .) [*Rhetorical* 8].

4. If one renounces one group, it is imperative that there be a new group to join to make up for the lost identity of the old. See Giroux, for example. Gresson calls this trend the "recovery school of whiteness" (39).

5. See Henke, for example:

   As a genre, life-writing encourages the author/narrator to reassess the past and to reinterpret the intertextual codes inscribed on personal consciousness by society and culture. Because the author can instantiate the alienated or marginal self into the pliable body of a protean text, the newly revised subject, emerging as the semifictive protagonist of an enabling counternarrative, is free to rebel against the values and practices of a dominant culture and to assume an empowered position of political agency in the world. (xv–xvi)

6. See my discussion of Douglass, in which I analyze simplified readings of the 1845 *Narrative* and call into question the limits of literacy narratives in forming counterhegemonic subjectivities.

7. Hartigan raises serious questions about antiracism as a filter for analyzing stories of whiteness suggesting that antiracism as a methodology creates a scenario "where [the subject's] suspicions might never be fully expressed, examined, or disengaged through antiracism's activist solutions. . . . I think it is important to recognize that the significance of race in certain situations exceeds individuals' efforts, whether avowedly political or not, to engage its unruly range of potential meanings and implications" (*Odd* 251–52).

8. Again my observations coincide with Hesse's: "what is happening is a movement from general to more specific exposition" ("Stories" 183).

9. According to Scott Russell Sanders, "Orwell forcefully argued . . . [that] such a bypassing of abstraction, such an insistence on the concrete is a politically subversive act" (33).

10. See Chapter 3 for a discussion of whiteness as melancholic kitsch.

11. In this particular autobiographical essay of Frankenberg's, she, in a metatextual strategy similar to Worsham's, analyzes her own story about whiteness and concludes that "the burden of my narrative was one of redemption of my

white self" noting that it "protests my own 'innocence' . . . as in 'youthful, naive.'" But here again, as in Worsham's case, Frankenberg's self-consciousness does not alleviate the problem as she goes on to claim that despite her best intentions the narrative exhibits "sickening aspects" (6). In so doing the narrating consciousness bolsters ethical authority by laying claim to the injury of her white status: she confesses that her subjectivity is sickening. The irony of course is that her own narrative efforts "betray" her in a similar way to what she observes in Roediger's language.

NOTES TO CHAPTER 2

1. See the discussion of Robyn Wiegman's essay, "Whiteness Studies and the Paradox of Particularity," as well as our discussion of Mike Hill's *After Whiteness: The Unmaking of an American Majority* in the Introduction.
2. See William Jones's "Basic Writing: Pushing Against Racism" (72–80) and Jerrie Cobb Scott's "Literacies and Deficits Revisited," *Journal of Basic Writing* 12.1 (1993): 46–56.
3. See Dian Schaffhauser's 13 Oct. 2010 online article in *Campus Technology*, where she discusses the plan to tackle "remediation": <http://campustechnology.com/articles/2010/10/13/new-blackboard-and-k12-project-to-tackle-cc-remediation.aspx>.
4. See New Jersey Department of Education statistics: <http://www.state.nj.us/education/data/enr/enr10/stat_doc.htm >.
5. See Karen Brodkin's *How the Jews Became White Folks and What That Says About Race in America* (30).
6. See Du Bois's discussion of race and labor in his *Black Reconstruction in America 1860–1880* New York: Atheneum, 1969.
7. Qtd. in Keith Gilyard and Elaine Richardson, "Students' Right to Possibility," *Insurrections: Approaches to Resistance in Composition Studies*. Ed. Andrea Greenbaum. New York: SUNY P, 2001.
8. See, for example, her uses of language in her book, *Borderlands/La Frontera: The New Mestiza*.
9. See Jon-Christian Suggs's *Whispered Consolations: Law and Narrative in African American Life*. Ann Arbor: Michigan UP, 2000, for an extended interpretation of this passage.
10. See Ralph Ellison's "Twentieth Century American Fiction and the Black Mask of Humanity."
11. See William Jones's "Basic Writing: Pushing Against Racism" where he argues that "racism situates basic writing programs as Jim-Crow way stations for minority students by insisting on a hierarchy of intelligence among races."

NOTES TO CHAPTER 3

1. Student resistance is much discussed in critical pedagogy especially with regard to race (see Chapter 5). Analouise Keating, for example, finds that such resistance requires that race be approached obliquely:

   I rarely begin a course or a unit by focusing specifically on 'race' or on any other social identity category; instead, I start with thematic and aesthetic issues and give students specific suggestions, topics to reflect on as they read. I have learned that these topics should not foreground 'race,' for to do so often makes students defensive and triggers various status-quo stories. I plan classroom discussion carefully, and lead

> students through questions designed to assist us in becoming aware of how they have unconsciously operated within a 'white' reading framework. . . . I find it effective to begin with seemingly "universal" topics (such as quest motifs, childhood, and so forth), rather than with "race" or any other social identity category. (91)

2. Fish, adopting the persona of the curmudgeon, demands that academics "do your job" and excoriates writing instructors for polluting their class with provocative "ideas" and "content" (40–49). His proposed remedy, which he enacts in his first-year writing courses, is to have students create their own invented language and devise ways for teaching its grammar and syntax. By teaching students about linguistic structure, he believes their writing will improve although he admits to being unclear about the connection. Arguably, his class has at least as little to do with *writing* as any class he criticizes. I do agree with Fish that our attempts to teach writing are impeded by the influence on discourse of "well-worn and terminally dull arguments one hears or sees on every radio and TV talk show" (41). Indeed, this is precisely my point about Imus and other "controversies."

3. Despite such popular beliefs that delimit writing instruction to craft-based issues of mechanics and structure, I have ironically found equal resistance on the part of students to reducing writing to a discussion of generic features, such as, for example, when I ask them to try to theorize the attributes of the personal essay in a particular piece of writing that distinguish it generically from other types of writing. Students resist talking about how the writing is constructed and instead wish to focus on what the writing is about—i.e., the ideas and opinions expressed. The persistence of this tendency suggests that fracturing writing instruction from content is at least on some level as counterintuitive as the social epistemic rhetoric disallowed in current traditionalism and discredited as invalid writing pedagogy by Fulkerson and others.

4. See their textbook, *They Say/I Say* in which they argue for a fill-in-the-blank approach to demystify academic rhetoric and argument for students. Although the authors bill their approach as a progressive, student-centered, and dialogic method that provides a pragmatic means of situating writing as conversation, the philosophy of which is fairly unassailable, the templates themselves are arguably reductive—even reactionary—rather than radical, not to mention misleading in the promotion of (to my mind) the mistaken belief that abstraction in academic discourse amounts to no more than Orwellian obfuscation. This ultimately impoverished view of rhetoric as "moves" or language games plagues the field of composition and rhetoric and panders to the belief of writing and rhetoric as a formulaic activity, again devoid of political significance.

5. For an example of the extensive reign of political kitsch see Westbrook's discussion, where he sees kitsch in a variety of political agendas in France. He coins the term "bovéism, signifying a complacent nostalgia for an idealized past," after the antiagribusiness activist José Bové, to describe the kitsch tendency in leftist politics: "It is precisely the decline of the traditional binary between Left and Right . . . which requires new categories of analysis. Bovéism, presented here as a cultural politics of kitsch, is a provisional attempt to find such a vocabulary" (426).

6. Seshadri-Crooks offers a Lacanian explanation of difference to account for whiteness in opposition to materialist explanations such as Roediger's. Nonetheless, her analysis too centers around the question of falseness (although she is careful to point out that here the idea of fantasy is not a synonym for falseness): "The assumption made by every subject of race that Whiteness is a transcendental signifier that promises absolute wholeness and being is

false. . . . The fantasy of Whiteness is false because it is not fundamental. . . . Unlike sexual difference, there is nothing fundamentally irresolvable about race or its master signifier" (61).

7. See his chapter 1 for discussion of the trope of hollowness as well as McBride's discussion of Hermann Broch, whose understanding of kitsch is also linked to this idea. Broch describes Vienna "as the capital of a gangrenous empire whose disintegration uncovered its actual, hollow core" (McBride 284).

8. See Ryden, "Bourgeois" and "Politeness." Discussions of the application of kitsch range from analyses of art, such as Broch's observation, "Kitsch is the element of evil in the value system of art" (63) or Greenberg's belief that "the peasant will go back to kitsch when he feels like looking at pictures, for he can enjoy kitsch without effort" (18) to broader theorizations such as Katherine Lugg's *Kitsch: From Education to Public Policy* to Kundera's often-quoted meditation on the metaphysical "kitsch tear":

    Kitsch causes two tears to flow in quick succession. The first tear says: how nice to see children running on the grass! The second tear says: how nice to be moved, with all of mankind, by children running on the grass! It is the second tear which makes kitsch kitsch. The brotherhood of man on earth will only be possible on a base of kitsch." (*Unbearable* 251)

    Kundera characterizes kitsch here as a movement from particular experience to systematized generality, a point emphasized by Musil, according to McBride, who characterizes Musil's view as one where "kitsch configures itself as an aesthetic modality that shuns the task of presenting singular experience and instead reifies it in ready-made formulas" (286) to turn sentiments into concepts (290).

9. This nostalgic variety contrasts with the melancholic response we see in the description made by Roediger and others of whiteness's inauthenticity. In those descriptions, whiteness seems to be in a state of ruin. See discussion of nostalgic and melancholic kitsch in this chapter on pages 78–79.

10. See Introduction for an overview of Wiegman's discussion of particularity with regard to whiteness. Wiegman sees particularity as the means through which whiteness continues to reconstitute itself, thus aligning whiteness with a view of kitsch similar to Westbrook's. See note 5.

11. Greenberg, along with Celebonovic, attributes a class dimension to kitsch, seeing it as working class and bourgeois, respectively (and contradictorily). Greenberg sees kitsch, which he groups with folk art, as emanating from the masses, i.e., "peasant" desire. His articulation, however, in his touchstone essay on avant-garde and kitsch, is essentially modernist in its conception of the aesthetic binary between art and kitsch in relation to authenticity and has been critiqued for its implied elitism that dismisses mass culture. Lisa Otty describes Greenberg's view of kitsch as "a drip-feed of pre-digested information" as opposed to his vision of the avant-garde, "in which society moves towards a more *authentic* future" of resistance (41, emphasis added).

    The relationship between kitsch and class is an important one in light of a trend to recuperate kitsch from elitist classifications. Calls to read kitsch sympathetically as the democratic expression of popular art rather than pejoratively come from feminists such as Hoberman who argue for kitsch's importance as a means of connectivity in the feminine sphere, similar to Binkley who sees it as representing an aesthetic of "embeddedness," and postmodernists who, honoring "the demise of the hegemonic discourse of aesthetic autonomy" (McBride 282) find the highbrow/lowbrow binary set up by Greenberg and others that posits a "pure" art form as itself artificial, and, I would argue, therefore, its own sort of kitsch.

In addition to Hoberman, Binkley, and McBride, see Otty, Gurstein, Mukhopadhyay, and Banita for descriptions of the controversy surrounding elitism and the concept of kitsch. Otty, for example, explains:

> Greenberg's thought fell out of fashion as the twentieth century progressed and it became increasingly clear not only that mass culture was here to stay but that it required more thorough consideration. . . . Greenberg's modernist formalism, and indeed aesthetics more generally, appeared as elitist, conservative and largely irrelevant to contemporary culture.
>
>   In contrast, the embrace of mass culture . . . came to be seen as representative of a new, more democratic spirit in the art world. (42)

In this same vein, Gurstein describes the highbrow/lowbrow dilemma: "critics fear that commercial entertainment numbs and demoralizes consumers as it coarsens taste and lowers standards; defenders believe that popular entertainment speaks to the desire of ordinary people and . . . can be 'subversive' of the status quo" (136). Likewise Mukhopadhyay troubles the distinction between Indian folk art and kitsch by arguing that traditional Bengali scroll painting, an ephemeral art form, which blends 9/11 kitsch and traditional elements, is in effect a transcultural engagement forming a new autoethnographic idiom. Banita sees Azar Nafisi's antikitsch efforts in the celebrated *Reading Lolita in Tehran* as failing when the memoirist falls back on the antidote of an uninterrogated faith in monolithic Western Literature that effectively reinscribes a kind of high brow, belletristic kitsch in its uncritical celebration of Western humanism.

12. Nabokov identifies in an interview for *Paris Review* a list of kitsch: "Freudian symbolism, moth-eaten mythologies, social comment, humanistic messages, political allegories, overconcern with class or race, and the journalistic generalities we all know" (qtd. in Banita 98).

13. See Ryden, "Bourgeois."

14. The title of this subsection makes reference to a painting by the twentieth-century artist Jared French, entitled *Washing the White Blood from Daniel Boone*. See Afterword.

15. Sontag's essayistic exploration of camp is intended to be just that—explorative rather than definitive in its assertions about what constitutes camp. As such, it contains contradictions. While she on the one hand declares that camp puts "irony over tragedy" (115) and is an enactment of the notion of "Being-as-Playing-a-Role" (109), she also states that "pure examples of Camp are unintentional: they are dead serious. The Art Nouveau craftsman who makes a lamp with a snake coiled around it is not kidding, nor is he trying to be charming. He is saying, in all earnestness: Voila! the Orient!" (110–11). Thus she defines camp as "seriousness that fails" (112), yet later on insists that "Camp is playful, anti-serious" (116).

16. Such a reading would suggest melancholic kitsch with its emphasis on the "ruin" of masculinity, but the parodic element that undercuts any possibility of wistfulness puts the remarks in the terrain of something like a camp compliment, in which Imus and the co-host attempt to admire the "toughness" of the players through the gendered and raced insult.

17. In her discussion of enthymemic whiteness, Ratcliffe analyzes an email sent to her by a graduate student who thinks through her response to a white stand-up comedian's use of what initially seems to the student to be racist humor. The student's first response is that she is "aghast" ("In Search" 283), but she eventually concludes that this response is steeped in her own whiteness that silences mentions of racialization as impolite. Ratcliffe sees the student questioning the enthymemic structure of whiteness here in which "race is not to be talked,

or joked, about. However, . . . [the student] questions her performance of this enthymeme . . ., and as she does so, she begins making whiteness visible" (285).

18. See Ogletree's discussion of Professor Gates' arrest.

19. The story, published in 1973, describes a group of urban African-American youth, reluctantly in the process of being "educated" by a woman in the neighborhood who takes them to the New York City luxury toy store, F.A.O. Schwartz, with the intent of shocking the children into critical awareness about their capitalist society's racist structure. In teaching this story, I have discovered that cultural narratives of consumerism and meritocracy are so strong as to interfere with students' ability to understand the story and that these narratives produce misreadings, ones in which students understand the story's "lesson" to be that if the children were to go to school and work hard, they would one day be able to buy expensive toys.

NOTES TO CHAPTER 4

1. I have changed the acronym of the institution. Further, my experiences were sixteen years ago, and are not evidence of what any particular college or university may be doing in terms of writing instruction today outside of the university where I work.

2. I have changed the acronym of the institution.

3. I have changed the name of the student.

4. The principal architects of New Criticism, John Crowe Ransom, Allen Tate, and Robert Penn Warren, railed against a rapidly industrializing U.S. in the 1920s and in response, referring to themselves as "Agrarians," wrote a manifesto, "I'll Take My Stand" (1930). This movement was unsuccessful, and they later came up with New Criticism as an expression and definition of themselves. For a comprehensive discussion of New Criticism's harmful effects on progressive, left-leaning, or otherwise literature authored by non-whites and women, see Barbara Foley's *Radical Representations: Politics and Form in U.S. Proletarian Fiction, 1929–1941* (3–6). For instance, borrowing from Jane Tomkins, Foley points out that New Criticism "is routinely seen as an ideological maneuver rationalizing a conservative and exclusionary concept of literary value" (3). She goes on to say:

> Texts by women and people of color have thus far been the principal beneficiaries of the demise of New Criticism and the gate-crashing democratization in U.S. cultural studies. In recent years, however, there has also been a significant renewal of interest in the Depression-era literary radicals whose influence the New Critics set out to combat. (5)

While she suggests that New Criticism had all but been rejected as a literary interpretive force in 1994 when she was writing, actual events suggests Foley's prediction somewhat premature. As I point out in my essay, New Criticism is the predominant interpretive lens most teachers use in their writing classes, and it's the one typically used by the textbook industry in the scaffolding and framing questions that accompany readings. Also significant is Foley's observation that New Criticism's task, to a great extent, was to limit the literary influence of radicals on the left. Citing Gorham Davis, who wrote in 1930, Foley notes, ". . . the Agrarians had triumphed in the realm of literary theory. According to the emerging New Critical evaluative standards, "holding liberal-democratic-progressive views with any conviction made one incapable of appreciating imaginative literature at all" (4). Other readings existed, but only a New Critical one would be considered legitimate and in many ways neutral and normal, like whiteness.

5. See Ira Shor's essay "Our Apartheid: Writing Instruction and Inequality" and *Mike Hill's After Whiteness: The Unmaking of an American Majority*, where they both argue convincingly about the structurally based economics of higher education which makes adjunct labor, especially in English departments, so lucrative both for the department and the institution.

6. In his text, Bartholomae refers to the student as both the "basic writer" and the 'other'. He is explicitly using the language of postcolonial theory, citing Gayatri Spivak's famous essay, "Can the Subaltern Speak?" in his epigraph as he sees that just as in the colonial context the subaltern is a location against which the occident comes into being, so too is the basic writer (and Basic Writing) a location against which the "normal" whiteness in writing and writing instruction comes into being. While his argument specifically refers to the basic writer, it seems equally applicable to those students who enter composition classes and must conform to a language that is positioned in opposition to their own as is often the case with the white middle-class dialect that minority students must successfully mimic in order to get out of their composition class. Hence, my inclination to see the pedagogy of the EC adjuncts in colonial terms is underscored by Bartholomae's argument.

7. Corbett goes on to say:

> In modern times, the enthymeme has come to be regarded as an abbreviated syllogism—that is, an argumentative statement that contains a conclusion and one of the premises, the other being implied. . . . The essential difference [between a syllogism and an enthymeme] is that the syllogism leads to a necessary conclusion from universally true premises but the enthymeme leads to a tentative conclusion from probable premises. (60)

In Corbett's reckoning of the enthymeme, the rhetor relies on information that is readily available to the audience; information that we may reasonably sum up as the sociocultural consciousness of the given community or their common places. This information is used by the rhetor to achieve his/her aim of delivering a persuasive speech or pronouncement.

8. To flesh out her point, Poster borrows from George Kennedy's work, drawing a distinction between primary and secondary rhetoric and arguing that primary rhetoric is the conception of rhetoric as held by the Greeks when the art of rhetoric was "invented." It was primarily an art of persuasion as used in civic life. She argues that the enthymeme is secondary rhetoric. It is a rhetorical technique (Poster 8). We might also say that it refers to a method of analyzing technique so we might refer to something as being "enthymematic" when we're trying to discover how someone has put their argument together. She continues,

> Any . . . assertion about the centrality or marginality of [the enthymeme] within the rhetorical tradition must be approached as reflecting not so much absolute transcendent conditions of history, but rather the relationship of the historical tradition to the historicist position of the writer performing the act of canon construction. (9)

By "centrality or marginality" Poster refers to what amounts to a series of misunderstandings about the nature of the enthymeme, which results in the term variously being marginalized or its centrality to rhetoric rendered questionable in much of the scholarship on the rhetorical tradition. She argues convincingly that the use of the term itself has changed over time in part because of the various languages and cultures that it has been situated in; it's not the term that is unstable, it is language itself that is unstable reflecting, in some ways, the very complexity of language that my pedagogy encourages students to see and that some of my colleagues' pedagogy inside and outside of composition and rhetoric seems to elide.

9. The idea that students write even personal or autobiographical texts in a generic way is a central feature of the "Bartholomae Elbow" debates, where Bartholomae makes this charge against that kind of teaching and writing product as something he rejects. His position is that in many ways students are reproducing power structures that are in effect idealized fiction. His objective in Freshman Composition, he argues, is to remove those fictionalized narratives from the students' repertoire in favor of original student writing. He believes that students must first master the language of academia in order to use it to challenge its hegemonic position. See also Wendy's first chapter in this book, "Confessing Whiteness," where she discusses the generic nature of personal narrative.

10. See "Interrogating the Monologue: Making Whiteness Visible," *CCC* 52.2 (Dec. 2000): 240–59, where, in dialogue with Wendy, I first discuss Hykine's poem.

11. See my Chapter 2 for a full discussion of how whiteness functions to make the white working class invisible in various ways.

12. See Wendy's Discussion of Normann and Norma in Chapter 3.

13. See the essay's introduction, where Wiegman argues that the working-class white male, in the form of the minoritized designation of "white trash," establishes ethical authority through claiming a "harmed and discriminated whiteness" (146) that, according to progressive liberal discourse, can best be alleviated by claiming an antiracist subjectivity through class alliance. This is, in fact, one way of critiquing "C.P. Ellis," who Amanda identifies with on several levels.

14. See Cheryl Harris's "Whiteness as Property," *Harvard Law Review* 106 (June 1993): 1707–91, particularly 725, 1773, for a full discussion of how whiteness became a property right protected by the narrative of U.S. law, and how it persists in the present day.

NOTES TO CHAPTER 5

1. This chapter was first published in slightly altered form as an essay in *disClosure: a Journal of Social Theory* 16 (2007): 111–30.

2. Affect (as differentiated from emotion), such as core affect, is described by Russell as "that neurophysiological state consciously accessible as the simplest raw (nonreflective) feelings evident in moods and emotions. . . . Core affect is primitive, universal, and simple (irreducible on the mental plane). It can exist without being labeled, interpreted, or attributed to any cause" (148). Despite this "rawness," Clough stresses that affect's connection with bodily response should not be regarded as "presocial." Citing Massumi, she points out that affect involves "a reflux back from conscious experience to affect, which is registered, however, as affect" and that it always exists "in excess of consciousness" (2). Micciche further clarifies, "affect names preverbal, visceral conditions that *encompass* emotion and feeling." Despite these distinctions, for the purposes of the discussion here, I follow suit with Micciche, who acknowledges that "you may sometimes catch me slipping among these terms simply because they are linked in their capacity to signify emotive functions, and they offer a more textured, because more varied, vocabulary to me" (*Doing* 15, emphasis added).

3. This threaded discussion took place in the context of a first-year writing course whose theme was an investigation of "Cultural Canons: What

We Study and Why." *Huck Finn* was being considered as a text with a "troubled" history.

4. Quoted in hooks ("Wings" 39).

5. Despite its constructed quality, race can be described in ontological as well as epistemological terms. The philosopher John H. McClendon III makes this point when he argues:

> What if we think of race in reference to it being a social category? We thereby uncover that its ontological basis is not the product of nature and instead is linked to social reality. What about other forms of socially derived phenomena, commonly studied by the social sciences? Being in nature does not limit the boundaries of reality. Social reality, though distinct from natural reality, is nevertheless real. Race derives its ontological status from social reality. (213–14)

While I would maintain that the relationship between the "social" and the "natural" is more dialectical than it is "distinct" (see Seshadri-Crooks discussion of the interplay of biology and racialization 11–20), McClendon's assertion, derived from David Theo Goldberg's work, is useful in countering reactionary appropriation of critical race theory's insights into the "fiction" of race for the purposes of reasserting white hegemony. If race itself is not "real," the argument goes, then racism too cannot exist. Granting race ontological status underscores that while race is a social category with epistemological status, the material effects of *racism* are quite "real" in the manifestation of its "changing same quality" (Bonilla-Silva 9) as discussed in the Introduction of this book.

6. In *After Whiteness*, Mike Hill tells us that "It has become a common enough charge that the spate of work that amassed on whiteness throughout the 1990s has served to exacerbate the problem of white hegemony that it only pretended to unmask" and that this has happened "contrary to . . . best intentions" (16).

7. Daniels makes this observation in her review of two books that attempt to plumb the depths of whiteness: *White Racism* by Joe R. Feagin and Hernan Vera; *Memoir of a Race Traitor* by Mab Segrest.

8. Although CRT began as a movement within legal studies, it "has had a galvanizing effect not only within the narrow world of legal academia, but also on the public discourse on race more generally." Critical Race Theory attempts to "expose and dismantle [the normative supremacy of whiteness in American law and society] . . . from an explicitly race-conscious and critical 'outsider' perspective" (Valdes, et al. 1).

9. Katula explains that no such ethical dilemma would have existed in the duty-based, public spirit-oriented rhetoric of Quintilian's "good man speaking well" if emotional appeal were used to achieve what is best for the community.

10. See, for example, Cathy Caruth's socially inflected understanding of trauma.

11. See Chapter 4 for an analysis of Jackson's discussion on whiteness and the enthymeme with regard to cultural hegemony.

12. Stearns and Stearns use the term "emotionology" to distinguish cultural standards of emotion from merely individual experiences of it.

13. In *Rethinking Racism*, Seibel-Trainor makes a case for an opposite interpretation of the relationship of emotion to racism. She reads manifestations of student racism as examples of "emotioned" institutional discourse "that are not necessarily about race per se. Students become convinced of such beliefs in part through the routines and culture of schooling, and they draw from them when confronted with matters of race" (3). Students in effect

programmatically misapply their indoctrination into individualism and the work ethic to arguments about race. The emotional commitment does not stem from racism but rather response to race is absorbed into a greater cluster of emotion. This process would seem to be one of the means through which whiteness maintains itself, but Joe's case seems to function differently. I am arguing here that his rhetoric carefully disguises his originating emotional commitment to whiteness.

14. Megan Boler points out that feminist consciousness raising is an underrated and insufficiently acknowledged example of a paradigm of political emotion:

> we need to right the historical record, and acknowledge that the feminist politics of emotion paved the way for radically reconceptualizing emotions in education and scholarship. Contemporary discussions of feminist poststructuralism and theories of subjectivity more often than not fail to acknowledge the historical roots of consciousness-raising and feminist pedagogies. Feminists of the 1970s and 1980s deserve credit for catalyzing a radical paradigm shift that put emotions on the political and public map as a key to social resistance. (123)

15. An example of such passive empathy recentering whiteness can be found in Martha Nussbaum's treatment of the role of compassion in multicultural education to cultivate good citizenry:

> Compassion requires demarcations: which creatures am I to count as my fellow creatures, sharing possibilities with me? ... Rousseau argues that a good education, which acquaints one with all the usual vicissitudes of fortune, will make it difficult to refuse acknowledgment to the poor or the sick, or slaves, or members of lower classes. It is easy to see that any one of those might really have been me, given a change in circumstances. ... it is all the more urgent to cultivate the basis for compassion through the fictional exercise of imagination—for if one cannot in fact change one's race, one can imagine what it is like to inhabit a race different from one's own. (*Cultivating* 92)

Nussbaum's use of "one" (and "we" throughout her book) fixes this ethical compassion as a white concern, for clearly it is white people who suffer from a lack of DuBoisian double consciousness and are in need of remediation in "imagination." Her depiction points to the problem of conceiving of justice in terms of white empathy/ sympathy/ compassion, as such a move preserves the position of power of the white subject.

16. See Jones's discussion of sympathy versus empathy, in which the former is described as "our awareness and participation in suffering" and the latter as "our ability to comprehend mental states of another" (67–68).

NOTES TO CHAPTER 6

1. I have changed the name of the student.
2. See Bonilla-Silva (2) for a discussion of redlining and the role of realtors and homeowners who, as Bonilla-Silva says, through a variety of exclusionary practices limit entry of blacks and dark-skinned Latinos into white neighborhoods. See also Cheryl Harris's "Whiteness as Property," *Harvard Law Review* 106 (June 1993): 1707–91, for a discussion of the contemporary property interests in whiteness white people still maintain as a result of U.S. law.
3. See our Introduction (1) where we discuss Kozol's as well as Bonilla-Silva's assessment of *de facto* segregation in the present day.
4. See *Playing in the Dark: Whiteness and the Literary Imagination* (39).

5. See Martin E. Spencer's "Multiculturalism, 'Political Correctness' and the Politics of Identity," where he points out that in 1991 the then New York State commissioner of education, Thomas Sobol, called for a multicultural curriculum which would ask questions such as "'What is an American?' 'Who am I?' 'What is/are my cultural heritages'" (Sobol qtd. in Spencer 547).

6. See Barbara Foley's excellent new book on Ralph Ellison, *Wrestling with the Left: The Making of Ralph Ellison's Invisible Man*. Durham: Duke UP, 2010.

7. See Harris (1707–91) for a discussion of the contemporary property interests in whiteness white people still maintain as a result of U.S. law.

8. See Max van Manen's *Researching Lived Experience: Human Science for an Action Sensitive Pedagogy*. Albany: SUNY Press, 1990.

Bibliography

Abu-Lughod, L. and Catherine Lutz, eds. *Language and the Politics of Emotion.* Cambridge: Cambridge UP, 1990.

Achebe, Chinua. "An Image of Africa: *Conrad's Heart of Darkness.*" *The Story and Its Writer.* Ed. Ann Charters. 6th ed. New York: Bedford, 2003. 1447–52.

Ahmed, Sara. *The Cultural Politics of Emotion.* New York: Routledge, 2004.

Alcorn, Marshall W. "Ideological Death and Grief in the Classroom: Mourning as a Prerequisite to Learning." *Journal for the Psychoanalysis of Culture and Society* 6.2 (2001): 172–80.

Alexander, Michelle. *The New Jim Crow: Mass Incarceration in the Age of Colorblindness.* New York: New Press, 2010.

Allen, Theodore. *The Invention of the White Race.* Vol. 1. London: Verso, 1994.

Althusser, Luis. *Lenin and Philosophy.* New York: Monthly Review, 1971.

Anzaldúa, Gloria. *Borderlands/La Frontera: The New Mestiza.* San Francisco: Aunt Lute Books, 1987.

Aristotle. *Rhetoric. The Complete Works of Aristotle: The Revised Oxford Translation.* Ed. Jonathan Barnes. Trans. W. Rhys Roberts. Princeton: Princeton UP, 1984. 2152–69.

Aronowitz, Stanley. "Between Nationality and Class." *Harvard Educational Review* 67.2 (1997): 188–207.

Asadullah Samad, Anthony. "Don Imus: Who You Calling 'Nappy-Headed Hos'?" *Sentinel* [Los Angeles, CA] 12–18 April 2007: A7. Black Newspapers.

Awkward, Michael. *Burying Don Imus: Anatomy of a Scapegoat.* Minneapolis and London: U of Minnesota P, 2009.

Bacon, Jen. "Getting the Story Straight: Coming Out Narratives and the Possibility of a Cultural Rhetoric." *World Englishes* 17.2 (1998): 249–58.

Baldwin, James ."If Black English Isn't a Language, Then Tell Me, What Is?" *New York Times* 29 July 1979: 19. Print.

Bambara, Toni Cade. "The Lesson." *Gorilla, My Love.* New York: Vintage, 1992.

Banita, Georgiana. "Affect, Kitsch and Transnational Literature: Azar Nafisi's 'Portable Worlds.'" *Semiotic Encounters: Text, Image, and Trans-Nation.* Ed. Sarah Sackel, Walter Gobel, and Noha Hamdy. Amsterdam and New York: Rodopi, 2009.

Bartholomae, David. "The Tidy House: Basic Writing in the American Curriculum." *Journal of Basic Writing* 12.1 (1993): 4–21.

Bean, John C. *Engaging Ideas.* San Francisco: Jossey Bass, 2001.

Beech, Jennifer. "Redneck and Hillbilly Discourse in the Writing Classroom: Classifying Critical Pedagogies of Whiteness." *College English* 67.2 (2004): 172–86.

Bennett, Lerone. *The Shaping of Black America: The Struggle and Triumphs of African Americans 1619–1990s.* New York: Penguin, 1993.

Berger, Maurice. *White Lies: Race and the Myths of Whiteness.* New York: Farrar, 1999.

Berlin, James. "Rhetoric and Ideology in the Writing Class." *College English* 50.5 (1988): 477–94.

Bettinger, Matthew. "Drunk on Hysteria: It's Finally Time to Integrate Public Schools." *The Justice* 8 April 2003. 12 Feb. 2008 <http://www.thejusticeonline. com/news/2003/04/08/>.

Binkley, Sam. "Kitsch as a Repetitive System: A Problem for the Theory of Taste Hierarchy." *Journal of Material Culture* 5 (2000): 131–52.

Bishop, Wendy. "Writing Is/And Therapy? Raising Questions about Writing Classrooms and Writing Program Administration." *Journal of Advanced Composition* 13.2(1993) <http://www.jacweb.org/Archived_volumes/Text_articles/v13_12Bishop.htm>.

Bitzer, Lloyd F. "Aristotle's Enthymeme Revisited." *Quarterly Journal of Speech* XLV (Dec. 1959): 399–408.

Bizzell, Patricia and Bruce Herzberg. *The Rhetorical Tradition: Readings from Classical Times to the Present.* 2nd ed. New York: Bedford St. Martins, 2001.

Bloom, Lynn Z. "Freshman Composition as a Middle-Class Enterprise." *College English* 58.6 (1996): 654–75.

Bohm, David and F. David Peat. "Dialogue and Culture." *Science, Order, and Creativity.* New York: Bantam, 1987. < http://cogweb.ucla.edu/CogSci/Bohm_Peat_87.html>.

Boler, Megan. *Feeling Power: Emotions and Education.* New York and London: Routledge, 1999.

Bonilla-Silva, Eduardo. *Racism without Racists: Color-blind Racism and the Persistence of Racial Inequality in the United States.* Lanham, MD: Rowman, 2003.

Brennan, Christine. "Rutgers Women Block Imus' Shot with Classy Stand." *USA Today* 10 April 2007 <http://www.usatoday.com/sports/columnist/brennan/2007-04-10-brennan-rutgers_N.htm>.

Broch, Hermann. "Notes on the Problem of Kitsch." Dorfles 49–67.

Brodkin, Karen. *How the Jews Became White Folks and What that Says about Race in America.* New Brunswick: Rutgers, 1998.

Bruch, Patrick and Thomas Reynolds. "Critical Literacy and Basic Writing Textbooks:Teaching Toward a More Just Literacy." *BWe: Basic Writing* e-journal 2.1 (2000). <http://orgs.tamu-commerce.edu/cbw/asu/journal_3_spring2000.thm#critical>.

Burgess, Susan. "Did the Supreme Court Come Out in Bush v. Gore? Queer Theory and the Performance of the Politics of Shame." *Differences: A Journal of Feminist Cultural Studies* 16.1 (2005): 126–46.

Carter, Julian B. *The Heart of Whiteness: Normal Sexuality and Race in America, 1880–1940.* Durham and London: Duke UP, 2007.

Caruth, Cathy. *Unclaimed Experience: Trauma, Narrative, and History.* Baltimore: Johns Hopkins, 1996.

Celebonovic, Aleksa. *Some Call it Kitsch: Masterpieces of Bourgeois Realism.* New York: Abrams, 1974.

Cheng, Anne Anlin. *The Melancholy of Race.* Oxford: Oxford UP, 2000.

Chesnutt, Charles. "The Wife of his Youth." 12 Feb. 2008 <http://etext.virginia.edu/toc/modeng/public/CheWife.html>.

Chirrey, Deborah A. "'I Hereby Come Out': What Sort of Speech Act is Coming Out?" *Journal of Sociolinguistics* 7.1 (2003): 24–37.

"Chris Christie Victory Speech." C-Span. 3 Nov. 2009 <http://www.c-spanvideo. org/program/289788–1>.

Cicero. *De Oratore*. Trans. E. W. Sutton and H. Rackham. Cambridge: Harvard UP, 1959.

"Class in the Classroom: Transcription of an American Studies Association Workshop." *Radical Teacher* 46 (1995): 46.

Clough, Patricia Ticineto. "Introduction." *The Affective Turn: Theorizing the Social*. Ed. Patricia Ticineto Clough and Jean Halley. Durham and London: Duke UP, 2007: 1–33.

Connors, Robert. "Teaching and Learning as a Man." *College English* 58.2 (1996): 137–57.

Corbett, Edward P. J. *Classical Rhetoric for the Modern Student*. 3rd ed. New York: Oxford UP, 1990.

Crowley, Sharon. "Response to Edward M. White's 'The Importance of Placement and Basic Studies.'" *Journal of Basic Writing* 15.1 (1996): 88–91.

Crowley, Sharon and Debra Hawhee. *Ancient Rhetorics for Contemporary Students*. 4th ed. New York: Pearson, 2009.

Curry, Renee. *White Women Writing White: H. D., Elizabeth Bishop, Sylvia Plath, and Whiteness*. Westport, CT: Greenwood, 2000.

Daniels, Jessie. "The White Problem." Review of *White Racism*, by Joe R. Feagin and Hernan Vera and *Memoir of a Race Traitor*, by Mab Segrest. *Minnesota Review* 47 (1997): 199–204.

Dews, C. L. Barney and Carolyn Leste Law, eds. *This Fine Place So Far from Home: Voices of Academics from the Working Class*. Philadelphia: Temple UP, 1995.

Dorfles, Gillo, ed. *Kitsch: The World of Bad Taste*. New York: Bell, 1975.

Du Bois, W.E.B. *Black Reconstruction in America 1860–1880*. New York: Atheneum, 1969.

Dyer, Richard. *White*. London and New York: Routledge, 1997.

Dyson, Anne Haas and Geneva Smitherman. "The Right (Write) Start: African American Language and the Discourse of Sounding Right." *Teachers College Record* 111.4 (2009): 973–98.

Ellison, Julie. "A Short History of Liberal Guilt." *Critical Inquiry* 22 (1996): 343–71.

Ellison, Ralph. *Invisible Man*. New York: Vintage Books, 1995.

———. "Twentieth-Century Fiction and the Black Mask of Humanity." *Shadow and Act*. New York: Vintage, 1964. 22–44.

Felman, Shoshana. "Education and Crisis, or the Vicissitudes of Teaching." *Trauma: Explorations in Memory*. Ed. Cathy Caruth. Baltimore: Johns Hopkins, 1995. 13–60.

Fergus, Devin. *Liberalism, Black Power, and the Making of American Politics 1965–1980*. Athens and London: U of Georgia P, 2009.

Fienberg, Lorne. "Charles W. Chesnutt's 'The Wife of His Youth': The Unveiling of the Black Storyteller." *American Transcendental Quarterly* 4.3 (1990): 219–37.

Finkelstein, Norman G. "Daniel Jonah Goldhagen's 'Crazy' Thesis: A Critique of Hitler's Willing Executioners." *New Left Review* I/224 (1997): 39–87.

———. *The Holocaust Industry*. New York and London: Verso, 2000.

Fish, Stanley. *Save the World on Your Own Time* Oxford: Oxford UP, 2008.

Fishman, Stephen M. and Lucille McCarthy. "Teaching for Student Change: A Deweyean Alternative to Radical Pedagogy." *College Composition and Communication* 47.3 (1996): 342–66.

Foley, Barbara. Radical Representations: Politics and Form in U.S. Proletarian Fiction, 1929–1941. Durham: Duke UP, 1993.

Foucault, Michel. *The History of Sexuality, Vol. 1: An Introduction.* Trans. Robert Hurley. New York: Random, 1978.

Frankenberg, Ruth, ed. "Introduction: Local Whitenesses, Localizing Whiteness." *Displacing Whiteness: Essays in Social and Cultural Criticism.* Durham: Duke UP, 1997. 1–33.

———. "The Mirage of an Unmarked Whiteness." *The Making and Unmaking of Whiteness.* Ed. Birgit Brander Rasmussen, et al. Chapel Hill: Duke UP, 2001. 72–96.

———. "When We Are Capable of Stopping, We Begin to See": Being White, Seeing Whiteness." *Names We Call Home.* Ed. Becky Thompson and Sangeeta Tyagi. London and New York: Routledge, 1996. 3–18.

———. *White Women, Race Matters: The Social Construction of Whiteness.* Minneapolis: U of Minnesota P, 1993.

Frye, Marilyn. "On Being White: Toward a Feminist Understanding of Race and Race Supremacy." *The Politics of Reality: Essays in Feminist Theory.* Trumansburg, NY: Crossing, 1983. 110–27.

Fulkerson, Richard. "Composition at the Turn of the 21ˢᵗ Century." *College Composition and Communication* 56.4 (2005): 654–87.

Gallagher, Charles. "White Reconstruction in the University." *Socialist Review* 94.1/2 (1995): 165–87.

Garner, Steve. *Whiteness: An Introduction.* London and New York: Routledge, 2007.

Gilyard, Keith. "Basic Writing, Cost Effectiveness, and Ideology." *Journal of Basic Writing* 19.1 (2000): 36–42.

———. "Higher Learning: Composition's Racialized Reflection." *Race, Rhetoric, and Composition.* Ed. Keith Gilyard. Portsmouth, NH: Boynton Cook, 1999. 44–52.

Giroux, Henry. "Racial Politics and the Pedagogy of Whiteness." *Whiteness: A Critical Reader.* Ed. Mike Hill. New York and London: New York UP, 1997. 294–315.

Goldthwaite, Melissa. "Confessionals." *College English* 66.1 (2003): 55–73.

Goodburn, Amy. "Racing (Erasing) White Privilege in Teacher/Researching Writing About Race." *Race, Rhetoric, and Composition.* Ed. Keith Gilyard. Portsmouth, NH: Boynton Cook, 1999: 67–87.

Graff, Gerald and Cathy Birkenstein. *They Say/I Say: The Moves that Matter in Academic Writing.* New York and London: Norton, 2006.

Greenberg, Clement. "Avant-Garde and Kitsch." *Art and Culture: Critical Essays.* Boston: Beacon, 1961. 3–21.

Gresson, David Aaron. *America's Atonement: Racial Pain, Recovery Rhetoric, and the Pedagogy of Healing.* New York: Lang, 2004.

Grimaldi, William A. *Studies in the Philosophy of Aristotle's Rhetoric.* Hermes Einzelschriften 25. Wiesbaden: Franz Steiner, 1972.

Gurstein, Rochelle. "Avant-garde and Kitsch Revisited." *Raritan* 22.3 (2003): 136–58.

Guyatt, Nicholas. "Movement and Rootedness." Review of *The Making of African America: The Four Great Migrations* by Ira Berlin and *The Political Worlds of Slavery and Freedom by Steven Hahn: The Nation* 14 June 2010: 35–40.

Harris, Cheryl I. "Whiteness as Property." *Harvard Law Review* 106 (1993): 1707–91.

Hartigan, John. "Establishing the Fact of Whiteness." *American Anthropologist* 99.3 (1997): 495–505.

———. *Odd Tribes: Toward a Cultural Analysis of White People.* Durham and London: Duke UP, 2005.

Hedges, Chris. *Death of the Liberal Class.* New York: Nation, 2010.

Heilker, Paul. *The Essay: Theory and Pedagogy for an Active Form*. Urbana: NCTE, 1996.

Henke, Suzette. *Shattered Subjects*. New York: St. Martin's, 1998.

Hesse, Douglass. "The Place of Creative Nonfiction." *College English* 65.3 (2003): 237–41.

———. "Stories in Essays, Essays as Stories." *Literary Nonfiction: Theory, Criticism, Pedagogy*. Ed. Chris Anderson. Carbondale: Southern Illinois UP, 1989.

Hill, Mike. *After Whiteness: Unmaking an American Majority*. New York and London: New York UP, 2004.

Hindman, Jane E. "Making Writing Matter: Using the 'Personal' to Recover[y] an Essential[ist] Tension in Academic Discourse." *College English* 64.1 (2001): 88–108.

———. "Thoughts on Reading the Personal: Towards a Discursive Ethics of Professional Critical Literacy." *College English* 66.1 (2003): 9–20.

Hoberman, Ruth. "Aesthetic Taste, Kitsch, and *The Years*" *Woolf Studies Annual, Vol. 11.* New York: Pace UP, 2005. 77–98.

Hoffman, Adina. "Lives on the Ground." Review of *A Tale of Love and Darkness*, by Amos Oz, *Once Upon a Country*, by Sari Nusseibeh with Anthony David, *Palestinian Walks*, by Raja Shehadeh, and *Dark Hope*, by David Shulman. *The Nation* 18 Feb. 2008: 23–28.

Holmes, David G. "Fighting Back by Writing Black." *Race, Rhetoric, and Composition*. Ed. Keith Gilyard. New Hampshire: Boynton Cook, 1999. 53–66.

hooks, bell. "Representations of Whiteness in the Black Imagination." *White: Essential Readings on the Other Side of Racism*. Ed. Paula S. Rothenberg. New York: Worth, 2002: 19–23.

———. "Representing Whiteness: Seeing Wings of Desire." *Zeta* 2 (1989): n.pag.

———. *Teaching to Transgress: Education as the Practice of Freedom*. New York: Routledge, 1994.

Horner, Bruce and Min-Zhan Lu. "The Birth of Basic Writing." *Representing the "Other": Basic Writers and the Teaching of Basic Writing*. Urbana, IL: NCTE, 1999. 3–29.

Ignatiev, Noel. *How the Irish Became White*. New York: Routledge, 1995.

———. Interview. "Treason to Whiteness is Loyalty to Humanity." *Utne Reader* 66 (Nov./Dec. 1994): 82–87.

"Imus Becomes a Proxy Issue for Talk Show Hosts." journalism.org <http://www.journalism.org/node/5153>.

Jackson, Matthew. "The Enthymematic Hegemony of Whiteness: The Enthymeme as Antiracist Rhetorical Strategy." *Journal of Advanced Composition* 26.1 (2006): 601–41.

Jacobs, Dale and Laura Micciche, eds. *A Way to Move: Rhetorics of Emotion and Composition Studies*. Portsmouth, NH: Boynton Cook, 2003.

Jones, Janine. "The Impairment of Empathy in Goodwill Whites for African Americans." Yancy 65–86.

Jones, William. "Basic Writing: Pushing Against Racism." *Journal of Basic Writing* 12.1 (1993): 72–80.

Jordan, Winthrop. *White Over Black: American Attitudes Towards the Negro 1550–1812*. Chapel Hill: U of North Carolina P, 1968.

Kamler, Barbara. *Relocating the Personal*. Albany: SUNY, 2001.

Katula, Richard A. "Quintilian on the Art of Emotional Appeal." *Rhetoric Review* 22.1 (2003): 5–15.

Keating, AnaLouise. *Teaching Transformation: Transcultural Classroom Dialogues*. New York: Palgrave/Macmillan, 2007.

Kolchin, Peter. "Whiteness Studies: The New History of Race in America." *The Journal of American History* 89.1 (2002). 12 Feb. 2008 <http://www.history-cooperative.org/journals/jah/89.1/kolchin.htm>.

Koziak, Barbara. *Retrieving Political Emotion: Thumos, Aristotle, and Gender.* University Park: Pennsylvania State UP, 2000.

Kozol, Jonathan. *Shame of the Nation: The Restoration of Apartheid Schooling in America.* New York: Crown, 2005.

Kulka, Tomas. *Kitsch and Art.* University Park: Pennsylvania State UP, 1996.

Kundera, Milan. *The Book of Laughter and Forgetting.* Trans. Michael Henry Heim. New York: Harper, 1994.

——. *The Unbearable Lightness of Being.* Trans. Michael Henry Heim. New York: Harper, 1999.

Lagapa, Jason. "Parading the Undead: Camp, Horror and Reincarnation in the Poetry of Frank O'Hara and John Yau." *Journal of Modern Literature* 33.2 (2010): 92–113.

Landsman, Julie. *A White Teacher Talks About Race.* Lanham, MD: Scarecrow, 2001.

Leonardo, Zeus. *Race, Whiteness, and Education.* New York and London: Routledge, 2009.

Lindquist, Julie. "Class Affects, Classroom Affectations: Working through the Paradoxes of Strategic Empathy." *College English* 67.2 (2004): 187–209.

Linkon, Sherry Lee and John Russo. "New Working-Class Studies." *Minnesota Review* 63/64 (2005): 81–96.

Lu, Min-Zhan. "Conflict and Struggle: The Enemies or Precautions of Basic Writing?" *College English* 54.8 (1992): 887–913.

Lugg, Katherine. *Kitsch: From Education to Public Policy.* New York: Garland, 1999.

Lupica, Mike "Their Face of Grace Outshines Vile Insult." *New York Daily News* 11 April 2007 < http://www.nydailynews.com/news/2007/04/11/2007-04-11_their_face_of_grace_outshines_vile_insul-4.html>.

Lynn, Steven. *Texts and Contexts: Writing About Literature with Critical Theory.* 6th ed. New York: Pearson, 2011.

Marshall, Ian and Wendy Ryden. "Interrogating the Monologue: Making Whiteness Visible." *College Composition and Communication* 52.2 (2000): 240–59.

McBride, Patrizia C. "The Value of Kitsch: Hermann Broch and Robert Musil on Art and Morality." *Studies in Twentieth and Twenty-First Century Literature* 29.2 (2005): 282–301.

McClendon, John H. III. "On the Nature of Whiteness and the Ontology of Race: Toward a Dialectical Material Analysis." Yancy 211–26.

McIntosh, Peggy. "White Privilege and Male Privilege: A Personal Account of Coming to See Correspondences Through Work in Women's Studies." *Critical Race Theory: Looking Behind the Mirror.* Ed. Richard Delgado and Jean Stefancic. Chicago: Temple UP, 1997. 291–99.

McKinney, Karyn D. *Being White.* New York and London: Routledge, 2005.

Melville, Herman. "The Whiteness of the Whale." Chapter 42. *Moby Dick.* Project Gutenberg.<http://www.gutenberg.org/files/2701/2701-h/2701-h.htm#2HCH0042>.

Micciche, Laura. *Doing Emotion.* Portsmouth, NH: Boynton Cook: 2007.

Miller, Keith D. "Plymouth Rock Landed on Us: Malcolm X's Whiteness Theory as a Basis for Alternative Literacy." *College Composition and Communication* 56.2 (2004): 199–222.

Minh-ha, Trinh T. *Woman, Native, Other: Writing Postcoloniality and Feminism.* Bloomington: Indiana UP, 1989.

Morrison, Toni. *Playing in the Dark: Whiteness and the Literary Imagination.* Cambridge: Harvard UP, 1992.

———. *Song of Solomon.* New York: Plume, 1987.

Mukhopadhyay, Bhaskar. "Dream Kitsch—Folk Art, Indigenous Media and 9/11': The Work of Pat in the Era of Electronic Transmission." *Journal of Material Culture* 13.1 (2008): 5–34.

Mutnick, Deborah. "The Strategic Value of Basic Writing: An Analysis of the Current Moment." *Journal of Basic Writing* 19.1 (2000): 69–83.

Newkirk, Thomas. *The Performance of Self in Student Writing.* Portsmouth: Heineman, 1997.

Newman, John Henry. *The Idea of a University.* Ed. Frank M. Turner. Binghamton: Yale UP, 1996.

Nussbaum, Martha. *Cultivatins Humanity: A Classical Defense of Reform in Liberal Education.* Cambridge, MA and London: Harvard UP, 1997.

———. *The Therapy of Desire: Theory and Practice in Hellenistic Ethics.* Princeton: Princeton UP, 1994.

Nyong'o, Tavia. "Racial Kitsch and Black Performance." *The Yale Journal of Criticism* 15.2 (2002): 371–91.

Ogletree, Charles. *The Presumption of Guilt: The Arrest of Henry Louis Gates, Jr. and Race, Class and Crime in America.* New York: Palgrave, 2010.

Olalquiaga, Celeste. *The Artificial Kingdom.* New York: Pantheon, 1998.

Ong, Walter. "The Writer's Audience Is Always a Fiction." *PMLA* 90.1 (1975): 9–21.

Orwell, George. "Shooting an Elephant." Project Gutenberg Australia. <http://gutenberg.net.au/ebooks02/0200141.txt>.

Otte, George and Rebecca Williams Mlynarczyk. *Basic Writing.* West Lafayette, IN: Parlor, 2010.

Otty, Lisa. "Avant-Garde Aesthetics: Kitsch, Intensity, and the Work of Art." *Litteraria Pragensia* 16 (2006): 36–57.

Perl, Sondra and Mimi Schwartz. *Writing True: The Art and Craft of Creative Nonfiction.* New York: Houghton, 2006.

Poster, Carol. "A Historicist Reconceptualization of the Enthymeme." *Rhetoric Society Quarterly* 22.2 (1992): 1–24.

Pratt, Mary Louise. "Arts of the Contact Zone." *Profession* (1991): 33–40.

Prendergast, Catherine. "Race: The Absent Presence in Composition Studies." *College Composition and Communication* 50.1 (1998): 36–53.

Puente, Maria. "Outrage Over Imus shows Societal Shift." *USA Today* 12 April 2007 <http://www.usatoday.com/life/people/2007-04-12-imvs-language_N.htm>.

Quandhal, Ellen. "A Feeling for Aristotle: Emotion in the Sphere of Ethics." Jacobs and Micciche 11–22.

Quitman Troyka, Lynn. "How We Have Failed the Basic Writing Enterprise." *Journal of Basic Writing* 19.1 (2000): 113–23.

Ratcliffe, Krista. *Rhetorical Listening: Identification, Gender, Whiteness.* Carbondale: Southern Illinois UP, 2005.

———. "In Search of the Unstated: The Enthymeme and/of Whiteness." Response Essay. *Journal of Advanced Composition* 27 (2007): 275–90.

Raymond, James C. "Enthymemes, Examples, and Rhetorical Method." *Classical Rhetoric and Modern Discourse.* Ed. Robert J. Connors, Lisa S. Ede, and Andrea A. Lunsford. Carbondale: Southern Illinois UP, 1984. 140–51.

"Reid Apologizes for 'Negro Dialect' Comment." CNN. <http://politicalticker.blogs.cnn.com/2010/01/09reid-apology-for-negro-dialect-comment/?fbid=E4L1JvSflfq>.

Roediger, David. *Wages of Whiteness: Race and the Making of the American Working Class.* Rev. ed. New York: Verso, 1999.

Russell, James A. "Core Affect and the Psychological Construction of Emotion." *Psychological Review* 110.1 (2003): 145–72.

Ryden, Wendy. "Bourgeois Realism or Working Class Kitsch? The Aesthetics of Class in Composition." *Open Words: Access and English Studies* 1 (2007): 4–23.

———. "Conflict and Kitsch: The Politics of Politeness in the Writing Class." Jacobs and Micciche 80–91.

———. "Conflicted Literacy: Frederick Douglass's Critical Model." *Journal of Basic Writing* 24.1 (2005): 4–23.

Said, Edward. *Orientalism*. New York: Vintage, 1978.

Sanders, Scott Russell. "The Singular First Person." *Essays on the Essay: Redefining the Genre*. Ed. Alexander J. Butrym. Athens: U of Georgia P, 1989.

Saxey, Esther. *The Homoplot: The Coming-Out Story and Gay, Lesbian and Bisexual Identity*. New York: Lang, 2008.

Scott, James C. *Domination and the Arts of Resistance*. New Haven: Yale UP, 1990.

Sedgwick, Eve. *The Epistemology of the Closet*. Berkeley: U of California P, 1990.

Segrest, Mab. "The Souls of White Folks." *The Making and Unmaking of Whiteness*. Ed. Birgit Brander Rasmussen, et al. Chapel Hill: Duke UP, 2001. 43–71.

Seibel-Trainor, Jennifer. "Critical Pedagogy's 'Other': Constructions of Whiteness in Education for Social Change." *College Composition and Communication* 53.4 (2002): 631–50.

———. *Rethinking Racism: Emotion, Persuasion, and Literacy Education in an All-White High School*. Carbondale: Southern Illinois UP, 2008.

Seshadri-Crooks, Kalpana. *Desiring Whiteness: A Lacanian Analysis of Race*. London and New York: Routledge, 2000.

Shaughnessy, Mina. *Errors and Expectations*. New York: Oxford UP, 1979.

Shor, Ira. "Our Apartheid: Writing Instruction and Inequality." *Journal of Basic Writing* 16.1 (1997): 91–104.

———. *When Students Have Power*. Chicago: U of Chicago P, 1996.

———. "Why Teach About Social Class?" *Teaching English in the Two Year College*. 33.2 (2005): 161–70.

Sledd, James. "Bi-Dialectalism: The Linguistics of White Supremacy." *English Journal* 58.9 (1969): 1307–29.

Sleeter, Christine. "How White Teachers Construct Race." *Race, Identity and Representations in Education*. Ed. Cameron McCarthy and Warren Crichlow. New York: Routledge, 1993. 157–71.

Sontag, Susan. "Notes on Camp." *Against Interpretation: A Susan Sontag Reader*. Introduction by Elizabeth Hardwick. New York: Farrar, 1982. 105–19.

Spencer, Martin E. "Multiculturalism, 'Political Correctness' and the Politics of Identity." *Sociological Forum*. Spec. issue of *Multiculturalism and Diversity* 9.4 (Dec. 1994): 547–67.

Spigelman, Candace. *Personally Speaking: Experience as Evidence in Academic Discourse*. Carbondale: Southern Illinois UP, 2004.

Spivak, Gayatri. *Outside in the Teaching Machine*. New York and London: Routledge, 1993.

Stearns, Carol and Peter Stearns, eds. *Anger: The Struggle for Emotional Control in American History*. Chicago: U of Chicago P, 1986.

Storrs, Debbie. Review of *The Making and Unmaking of Whiteness*. Ed. Birgit Brander Rasmussen, et al. *Contemporary Sociology* 31.5 (2002): 570–72.

Strickland, Donna and Ilene Crawford. "Error and Racialized Performances of Emotion in the Teaching of Writing." Jacobs and Micciche. 67–79.

Swiencicki, Jill. "The Rhetoric of Awareness Narratives." *College English* 68.4 (2006): 337–55.

Thandeka. *Learning to Be White: Money, Race, and God in America.* New York: Continuum, 1999.

Valdes, Francisco, Jerome McCristal Culp, and Angela P. Harris, eds. *Crossroads, Directions, and a New Critical Race Theory.* Philadelphia: Temple UP, 2002.

van Manen, Max. *Researching Lived Experience: Human Science for an Action Sensitive Pedagogy.* Albany: SUNY P, 1990.

Verhovek, Sam Howe. "Clash of Culture Tears Texas City." *New York Times* 30 Sept. 1997: A14.

Villanueva, Victor. "Maybe a Colony: And Still Another Critique of the Comp Community." *Journal of Advanced Composition.* Spec. issue of *Race, Class, Writing* 17.2 (1997): 183–90.

———. "The Rhetorics of the New Racism or The Master's Four Tropes." *FYHC: First-year Honors Composition.* <http://www.fyhc.info/lead-article.asp>.

———. Symposium Collective. "The Politics of the Personal: Storying Our Lives Against the Grain." *College English* 64.1 (2001): 41–62.

Walker, Jeffrey. "Pathos and Katharsis in Aristotelian Rhetoric: Some Implications." *Rereading Aristotle's Rhetoric.* Ed. Alan G. Gross and Arthur Walzer. Carbondale and Edwardsville: Southern Illinois UP, 2000. 74–92.

Walzer, Arthur. "Aristotle's *Rhetoric,* Dialogism, and Contemporary Research in Composition." *Rhetoric Review* 16.1 (Fall 1997): 45–57.

Wang, Yong. "The Homosexual Subject: Coming Out as a Political Act." *Journal of Men, Masculinities, and Spiritualities* 1.3 (2007): 235–49.

Westbrook, John. "Cultivating Kitsch: Cultural Bovéism." *Contemporary French and Francophone Studies* 6.2 (2002): 424–35.

Whiteside, Kelly. "Rutgers Coach Has History of Standing Firm." *USA Today* 10 April 2007 <http://www.usatoday.com/sports/college/womensbasketball/2007-04-10-stringer_N.htm>.

Wiegman, Robyn. "Whiteness Studies and the Paradox of Particularity." *boundary 2* 26.3 (1999): 115–50.

Worsham, Lynn. "After Words." *Feminism and Composition Studies.* Ed. Susan Jarratt and Lynn Worsham. New York: MLA, 1998. 329–56.

———. "Going Postal: Pedagogic Violence and the Schooling of Emotion." *Journal of Advanced Composition* 18.2 (1998): 213–45.

Yancy, George, ed. *What White Looks Like: African American Philosophers on the Whiteness Question.* New York and London: Routledge, 2004.

Zandy, Janet, ed. *Liberating Memory: Our Work and Our Working-Class Consciousness.* New Brunswick, NJ: Rutgers, 1995.

Index